DANGEROUS CROSSROADS

I0096110

DANGEROUS CROSSROADS

Europe, Russia, and the Future of NATO

HALL GARDNER

BLOOMSBURY ACADEMIC
NEW YORK • LONDON • OXFORD • NEW DELHI • SYDNEY

BLOOMSBURY ACADEMIC
Bloomsbury Publishing Inc
1385 Broadway, New York, NY 10018, USA
50 Bedford Square, London, WC1B 3DP, UK
29 Earlsfort Terrace, Dublin 2, Ireland

BLOOMSBURY, BLOOMSBURY ACADEMIC and the Diana logo
are trademarks of Bloomsbury Publishing Plc

First published in the United States of America by ABC-CLIO 1997
Paperback edition published by Bloomsbury Academic 2025

Copyright © Hall Gardner, 1997

All rights reserved. No part of this publication may be reproduced or
transmitted in any form or by any means, electronic or mechanical,
including photocopying, recording, or any information storage or retrieval
system, without prior permission in writing from the publishers.

Bloomsbury Publishing Inc does not have any control over, or responsibility for,
any third-party websites referred to or in this book. All internet addresses given
in this book were correct at the time of going to press. The author and publisher
regret any inconvenience caused if addresses have changed or sites have
ceased to exist, but can accept no responsibility for any such changes.

A catalog record for this book is available from the Library of Congress.

ISBN: HB: 978-0-2759-5857-2
PB: 979-8-7651-4191-5
ePDF: 978-1-4408-2316-9

To find out more about our authors and books visit www.bloomsbury.com
and sign up for our newsletters.

"Upon the breaking and shivering of a great state and empire, you may be sure to have wars."

Sir Francis Bacon, Vol. LVIII of *Vicissitudes of Things*

Contents

Preface

Dangerous Crossroads was written to further explicate some key points made in my first book, *Surviving the Millennium*. The fundamental concern of this work is to question whether the United States, Europe, and Russia will ultimately be able to formulate a truly inclusive and comprehensive system of European security.

The book argues that once NATO enlarges to include Poland, the Czech Republic, and Hungary, it will soon find itself torn between two conflicting imperatives. NATO will need to work with Russia, Ukraine (and other non-NATO states) to forge a comprehensive system of regional security on the one hand, but concurrently integrate its new members into its exclusive military command on the other—with a predilection to invest far greater resources into the latter. Moreover, the effort to concentrate NATO's formidable power into Central Europe risks the overextension of NATO capabilities; the United States may well lose sufficient flexibility to deal effectively with potential crises arising in the Mediterranean, the Persian Gulf, or East Asia. (At the same time, should Russia become a real threat, then NATO may find itself precariously overexposed by its own forward deployment.)

Although NATO and Russia have promised to maintain mutual transparency in creating and implementing defense policy and military doctrines in the historic May 1997 NATO-Russia Founding Act (the final outcome of the proposed NATO-Russia Charter), Russia may increasingly feel itself alienated from issues that affect its perceived "vital" security interests. As the integration into NATO's military command structure is, by necessity, an exclusive process, it may prove increasingly difficult for NATO and Russia to agree to conjoint power sharing arrangements, going beyond mere consultations, *for the entire region*. Accordingly, NATO-Russian relations could enter a highly volatile phase—a dangerous crossroads—once new NATO members move beyond the positive aspects of military reform and regional reinforcement and then develop an initial capability to conduct Article V missions (to be achieved between the years 1999 and 2001). The U.S. Department of Defense expects new members to reach a more mature capability around 2009—at roughly the same juncture that Russia is expected to have revamped and modernized its own military forces.

Dangerous Crossroads proposes a Euro-Atlantic compromise as an alternative to NATO enlargement. This non-exclusive alternative would involve the extension of NATO security guarantees, but not its integrated military command, to a select group of states that form the core of a militarily integrated Euro-Atlantic Defense and Security Identity. This option is intended to forestall the possible isolation of Russia, Belarus, or other states not accepted as "full" NATO members, as it would represent a truly inclusive system of regional defense backed by *conjoint* NATO, EU/WEU, and Russian security guarantees. As Romania and Slovenia, as well as Poland, the Czech Republic, and Hungary could enter as core members concurrently, this option seeks to strengthen regional cooperation, and help mend apparently burgeoning transatlantic disputes (the rift between France and NATO), thus preventing the possible breakdown of NATO's political consensus. This proposal could represent a fallback position should the U.S. Senate, or other allied parliaments, not ratify the July 1997 plan to bring Poland, the Czech Republic, and Hungary into NATO as "full" members.

I would like to thank Graeme Auton, Chris Coker, Art Hoffman, Bob Jackson, Helmut Wagner, and other members of the *Committee on Atlantic Studies* for their encouragement, as well as Marcel van Herpen of the *Cicero Foundation*. James Harris McCall of the *School of Advanced International Studies* provided writings of Paul H. Nitze and other crucial contributions. Steven Ekovich helped to introduce me to key American figures involved in the NATO enlargement debate (as did the U.S. Information Service). Andrei Grachev provided valuable perspectives and documentation on Russian foreign policy. My former students, Marc Glaeser, Robert J. Scharf, and Trung Latieule continued to assist my efforts, even after graduation. And last, but not least, I want to thank those who did the dirty work, not only proofreading and typing, but also research and translations, Nicole Dewar, Elisabeth Kwok, Natalie Lechmanova, Ashley Maxon, and Florent Palluault. Belated thanks to my first production editor at Praeger, Sally M. Scott, for her work on *Surviving the Millennium* (which had a rough birth during a time of family crisis), and of course, special thanks to the production editor of this work, David Palmer, and those at Praeger who assisted him. And for my family who put up with yet another project. The views expressed are, of course, my own responsibility.

Acronyms

ABM	anti ballistic missile
APC	Atlantic Partnership Council
AGH	Ad Hoc Group (NACC)
AID	(US) Agency for International Development
ALCM	air-launched cruise missile
APEC	Asia-Pacific Economic Cooperation
ASEAN	Association of Southeast Asian Nations
AWACS	Airborne warning and control system
Benelux	Belgium-Netherlands-Luxembourg
BMD	ballistic missile defense
CBO	Congressional Budget Office
CCS	cooperative-collective security
CDU/CSU	Christian Democratic Union/Christian Socialist Union
CFE	Conventional Forces in Europe (treaty)
CFSP	Common Foreign and Security Policy (EU)
CIA	Central Intelligence Agency
CIS	Commonwealth of Independent States
CJTF	combined joint task forces
COB	colocated operating bases
C^4I	command, control, communications, and computers
DSI	defense and security identity
EC	European Community
ESDI	European security and defense identity
EEC	European Economic Community
EFTA	European Free Trade Agreement
EU	European Union

GAO	Government Accounting Office
GATT	General Agreement on Tariffs and Trade
GDP	gross domestic product
GNP	gross national product
G-7/ G-8	Group of Seven; Group of Eight
ICBM	intercontinental ballistic missile
IFOR	Implementation Force
IGC	Intergovernmental Conference (EU)
IMF	International Monetary Fund
INF	intermediate-range nuclear forces
IPP	Individual Partnership Program (PfP)
IRBM	intermediate-range ballistic missile
KGB	Committee of State Security (Komitet gosudarstvennoi bezopasnosti)
MFN	most-favored nation
MIRV	multiple independently targeted reentry vehicles
NACC	North Atlantic Cooperation Council
NASA	National Aeronautics and Space Administration
NATO	North Atlantic Treaty Organization
NPT	Non-Proliferation Treaty
OECD	Organization for Economic Cooperation and Development
OSCE	Organization for Security and Cooperation in Europe
PfP	Partnership for Peace
PMSC	Political-Military Steering Group (PfP)
PRC	People's Republic of China
RAND	RAND [Research and Development] Corporation
SACEUR	Supreme Allied Commander Europe
SFOR	Stabilization Force
SHAPE	Supreme Headquarters Allied Powers Europe
SLBM	submarine-launched ballistic missile
START I/II	Strategic Arms Reduction Talks
START III	Strategic Arms Reduction Talks
UK	United Kingdom
UN	United Nations
UNCTAD	UN Conference on Trade and Development
UNPREDEP	UN Preventive Deployment Force
UNRRA	UN Relief and Rehabilitation Administration
UNSC	UN Security Council
UNTAES	UN Transitional Administration in Eastern Slavonia
USSR	Union of Soviet Socialist Republics
WEU	Western European Union
WTO	World Trade Organization

DANGEROUS CROSSROADS

General Introduction

"IN," "OUT," "DOWN," AND "HAPPY"

The remark by NATO's first Secretary-General, Lord Ismay, that NATO was created for a threefold purpose—"to keep the Americans in, the Russians out, and the Germans down"[1]—has been widely cited, if not overused and abused, in the aftermath of the Cold War. Lord Ismay's depiction (plus the less widely cited addendum, "to keep the French happy")[2] does indeed express some partial truths, as do all clichés, but it still fails to address the full complexity of Cold War interrelationships, much less foresee the profound changes of the post–Cold War era.

The first factor that cliché failed to illuminate was that Germany would not tolerate being kept "down" and partitioned forever. In effect, Bonn would be able to rebuild its political and economic capabilities, as well as its global status, under a pro-Western NATO aegis which would permit West Germany ultimately to demand unification on its terms and not those of Soviet-backed East Germany—much as former German Chancellor Konrad Adenhauer had originally envisioned. Once Bonn did achieve unification, it would be able to achieve a greater political, if not military, role in European and global politics, one better corresponding to its political-economic will and capabilities.

The second, and most often overlooked, factor was that Moscow itself possessed both a legal and tacit role in keeping the Germans "down." In effect, the Allied-Soviet division of Germany served to "double contain" the potential political-economic and military power capabilities of Germany and Europe as a whole.[3] Successful Western efforts to pressure Moscow out of a role in keeping Germany "down" (which had indirectly provided Moscow a role in keeping *both* Western *and* Eastern Europe "down") consequently risked new uncertainties arising from demands for German/European unity. New security concerns would include the potential unleashing of territorial disputes or irredentist claims throughout the former Soviet bloc, at the same time that an expanding Germany/Europe could potentially isolate Moscow from Europe altogether. Loss of control of regions deemed "vital" to Soviet/Russian security interests would accordingly lead Moscow to demand a significant degree of *power sharing* in regard to any new system of Central and Eastern European security proposed by the United States or the European Union.

The third factor was that keeping the Americans "in" was a largely artificial geopolitical arrangement whereby the Americans were reluctantly drawn back into European affairs by Europe's inability to resolve its own conflicts. In a word, the American role in guaranteeing European security could not be considered "permanent," and, as a corollary, any enlargement of the American role would risk an "overextension" of American political will and capabilities. Alternatively, if the United States did decide to involve itself further in European security, Washington would demand that it do so largely on NATO's terms and in accord with American global interests.

In regard to the addendum, the French would never be "happy." On the one hand, NATO did help to keep Germany "double contained" (at least until 1989). On the other hand, NATO never really promised to defend French security interests, particularly in regard to Algeria and the *l'espace euro-méditerranéen*. Following German unification, however, France began to look back to NATO, partly as a means to sustain the "double containment" of potential German political-economic and military power. In return, Paris demanded a "Europeanization" of NATO so that the latter would reform itself to focus more closely on French security concerns in particular and concurrently provide greater support for European "power sharing" in general.

It is thus in this context that German unification—not so accidentally followed by Soviet collapse—has raised significant questions in regard to the American role in European and global security. On the one hand, the proposed enlargement of NATO risks overextending the American commitment to Europe. On the other hand, not to enlarge NATO, or else not to engage in a concerted effort to implement a new, comprehensive system of European security, risks the rebirth of regional tensions and conflicts—if not a recidivist return of Russian subterfuge and expansionism. At the same time, the United States cannot continue to bear the predominant role in any new system of European security: a united Germany and an expanding European

Union should be expected to pull more of their own weight in European security affairs, in terms of both "power" and "responsibility" sharing.

NEW PROPOSALS FOR EUROPEAN SECURITY

Among the many disputes afflicting the U.S.-Russian relationship, the question of NATO enlargement is the most contentious. NATO enlargement represents the critical issue that is likely to determine whether Moscow and Washington can forge a closer entente in the near future or the post–1991 détente will soon deteriorate into renewed confrontation and mutual imprecations. In essence, U.S.-Russian relations stand at a historic—yet dangerous—crossroads.[4]

Following the Soviet implosion in 1991, three very different proposals to cope with security dilemmas and uncertainties for non-NATO Central and Eastern European countries (including Finland, Sweden, the Baltic states, and Austria) have been outlined. A fourth option has been given less attention than it deserves.

The first approach is the "NATO maximalist" approach, which plans to expand NATO membership into Central Europe as soon as possible. NATO maximalists have tended to dominate the public debate, although they themselves are divided as to precisely which Central and Eastern European states should ultimately enter NATO. Poland, the Czech Republic, and Hungary are generally mentioned. Slovakia, which was given strong congressional support in 1994, largely disappeared from the list by 1995–96. France has pressed for the inclusion of Romania; Italy has pressed for Slovenian membership. An even more assertive "neo-containment" option has pressed for the incorporation of the three Baltic States and Ukraine, in addition to Poland, the Czech Republic, Hungary, among others. This latter option argues that NATO must enlarge its membership as rapidly and as to as many countries as possible so as to preclude the possibility that Russia might ultimately seek to re-incorporate these regions into its sphere of influence and security.

The second is the so-called evolutionary "WEU-first" approach, which argues that NATO should *extend* security guarantees (but not "full" membership) to states that join the European Union (EU) and then the West European Union (WEU). In general, this approach seeks to reduce U.S. commitments and costs; it argues that Europeans should primarily handle "European" security concerns, while the United States should concern itself with global ones. A not-so "evolutionary" version of the "WEU-first" approach, however, seeks to encourage "Europeans only" successors to NATO. This approach proposes that the United States should, in effect, *threaten* isolationism in an effort to shock the European Union (EU) and the West European Union (WEU) into strengthening the EU's Common Foreign and Security Policy (CFSP) and into upgrading European defense capabilities.

The third option is the "NATO self-limitation" approach, which argues that a non-threatening NATO can enlarge into Central and Eastern Europe *with* Russian consent. A new system of transatlantic security can be formed by forging "bridges" between NATO and non-NATO members, and then finalized by the signing of a joint NATO-Russian security accord or a "NATO-Russian Charter" leading to the formation of a joint NATO-Russian Council. This approach advocates at least four "parallel" tracks, which should take place simultaneously: (1) the "internal adaptation" or reform of the Atlantic Alliance to permit greater sharing of "power" and "responsibility" for NATO allies in Western Europe; (2) the extension of invitations to begin NATO accession talks for states of Central Europe; (3) a strategic entente with Ukraine; and (4) an intensive dialogue with Russia resulting in the formulation of a NATO-Russian Charter. At least on the surface, this option appears to be more in favor of cooperation with Russia than is the NATO maximalist approach.

The fourth alternative envisions the strengthening of the Partnership for Peace (PfP) initiative to form a militarily integrated system of "cooperative-collective security" (CCS) for Central and Eastern Europe, which would involve much closer cooperation between the UN, OSCE, NATO, the WEU, and Russia through a strengthened Atlantic Partnership Council. (The latter, proposed in late 1996, brings together the North Atlantic Cooperation Council [NACC] and the Partnership for Peace initiative [PfP].) The cooperative-collective security approach does not necessarily exclude the possibility of NATO enlargement. It only argues that any comprehensive system of European security that seeks to guarantee the *legitimate* security concerns of *both* NATO *and* non-NATO members should preferably be implemented *prior to* taking any steps toward NATO enlargement. The CCS approach argues that any enlargement of NATO's "full" membership should (1) not result in an overextension or hypertrophy of NATO's integrated military command and political consensus; (2) not provoke a backlash among states not accepted as "full" members of NATO; and (3) work to support and strengthen a comprehensive militarily integrated system of European security that *builds upon* the existing *regional* defense and security concerns of each of the states in Central and Eastern Europe.

Dangerous Crossroads will essentially argue that: (1) the "NATO maximalist" approach not only risks alienating both Russia and Belarus but also states such as Ukraine, the Baltic states, among others, which would not initially be granted "full" NATO membership. Even the possible incorporation of Poland, the Czech

Republic, Hungary, Romania, and Slovenia (at a maximum on the first round) into NATO as "full" members is not sufficient *by itself* and will not secure European and global stability in the long term. Most crucially, granting "full" NATO membership to the former Soviet–bloc states risks the overextension of NATO's political consensus and resources.

(2) Despite the claims that it represents an "evolutionary" approach, the "WEU-first" approach is still likely to aggravate U.S.-EU/WEU-Russian relations. First, the EU has hesitated to expand (largely due to the costs involved). Second, it is not clear that once new EU members are accepted they will necessarily obtain WEU or NATO security guarantees. As the WEU has been highly dependent upon NATO assets, WEU actions in support of EU members could implicate NATO members. NATO and the EU/WEU could disagree over which states deserve security supports, and over how those states should be defended, in the case of a significant confrontation. At the same time, a hesitantly expanding EU/WEU may well be regarded by Moscow as absorbing former Soviet (or czarist Russian) spheres of influence and security, affording Moscow time to obstruct the process.

(3) The NATO "self-limitation" approach (like the NATO maximalist concept) risks an overextension of NATO resources, if not the political will to act. Despite American promises that NATO enlargement is not aimed "against" Russia or any other country, expansion could well be viewed by those states not accepted as enhancing the *actual* and *potential* capabilities of those states that join, relative to their regional rivals. Secondly, although NATO has affirmed that the purpose of its enlargement is "peaceful" and "defensive," a truly adequate defense aimed at sustaining NATO's Article V security guarantee may well entail a significant offensive capability. Thirdly, the expansion of NATO membership could be interpreted as a *preclusive* act intended to significantly limit the diplomatic, economic, and military interaction of Russia or other non-member states with those states which enter NATO as "full" members.

There is a significant risk that even the proposed "NATO-Russian Charter" may not allay Russian suspicions of "encirclement" particularly if Russia sees itself being pressured into an agreement against its interests or if the process of NATO enlargement *precedes* the final formulation of an in-depth NATO-Russian security treaty. It may be very difficult to persuade Moscow, for example, that the proposed initial membership of Central European states in NATO's political structures will not be followed by their eventual membership in NATO's integrated military command. To be successful, a NATO-Russian Charter must go beyond mere consultation and involve Russia in active cooperation in areas that affect its *legitimate* security concerns. Finally, there is added risk in the fact that the decision to enlarge NATO's integrated command could come at a time when Boris Yeltsin's (or another leader's) authority is in question, thus provoking a crisis in the Russian leadership.

(4) It will accordingly be argued that it is premature to begin steps toward NATO or WEU enlargement without having first initiated a systematic cooperative-collective security approach, one involving the step-by-step effort to integrate thoroughly Central and Eastern Europe *and* Russia into a new global concert. Russia should preferably be actively involved in the formation of a new system of cooperative-collective security *prior* to the enlargement of NATO's "full" membership, so that NATO enlargement becomes part of an integral aspect of European security and plays a truly supportive—and not divisive—role in sustaining peace in Europe. From this perspective, the proposed Atlantic Partnership Council should expand PfP activities into a full-fledged Euro-Atlantic Defense and Security Identity (under a general UN or OSCE mandate) in the period 1997–99. This action should take place before any new member is to fully come on board—so as to help reduce the potential gap in power differential between NATO and non-NATO members, and particularly as a piecemeal approach is more likely to exacerbate than abate European and global tensions. (For details, see Chapter 11.)

In July 1997, NATO did promise "full" membership to Poland, the Czech Republic, and Hungary by 1999, and to consider the membership of Romania, Slovenia, and the Baltic states sometime in the near future. Yet it should still be shown specifically how that enlargement will *not* infringe upon *legitimate* Russian security interests. If NATO is to expand without ultimately provoking a backlash in Russia, then it must be shown how the enlargement of NATO's "full" membership will effectively work to support the national security interests of Russia itself—for example, in "double containing" the power of states that might represent potential "threats" to Russia or its allies.

In effect, any future system of European security must be truly comprehensive and designed to forestall a possible backlash by those states not accepted as NATO members. The cooperative-collective security approach represents an effort to formulate a viable compromise between a potentially provocative and precipitous unilateral NATO enlargement (without compensating measures or without the inclusion of Russia or other states in key aspects of the decision-making process that affect their "vital" interests) and the option of taking no steps at all. Concurrently, the system of cooperative-collective security must be made acceptable to the U.S. Congress and the parliaments of NATO members. U.S. congressional failure to ratify the process of NATO enlargement (or to support any proposed system of security that directly or indirectly involves NATO) could undermine the credibility of NATO itself.

Dangerous Crossroads thus focuses on developing a system of cooperative-collective security for Europe as a first step toward the implementation of a new system of global security. In the effort to forge a global concert, the book proposes a plan to draw the leading powers of Germany, Japan, and Russia (and ultimately China) into greater support for viable systems of cooperative-collective security in Europe and Asia, and to strengthen the "interlocking" interaction and coordination among NATO, the UN, OSCE, EU/WEU, and Russia. The ultimate purpose is to upgrade the role of Germany/Europe, Japan, and Russia in both European and global security, but without pushing the United States into a populist isolationism that could embolden revisionist and revanchist movements throughout the Eurasian continent, possibly resulting in a repetition of the horrors that plagued Europe in the first half of the twentieth century.[5]

Dangerous Crossroads examines the global ramifications of the NATO-Russian relationship. Chapter 1 discusses the nature of the U.S.-Russian relationship as it interfaces with the Partnership for Peace initiative. The latter has been intended to draw formerly rival militaries into mutual cooperation and respect, and to enhance the military professionalism of all participating states. The chapter also seeks to clarify the definition of "full" NATO membership and proposes the concept of *extending* "conjoint" NATO-WEU-Russian security guarantees to new "associate" members, which would participate in a Euro-Atlantic Defense and Security Identity (DSI).

Chapter 2 argues that NATO should not consider expansion into Central and Eastern Europe until it sets its own house in order. NATO has just begun to formulate a new relationship with Western European countries and particularly with France. What NATO calls its "internal adaptation" involves the creation of a European Security and Defense Identity (ESDI), whose precise nature has been subject to debate. In addition, the formation of Combined Joint Task Forces (CJTF) permits NATO to work side-by-side with non-NATO troops, for example, including Russian and Ukrainian forces. The chapter also examines the geostrategic implications of EU/WEU enlargement and the key questions involving the European Union's Common Foreign and Security Policy and French concepts of "concerted deterrence," as well as the long-term implications of German unification. It is argued that demands for NATO expansion are partly intended to "double contain" potentially independent German and European political-military capabilities.

Chapter 3 looks at the geopolitical ramifications of proposed NATO enlargement into Central and Eastern Europe. It analyses and critiques the demands of the U.S. Congress for NATO to expand into Central Europe. The chapter examines issues regarding the new security concerns of the formerly neutral states, such as Austria, Finland, and Sweden; the reluctance of Central and Eastern European states, such as Poland, to enter into "conjoint" NATO-Russian security guarantees; and the question of whether the "lines" presently being formed in Europe will be "permeable" or "impermeable."

Chapter 4 argues that Russian acceptance of any formal NATO-Russian Charter will depend primarily upon whether NATO's actions are perceived as truly bolstering Russian security (and the status of the Russian military within Russia and the Commonwealth of Independent States), or as actually threatening to undermine Russia's precarious stability. The chapter also examines the relations between the central Moscow government and the various regions and republics, focusing on the apparent inability to form a positive balance between the powers of the central government and those of the regions. The chapter analyses Russian domestic politics, and it questions whether the present pro-Western "national-democratic" leadership can constrain the Russian military and forestall the rise to power of revanchist factions.

Chapter 5 examines relations among former Soviet–bloc states and present CIS members, as Russia continues to seek *primacy*, if not *hegemony* or *dominance*, over states of the former Soviet Union. In particular, it focuses on Polish-Belarusian-Ukrainian relationships with Russia, but also explores relations between Russia, Kazakhstan, and CIS states in Central Asia. It is argued that NATO enlargement risks impelling Russia toward tighter hegemonic controls, whereas the cooperative-collective security approach would permit Russia to relax its efforts to obtain *hegemony*. The chapter also explores the question of whether G-7 assistance can ultimately help stabilize Russia and the CIS states.

Chapter 6 analyses Russia's "Eurasian" strategy, and it questions whether Moscow will make good on its threats to forge a closer military-technological alliance with China, Belarus, Kazakhstan, India, Iran, Iraq in counter-response to NATO enlargement. At the same time, it is argued that a NATO-EU/WEU-Russian-Japanese entente could help contain China and other potentially anti–Western states and movements, which could opt for more assertive political-military strategies, regardless of Russian strategy. In addition to helping to prevent regional powers from playing the interests of the United States and Russia against one other, a NATO-EU/WEU-Russian-Japanese entente could also help to forestall the formation of new "encircling" alliances not under the control of either Moscow or Washington.

Chapter 7 discusses the Alliance's nuclear strategy and points out how enlargement (without Russian inputs) risks jeopardizing the START II Treaty, the INF accords, the ABM Treaty, and the Conventional Forces in Europe (CFE) agreements—despite NATO promises not to deploy nuclear weapons on the territory of new members. It is argued that these treaties are interrelated and that if either the United States or Russia refuses to abide by any one agreement, the others may also be jeopardized. The chapter also analyses the vital question of "Article V" security guarantees (which could require a significant "forward" capability to provide adequate reassurance) for new and old members of NATO and outlines possible scenarios in the case that conflict does break out.

Chapter 8 analyses the failure of the EU and UN to resolve the Yugoslav crisis and the difficulties involved in actualizing an effective concerted relationship among the United States, United Kingdom, France, Germany, and Russia through the belated establishment of the Contact Group in 1994, followed by the deployment of the multinational Implementation Force under a general UN mandate but under NATO operational controls. The chapter argues that the crisis in the former Yugoslavia represents the testing ground for a future system of cooperative-collective security throughout all of Europe, as NATO, the WEU, the UN, the OSCE, Russia, Ukraine and other non-NATO countries each play a role. At the same time, however, Moscow's participation in NATO activities in the former Yugoslavia does not necessarily guarantee its acceptance of NATO enlargement.

Chapter 9 critiques the "NATO maximalist," "WEU-first," and "NATO self-limitation" approaches to Central and Eastern European security, as well as the corresponding views of former Senator Robert Dole, Senator Sam Nunn, and former National Security Advisor Zbigniew Brzezinski, among others, in regard to issues involving NATO and EU/WEU enlargement. It is argued that any future system of security for Central and Eastern Europe must concern itself with NATO's integrated military command and its ability to cope with new members and sustain political consensus; the Russian response to NATO enlargement; the precise nature of security assurances or guarantees granted to Central and Eastern European states; the relationship of NATO and the proposed Atlantic Partnership Council to the UN and OSCE, as well as to the EU and WEU; and American congressional reaction to any security commitment promised, not to overlook the costs of any proposed system of European security.

Chapter 10 explores the complexities involved in strengthening international regimes and argues for closer "interlocking" coordination between NATO, the UN, OSCE, the EU/WEU, and Russia. The fact that NATO forces have operated in interaction with the UN in Eastern Slavonia in former Yugoslavia, for example, represents one model of "interlocking" cooperation between NATO and international regimes that could be applied more generally throughout Central and Eastern Europe as a whole. The chapter likewise looks at issues involving the UN/OSCE role in the Russian "near abroad." Additionally, it argues for German and Japanese membership on the UN Security Council, as a means to strengthen the commitments of the these increasingly influential states to a global system of cooperative-collective security. Such a global system of security (based upon a NATO-European-Russian-Japanese entente) would seek to manage carefully the rise of China, and adjudicate actual or potential disputes or conflicts throughout the world.

Chapter 11 first critiques the potential costs of NATO expansion, as outlined by the Congressional Budget Office (CBO) and the White House. Rather than forcing NATO member states alone to bear the security burden, it is argued, the costs of any new system of European security should be spread out among the participating members of NATO's Atlantic Partnership Council and the OSCE. Secondly, the chapter argues for the implementation of a comprehensive system of cooperative-collective security that seeks to break the impasse between Russia and the United States over the issue of NATO enlargement. It proposes to guarantee the safety of Central and Eastern European states by forming a Euro-Atlantic Defense and Security Identity (DSI) under a general OSCE or UN mandate (but under the operational control of a strengthened Atlantic Partnership Council that would involve the full input and participation of non-NATO members such as Russia and Ukraine). The proposal does not necessarily preclude the enlargement of "full" NATO membership, but it does argue that a comprehensive cooperative-collective security regime—backed by NATO, EU/WEU, and Russian security guarantees—should be implemented prior to the proposed enlargement of NATO's "full" membership to Poland, the Czech Republic, and Hungary by 1999, the year of NATO's fiftieth anniversary. At the same time, however, it is also argued that NATO should prepare for the possible contingency that the U.S. Senate, or another allied parliament, might not ratify NATO's plans for enlargement, in which case a "Euro-Atlantic compromise" has been proposed as a possible fallback option.

CHAPTER 1

NATO and Russia: The Partnership for Peace

THE PARTNERSHIP FOR PEACE

The American Partnership for Peace (PfP) initiative represents an ambitious yet ambiguous strategy. Despite its declared intent[1] and its significant efforts to establish confidence among former antagonists, the PfP initiative has yet to be formulated in such a way as simultaneously to incorporate legitimate Russian security interests and guarantee the security of Central and Eastern European states. NATO documents have called for an "inclusive" and "comprehensive" system of European security; yet the public discussion surrounding NATO enlargement has taken a piecemeal and "NATO or nothing" character. Demands that particular Central European states enter NATO as "full" members appear to imply that those states that are not in the first wave of NATO enlargement will not be granted "hard" security guarantees. The dilemma is that proposed NATO enlargement risks exposing states that do not enter on the first round to continued uncertainty and instability—that is, unless the United States, the EU/WEU, and Russia can work in concert to design a larger and more comprehensive system of security either concurrently or preferably prior to the enlargement of NATO's "full" membership.

The Partnership for Peace (which is said to have originated in SHAPE headquarters in March–April 1993 as the "Partnership for Peacekeeping") was first presented to the NATO allies in October 1993. It grew out of the London Summit of 1990, which announced the end of the Cold War, and the November 1991 NATO summit which instituted the North Atlantic Cooperation Council. The PfP was intended to bring the NACC out of the realm of discussion and into the realm of practicality. In June 1994, the NATO foreign ministers decided that the PfP's Political-Military Steering Committee (PMSC) and the NACC Ad Hoc Group (AHG) should closely coordinate their activities, along with those OSCE states that sustained an interest in peacekeeping and cooperation with the NACC. NATO also recognized that, due to the declining size of forces its members were willing to provide, all future "out of area" operations would, by necessity, be "multinational" in character. The PfP (plus the NACC) was thus designed to guarantee a modicum of interoperability, to meet the needs of an enlarged NATO and partner states.[2] In September 1996, an enhanced PfP or "PfP plus" was initiated that could potentially permit greater regional defense preparations among PfP participants. It was estimated that between fifteen to twenty out of twenty–seven PfP participants would join an enhanced PfP. In late 1996, it was proposed that NACC and the PfP be merged to form the Atlantic Partnership Council. This proposal (to be finalized at the July 1997 NATO summit in Madrid) was intended to permit all NACC members to participate in the planning, preparation, and implementation of PfP peacekeeping missions and exercises. NATO alone would no longer plan and administer PfP activities.

According to its authors, the purpose of PfP was threefold: (1) to address the security concerns of many of the Central and Eastern European states seeking closer relations and eventual membership in NATO; (2) not to destabilize the delicate political environment in the former Soviet Union; and (3) not to jeopardize the alliance itself.[3] While the above is true, the PfP initiative can also be said to have represented an effort to forge a domestic compromise between those who advocated a more expansionist approach in favor of NATO enlargement, and those who supported compromise with the new Russia; it was also an attempt to buy time. Both the State Department and National Security Council were internally split on the issue.[4]

The PfP seeks to establish more cooperative military relations among potential rivals, to increase the transparency of defense budgets, to establish democratic controls over defense forces, and to engage in peacekeeping exercises. The PfP has hoped to bring Central and Eastern European states, as well as Russia, into political-military cooperation with the United States and to reinforce the military professionalism of all the participating elites, so as to reduce the possibilities of conflict. The PfP initiative also proposed NATO consultations "with any active participant in the Partnership if that Partner perceives a direct threat to its territorial integrity, political independence, or security." It thus promises "soft" security assurances, similar to those of Article IV of the Washington Treaty, but does not promise "hard" security guarantees as promised by Article V.[5]

NATO claimed that it would provide a transparent process, but the key questions as to exactly who would enter (and in what order) remained unanswered. The so-called Visegrad states (Poland, the Czech Republic, Hungary, and Slovakia) were first proposed for "full" NATO membership by Germany in 1993, roughly at the same time the PfP was being formulated. These same states were later given support by the U.S. congressional NATO Participation Act of 1994. (By 1995–96, however, Slovakia seemed to have been dropped from the list.)

States as diverse as Albania, Bulgaria, Estonia, Latvia, Lithuania, Malta, Romania, and Slovenia, have also expressed interest in a closer relationship with NATO, if not "full" NATO membership itself. In May 1996, the three Baltic states (supported by Norway, Sweden, and Finland) issued a joint declaration asserting that all three Baltic republics will apply together for EU and NATO membership. Romania has been proposed by France as a potential member on the first round of enlargement; Slovenian membership has likewise been supported by Italy. Canada has proposed Poland, the Czech Republic, Hungary, Romania, and Slovenia for membership. (American advocates of rapid NATO enlargement have generally argued that states such as Romania, Slovenia, and the Baltic republics should enter NATO, but on a proposed second round.) In early 1997, Bulgaria surprised NATO by proposing itself as a possible candidate.

Even neutral and formerly neutral states have sought a closer relationship with NATO. Austria and Sweden began to express interest in a closer relationship with NATO in early 1996; at the same time, Finland began to inquire discreetly as to the possibility of a closer relationship with NATO, given changes in Helsinki's external environment and membership in the EU. NATO Secretary-General Javier Solana visited Sweden and Finland in October 1996—the first time a NATO secretary-general had visited these states. Neutral Switzerland joined the PfP in December 1996.

In regard to Russia, Boris Yeltsin first proposed Russia's interest in belonging to NATO in December 1991 (Russia has yet to make a formal application for "full" membership). The United States subsequently asked Russia to participate in the Partnership for Peace (PfP) and the Individual Partnership Program (IPP); Washington also agreed to let Moscow opt for an special status in relationship to NATO and appeared to promise eventual "full" membership in the Alliance. On the other hand, Russia chose to stall on signing the Individual Partnership Program of the PfP in 1994. By October 1996, Moscow was concerned with the fact that should it apply for "full" NATO membership, it might either be turned down or be told to wait. As Moscow has found it doubtful that it would be accepted as a "full" member, it has not seen much difference between being rejected and being told to wait—both may cause an anti–NATO backlash.[6] Moscow's leadership appeared split between those who supported Russian membership in NATO's political structures (similar to the French model) and those who opposed entering NATO altogether.

In December 1995 (and despite promises that it would make its decisions by late 1995), NATO decided that no public invitations to prospective members would take place before 1997. NATO's decision to postpone membership was ostensibly related to a need to engage in more extensive talks with potential applicants, review internal changes necessary for enlargement, and strengthen the PfP initiative.[7] Additional concerns included: (1) the poor state of civil-military relations within certain prospective member states; (2) problems resulting from "irredentist" claims of prospective members; (3) the decision to proceed with the Bosnian operation; (4) a reluctance to announce NATO enlargement prior to the 1996 Russian presidential elections; and (5) debates concerning how to keep Moscow in the peace process in the former Yugoslavia.

Then, in late October 1996 prior to the presidential elections, in a speech delivered in Detroit intended to attract roughly 20 million voters of Central and Eastern European ethnic origin concentrated in the "rust belt" of roughly fourteen key states which account for 194 electoral votes, President Bill Clinton called for the first "full-fledged" members to join NATO by 1999 (the year of NATO's fiftieth anniversary).[8] Clinton's call, however, provided little time for a serious debate over the reasons for, and costs of, NATO enlargement.

AMERICAN AND RUSSIAN "SCHIZOPHRENIA"

In many ways, the ambiguity inherent in the PfP has resulted from the attempt to juggle the conflicting interests of Russia, the EU (plus potential EU and WEU members), the states of Central and Eastern Europe, and such key actors as Ukraine. The dilemma for the PfP and for U.S. diplomacy in general is not just how to provide adequate protection from a potential Russian revisionist or revanchist movement but also how to cope with tensions that could possibly spark conflict among Central and Eastern European states themselves.

American critics have, not surprisingly, described the PfP initiative as having unclear goals. Henry Kissinger, for example, has described the PfP as a "vague, multilateral entity specializing in missions having next to nothing to do with realistic military tasks."[9] From Kissinger's viewpoint, the PfP cannot both "propitiate" Russia and also ultimately draw Central European states into NATO, thus providing adequate security guarantees. Critics have accordingly dubbed the PfP as the "Partnership for Postponement" of NATO enlargement.[10] More moderate observers, however, have argued that the PfP represents a necessary "holding pen" until NATO members themselves forge a consensus as to how to enlarge and how to permit new states to meet the qualifications and responsibilities of membership.[11] In addition, NATO members such as France have demanded a readjustment of NATO's priorities, if not a "Europeanization" of NATO, in order to meet their burgeoning post–Cold War security concerns. (See Chapter 2.)

Criticism of the ambiguous nature of PfP consequently led President Clinton to declare in January 1994 that NATO enlargement would soon become a reality: "The question [was] no longer whether NATO will take on new members, but when and how."[12] In addition to implying that new NATO members would be "full" members and would obtain Article V security guarantees, President Clinton's statement avoided the more fundamental question as to "why" any new state should enter. President Clinton's statements may thus have represented an effort to assuage such domestic critics as presidential contender Robert Dole, who advocated the enlargement of NATO "sooner rather than later." (See Chapter 9.) At the same time, NATO itself appeared to stall on taking any final decisions.

Russian critics have joked that the PfP will implement "such an army of peacekeepers and rescuers in Europe that there may not be enough armed conflicts and catastrophes."[13] Russian observers argue that the primary motivation for the PfP stems from a deep-rooted anti–Russian bias, and that NATO is still geared toward "containment." It is believed that the PfP will ultimately result in a new arms race between those who belong to the PfP (and then to NATO), and those who do not make the grade. Moreover, they worry that Russian arms will not be included in NATO's integrated forces, which would exclude Russia from its former Soviet arms markets and a significant source of hard currency.[14] NATO expansion may also undermine the 1990 CFE agreement, if not bring NATO's military-technological infrastructure closer to Russian borders. (This latter argument represented an effort to obtain arms reductions and to renegotiate the CFE Treaty—signed by the Soviet Union and Warsaw Treaty Organization in 1990—to reflect better the reality of the Soviet collapse and contemporary Russian security concerns.)

More subtly, Russian critics argue that the PfP is designed to implement the Partnership on a strictly individual basis with particular countries within the Commonwealth of Independent States (CIS). In such a way, the PfP could play off the interests of one CIS state against another (particularly Ukraine versus Russia) and thus ultimately undermine political, military, and economic cooperation among the CIS states. Likewise, PfP activities might be expanded in a way that collides with Russian interests. Russia might have to accept the demand to deploy peacekeeping forces, for example, in regions where Russia does not want such forces. The PfP might likewise attempt to draw Russia into a defense of U.S. interests alone; it might, for example, seek to draft Russia as a gendarme against China and pan-Islamic movements in a way that serves American, and not Russian, interests. Another ulterior purpose of the PfP (according to Russian critics) was an attempt to forge a "Baltic–Black Sea" alliance and a new *cordon sanitaire* against Russia.[15] Russian critics see the formation of a Polish-Ukrainian "strategic partnership," combined with Polish, Baltic state, and other Central and Eastern European efforts to join NATO, as a potential new "encirclement" or "double buffer zone."[16] Such a possibility would in turn force Moscow to boost defensive precautions and result in a new "cold peace," as Boris Yeltsin claimed at the OSCE Budapest summit in December 1994.

General Leonti Shevtsov (leader of the Russian forces engaged in IFOR to implement the 1995 Dayton Agreement) has further argued that the PfP originated in part as a response to the demands of the Central and Eastern European states whom the Soviet Union had "oppressed for fifty years." These states have got "NATO by the throat and are asking for urgent help. And NATO replied in a typical Russian manner: it promised too much and is now bending over backwards to find a solution. . . . But they don't want to spoil relations with Moscow." General Shevtsov argues that since the collapse of the Warsaw Pact, NATO has been fighting for its very survival: NATO needs a new mission in order to justify its heavy toll on the American and European taxpayer. General Shevtsov asserts that "if Bosnia had not existed, NATO would have invented it."[17] (This Russian critique appears justified by Senator Richard Lugar's demand that NATO must "go out of area or out of business.") While supporting PfP and Russian participation in IFOR, even General Shevtsov has threatened that Russia "will strike back" if NATO expands up to the Russian border.

Despite similar criticism, and after some bargaining and threats, Moscow did sign the PfP framework document in June 1994. In April 1994, Russian Foreign Minister Andrei Kozyrev had categorically denied that Russia wanted special status within the PfP structure. At the same time, he had made it clear that Russia did hope to establish and sustain a closer entente relationship with NATO—a 16-plus-1 relationship. The PfP document thus seemed acceptable to Moscow in that it appeared to promise a far-reaching NATO-Russian relationship both inside and outside the Alliance, including the sharing of information on issues of European political security, plus cooperation in peacekeeping.

Critics on both sides attacked the agreement. The fact that

throughout the spring of 1994 Kozyrev proposed the formulation of conjoint NATO-Russian security guarantees to Central and Eastern European states raised the fears of those countries that NATO and Russia intended to establish a condominium. NATO spokespersons accordingly emphasized that PfP did not represent a "NATO-Russian condominium" or a "Yalta II." NATO spokespersons also emphasized that Russia was not to have any voice in the NATO decision-making process—a statement which, to Russian ears, implied that Russia would not be under consideration as a "full" member of the Alliance. Moreover, Western critics of PfP feared that Moscow could still use its special relationship within the PfP to pressure other members.

For its part, Moscow accused Washington of attempting to break its previous promises. Expansion was regarded as violating the "gentleman's agreement" made with Mikhail Gorbachev not to enlarge NATO. Western failure to implement a European Security Council, as promised by the 1990 Paris Charter, was accordingly regarded as breaking mutual trust.[18] NATO enlargement was also regarded as jeopardizing Russo-German relations, as it would violate the 1990 German-Soviet Treaty of Good Neighborliness, Partnership, and Cooperation, which stated "if one of the two states should become the target of aggression, then the other side will give the aggressor no military aid or support."[19] In 1990, Bonn had argued that NATO was a defensive alliance and would not attack Moscow. Proposals to enlarge NATO thus raised questions as to Bonn's obligations if conflict were to erupt between Russia and a new NATO member.

Not only did Moscow argue that the United States would violate previous agreements by enlarging NATO but it continued to press for a new system of European security that appeared to minimize the role of NATO. In May 1994, General Pavel Grachev, then defense minister, proposed the creation of a bloc-free system to be coordinated by the NACC and OSCE. The Russian military leadership likewise raised demands for special treatment as a "great" power, with special rights and responsibilities over the CIS territories. Moscow additionally sought an indirect *droit de regard* over the NATO decision-making process—a demand not acceptable to NATO foreign ministers.[20] The fact that the Russian elite demanded a strategic partnership with NATO closer than that granted by PfP—if not the replacement of NATO and the EU/WEU by an all-European system of security— accordingly met with American opposition. Henry Kissinger, for example, had previously denigrated Boris Yeltsin's "Charter for American and Russian Partnership and Friendship" as well as his calls in July 1992 for a stronger OSCE and for a "Euro-Atlantic Peacekeeping Capability" as "downgrading NATO."[21] (See Chapter 10.)

By December 1994, in response to intense criticism of Russian policy toward the PfP, Moscow appeared to reverse its support for it. At the meeting of NATO foreign ministers, former Foreign Minister Kozyrev balked at formally signing the PfP Individual Partnership Agreement or an agreement on special NATO-Russian ties. The latter represented a symbolic bilateral protocol (not legally binding) which underscored that Russia could cooperate with the United States on an equal basis with the other major European states. The protocol also permitted active consultation and participation with NATO; Moscow, however, believed that even this accord did not fully meet its demands for rough geopolitical parity with the United States and EU, as a politically "equal" decision-making power.

Accordingly, up until June 1994 it appeared that the "pros" of signing-on to the PfP appeared to overrule the "cons." Moscow thus carefully considered the prospects of greater political and economic cooperation with the West and also the fact that the more Russia supported the PfP, the more it should gain in the Individual Partnership. (States that accept the Individual Partnership are to be granted special advantages in accordance with their military capabilities and financial input, as well as their willingness to pursue shared objectives.) In addition, Russian proponents of the PfP argued that Russian membership in the Partnership would actually help to stall NATO's expansion eastward, if not deflect a new "encirclement."

Between July and December 1994, however, Moscow (not entirely because of pressure from domestic hard-liners) began to argue that the PfP might not in fact stall NATO's expansion eastward; it then began a new delaying tactic, the refusal to sign-on to PfP. Ostensibly, Kozyrev's decision not to endorse the PfP Individual Partnership Agreement was necessary in order to examine in greater detail NATO's proposals for enlargement. NATO (under U.S. directives) had ordered a intensive twelve–month study of what would be required for the eastward expansion; after eighteen months, prospective members would be told if they met the appropriate criteria for joining NATO. The study was to look at budgets, the nature of nuclear guarantees, and the logistics of adding new members. Kozyrev argued that the study appeared to indicate that NATO had abandoned its "go slow" approach; Moscow would need time to analyze the implications.[22]

THE REASONS BEHIND MOSCOW'S INITIAL REFUSAL TO SIGN-ON TO THE INDIVIDUAL PARTNERSHIP AGREEMENT

Moscow's actions should be seen in their full context. On the one hand, both President Yeltsin and Foreign Minister Kozyrev warned against unilateral NATO expansion as tending to the exclusion and isolation of Russia. On the other hand, the fact that Boris Yeltsin appeared to offer the possibility of NATO membership for Warsaw on 25 August 1993 (and for Prague on 26 August) but then reversed himself on 30 September (in the midst of his crackdown on the Russian parliament) continued to raise suspicions. Washington accused Moscow of being "schizophrenic." In August 1993 Yeltsin had stated in Warsaw that there was no longer any "place for hegemony and diktat, the political psychology of Big Brother and Little Brother" in the relationship between Russia and Poland. In addition to promising the withdrawal of Russian forces ahead of schedule, a joint Polish-Russian declaration stated "in the long-term such a decision [to join NATO] does not go against the interests of other states, including Russia."[23]

Again indicating a pro-Western position, Russia made no protest in regard to American and German military cooperation agreements reached with Ukraine between June and August 1993. By June 1993, after intense lobbying by Polish-Ukrainian groups in support of Kyiv (Kiev) in the spring, and in fear that U.S. policy had alienated Kyiv, the Clinton administration sought to "turn the page" in U.S.-Ukrainian relations.[24] Likewise, in June 1993 Germany signed agreements promising military cooperation with Kyiv. Chancellor Helmut Kohl stated that he would not give preference to Russia over Ukraine; the latter had received over half of its foreign aid from Germany. Bonn stressed the importance of Ukraine signing the Non-Proliferation Treaty (NPT) and ratifying START I in accordance with U.S. policy.[25] (In addition, the Ukrainian Republican party proposed the creation of a Baltic–Black Sea Union in mid-August 1993, while Belarus political elites proposed the formation of a belt of "neutral" states in Europe, with Minsk as the capital.)

What was suspicious in Russian eyes was that fact that the Ukrainian foreign minister, Anatoly Zlenko, visited NATO headquarters in mid-September 1993 and expressed strong support for NATO enlargement. Although Ukraine, he stated, was yet not ready to join, he expressed hope that NATO expansion would not stop at the Ukrainian border.[26] Kyiv argued that Moscow would eventually be able to force it into dependence if Ukraine did not ultimately become a NATO member, or obtain security guarantees from NATO stronger than those promised by PfP. Concurrently, Kyiv threatened to retain its nuclear armaments if not granted some form of guarantee by the United States or EU (or even China) against Russia or other hostile states.

Toward the end of September 1993—a time, not so accidentally, when Moscow had been focusing its attention on the parliamentary *pronunciamento*—the resignation of Kyiv's "pro-Russian" prime minister Leonid Kuchma was accepted. Kuchma was considered "pro-Russian" due to his argument that Ukraine must reestablish trade links with Russia or else face collapse. His opponents argued that if Ukraine did not sustain economic autonomy, Moscow could reassert its hegemony over Kyiv. Later that month, the new Ukrainian president, Leonid Kravchuk, assumed direct control of the Ukrainian Council of Ministers by decree. Kravchuk promised Moscow that Kyiv would remain in the CIS, but he added that he would also seek security guarantees from other states, in particular, Poland or the People's Republic of China (PRC), if the United States did not grant formal security guarantees in exchange for Ukrainian denuclearization. Ukrainian newspapers were speaking of a nuclear umbrella over Central and Eastern European states at the same time that Warsaw and Kyiv were discussing a strategic partnership.[27] While Kravchuk spoke of retaining an Ukrainian nuclear deterrent, Polish leader Lech Walesa attempted to manipulate the issue of Ukrainian nuclear disarmament in an effort to obtain a precise timetable for Polish membership in NATO.

It was then, on 30 September, during events that led to his forceful crackdown on the Russian parliament, the Yeltsin leadership reversed itself and warned against NATO expansion to the exclusion of Russia. Suspicions had been raised in Moscow that Washington and Bonn, despite promises to the contrary, intended to play Ukraine against Russia. The Russian military consequently regarded American offers to modernize Ukrainian conventional military capabilities in exchange for the elimination of Ukrainian nuclear weapons as an act of "encirclement," particularly as Ukraine was left with an excess of top-of-the-line former Soviet military forces and equipment. The potential "threat" of a Baltic–Black Sea alliance of states (such as Ukraine, Poland, and the Baltic states, if not Belarus and others) thus had become unnerving for Moscow, particularly at a moment when Yeltsin was being confronted with a parliamentary *pronunciamento*.[28] The Russian military argued that Washington appeared to be promising NATO security guarantees to Kyiv; Yeltsin was accordingly impelled to grant concessions in order to gain reluctant military support for his September–October 1993 crackdown on Russian parliament.[29]

Once Moscow appeared to reverse itself, Washington dubbed its actions "schizophrenic." Interestingly, however, Moscow did not signal a complete abandonment of ties to NATO. Despite Russian concerns, former foreign minister Kozyrev called for a NATO-Russian "system of overlapping security guarantees"—involving a conjoint NATO-Russia nuclear guarantee for Central and Eastern European states. This latter fact suggested that Russia was not entirely opposed to NATO enlargement. Moscow seemed ready to accept the extension of NATO's political-security guarantees (but not military infrastructure), provided that its legitimate security concerns were taken into account. (After the Russian offers, Central and Eastern European states feared the possibility of a NATO-Russian condominium. In general, these states have opposed proposals involving "buffer" zones, as well as NATO-Russian "cross security guarantees." [See Chapter 3.])

OTHER CONCERNS

Moscow's initial decision not to sign-on to the PfP Individual Partnership may have also represented a negative response to the Republican victory in the November 1994 U.S. congressional elections, and to the general toughening of Democratic party policy toward Russian interests. Among other issues, the Brown Amendment, which was passed prior to the November 1994 elections, raised Russian suspicions, because it permitted the Central European states of Poland, the Czech Republic, Hungary, and Slovakia privileges in logistics and weapons acquisitions normally reserved for NATO members. (The Brown Amendment overturned President George Bush's decision to freeze high-tech and arms sales to Central European states in order to prevent this region from becoming a source of friction between Moscow and Washington.) Along with proposing the sale of F-16 fighter aircraft to Poland, the Brown Amendment appeared to be an effort to force Moscow to acquiesce to NATO membership for Central European states—prior to the formulation of a full-fledged entente with Moscow.

President Clinton's proposals to raise U.S. defense spending by $25 billion over a six-year period (to improve force readiness, military pay and the quality of military life, and to modernize military technology as deemed necessary for the twenty–first century) may have also raised Russian suspicions, in the context of NATO proposals for eastward expansion. Key Republican Party leaders, such as Senator Robert Dole and the chairman of the Senate Foreign Relations Committee, Jesse Helms, were perceived by Moscow as either blatantly anti–Russian or not willing to work with Russia (or even European allies) within the confines of international regimes. Republicans expressed an intent to reverse the "Russia first" strategy of Presidents Bush and Clinton. (See Chapter 5.) Additional aid to the Central European states was, in many ways, intended to impel these states into regional defense cooperation among themselves through, for example, air defense cooperation.

The extension of "enhanced" or "associated" membership for Central and Eastern European states into the Western European Union, plus the incorporation of states such as Finland into the EU, also raised Moscow's concerns. Although their "full" participation in NATO or the WEU did not appear likely in the near future, Moscow feared that such countries as Finland, Sweden, Austria, or other new EU members would ultimately acquire WEU and then NATO membership through the "kitchen entry." Moscow accordingly asked to be informed of any security accords reached between the EU/WEU and any Central or

Eastern European state.

Moscow's initial opposition to the PfP may have also represented a protest against President Clinton's threats to end U.S. support for the arms embargo of Bosnian Moslems and against U.S. threats (in part in response to Republican demands) to augment NATO air strikes against Bosnian Serb positions. In April 1994, following NATO airstrikes on Bosnian Serb positions, Yeltsin had threatened not to sign-on to the PfP. Moscow likewise stated its intent to block NATO's use of Central Europe, such as Hungarian airspace and facilities, to stage activities that might ultimately oppose Russian interests or allies (even if these actions were not at that time directed against Russia itself).

An additional reason for not entering the PfP stemmed from the projected military operation in Chechnya. Russia did not want to engage itself in defense commitments with the West at the same time that it was planning a significant military intervention in Chechnya. The December 1994 intervention there not only stalled a NATO-Russian partnership but also weakened Russian credibility in regard to its proclaimed support for international mediation and for the OSCE as a cooperative-collective security organization. (See Chapter 10.)

Despite criticism from Russian hard-liners, Foreign Minister Kozyrev did keep open the door to Russian participation in the PfP. At the same time, however, he intended to strengthen Russia's bargaining position with NATO by not signing-on to the PfP Individual Partnership or the special bilateral protocol on NATO-Russian relations of December 1994. By February 1995, however, the Russian deputy foreign minister, Georgi Mamedov, was sent to Washington to start negotiations over the conditions for NATO enlargement. In March, at his Geneva meeting with U.S. Secretary of State, Warren Christopher, Kozyrev did set some preconditions for NATO's expansion. First, Moscow could accept NATO's eastward expansion if the United States, the EU, and Russia updated the 1990 Conventional Forces in Europe Treaty. As the CFE was based on the obsolete principle of "parity" between NATO and the Warsaw Treaty Organization, the total count would now refer to national forces, not rival blocs. Second, the United States needed to formulate a firm treaty recognizing Russia's legitimate security interests in a number of areas. These would include the nondeployment of foreign military bases and nuclear weapons in eastern countries; the nonextension of NATO's military organization to the Baltic states and other former Soviet republics; and Russia's equal participation in programs relating to logistical and technical support for the armed forces of former Warsaw Pact states that became NATO members. Third, Russia would demand that all peacekeeping operations in Europe be transferred to the exclusive jurisdiction of the OSCE. The Russian Federation's territorial integrity, including Kaliningrad, would be guaranteed. Fourth, the new security architecture of Europe required a formal codification of NATO-CIS relations by which Russia could preserve its subregional security system with CIS states and resolve disputes with Ukraine. In addition, a reformulation of principles governing the partnership with the United States was also required so that the sides would deal with each other as equal partners (not sixteen plus one, but one plus one).[30]

Later that month, Kozyrev warned of a possible tougher Russian policy. Although stressing the importance of continued U.S.-Russian cooperation, he argued that the U.S.-Russian "honeymoon" had ended, "not in divorce, but in a growing inability to resolve the problems that we face."[31] The problem was that Boris Yeltsin had become convinced (in large part due to military opposition) that Kozyrev's proposals represented hasty concessions that appeared to condone NATO's expansion altogether. Yeltsin's actions indicated that the post–1991 U.S.-Russian relationship could not at all be characterized as a "honeymoon," as Kozyrev had expressed it. Washington and Moscow had yet to be "married" in a formal entente of active policy coordination, which would evolve beyond mere consultation and détente. Rather, the United States and Russia were still in the midst of a torrid dating game in which the Russians were threatening to accuse the Americans of "date rape." Kozyrev's days were numbered.

Before the May 1995 summit, President Clinton drafted a letter to President Yeltsin stating that Washington had no objection "in principle" to Russia ultimately joining NATO as a "full" member of the alliance. President Clinton promised to slow down steps toward NATO enlargement (despite congressional pressure to expand Alliance membership as soon as possible), and he proposed "a broad, enhanced NATO-Russia dialogue and cooperation going beyond PfP," to begin on 31 May 1995. Regardless of Washington's promises, Russian critics immediately denounced this effort (as well French proposals in April 1995 for a NATO-Russian "non-aggression" pact) as a ploy to cajole Russia into accepting NATO's unilateral expansion into Central and Eastern Europe. Moreover, Washington's offer appeared disingenuous; it seemed doubtful that NATO would help defend the Russo-Chinese border or engage in actions in Central Asia against pan-Islamic, pan-Turk, or various independence movements. It was furthermore unlikely that Russia would want to play the role of gendarme in these regions in accord with American interests, or that it would want to reveal its military secrets and weaknesses. On this basis, Moscow could in its turn call American policy "schizophrenic"—in the sense that Washington's promise of Russian membership in NATO appeared insincere.

Moscow finally signed the Individual Partnership Program and bilateral accord on 31 May 1995, but not without significant reservations. Kozyrev warned the NATO allies of the need (from the Russian perspective) to transform NATO "from a military alliance to a political organization with corresponding changes in NATO institutions and basic documents." Kozyrev furthermore stated that "preserving NATO as a purely military bloc would run counter to the trends of molding a single Europe. In this case we would need to clarify whom NATO is going to defend itself against. . . . If one has in mind Russia, it is obvious that this would mean creating new dividing lines in Europe. If, however, one has in mind a third party threat, Russia and NATO could tackle the issues jointly together with other European institutions. . . . Russia's position regarding NATO expansion has remained unchanged. We continue to believe that it does not meet either the interest of Russia's national security or the interest of European security as a whole. Furthermore, the hasty resolution of the issue may threaten the establishment of truly mutually advantageous and constructive relations between Russia and NATO and the usefulness of Russia's partnership in the PfP. It will not create greater stability or security either."[32]

By this statement, Kozyrev outlined the continued Russian opposition to a NATO expansion that did not take into account specific Russian interests. However, he did not rule out the possibility of Russia working with a reformed NATO, thus raising the question of whether NATO itself could accept Russian proposals for reform. In addition, he hinted at the possibility of a compromise "in which Russia and NATO could tackle the issues jointly together with other European institutions." Yet, Kozyrev warned if the two sides could not soon work out a compromise Moscow might call off its participation in the PfP, and a further deterioration in U.S.-Russian relations could result in new "dividing lines" in Europe.

Following Kozyrev's dismissal, the new Russian foreign minister took a slightly different tack. Since January 1996, Yevgeny Primakov has taken a position that appears tougher but thus far kept open the door to compromise. In December 1995, as chief of foreign intelligence, Primakov had stated that NATO expansion would create a "security threat" for Russia and that his organization would try to find the true motives for NATO enlargement and to block that expansion. Primakov also warned that although Russia no longer had an obvious "main opponent" but that it would seek to prevent the emergence of a "global hegemony," a rather clear reference to the United States.[33] In late January 1996, Boris Yeltsin sent a long communiqué to Bill Clinton outlining his opposition to NATO enlargement.

At the 4 June 1996 NATO summit (held prior to the Russian presidential elections), Western leaders gave the impression that a NATO-Russian compromise deal was in the making. Primakov, for his part, noted that Western leaders seemed to recognize "for the first time" that NATO could not expand "without an intensive dialogue with Russia" about the terms of that expansion.[34] One significant indication of a possible compromise was that NATO ministers met with Primakov prior to meeting with Central and Eastern European foreign ministers, thus suggesting a decision to consider Russian interests before those of Central and Eastern Europe.

Yet in reconfirming his previous statements, after the 4 June 1996 meeting of NATO/NACC foreign ministers, Primakov asserted that Moscow would oppose any expansion of NATO's military infrastructure. He stated that Moscow would not only oppose the deployment of NATO troops in Central Europe but would oppose joint military command structures, air defense systems, intelligence sharing, and "similar measures." At the same time, Primakov noted that Moscow would accept the "political enlargement" of NATO, which led Western commentators to believe that Moscow's policy had changed. Primakov's statements, however, really reiterated Kozyrev's proposals for a NATO-Russian "system of overlapping security guarantees." In April 1996, Primakov likewise proposed the establishment of conjoint NATO-Russian security guarantees for the Czech Republic, Slovakia, Hungary, and Poland. (These proposals had been rejected by each of these states, as well as by Washington.[35] Concurrently, Primakov also opposed "full" NATO membership for Finland, the Baltic States, Sweden, or Austria.)

The key difference between Foreign Minister Primakov and his predecessor, however, was that Primakov appeared less insistent that NATO reform itself into a "political organization" and that the OSCE and NACC should form an "all-European security regime." Primakov— while adamantly opposing the expansion of NATO's military infrastructure closer to Russia's borders—thus appeared more willing to deal with NATO as a military organization. Moreover, he appeared to de-emphasize the role of the OSCE as a "security" organization, although supporting it as a necessary "political" organization. Primakov emphasized that if NATO were to enlarge, new members should adopt either a "Norwegian" or "French" variant. (The analogy to France, however, would not seem appropriate for non-nuclear states, as Paris retains an independent nuclear deterrent!)

Washington, however, stated its opposition to any form of special arrangements. Official spokesmen argued against formalizing any special arrangements with Moscow that would involve the non-deployment of nuclear weapons (as has unilaterally been the case with Norway and Denmark). Washington also opposed any special arrangements with Russia in which NATO would not be permitted to forward deploy its forces, as was negotiated in the case with eastern

Germany. Special membership (in which states would participate in political, but not military, aspects of the alliance) along the lines of France and Spain was also ruled out.

Secretary of State Warren Christopher's Stuttgart speech on 6 September 1996 called for a "NATO-Russian Charter," to be formulated in parallel with invitations to potential NATO members in mid-1997. A NATO-Russian Charter would govern Alliance rules for deployments of weapons and troops in time of crisis, as well as establish groundwork for NATO-Russian cooperation on peacekeeping. Likewise, on 19 September 1996 the NATO Secretary-General, Javier Solana, stated that NATO was moving fast on key decisions involving enlargement, on enhancing PfP, and on a "renewed military structure for the future which will enable the full participation of all allies and reflect visibly a European Security and Defense Identity." He also expected a decision to invite several partners to begin membership negotiations at the NATO summit in Madrid in July 1997, "if all goes well." He furthermore observed that it was important to keep the door open for future members by intensifying the dialogue, and to upgrade and deepen the PfP so that a "PfP plus" should "generate the necessary reassurance that the security of an enlarged NATO and its Partners remains closely linked." He hoped that the experience of Russia and NATO working together in IFOR would mark "a key watershed" and that proposals for a "formal charter . . . would create standing arrangements for consultations and joint action between Russia and the Alliance. . . . Whatever the final form of our relations, the content of a Russia-NATO relationship will be substantial."[36] On the other hand, Defense Secretary William Perry specified that a charter should give Russia a voice, but not a vote, on sensitive matters. NATO had no plans to deploy nuclear weapons on the territory of new members, but Perry was concerned that Russia had not substantially reduced its arsenal of tactical nuclear weapons, deployed in the Russian north-west.[37]

NATO, accordingly opted in September 1996 to engage in three "parallel" tracks or convergent "vectors." These steps were to take place simultaneously: (1) the "internal adaptation" or reform of the Atlantic Alliance to permit greater sharing of "power" and "responsibility" for NATO allies in Western Europe; (2) the extension of invitations to begin NATO accession talks for states of Central and Eastern Europe; and (3) an intensive dialogue with Russia resulting in the formulation of a NATO-Russian Charter.[38]

The Russians, however, argued that the priority of the latter two "vectors" should be reversed. As then Security Council Secretary Alexander Lebed put it at his 7 October 1996 encounter with Secretary-General Solana in Brussels: "the problem should be tackled sequentially: first of all NATO re-organization, then working out

NATO-Russian relations and then following from that, deciding on whether NATO should be enlarged, in what order and how many countries."[39] Should NATO not give priority to NATO-Russian relations, Lebed warned, the Russian duma would probably put to question the whole context of arms control agreements, including START II, in the belief "that NATO enlargement will lead to enormous changes in the strategic climate."[40] Lebed noted that Russia was too weak to stop NATO from enlarging but still warned against NATO expansion without substantial Russian inputs. He argued that a NATO-Russian Charter was not sufficient unless it led to a treaty that was "very specific in terms of its legal implications" and that clarified "all the duties and rights of those who have signed that treaty."[41]

On 18 February 1997, following President Clinton's re-election, Secretary of State Madeleine Albright set a more rapid time table. She called for the accession agreements to be signed with new NATO members by December 1997, the establishment of a joint NATO-Russian Council (plus the formation of a joint NATO-Russian brigade), and the formation of the Atlantic Partnership Council before or at NATO's Madrid summit to be held in July 1997. A new CFE agreement was also proposed, as was the signing of a NATO-Ukrainian agreement intended to counter-balance the joint NATO-Russian Charter.

The Russian leadership, however, continued to publicly oppose Washington's actions. Russia continued to emphasize that the Baltic and CIS states must not belong to NATO—under any form. While Russia sought "full" membership in the G-7, the EU, the World Trade Organization, and the Organization for Economic Cooperation and Development, it would not trade the promise of American investment in Russia for NATO enlargement. Initially, Moscow demanded that the NATO-Russian Charter take the form of a legally binding international treaty, but then dropped that demand by 12 March 1997 in favor of an executive agreement, to be signed before NATO's July 1997 Madrid summit, either at the June G-7 meeting, or at a special NATO-Russian summit to be held at the end of May. The March 1997 Clinton-Yeltsin summit resulted in an executive agreement to pursue nuclear arms reductions under START III (an agreement which could be opposed by the Russian parliament); the summit itself was best characterized as an "agreement to disagree." Assuming that the NATO-Russian Charter is ultimately signed, such a charter will set the general parameters for NATO enlargement to take place, at the same time there is no guarantee that Russia will continue to sustain its agreement, nor is there any guarantee that the parliaments of all sixteen NATO members will ratify any proposed enlargement.[42]

In essence, NATO and Russia have thus far disagreed over the timing of NATO enlargement and over the formation of a comprehensive system of security for all of Central and Eastern Europe. NATO, on one hand, has insisted that its expansion is NATO's business alone; only by consistent and constant pressure, however, will Moscow finally accept its enlargement. On the other hand, Russia has accepted that it has no jurisdictional right to prevent NATO enlargement but has argued that pressure tactics will only exacerbate Russian political instability—if not result in a backlash with unpredictable consequences. The Russian position has thus been to postpone NATO enlargement for as long as possible, but, if NATO is to enlarge, to see the terms of that enlargement thoroughly negotiated beforehand and on the basis of conjoint NATO-Russian power sharing—if possible.

Although Russia could ultimately accept NATO enlargement without a destabilizing backlash, this possibility depends upon which states enter NATO, the conditions for entry, and how truly "substantial" NATO's promises of consultation and active cooperation are. The Russian elite want to be certain that NATO enlargement is framed in such a way as to incorporate "vital" Russian interests and that the NATO club is in fact inclusive, rather than exclusive. At the same time, two other questions remain vital. The first is whether the Russian leadership in power when NATO announces its enlargement is secure and legitimate. As the question of NATO enlargement is intimately connected to the Russian image of prestige, expansion could represent a severe loss of face for Russia's "democratic" leadership. The second question revolves around the global interests of Russia; how the Russian leadership perceives the global geostrategic relationship at the time of NATO expansion will significantly affect the Russian decision-making process in that regard. Not only is Moscow concerned with NATO's formidable military capabilities, but it is also concerned with how new NATO members might use their links to the Atlantic Alliance to advance their own geopolitical interests, in possible opposition to the interests of Russia itself or its allies. It is also concerned with how its allies, such as Belarus, might react.

At the same time, it is not clear that U.S. policy has been moving in the appropriate direction. It is not entirely accidental, for example, that Warren Christopher's September 1996 speech came exactly fifty years after Secretary of State James Byrnes's Stuttgart speech, which, by supporting West German claims to unification, was one of the opening salvos of the Cold War. Christopher tried to put a better light on the occasion by observing, "Then we had won the war, but not won the peace. . . . Now we have prevailed in the Cold War, but we've not fully made the adjustment and adaptation to the peace."[43] Yet, despite Washington's disclaimer that it has stated an intention to adapt to the peace, it is still not at all certain that Washington has come to understand its previous mistakes. In effect, much as Washington backed Bonn's claims at the advent of the Cold War, it has, since 1991, been attempting to secure German *and* European unification through the process of NATO enlargement. Washington has consequently risked once again alienating Moscow unless a compromise—that is solid enough to last well into the next millennium—can be found.

THE QUESTION OF "FULL" MEMBERSHIP: A WAY TO COMPROMISE?

In many ways, the NATO-Russian dispute hinges on the question of "full" membership. Although the public debate has revolved around the question of "full" membership in NATO, it is still not entirely clear exactly what responsibilities and duties "full" NATO membership entail. On the one hand, the September 1995 *Study on NATO Enlargement* has stated that all new members will be considered "full" members. The fact that "full" membership was not defined in the Washington Treaty, however, raises a degree of ambiguity as to the status of new applicants and what requirements (particularly those related to nuclear weapons) will be placed on them. Norway as a "full" member opted for a non-nuclear status and for the non-permanent deployment of foreign forces (at least in "peacetime") by a unilateral decision (which could be revoked). On the other hand, France as a "full" member has retained its own nuclear deterrent but has not participated in NATO's integrated military command since 1964.

Does "full" membership necessarily entail participation in NATO's integrated military command? Could NATO adopt an additional category of "associate"[44] membership, as its Individual Partnership Program or its experiment in the former Yugoslavia with Combined Joint Task Forces involving non-NATO countries may suggest? Assuming Moscow cannot belong to NATO's political committees, could Russia then join NATO as an "associate" member by participating within a strengthened Atlantic Partnership Council, but not become an integral part of NATO's integrated military command? Could Russia and all other states that participate in a new European system of cooperative-collective security involving conjoint NATO-WEU-Russian security guarantees be considered as "associate" members?

From the Russian perspective, even if "full" NATO membership for states other than Russia does not mean the necessity to deploy nuclear weapons or foreign forces in "peacetime," the concept still implies that NATO has exclusive influence over the defense and security matters of each state that joins. Moscow would accordingly have no input into NATO actions that might affect its perceived vital interests and thus could be excluded from participating in such issues. (What one side might consider a condition of "peace," for example, could be considered preparation for war by another.) Moreover, as Moscow doubts that it would be permitted to join NATO's integrated military command as a "full" member, it has raised the question as to whether it could share security responsibilities with NATO by establishing conjoint NATO-Russian security guarantees for Central and Eastern European states. (See Chapters 2 and 3.) From this perspective, Moscow has not absolutely opposed NATO enlargement; on the contrary, it has sought a power-sharing arrangement with an enlarged NATO.

Unless the concept can be diplomatically (if not legally) redefined in light of the new post–Cold War geostrategic environment, as well as the substantial reforms taking place within NATO itself, "full" membership means exclusive NATO power and influence over all members' security concerns, and that all "full" members have a right (if they so choose) to participate in NATO's integrated military command and nuclear planning (at whatever time they choose). An "associate" membership, if such a concept could be adopted, would imply that select states could obtain NATO security guarantees and participate in certain political aspects of the NATO decision-making process in specific areas, but they would not be directly involved in the integrated military/nuclear aspects of NATO's contingency planning. As "associate" membership would imply the *extension* of NATO security guarantees to a selected state or group of states (such as states that enter the WEU or, as proposed in this book, a *hierarchy* of states that participate in an Euro-Atlantic Defense and Security Identity), it could thus permit greater power sharing among NATO and non-NATO members, but without exposing NATO's integrated military command. Accordingly, "associate" states that play key roles in the development of an Euro-Atlantic DSI could ultimately be designated as "full" NATO members depending upon the extent of their contributions. In essence, the proposal to establish an Euro-Atlantic DSI argues that it would be wiser to forge a militarily integrated regional system of defense that incorporates as many states as possible as "associate" members *prior to* the enlargement of NATO's "full" membership.

The issue of what constitutes "full" membership in NATO is of particular concern for the U.S. Congress. For a state to become a "full" member of NATO means a revision of the North Atlantic Treaty, which requires a potentially difficult-to-achieve two–thirds majority vote in the Senate. On the other hand, for NATO to extend security guarantees to new "associate" member states would require a more readily obtainable simple majority in both houses of Congress by joint resolution. In addition, the differences between the material costs of enlarging NATO's "full" membership versus those costs involved in *extending* NATO security guarantees to new or "associate" members would have to be debated by both Houses. (See Chapter 9.)

CHAPTER 2

Europe: Widening With or Without Deepening?

A COMMON FOREIGN AND SECURITY POLICY?

The collapse of the Soviet empire, as-yet-unabated U.S.-Russian tensions, and American nuclear and conventional arms retrenchment and demands for European "responsibility sharing," have combined to generate anxiety among the major U.S. allies. In the past, the Soviet "threat" was part of the glue that provided allied political cohesion. Now, however, following German unification and Soviet implosion, that glue needs re-adaptation. It would be preferable for NATO to set its own house in order before it enlarges its membership.

Fears of possible U.S. isolationism (or, really, U.S. reluctance to support "vital" European security concerns) have, on one hand, led NATO allies to develop more independent defense capabilities. On the other hand, they have also sought the "Europeanization" of NATO through Combined Joint Task Forces and a European Security and Defense Identity. Western European allies (and France in particular) have demanded a reform of NATO's command structure to elicit greater input in areas that concern their general interests.

At the same time, however, Europeans have yet to forge a Common Foreign and Security Policy, following the December 1991 Maastricht Treaty. The efforts to forge a wider European Economic Area, European Monetary Union, a West European Union more independent of NATO, and multinational Euro-forces represent steps toward a new European unity, but one that is a long way from being actualized. The 1996–97 Intergovernmental Conference will attempt to resolve key issues, most crucially the formulation of a CFSP and the extent of EU expansion—involving security guarantees to be granted to new EU members.

Moreover, it is clear that Washington has looked less to its Cold

War "special relationship" with the United Kingdom and more to
Germany at least since 1989—raising new security issues. (U.S. pressure
on the United Kingdom to forge a settlement with the Irish Republican
Army, for example, appears indicative of the downgrading of the
British position in the "special relationship.") In some ways, the UK
and France have formed an axis (to a certain extent linked to Russia)
intended to counterbalance the new U.S.-German relationship. At the
same time, France's new rapprochement with NATO has been partly
intended to offset German influence within the Atlantic Alliance as
well as to assert French interests in the *l'espace euro-méditerannéen*.

While Bonn has been active politically (and economically), it has
been reluctant to engage itself in a greater defense role, due to
historical and political-legal constraints, and also to its preoccupation
with the costs and problems of German unification. This is true despite
the fact that the legislature did in July 1994 support a reinterpretation
of the German Basic Law permitting German troops to be used in UN or
OSCE out-of-area missions, and opening the door to the possibility
that German forces could ultimately be integrated into a European
system of cooperative-collective security. (A decision to deploy troops
needs a simple majority vote of the *Bundestag*.) Ironically, however,
the newly active German foreign policy (without a corresponding
military role) has, in many ways, upset efforts to achieve a CFSP.

At present, West European states must weave their policies between
the conflicting interests of: (1) American Atlanticism (possibly moving
into isolationism, really "selected interventionism"); (2) German
Mitteleuropa schemes (which seek to draw Central Europe into the EU
and NATO as soon as possible); (3) Russian retrenchment (accompanied
by Russian claims to the former Soviet, if not czarist, "near abroad");
and (4) actual or potential Central and Eastern European disputes.
Although there has developed a general consensus that *deepening* is a
precondition for *widening*, it is still not clear precisely what forms of
deepening will be necessary to cope with the fact that Europe has
increasingly found itself *drawn* into ever-wider political-economic and
security concerns—and dangers. The fact that Europe has not yet been
able to forge a CFSP vis-à-vis the newly independent states of the
former Soviet Union, the 1991 Persian Gulf War with Iraq, or even the
1991 civil war in Yugoslavia in Europe's own backyard, has weakened
relations among the European states themselves, in addition to
straining EU/WEU relations with NATO and the United States.

RESPONSIBILITY SHARING

As Europe cannot yet defend itself without NATO supports, it
should be self-evident that NATO should not consider the question of

enlargement until it addresses the concerns of its present allies regarding American intent to defend their vital interests. Emphasis upon what former Secretary of State James Baker once called "responsibility-sharing" (really a euphemism for the earlier term, "burden sharing") without necessarily permitting "power sharing" has exacerbated inter-allied geostrategic and political-economic tensions.[1]

U.S. insistence upon "responsibility-sharing" has increasingly put the onus of defense upon Western Europe; concurrently, European states seek greater influence in decision-making *power* if they are, in fact, going to substantially increase their proportion of the defense "responsibilities." The issue is not merely that of domestic pressures against greater military spending: the Europeans want to be certain that any new systems of defense will serve their so-called "all-European" political interests. In this regard, the WEU (which involves NATO members) has tended to play a role as an intermediary between NATO and the EU. The EU and WEU have, however, generally seen their limitations in the crisis in the former Yugoslavia; they have thus seen the need for close cooperation with NATO.

In view of American nuclear and conventional force withdrawals from continental Europe, both France and Germany have sought a European defense policy more independent of NATO. Should Washington ultimately retract its military forces from European territory, then defense may well be spread too thin. U.S. troop strength dropped from roughly three hundred thousand in 1989, to two hundred and twenty thousand in 1992, to one hundred thousand by 1995. In the "burden-sharing amendment" to the 1993 Defense Authorization Bill, Congress cut $3.5 billion out of defense spending so as to impel Allies to boost their defense responsibilities. The House also sliced the Pentagon's proposal to deploy one-hundred and fifty-thousand troops, to one hundred thousand. (At the same time, the House threatened to cut U.S. forces stationed in Europe to fifty thousand, if not to twenty-five thousand.) President Clinton's 1994 calls for a $25 billion American defense increase were consequently intended to assuage NATO and European concerns; Clinton accordingly reaffirmed the promise to sustain a U.S. troop presence of one hundred thousand men.

In addition to efforts to forge a stronger political-economic union (likely resulting in a greater competition with the United States), the EU has insisted on the development of the Euro-corps, which is to be relatively independent of the United States and NATO. At the same time, however, Western Europeans have insisted on greater autonomy for the WEU within NATO itself. In general, Europeans, particularly the French, insist that NATO must reform itself in order to establish an ultimately more effective U.S.-EU/WEU relationship, particularly as Europeans have complained that U.S. actions have tended to marginalize the question of a more independent ESDI and put on hold a strengthening of WEU defense capabilities. Washington, however, has continued to use NATO channels to deal with the EU, in part due to the latter's inability to forge a coherent CFSP.[2]

Although the EU seeks a more independent foreign and security policy, it does not yet have the means to achieve it. As of June 1996, the WEU was roughly eighty percent dependent upon NATO logistics; hence, Europe cannot act without U.S. military support until the EU/WEU builds a greater capacity. In particular, the EU/WEU needs access to satellite surveillance capabilities, C^4I, heavy logistics, long-range air and sea-lift, all-weather aviation, amphibious capabilities, large-deck aircraft carriers, and missile defenses. (Except for NATO's Airborne Warning and Control System [AWAC], most NATO assets not controlled by Europeans allies belong to the United States, especially intelligence systems and heavy airlift.)[3] Until the EU/WEU develops its own assets (in many ways duplicating American capabilities), or else acquires satellite and airlift capabilities from Russia or Ukraine, U.S. aircraft carriers and logistics could, depending on the political-military situation, be put on a lend-lease arrangement.

In an effort to offset dependence upon Alliance assets (as well as to prepare for the possibility of the United States moving into "selective interventionism"), the EU/WEU has taken steps to develop its own capabilities. In the June 1992 Petersberg Declaration, the WEU Council proposed force development for humanitarian, peacekeeping, and crisis management. France and Germany in particular have hoped to establish a more significant all-European force by the turn of the century—symbolized by the 14 July 1994 (Bastille Day) presence of German troops on the Champs d'Elysées. The Eurocorps is on its way to becoming a significant army of thirty–five to forty thousand men (initially starting at fourteen thousand). Operational since 1995, it is no longer considered a "language school." The Eurocorps is open to all EU members: actions taken by the Eurocorps need the unanimous approval of all participating members. The UN or OSCE, for example, could ask the Eurocorps to enter Bosnia if the United States did not want to engage itself further. France, Italy, and Spain also agreed in May 1995 to create two new joint forces for the WEU: Euroforce and Euromarforce. Although independent, French units of the Eurocorps can also come under NATO's operational command (going beyond more limited operational control)—as agreed to by France in 1993 in exchange for closer participation with NATO.

An additional area of dispute concerns access to satellite intelligence, which has proved a key to information control (and disinformation). President François Mitterrand opted to develop an EU satellite system, Hélios, after the United States showed satellite pictures of Iraqi targets to Paris but did not permit France to use them. Moreover, in November 1994, President Clinton cut off U.S. satellite intelligence to allies, notably the UK and France, that dealt with ship movements in the Adriatic. (At the time, Washington sought to end the arms embargo imposed on Bosnia.) The issues of who controls satellite information, exports (for example, to Saudi Arabia), and satellite image commercialization have led Europe to develop its own program in competition with the United States and Russia.[4]

From a defense standpoint, Soviet collapse, combined with a gradual U.S. retrenchment, has tended to divide European maritime and continental states. Franco-German continental interests do not necessarily coincide with British and Italian maritime interests. In part because of their vulnerability as maritime powers, both Britain and Italy have attempted to elicit a strong naval commitment from NATO. Soviet disaggregation may have largely eliminated the threat of Moscow's unified conventional forces in the Central European theater but it did not eliminate Russian military pressure on Europe's northern and southern flanks. (See Chapter 7.)

THE EUROPEANIZATION OF NATO

Ironically, despite earlier tensions which manifested themselves during the Bush administration, the crisis in the former Yugoslavia at least *initially* strengthened the NATO/WEU relationship; it also led to a French-American rapprochement. Yet as Europeans increasingly demanded power sharing within NATO, the Bush administration hesitated, fearing a European "caucus" inside NATO. It thus sent strong signals of opposition to any effort to develop a major European nuclear/conventional force politically independent of NATO. The Clinton administration, however, appeared to encourage European efforts to forge CJTF, and to create "separable, but not separate" forces, as well as efforts to form a ESDI in January 1994; nonetheless, it continued to debate the issue until June 1996. Concurrently, the January 1994 American proposals to enlarge NATO may have represented an effort to "double contain" German and Western European interests in the assumption that if key Central European countries did join NATO, then they would continue to support U.S. geostrategic interests and thus counterbalance those of Western Europe (and that they would not eventually forge their own Central European "caucus" within NATO).

During this time NATO and the WEU coordinated activities in the former Yugoslavia. Both maintained the arms embargo (although U.S. policy-makers ended American participation in the embargo in November 1994). NATO's integrated military command was also used to maintain the no-fly zone over Bosnia (operating with France under

SHAPE's integrated command). NATO operated in Hungarian airspace, as well as in Albanian territorial waters (both upsetting Moscow)—in addition to engaging in joint NATO/UN and NATO/WEU operations.[5] At the same time, NATO accepted a greater role for the WEU (and for non-NATO and non-WEU members, such as Russia and Ukraine) in Bosnia through Operation "Joint Venture."[6]

Finally, in June 1996, NATO restated its intention to make the collective assets of the alliance available for WEU operations as promised in January 1994. In Berlin, on 3 June 1996, the North Atlantic Council (NATO's senior intergovernmental decision-making body) resolved to go forward with ESDI and CJTF, as well as to establish a Policy Coordination Group. The latter was designed to ensure that any new NATO missions would be under the oversight of political decision-makers, particularly in complex political situations, such as those presented in Bosnia. France in particular argued that the North Atlantic Council should take the prime role in shaping NATO policy, so that the military decision-making bodies would be de-emphasized.[7]

The June 1996 Berlin accord of NATO foreign ministers promised a substantial reform, but one that still needs to be worked out in practice. The WEU may be able to deploy up to 70,000 NATO forces, with air support and use of American satellite intelligence and technical expertise. Both the United States and EU will have to agree on NATO assets being placed at the disposal of the WEU; but Washington is not to engage the Alliance without the concurrence of the Europeans. Although NATO and Washington are to be informed as to the nature of WEU activities, the United States and the North Atlantic Council should not have any *droit de regard* over WEU actions with NATO's assets—as argued by Paris.[8] The French have been concerned that the United States could withdraw assets once loaned out, particularly as it is unlikely that United States would permit the WEU to use American assets at will. In addition, to make up for WEU weakness relative to NATO, the role of the WEU as a defense arm of the EU is to be enhanced. Moreover, detailed discussions among NATO, the WEU, UN, and the OSCE would precede actions, which could include crisis management, peacekeeping, and, in certain cases, collective defense.[9]

In addition to disagreements over how to share NATO assets, debate has revolved around reform of the NATO command structure. A European adjoint to the NATO Supreme Commander in Europe (SACEUR) was envisioned. The French also demanded that both NATO's southern and northern commands be rotated among the European allies, otherwise France would not return to NATO's military committees as a "full" partner. (The United States retains the Atlantic and European commands, but France argued that the two key regional commands should be under European leadership.) According to the

French defense minister Charles Millon, European control of the southern and northern commands would give Europe "permanent and irreversible visibility."[10]

Delay in the decision to implement CJTF and ESDI occurred in part due to the fact that U.S. General George Joulwan, NATO Supreme Allied Commander, Europe, feared that if European NATO commanders "wore WEU hats" (as well as their individual national hats), divided loyalties might weaken NATO's command structure. "Multiple hatting" could theoretically permit WEU countries to use the NATO command structure to organize military operations under a European aegis. (General Joulwan himself wears both an American and a NATO hat.) Other U.S. officials, however, argued that such a change was absolutely necessary to engage France, and the European countries in general, in a new system of security for all of Europe, to permit NATO allies to engage more easily in "out of area" operations, and to strengthen U.S. domestic support for NATO by showing that the EU was ready for greater "responsibility" and "power" sharing.[11]

The key disagreement has accordingly been over who shall head the key southern command, involving political military influence over former Yugoslavia and the rest of the *l'espace euro-méditerranéen*. The proposal that the latter region be divided into separate European and American commands represents one possible compromise. From the French (and European) perspective, it was crucial to renovate the Alliance (thus providing greater European "power sharing") in order to permit the development of a new system of security in Europe.[12] At the same time, Defense Minister Millon warned at the NATO foreign ministers meeting at Bergen, Norway, in September 1996 that France insisted upon a thorough reform of the Alliance command structure, or it would go back to its previous Gaullist position—and thus remain outside NATO's Military Committee, which France sought to rejoin in December 1995. Paris also threatened not to support NATO enlargement over the issue. (See discussion below.)

TOWARD A EUROPEAN NUCLEAR FORCE?

NATO's nuclear forces have been reduced by roughly eighty percent from their Cold War level. They consist primarily of some 480 nuclear free-fall bombs, stationed at thirteen sites in seven allied countries. Although a portion of the American nuclear submarine fleet remains committed to NATO, there are no ground-based systems that provide visible "reassurance" to NATO allies. The steep reduction of American nuclear weapons has raised questions as to the extent of the U.S. commitment to Europe, particularly as Washington has dubbed such devices as "weapons of last resort."[13]

The threat of the United States ultimately moving toward "selective interventionism," and Moscow's more assertive policies toward the "near abroad," have accordingly led Europe to intensify its efforts to develop an adequate and coordinated nuclear deterrent, one that could ultimately operate in coordination with the American deterrent, or possibly alone. However, the UK and France have not yet seen eye-to-eye on European nuclear strategy. Britain retains "full" membership in NATO's Nuclear Planning Group; France is not yet part of NATO's integrated military command, although it has rejoined NATO's Military Committee. In the past, British and French nuclear cooperation had been handicapped by London's "special relationship" with Washington and NATO's integrated military command. At the same time, it may be possible for Britain to opt out of NATO command in case of "supreme national emergency"—implying the hypothetical possibility of linking the British deterrent to that of the French, independent of the Americans. Thus far, however, London and Paris have yet to formulate what Paris has called "concerted deterrence," involving closer Anglo-French, and possibly German, nuclear cooperation. (In October 1995, British Prime Minister John Major and French President Jacques Chirac did promise to deepen their cooperation through the Franco-British Joint Nuclear Commission and to strengthen Europe's contribution to overall nuclear deterrence.)

Since 1979, France has looked increasingly to Germany to co-finance its *force de frappe*. Germany would agree (1) if France agreed to enlarge its defense "sanctuary" and participate in the forward defense of Germany, and (2) if Bonn would be permitted some say in the decision to use the nuclear trigger—particularly in regard to tactical nuclear weapons or targets located on German territory. Germany may ultimately demand a "dual key" arrangement (at the same time that Britain and France more closely coordinate nuclear strategy), with the unspoken threat that Bonn may unilaterally develop a nuclear capability. In December 1996, Paris and Bonn secretly signed a "common strategic concept" aimed at forming a concerted defense, involving nuclear dissuasion in the European context, and formalizing their relation of "parity."[14] The strategic concept also reaffirmed their commitment to NATO and the WEU. In the same month, the foreign ministers of France, Germany, and Poland (members of the "Weimar triangle") discussed security cooperation and EU enlargement.

In addition to looking more closely at the UK and Germany, France has also in many ways been looking to NATO (and NATO to France). In 1991, France participated in the drafting of NATO's first unclassified strategy, "The Alliance's New Strategic Concept," and consequently approved it, although Paris did not belong to the Alliance's integrated military command. Whereas President Mitterrand had generally promoted a pan-European security framework, largely excluding the United States, France entered NATO's Military Committee in April 1993 (in response to the crisis in former Yugoslavia) and as a means to support the Balladur initiative (June 1993 to April 1995) on Eastern European security. In December 1995, the new French foreign minister, Hervé de Charette, stated that France was to participate as a normal member of NATO's Military Committee, and Defense Minister Charles Millon stated that France was prepared to discuss a role in the NATO's Nuclear Planning Group but wanted to be certain that NATO reform was well underway before joining. France stated that it was prepared to enlarge its nuclear "sanctuary," but not necessarily to new EU members. France's nuclear umbrella may accordingly extend to Germany, Italy, the Benelux countries, and Spain, with the UK as a strategic partner, but not to new EU/WEU members.[15]

France's rapprochement with NATO represented an effort to reform NATO from the inside (rather than from the outside). It is also apparent that France seeks to share the assets of the Alliance due to an overall decline in French defense expenditure. (In February 1996, France announced its decision to end conscription and switch to an all professional army. Overall non-civilian troop strength was reduced from 500,000 to 350,000; a projection force of fifty to sixty thousand troops was established. France also opted to close eighteen land-based ICBM silos, and dismantle thirty Hades tactical nuclear weapons, originally designed to strike East German territory.) In political-military terms, France hopes to compensate for its relatively limited role in the Persian Gulf War and in Bosnia. France likewise intends to influence the debate over NATO enlargement, and to make certain that French/EU interests are upheld. And finally, France's rapprochement with NATO may also be intended to round out the U.S.-German "special relationship," and to strengthen the French role in the "double containment" of Germany through a dual NATO/WEU aegis.

Closer French ties to NATO thus appear, on one hand, intended to keep the United States from moving into "selected interventionism" and, on the other, to make certain that French/EU security interests are ultimately backed by Washington. It appears doubtful that France can back the new EU members alone, that is, without U.S. nuclear support. In December 1994 Eduard Balladur, as French foreign minister, questioned whether Europe was ready to guarantee the frontiers of new EU members "without backing up this guarantee with a [U.S.] guarantee. . . . A positive response would constitute a major break in the Euro-Atlantic security balance. . . . Do we want this? Are our citizens ready for it?"[16] From this viewpoint, new EU members would not obtain French nuclear supports, unless likewise reassured by NATO.

As long as the EU/WEU is not prepared for a nuclear defense of its own expanding membership in concert with the United States, EU/WEU expansion could drag NATO into an unexpected crisis, particularly if the United States is not willing to offer all new EU/WEU members security guarantees. The Clinton administration did not send any strong signals to Europe in opposition to EU proposals to expand the West European Union to Central or Eastern European states—an expansion that might further dilute NATO's political cohesion and force planning. Bonn, in particular, had urged the Central European states to join the EU, WEU, and then NATO; ostensibly, Bonn did not want its eastern flank exposed to political-economic instability. Similarly, the Nordic states and Denmark have called for EU and NATO membership for the Baltic states. At the same time, however, neither NATO nor the WEU have appeared to be prepared to defend Finland or the Baltic States *if* called upon to do so. It is thus possible that the expansion of NATO activities may dilute the well-established force planning of the Alliance of thirteen members (not including the three that are not part of the integrated military command—France, Spain, and Iceland).

Whether the development of a more independent European military nuclear and conventional force will complement NATO strategy and strengthen the European pillar of the Alliance, as stated in the Maastricht Treaty on European Union, or whether divergent U.S.-EU political-military strategies will develop, depends largely upon whether the Americans and Europeans can agree on the range and nature of perceived threats.[17] Concurrently, should the United States move increasingly toward "selective interventionism," Germany may well seek a front seat in the Atlantic Alliance—as it appears doubtful that Bonn can be counterbalanced by Paris and London.

PROPOSALS FOR EU EXPANSION

The Intergovernmental Conference of 1996–97 intends to lay the foundations for European unity and expansion. The original Maastricht vision, involving "institutional variable geometry" and "varying speeds" of integration, opened a number of complex questions involving the inter-governmental decision-making framework and the implementation of a CFSP—all the more so as Europe seeks both to *widen* and *deepen*. The concern is that EU expansion threatens institutional, political-economic, and security overextension: as the original six-member European Economic Community (EEC) has grown to fifteen members. The expansion of the EU to incorporate the states (Sweden, Austria, and Finland, but not Norway or Iceland) that were originally in the European Free Trade Agreement (EFTA) has generally slowed progress to incorporate Central and Eastern European states. Should additional states enter the EU, this would raise substantial political-economic and security concerns. In its May 1994 white paper, the EU listed the legal and administrative steps that Poland, Hungary, the Czech Republic, Slovakia, Romania, and Bulgaria must take to align themselves with the EU's internal market. By June 1995, the three Baltic states signed a similar EU accord; Norway, Finland, and Sweden in May 1996 all pressed for membership of the Baltic states in the EU and NATO.[18] In addition to competition in agricultural produce, one of the most significant reasons for postponement of EU enlargement, however, is that the EU could face a politically unaffordable increase, up to 60 percent, in its budget for help to develop relatively deprived states.[19]

In July 1996, Chancellor Helmut Kohl pleaded with the EU to admit the Central European states, particularly Poland, as a matter of "existential" concern: "It would be disastrous for Germany if the EU were to end at the Oder-Neisse border."[20] While he warned against the expansion of NATO "too quickly" (unlike his position in 1994), he urged EU membership as soon as possible for the Czech Republic, Hungary, and Poland (he was not enthusiastic about Slovakia). In September 1996, President Jacques Chirac of France also called for Polish entry into the EU, by the year 2000; suggested a conference between NATO members and their new partners (for example, Russia) on states seeking NATO membership; and proposed a Franco-Polish-German summit, to be held in 1997.[21] Yet despite public proclamations to the contrary, France has preferred to deepen, rather than widen, the EU. The entry of Central European states will most likely occur long after the year 2000. Accordingly, the wider the EU becomes, the more actual and *potential* security challenges it will confront; yet, not to expand the EU also creates new uncertainties.

Not only does EU expansion create potential tension between NATO and the WEU, but it has also produced actual tensions within EU itself—between members of the EU and those of the WEU, particularly as the 1948 Brussels Treaty, which founded the WEU, is to expire in 1998—and as a new EU/WEU relationship has yet to be formulated. The problem lies in the fact that the EU and the WEU are functionally separate regimes, despite the fact that they are interrelated. On one hand, any member of the European Council can veto a request for action from the EU; on the other, the WEU grants formal security *guarantees* only to its members—which do not include all EU states. Moreover, a potential for crisis resides in the fact that Denmark, Ireland, Finland, Sweden, and Austria are "observers" and not full members of the WEU. Turkey, Iceland, and Norway are "associate" members of the WEU. This could create a schism between the EU and WEU (and with NATO) if any one of these states demands NATO or WEU assistance.[22]

FUTURE SCENARIOS FOR EUROPE

The future of European unity appears to be divided into at least three competing visions, which are to be debated at the Intergovernmental Conference (IGC) throughout 1996–97.[23] (1) The German Christian Democratic and Christian Socialist parliamentary group (the CDU/CSU) has proposed a federalist "two-speed" Europe involving a "hard" and "soft" core. (2) The essentially British proposal, most closely associated with Prime Minister John Major, envisions a "Europe à la carte" (which would essentially represent a looser association of European nations). (3) The French have outlined essentially two similar confederalist conceptions: "concentric European circles" (as proposed by Edouard Balladur) or the "Europe de patries" (as suggested by Jacques Chirac).

The German proposal (which is significant in that it represents one of the first German *political* initiatives of the post–1945 era) seeks to link foreign policy and monetary union: the economic "hard core" should correspond to those states which decide the Common Foreign and Security Policy. Originally, the German concept listed as forming the geostrategic and political-economic "hard core" France and Germany (the "core" of the "hard core") and the Benelux states. Largely in response to criticism, the CDU/CSU proposal has been modified to include any country that was willing *and* able to meet both monetary and defense requirements. The CDU/CSU idea envisions a "federal" structure (to some extent modeled on Germany itself!), in that it would grant more powers to the European Parliament. The latter would become the lower chamber of the EU parliament, with a reformed Council becoming the upper chamber. The European Commission would become the new European government.

Proponents have argued that such a proposal could lead to a more effective economic and monetary union. However, a "federal" European Union may have difficulties in directly or indirectly coordinating agreements on common objectives (international trade relations, the internal market, and the environment). It has thus been criticized as risking regional political and economic divergence between the "hard core" and the others if the "inner" and "outer" core ever refused to cooperate. For example, it might be difficult to prevent the "inner core" from separating itself from the "outer core" if the former did not want to subsidize the Common Agricultural Policy or the structural-fund aid to poorer areas. The German proposal has thus raised the prospect of a "multi-tier" European Union, in which an inner core of states (France, Germany, Belgium, and Luxembourg) would coordinate security, foreign, monetary, fiscal, budgetary, and socio-economic policies. If these "core" states were successful, they would attempt to bring the second tier (the UK, Denmark, and Italy, if not Spain) as well as the third (Portugal, Greece, and ultimately Central and Eastern European states) into line. At the same time—if successful—such a inner core would represent an even greater single market than the twelve-member EU did in 1992. The inner core would reap far greater benefits than would states outside the monetary union. A CFSP would then be decided and executed by a lesser number of significant powers, who would be willing and able to engage in whatever commitments were deemed necessary.[24]

The French offered a possible compromise involving Balladur's "concentric European circles" or Chirac's "Europe de patries." These proposals essentially accepted the concept of a geoeconomic "hard core" but looked toward a more *confederal* than *federal* model. Contrary to the German suggestions, the French suggested three or more concentric circles of countries and regions, which would correspond to different pillars of the EU. The first and widest circle would include Russia, Ukraine, and the three Baltic states; the second circle would include potential members, such as Central European states; and the third, the actual fifteen members. In general, the French position was in favor of EU enlargement, but only after the year 2000, once the EU had time to *deepen*.

The French divided the third circle of the actual fifteen members into two "hard cores": those states primarily concerned with security issues and those interested mostly in monetary cooperation. Members could join their preferred circle and not become involved in dimensions of the EU in which they had no national interests. Members of the hard core would determine whether other states could join; at the same time, the hard core would largely determine key policies, such as CFSP, without necessarily expanding the right of other states to majority voting or other initiatives. (In essence, Paris hoped to "Europeanize" the monetary system, in an effort to lessen the influence of the *Bundesbank*, Bonn wanted to make sure that any all-European currency was as good as—if not better than—the *Deutsche Mark*!)

Britain has particularly worried that "broadening" may mean "shallowing" in the key area of geostrategic decision-making. At the same time, the British have urged that countries reserve the right to "opt out"—an option that could undermine unity and result in indecision.[25] A key question thus remains as to whether all fifteen members should decide basic security issues (perhaps by majority vote) or a security council of five members (maybe with its presidency rotating among the fifteen) should take charge. Other proposals include a European Security Council open to all members willing to contribute to the general EU defense. Another possibility is to bring in the WEU as one of the multiple pillars of the EU.[26]

In many ways, the French proposal sought to synthesize elements of the British and German proposals—in what one hopes can become a true synthesis and not merely a mish-mash of competing national and institutional concerns. Moreover, the synthesis should not exclude the possible membership of states such as Turkey, Ukraine, and Russia—if these states are not to be alienated. Whereas French Socialists, such as François Mitterrand and EU president Jacques Delors, generally opposed too close an association of the EU with Russia and Central and Eastern Europe, the post–Socialist approach—if it follows that of classic Gaullist policy—is more open to the possibility of an even closer associate Russian membership with the EU (so as to counterbalance and "double contain" Germany). In general, the French and British proposals, as they are looser than those of the German federal model, permit greater cooperation with Central and Eastern Europe, and Russia in particular.

Each of these new proposals create significant questions as to how effective a CFSP can become—particularly as Europe has been increasingly drawn into expansion, willingly or not. In addition, a dilemma arises in that these three visions either disagree, or do not possess sufficient clarity, on the extent to which Central and Eastern European states should be integrated with the present EU. This is to say nothing of the vital question of Turkish membership, or that of Russian/Ukrainian and Baltic state relations with Europe.

TOWARD A "TRANSATLANTIC ORDER?"

The September 1995 *Study on NATO Enlargement* states that "the enlargement of NATO is a parallel process with and will complement that of the European Union," but there remains a fundamental disagreement as to how to proceed. Proposed NATO enlargement, for example, fails to address the need to resolve the potential conflict between EU (and possible WEU) enlargement to Finland and other Eastern European states on one hand, and U.S. congressional/German demands on the other to incorporate only Central European states into NATO. In any case, the precise security relationship among EU and WEU members (including EU members potentially striving for full WEU membership) has yet to be worked out. The United States and United Kingdom, for example, have opposed a merger of EU and WEU membership; both argue that the WEU should retain a separate identity. In fact, NATO and the WEU have yet to work out totally their differences over the ESDI and CJTF.[27] (See following discussion and also Chapter 9.)

As the EU continues to expand (bringing most Central and Eastern European states into associate or "enhanced" membership even without security guarantees), there is a real concern that U.S., EU/WEU, and

Russian policy may clash.[28] Whereas NATO moved quickly to establish institutional links with former Soviet republics through the North Atlantic Cooperation Council, the WEU acted only in late 1994 to institutionalize relations and to establish a partnership with Russia, Belarus, and Ukraine. Concurrently, the EU has expanded to include states such as Finland, which has a common border with Russia and which may expect *tacit* security support from the WEU—even if Helsinki does not become a full member and remains an "observer" but still participates in the CFSP. From this perspective, the EU (from a pan-European viewpoint) may seek to support states that the United States considers of only secondary importance (from its own global geostrategic perspective).[29]

French Foreign Minister's Alain Juppé's calls in February 1995 for a new "transatlantic order" represented an effort to check trends toward mutual protectionism and to draw the United States into a closer political-economic and security relationship (for example, to keep the United States in Europe). On the other hand, French proposals for a NATO-Russian "non-aggression pact" were an attempt to counterbalance U.S., German, and Russian interests, as became evident at the EU summit in March 1995 at Carcassone, France. The idea of a NATO-Russian non-aggression pact was subsequently dismissed by Washington as an European effort to "dictate" policy. At the same time, Juppé warned of a European veto on NATO eastward expansion: "If there is enlargement, then it will be agreed by 16 countries, not by one country."[30] Paris thus put Washington and Bonn on warning that the decision to expand NATO must be unanimous.

While apparently supporting the membership of Poland, the Czech Republic, and Hungary in NATO, Paris has also supported the membership of Romania, largely to the disapproval of Washington. Romania is regarded as a Francophile "Latin" island and counterbalance to Hungarian, German, Russian (and Ukrainian) influence in the region. Paris has argued that to admit Hungary in the first round would alienate Romania. The ethnic Hungarian minority in Transylvania might attempt to secede, believing itself to be backed by NATO. Moreover, Romanian membership would keep the door open to NATO membership for lesser countries in a proposed second round of enlargement (assuming there is a second round). And finally, according to the "checkers" argument, if Poland and Romania become members of NATO, then Ukraine, other Central European states, as well as the Baltic states, would be able to obtain indirect NATO supports, if not *de facto* membership. (See Chapter 9.)

At the same time, however, it has also been suggested that Paris has backed the membership of Romania for the purpose of stalling NATO enlargement. The French position was that NATO cannot afford to expand (either politically or economically) if it cannot obtain a political consensus among its present members. Moreover, NATO must adapt itself thoroughly to the new security threats posed by the post–Cold War disequilibrium. NATO must support France's interests in the *l'espace euro-méditerranéen* and work to counterbalance—if not "double contain"—German influence. NATO must not only support French interests in Central Europe but must also recognize legitimate Russian concerns.

In January 1996, Foreign Minister Hervé de Charette, the first foreign minister to meet the new Russian foreign minister, Yevgeny Primakov, accordingly expressed empathy for the Russian position in regard to NATO and agreed that Russian interests in both Central and Eastern Europe need attention.[31] Both Paris and London (in addition to Moscow) have been suspicious of ulterior German reasons for at least initially seeking the rapid expansion of NATO into Central Europe. (While Germany has softened its demands to expand NATO rapidly, Bonn has still sought to block a potential Russian veto on NATO's expansion: any agreement with Russia must be made *after* NATO began to take on new members, so as not to give Moscow a veto.) In February 1997, Paris backed Russian calls for a U.S., UK, French, German, Russian summit to discuss NATO enlargement prior to the July 1997 Madrid conference, and urged the United States to heed Russian concerns prior to the July 1997 NATO summit in Madrid. The French proposal was backed by Bonn, but not by Washington, which wanted to include all NATO members in the enlargement talks.

Despite stated intentions to cooperate, European-Russian military cooperation has gotten off to a poor start. In December 1994, German-Russian military exercises were called off due to the Russian intervention in Chechnya. In 1995, a Russian military cooperation agreement with Denmark was canceled for the same reason. Moscow has sought similar cooperation accords with the Baltic states to counterbalance defense agreements between Germany and the Baltic states. The latter have thus far rejected Moscow's overtures, as have Poland and Hungary. (Denmark, however, resumed military cooperation with Russia in 1996 once the war in Chechnya wound down, planning five activities in 1996, and six in 1997.)

Contrary to the view that EU expansion followed by WEU membership may appear less threatening than the growth of NATO,[32] Russia's Full Strategic Doctrine of November 1993 opposed the expansion of *any* blocs into former Soviet (and czarist) spheres of influence and security without simultaneous conjoint security guarantees with Moscow, even if these blocs were not perceived to be a "threat."[33] Moscow has accordingly asked to be informed about any defense agreements reached between the EU/WEU and Central and

Eastern European states. Russia has proposed a WEU-Russian Consultative Council (which would engage in joint naval manoeuvers, a WEU-Russian satellite system, joint cooperation on anti–tactical missile systems, and Russia-WEU arms cooperation).[34] The WEU has thus far agreed to *ad hoc* cooperation with Russia, but not to a formal Consultative Council. The Secretary-General of the WEU, José Cutileiro, met with Primakov for the first time in June 1996. While proposing greater cooperation with Russia, he admitted that there were "not many" areas where close cooperation was possible.[35] The WEU may hence appear just as discriminatory as NATO in Russian eyes—despite strong WEU support for Russian membership on the Council of Europe, for example.

At the same time, should the WEU ever really be in the position to offer any significant separate agreements with Russia, such actions would tend to be regarded with suspicion by Washington (as efforts to decouple Europe from NATO). By 1996, Italy and Russia, for example, entered into a defense cooperation agreement involving the joint development of radar planes, helicopters, and involving cooperation on security and arms control—the first of its kind for a NATO member.

Russia has additionally resented EU diplomatic intervention in former Soviet spheres of influence and security, the "near abroad." The Franco–German-inspired European Stability Pact (or Balladur initiative, finalized in 1995), intended to deal with security issues involving former Soviet-bloc states, was met rather coldly by Foreign Minister Kozyrev. The latter objected that he did not want to duplicate work already completed by the CSCE, an organization in which Russia is a member. (The European Stability Pact was intended as an exercise in preventive diplomacy and resulted in an agreement to support the status quo: no minor modifications of borders, and no collective or new minority rights.) In 1995 the Russian leadership had also ruled out a NATO-Russian "non-aggression pact," as proposed by France, arguing that Paris was using the proposal as a ploy to force Russia to accept NATO expansion. From Moscow's viewpoint, a non-aggression pact did not address the kind of regional conflicts that were likely to occur, in addition to which the pact seemed to imply that one or more of the parties had aggressive intent.

Moreover, Moscow believed it could play on U.S.-EU tensions to check NATO enlargement. The Russian defense ministry has believed that certain countries, such as Greece, Portugal, and Spain (Mediterranean countries closer to France than to Germany), were prepared to block NATO expansion if Moscow took a firm stand.[36] In February 1997, Italian Foreign Minister Lamberto Dini stated that "the eventual NATO expansion can only take place with the consensus of Russia and not against its will."[37] Norway (a non-nuclear NATO state with a three–hundred–kilometer border with Russia) was also perceived to be hesitant about NATO enlargement. Moscow has also regarded the neutral countries of Finland, Sweden, and Austria as ambivalent about NATO enlargement, despite strong Nordic support for Baltic state membership in the EU and NATO. (Throughout 1996, Foreign Minister Primakov warned all the former neutral states against joining NATO—a threat which could backfire by making these states even more willing to join.)

Moscow also has reason to believe that Turkey might not support NATO enlargement. Turkey does not see why it should pledge itself to defend Central European states, which are potential EU members, if Europe does not first extend full-fledged EU membership to Turkey. In December 1996, Turkish Foreign Minister Tansu Ciller met with Foreign Minister Primakov. It was speculated that Turkey may oppose NATO enlargement at the Madrid conference in July 1997, if Russia pledges not to support the Kurdish PKK. Foreign Minister Primakov, however, stated that Russia is not responsible for PKK actions. Primakov likewise rebuffed Turkish concerns with the sale of Russian S–300s (anti–missile systems somewhat similar to the U.S. Patriot) to the Greek controlled region of Cyprus. Moscow regarded the weapons as "defensive"; Ankara saw them as "undermining the peace." Moreover, Turkey has sought to block the transfer of NATO assets to the WEU— unless the EU/WEU comes to terms with Ankara on defense (and economic) issues.[38] (Washington could push for a greater Turkish role in WEU military planning, and it may attempt to press Ankara into making reforms in its human rights and economic policies so as to gain Turkish acceptance into the EU—a dubious prospect.)

Despite European calls for a closer relationship with Russia, and despite WEU support for the integration of Russia into the EU, Russia was initially refused entry into the Council of Europe (due to the appalling state of Russian prisons, police brutality, and human-rights violations). Moscow was also barred from the International Association of Constitutional Courts, ostensibly due to fact that the Russian Constitutional Court had not operated since its suspension in September–October 1993 and (according to Russian sources) to the politicization of its judges.[39] In December 1994, following its intervention in Chechnya, Russia's application for membership in the Council of Europe was suspended, but it was re-opened in 1995. Ukraine was consequently accepted into the Council of Europe *prior* to Russia and despite Kyiv's political-economic instability, lack of market-oriented reforms, and poor record in regard to prisoner rights and capital punishment. (Europe has regarded Ukraine as the key pivotal state. In May 1996, EU foreign ministers issued a statement—which could represent a significant step toward a CFSP—indicating that the

EU considered Ukrainian independence, territorial integrity, and sovereignty vital to European security.)[40]

Arguing that it was "better to integrate than isolate Russia," the Parliamentary Assembly of the Council of Europe then approved Russia's membership application, 164–35 with fifteen abstentions on 25 January 1996, despite the breakdown of negotiations in Chechnya and Russia's brutal intervention there. (Russia had yet to sign the European Human Rights Convention and adhere to the Council agreements on minority rights.) Russian revanchist Vladimir Zhirinovsky contended that "if a trend of hatred toward Russia prevails in Europe, Europe must know what our response will be."[41] Russian human rights activist Sergei Kovalev, however, warned that by voting in favor of Russian admission the Council would be assuming a very heavy responsibility, but that "an isolated Russia is more dangerous to itself and to the world than an integrated Russia."[42]

By May 1996, at his first Council of Europe ministerial conference, Yevgeny Primakov urged the EU to take stronger steps to protect Russian rights in the Baltic states and argued that the Council of Europe could represent a "cornerstone" for a new all-European security system "without dividing lines or blocs."[43] Rather than attempting to pressure Europe, Russia may seek to draw the EU (and WEU) away from U.S. influence. An alternative Russian foreign policy has accordingly been proposed by the Russian Council on Foreign Defense Policy. In brief, this alternative argues that Moscow should seek a strategic alliance with NATO, and test the rapprochement over a period of four to five years, in which NATO would promise not to enlarge. NATO would instead strengthen the PfP, among other actions meant to improve the NATO-Russian relationship. The Russian Council then urged that Russia make "maximum efforts . . . to establish [a] closer relationship" with the EU as well as with the WEU.[44] (This policy, however, could raise American concerns over Russian intentions ultimately to decouple European states from the Atlantic Alliance. To head off such a possibility, Washington must attempt to coordinate U.S., Russian, and EU/WEU policies through a cooperative-collective security approach. [See Chapter 11.])

THE LONG-TERM QUESTION OF EU ENLARGEMENT AND GERMANY

Although EU efforts to pursue greater economic, political, and strategic unification appear to represent a means to gain greater strategic-economic leverage vis-à-vis the United States (and Russia) and concurrently defend European interests as a whole, Europe is still far from unified. A number of issues threaten to weaken European unity, including: (1) a single market in financial services, transport, energy, telecommunications has yet to be implemented; (2) inter-governmental cooperation in regard fiscal and monetary policy (which in the long term could improve employment figures) has yet to be devised; (3) key protectionist centers of production and trade (such as agriculture and fishing) continue to oppose technocratic centralization and *étatisation*, which has been regarded as being imposed by Brussels; (4) the unemployment rate has hovered around 10–12 percent for the EU as a whole (roughly 18 million people), potentially causing socio-economic instability; (5) long-term inability to sustain the high costs of the European model of job security and social benefits due to global competition from the United States and Asia, resulting in socio-political conflict as benefits are cut; and (6) migration to Western Europe (from the former Soviet bloc, the former Yugoslavia, and from the south—the Maghreb, sub-Saharan Africa, and Turkey) could provoke the rise of ultranationalist and xenophobic movements.[45]

Serious concerns have been raised that ultimate failure to forge European unity could result in a schism between a protectionist south-west grouping led by France and a more liberal, internationalist, free-trade north-east grouping led by Germany. In this pessimistic scenario, Germany would be able to influence Scandinavian countries and Austria; France would look to the Mediterranean (Spain and Italy, most importantly, but also North African states, which are increasingly demanding French, more than German, attention due to the effects of immigration on France, as well as the rise of pan-Islamic movements, among other concerns). In addition, France and Germany would compete for influence over Central and Eastern European states. Both France and Germany would also look to influence Russia, which in turn could play divided European states against each other. The United States—if it did not move into "selected interventionism"—would also play off the interests of rival European countries, generally supporting the maritime "trading" states against continental "protectionist" states.

On one hand, an increasing measure of European self-reliance is absolutely necessary to keep the United States engaged on the continent. On the other, both the United States and Russia fear that EU expansion may result in protected markets or trade diversion, if not an exclusive EU sphere of influence and security. The EU has opposed both unilateral U.S. or Russian actions, but it has also opposed those actions that raise fears of a U.S.-Russian condominium. At the same time, the EU is concerned with the unilateral actions of its own members, particularly Germany.

Bonn has been accused of pursuing German unity at the expense of European unity—and at the expense of the European and global economies. Germany's late 1991 decisions to raise interest rates and recognize Croatian and Slovenian secession (without consulting fellow Europeans), combined with *Bundesbank* warnings against European monetary union and German actions in 1994 to cut back funding for EU activities, did not augur well for future European unity. German efforts to pursue *Ostpolitik* and to limit its military capability in exchange for German unification have also raised suspicions in Washington. Bonn has transferred roughly $700 billion in revenues to eastern Germany, and Germans may have to pay a 7.5 percent surcharge on their income tax for the foreseeable future to pay the costs of unification and continued subsidies to the east. Fourteen percent of the labor force is unemployed in the east versus eight percent in the west. The high costs of German unification, coupled with austerity measures necessary to reduce budget deficits to less than three percent of GDP and to lower the national debt to less than sixty percent of GDP, may make Germany less capable to support projects involving European monetary unification, for example.[46] Germany may no longer be able to support its "federal" model for Europe.

While German actions have caused worry in Washington, they have raised even more suspicion in Russia, despite (or because of) Germany's role as Russia's main financial benefactor. (Bonn provided Moscow with more than $75 billion in aid from 1990–96). German arms sales to Turkey, and fears of German support for the national independence of the Baltic states and such newly independent countries as Ukraine and Croatia, have led to Russian concern, as has Bonn's support for the Volga Germans and unofficial German claims to Kaliningrad (if not Polish territories). Since the breakup of the USSR, Germany has tended to play a policy of "equidistance" between Russia and Ukraine, but Bonn could well tilt closer to Kyiv, which has threatened to split away from the Russian-dominated CIS states. Russia fears losing political-economic influence over former Soviet spheres of influence and security, particularly as these newly independent states prefer the strong Western or German currencies—*Deutsche Marks über alles*—as opposed to hyperinflated rubles.

In addition to the dangers mentioned above (schism of Europe along a German-led free-trade North-East and a French-led protectionist South-East), the possible failure of France and Germany to evolve a common strategy could ultimately split Europe. This pessimistic scenario could leave Germany to seek out a more independent policy of *Sonderweg*, or a special way, between East and West, which would most likely result in Germany reaching out for a collaboration with Russia "at the expense of the countries in between" as the CDU/CSU has argued. It has thus been feared that Bonn may be tacitly threatening a separate Russian-German pact that might divide Europe and the Atlantic Alliance—if the NATO defense shield is not soon extended to cover Central European states (Poland, the Czech Republic, and Hungary) and thus provide a barrier against instability on Germany's eastern flank. Accordingly, fears of Germany pursuing a special path, plus concerns generated by former Russian Foreign Minister's Kozyrev's unfortunate remark in late 1994 calling for a Russo-German "axis" (among other signs of Russo-German policy collaboration), have in turn raised calls for an expansion of both NATO and the EU to check German expansionism. In effect, pan-Europeanism (backed by NATO) has sought to "double contain" pan-Germanism.

A potentially hegemonic Germany raises legitimate Russian security concerns. At the same time, it is not certain that Bonn can be "double contained" by an expanding European Union, with or without NATO. On the other hand, a shallow, but broader, European Union may permit Moscow to play European interests against each other. Moreover, a weak Europe may well decide to forge closer alliance relationships with Ukraine, China, Japan, or other powers. In 1995, the WEU opted to seek out stronger ties with ASEAN. In November 1993, German defense minister Volker Rühe called for closer defense consultation between Germany and Japan, raising concerns over a EU-Japanese "plutonium alliance." Once again, new European alliances could exacerbate traditional Russian fears of "encirclement."[47]

From this perspective, in order to "double contain" Germany (and keep it from reaching out to Russia or developing its own military potential), and in order to prevent Europe (as a politically unified region) from either splitting up or seeking out new alternative alliances, the whole process of EU enlargement really needs additional reinforcement. The EU does have a fundamental interest in *deepening*; on the other hand, it also has a fundamental interest in *widening*, to include as many states as possible, including Russia and Ukraine, if only on an "associate" basis. At the same time, however, an expanding EU/WEU is not really sufficient to "double contain" German potential; moreover, even NATO efforts to "double contain" Germany by expanding into Central Europe risk NATO's own overextension. Concurrently, if the United States moves into "selective interventionism," thereby impelling Europeans to concern themselves only with "European" security concerns, the Europeanization of NATO risks becoming its Germanization. From this perspective, German influence in NATO should be counterbalanced by that of France and the UK—including Russia as an "associate" member. What is thus needed is a cooperative-collective regime, under a general OSCE or UN mandate, that seeks to *channel* German energies into the establishment of a Euro-Atlantic Defense and Security Identity backed by NATO, the WEU, and Russia. (See Chapters 10 and 11.)

CHAPTER 3

NATO, Congress, and Central and Eastern Europe

POSSIBLE FAULT LINES IN POST-SOVIET EUROPE

The very discussion of NATO enlargement has caused what may be politically destabilizing debates in each of the states concerned. Moreover, once the Alliance finally decides upon enlargement, its very enlargement could provoke shifts in government leaderships and in power relations among states in the affected regions. New leaderships could bring to the forefront irredentist claims or territorial disputes that were previously and officially downplayed—particularly if a truly comprehensive system of security is not in place.

From this perspective, NATO must take into account: (1) unintended domestic consequences of NATO power projection that may result in political schisms among pro and anti–NATO factions within prospective NATO members; (2) the future power differential between those states which join NATO as "full" members and those which do not; (3) the ability of prospective NATO members, as well as non-NATO states, to use aspects of *strategic leveraging*[1] to manipulate NATO into backing their particular geopolitical interests; and (4) the geostrategic implications of different forms of irredentist claims or territorial disputes among Central and Eastern European states, including those directly affecting Russia or its allies, as well as disputes among NATO members themselves and with third parties. Concurrently, any NATO enlargement must take into consideration the fact that Russian pressures on the so-called "near" and "middle abroad" may not be related to the Russian ethnic diaspora alone but also to geostrategic, political-economic, and military-technological security concerns, such as access to Kaliningrad.

IRREDENTISM AND TERRITORIAL DISPUTES

The Alliance should carefully look at the nature of regional state interests and at the nature of the regional and global equipoise, in order to determine how NATO enlargement might affect those states which do or do not enter. The September 1995 *Study of NATO Enlargement* makes clear that states with "ethnic or territorial disputes, including irredentist claims, or internal jurisdictional disputes must settle those disputes by peaceful means in accordance with OSCE principles." First, it is not clear if states can totally resolve border questions and ethnic tensions in the near future. Second, it is possible that states could use NATO membership as a means to press for border revisions, potentially dragging NATO into a number of intramural and extramural disputes.

There are at least five interrelated categories of territorial disputes and irredentist claims that may affect NATO relations in the region. These claims (which may be backed officially by the regime in power, or else unofficially supported by political parties and powerful lobbies) are generally based upon historical borders, ethnic communities, linguistic ties, religious heritage, and other factors. Territorial disputes and political tensions may more simply arise out of undefined borders or the inability of states to protect their borders from illegal and unregulated trade, and drug or weapons trafficking.

The first category of irredentist claims or territorial disputes involves those directly or indirectly affecting Russia. These include Russian pressures on Central and Eastern European "front line" states considered within the "near" or "middle abroad." Russian pressures are not related entirely to the Russian ethnic diaspora but also involve geostrategic, political-economic, and military security concerns. These pressures, based in part on former czarist or Soviet claims, include claims to part or all of Ukraine and the Crimea; they also extend to potential or actual pressures on Belarus, Finland, the Baltic states, and Poland, not to mention other states in Central Europe. The Russian military presence in Moldova, for example, has partly been intended to pressure both Ukraine and Romania, in addition to supporting Russian ethnic groups in the Transdniester.

Central and Eastern European states fear the possibility of Russian political subterfuge and disinformation campaigns. They also fear the formation of "underground cells" or a "fifth column" of remaining Communist Party members or ethnic Russians, which may seek to destabilize their countries under orders from Moscow. Strong autonomy movements in eastern Ukraine and the Crimea have been regarded by Kyiv as backed by Moscow. For example, Russia has purportedly lent tacit support to miners in the Donbass region who had decided to strike for higher wages in a largely bankrupt Ukraine.

On the other side, this category also includes Moscow's suspicions of EU and Nordic support (including from NATO members Norway and Denmark) for Baltic state membership in the EU and NATO, as well as perceived foreign support for the autonomy or independence of regions inside Russia itself. These latter include Karelia, Komi, and Murmansk, if not St. Petersburg. Much as Germany has sought a NATO-backed security "buffer" in Central Europe between itself and "regional instability," the Nordic states have pressed for Baltic state membership in the EU and NATO as a security "buffer" and to prevent a "security vacuum"[2] that might permit Russia to dominate the region.

In general, the Nordic states of Sweden and Finland have been gradually shifting away from their Cold War position of "neutrality" (albeit with a pro-Western character) and toward a closer alignment with the EU. At the same time, because the EU does not yet possess an adequate nuclear deterrent and other military capability to defend these states against possible Russian aggression, Sweden and Finland have also looked toward a rapprochement with NATO, but without clamoring for NATO membership (as have the Baltic states). Finland has supported Estonia; Sweden has backed Latvia, while Denmark has supported Lithuania. Conversely, Russia may seek to play "divide and rule," if the Baltic states cannot settle their differences.

Problems stem from the remaining ethnic Russian presence, particularly in Estonia and Latvia. Whereas Lithuania has granted ethnic Russians (who made up only 9.4 percent of the population) automatic citizenship, both Estonia and Latvia have offered citizenship only to those families who had lived in the two states before 1940, and to their descendants. The rest have had to pass tests in language or constitutional and citizenship laws in order to be naturalized. Psychologically, Russians have generally seen themselves as having been relegated to second-class citizens, after having been placed in high positions by the Soviet government. In Latvia, Russians make up about 34 percent of the population, concentrated in its major cities; many Russians are well integrated into Latvian society. Latvian-Russian tensions have also resulted from the Latvian parliament's claims based on the 1920 Treaty of Riga that the Abrene territory was "unlawfully" incorporated into Russia in 1944, although these claims were ostensibly renounced in February 1996.[3]

Of those in the three Baltic states, Russian-Estonian tensions are probably the most tense, followed by those in Latvia and Lithuania, and for very different reasons. The Russian population in Estonia represents about 30 percent of the population, and it is concentrated in the border city of Narda—which is threatening to become a "state within a state." Estonians fear that this region could demand greater autonomy if the Russian population continues to grow. Critics of

Estonian policy have argued, for example, that the July 1996 decision to grant residence permits to former Russian officers, combined with simplified border crossings, could complicate hoped-for integration with NATO and the EU.[4]

Tension has resulted from Estonian claims based on the 1920 Treaty of Tartu, despite Estonian efforts to downplay these official claims to some eight hundred square miles of territory, including three cities. Changing its tactics (perhaps due to lack of U.S. and EU support), Estonia had begun to argue that it does not seek territory but wants its independence to be recognized fully; as long as Russia refuses to recognize the 1920 Treaty of Tartu, Baltic state independence remains "provisional." Baltic states accordingly believe that they have no real sovereignty and must therefore opt for NATO membership if they are not to be pressured into the CIS.[5] From its perspective, Moscow may not want to recognize the Treaty of Tartu for fear of being pressured into recognizing other interwar treaties, such as the 1921 Polish-Soviet Treaty of Riga, which advanced Polish claims into Lithuania, Belarus, and Ukraine. In addition, Russia has objected to Estonian parliamentary support for the Chechen resistance as interference in Russian domestic affairs. Thus despite Estonian efforts to reach a compromise, Russia threatened economic sanctions against Estonia in late 1996 and stated that it would not sign a border treaty. These threats were intended to secure the rights of Russian speakers in Estonia. In essence, Moscow seeks to forewarn NATO and suspects that both Latvia and Estonia will revive their territorial claims, particularly if NATO expands into Poland.

The independence of the Baltic states meant a loss of key Russian military bases. Tallinn and Paldiski (the former site of a nuclear submarine training base) in Estonia, and Liepaja, Riga, and Ventspils (site of a satellite listening post) in Latvia are no longer warm-water home ports for Russia. Accordingly, Lithuania is more affected by Russian geostrategic interests and transit routes to Kaliningrad than by problems with ethnic Russians. At the same time, Moscow and Vilnius possess disputes over about one-tenth of the Lithuanian border, while other disputes involve fishing rights.[6] Although Moscow has thus far opposed greater defense and economic integration among the Baltic states (and has attempted to play their interests against each other), greater Baltic integration could actually serve in long-term Russian interests as a "bridge" between the EU, Russia, and Belarus.

Although officially downplayed, German, Polish, or even Lithuanian claims to Russian Kaliningrad, among other issues, have likewise raised tensions. Kaliningrad represents the key to Baltic and Nordic stability, partially because Russian transit rights to and from Kaliningrad have yet to be fixed in a treaty. The Kaliningrad region also took the place of the Gulf of Finland as the key Soviet military base area (which permitted the Porkkala military base to be returned to Finland in 1956). The loss of harbors on the Baltic and Black Seas has increased the relative military importance of the Kola peninsula, and places pressure on the Nordic states.[7]

While Poland is not presently a threat to Russia, its surging economy and rapid population growth could possibly be regarded as a future "threat" to Russian interests (or to the interests of military elites within the Kaliningrad enclave alone). Accordingly, potential political, economic, and military instability in Kaliningrad would have significant ramifications in Poland and in the Baltic and Nordic states. Access to Kaliningrad, which represents the key Russian pressure point in Europe as well as a geostrategic bargaining chip in bargaining over NATO enlargement, has thus become a crucial issue for the Russian military and the Russian political elite. In February 1996, apparently without consulting Warsaw, Russia and Belarus advanced the idea of a transport corridor through Poland and Belarus, or else through Lithuania.[8]

There is also Polish-Lithuanian military cooperation, which involves a combined peacekeeping unit and an airspace management regime. This cooperation, in effect, works to forge a bilateral alliance that links the two countries strategically; thus if Poland enters NATO, Lithuania could not altogether be left out.[9] A significant crisis could erupt if Poland is brought into NATO and Lithuania denies Russia access rights. Lithuania could then appeal to Poland and NATO, despite the fact that it was not a member of NATO. (Such a crisis could represent a 1948–49 Berlin blockade, but in reverse.)

Moscow is also concerned with perceived support by Turkey, NATO member, for Tatarstan and Chechnya, among other republics inside the Russian Federation and Central Asian states of the CIS. Russia, for example, has accused Turkey of seeking to block Russian shares of Caspian Sea oil. Russian elites argue that the EU and Turkey have been trying to hamper CIS integration and to reduce Russia's influence in the Black Sea, the Transcaucasus, and Central Asia.[10] Ankara, on the other hand, regard Russia as supporting Armenia and the Kurdish PKK movement, among other anti–Turkish forces. (See Chapter 6.)

The second category includes irredentist claims or territorial disputes among Eastern European states against actual or potential Russian allies, such as Belarus, Moldova, Serbia, and possibly Bulgaria and Slovakia. Hungarians in former Yugoslavia (Vojvodina, Slovenia, and Croatia) have also been in the midst of disputes. Serbian refugees from other parts of the former Yugoslavia, for example, have been relocated in Vojvodina, which is a region with a high percentage of ethnic Hungarians. Romanian aspirations to unify with Moldova (efforts blocked by Russian support of the "Transdniester Republic") also fall into this category. Moldovan political groups appear split between those who want tight integration with Russia and the CIS (including those who support the secession of the "Transdniester Republic"), those who want to unify with Romania, and those who seek Moldovan independence. The latter two factions generally seek membership in NATO.[11] On the other side, Russia may seek to sustain permanent bases in Moldova to guard against NATO enlargement,[12] as well as to pressure Romania and Ukraine. Moldova itself does not want to become a "buffer" between the CIS and NATO—should Romania become a NATO member as has been proposed by France.

Perhaps most significant are potential tensions between Poland, Lithuania, Ukraine, and Belarus. Lithuania and Belarus possess conflicting geohistoric claims, although the two did sign an agreement on "On Good Neighborly and Friendly Relations" in February 1995. Since 1991, the Polish government has sought to establish positive diplomatic relations with both Belarus and Ukraine as a partial effort to wean these states away from Russian influence, but it has tilted more toward Ukraine than Belarus. This has been true despite potential irredentist claims to both Belarusian and Ukrainian territories based on the 1921 Polish-Soviet Treaty of Riga or eighteenth–century claims to "historic Poland." (Warsaw was the first capital to recognize Kyiv officially in December 1991.) About 300,000 Belarusians live in Poland, and 418,000 Poles live in Belarus. Poland could lay claims to Hrodna, but both sides have thus far sought to allay tensions. Concurrently, five million Russians exert strong political influence in Belarus.[13] For its part, Warsaw has realized that to open up irredentist claims could also elicit Bonn's claims to eastern territories (Silesia, Pomerania) granted by Stalin to Poland in the aftermath of World War II. Moreover, Warsaw has, somewhat ironically, opposed the repopulation of Kaliningrad by ethnic Germans migrating from the former Soviet Union and has thus permitted Russia to sustain a geostrategic pressure point in Western Europe, in order to calm fears of a German "encirclement."[14]

The third category represents irredentist claims or territorial disputes among Central and Eastern European states themselves. The Baltic states (often lumped together as allies) have sea border disputes with each other. Estonia has claimed the area around the key islands of Ruhnu and Kihnu as part of its economic zone, while Latvia has supported an equal division of the Gulf of Riga.[15] Additional actual or potential disputes include Polish, Hungarian, Slovakian, and Romanian claims to Ukrainian territory (such as Transcarpathia). Despite efforts to settle disputes, Polish-Lithuanian tensions remain, as do Hungarian tensions with Romania and Slovakia, among others. If political-economic crises continue to destabilize Ukraine, Belarus, or Poland itself, it is possible that Ukrainian Lvov and territories in Belarus could become thorns between Poland, Belarus, and Ukraine.

Issues involving Hungarian irredentism touch Slovakia, Ukraine, Romania, and Serbia. In many ways, Slovakia can be characterized as a "buffer" between Hungary, the Czech Republic, Ukraine, and the CIS.[16] Hungarian irredentist movements in particular have resulted from difficulties involving the assimilation of ethnic Hungarians into Slovakia and Romania after the partition of Hungary in the 1920 Treaty of Trianon. (Approximately three million ethnic Hungarians reside outside of Hungary.) The inclusion of Hungary, but not Slovakia, in NATO could well alienate the latter. Ukraine and Russia have ostensibly recognized collective Hungarian rights; Slovakia did as well, in 1994, although disputes over language laws and other issues have continued to perpetuate tensions.

Disputes between Romania and prospective NATO-member Hungary over Transylvania in particular may spark a potential conflict. Romanian defense minister Gheorghe Tinca stated that setting up NATO bases on Hungarian territory might encourage "Hungarian extremist forces" who dream of reviving Transylvania. According to Romanian spokespersons, the incorporation of Hungary into NATO without Romania could lead to "a climate of competition, mistrust, and instability," creating a new dividing line between NATO and Eastern Europe, and leaving Romania "vulnerable to other competing influences." Romania has sought up to $400 million in loans to embark on a military modernization program, ostensibly to make itself acceptable for NATO membership (but this policy also hedges bets in case Romania is not accepted).[17]

In addition to claims to northern Bukovina and southern Bessarabia, Romania also claims the potentially oil-rich Serpent Island, plus as much as 2,800 square miles on the Black Sea taken by the USSR in 1947 (now in Ukraine). Seeing themselves caught between Hungary, Moldova, Ukraine, and Bulgaria, Romanian spokespersons have seen NATO membership as the "only strategic option"; not to join would be a "disaster."[18] Romania and Hungary did, however, formulate a Basic Treaty in August 1996. In November 1996, the new Romanian government under President Emil Constantinescu and Prime Minister Viktor Ciorbea, however, did promise to settle these disputes. The government has been seeking a new association with Poland and Ukraine. Romania and Hungary have called for joint military cooperation (similar to the Franco-German initiative.) Romania hopes that its efforts to reduce its budget deficit and to resolve disputes with its neighbors will lead to EU and NATO membership.[19] Similarly, due to potential conflict with its neighbors, the Bulgarian president,

Zhelyu Zhelev, stated that NATO membership might help "unite" the population and help solve Bulgaria's national security problems![20]

The fourth issue concerns possible conflict of interest between prospective NATO members and states that either belong to the EU alone or belong to no major grouping. Russian threats to Finland and the Baltic states, for example, may concern EU/WEU spheres of security and influence but not *directly* those of NATO. NATO's involvement in former Yugoslavia could overstretch NATO's political consensus if war erupts again following the eventual withdrawal of U.S. or European forces. Turkey's support for Albania (coupled with bilateral U.S. military ties to Albania), coupled with indirect involvement in Serbian-held Kosovo, could become problematic (see below). Furthermore, NATO countries in southwestern Europe, such as France, may be more concerned with events in the Mediterranean and North Africa (the Maghreb) than with Central and Eastern Europe. An additional issue includes Italian claims to Istria, a territory shared by both Croatia and Slovenia.

The fifth category concerns disputes among NATO members themselves, with prospective NATO members, or with third parties. Most significantly, Turkey has threatened war if Greece enforces the extension of its territorial waters from six to twelve nautical miles. Ankara has opposed the sale of Russian S-300 surface-to-air missiles to the Greek-held section of Cyprus. Among other problematic issues, Turkish concerns involve Kurdish movements and Iraq, conflict between Armenia and Azerbaijan, insurrection in southern Albania in 1997 (seen as supported by ethnic Greeks), and conflicts in Bosnia, Kosovo, and Albania. (See Chapter 6.)

Despite the Czech-German peace treaty (1991–92), which ostensibly ended territorial claims, guaranteed both Czech and German rights, and officially recognized the "injustice" of the German expulsion from the Sudetenland, the treaty did not restore German property or ownership rights in the Czech Republic (unless Sudeten Germans renounce their German nationality for Czech). By April 1996, a new declaration had been formulated, and then signed by both governments in January 1997—despite statements by the German foreign minister Klaus Kinkel that German-Czech talks had been "disastrously bogged down" in January 1996.[21] While the German accord met with some domestic opposition, the Czech parliament ratified the accord after acrimonious debate in March 1997. The declaration includes German support for Czech membership in the EU and NATO. (Poland has likewise been concerned with the loyalty of the German population in Silesia and unofficial German claims to territories given Poland by Stalin.)

In many ways, the kind of issues that might confront a potentially overextended NATO necessitate adjudication through the UN or OSCE (backed by NATO, WEU, and Russian cooperation). Moreover, many of these potential disputes really cannot be thoroughly addressed until a cooperative-collective security regime is established, as unilateral NATO enlargement could well exacerbate regional tensions. Ethnic and territorial disputes (as well as questions involving civil-military relations) really cannot be resolved by the assumed panacea of NATO enlargement. Although "full" NATO membership may possibly help to adjudicate disputes among member states, help to secure international investment, and to a certain extent aid the transition to democratic structures (at significant risk of overextending NATO resources), NATO membership may concurrently exacerbate tensions among those states which do not join. NATO membership may thus tend to lend support to its newly joined members over non-member states rather than help to mediate effectively among the rival interests of all the disputing parties—in the assumption that NATO, the EU/WEU, and Russia cannot forge a more comprehensive system of cooperative-collective security for all of Central and Eastern Europe.

CONGRESS: FORCING NATO'S HAND

Although NATO has not publicly determined which states are to ultimately obtain NATO membership and security guarantees, the U.S. Congress has attempted to force NATO's hand, through the NATO Participation Act of 1994.[22] Not only has the public debate on the subject of NATO enlargement tended to antagonize Moscow and raise exaggerated expectations on the part of Central and Eastern European publics and elites, but NATO itself has left a number of key questions open. The promise of NATO membership has raised a not entirely healthy public debate throughout Central and Eastern Europe. The PfP has, for better or worse, created a race for entry into NATO, in which states fear that if they do not enter in the first wave they will be discriminated against.[23]

NATO's calls for an "inclusive" and "comprehensive" approach to European security issues appear to have fallen on deaf ears, as countries have generally been more concerned with their particular national security interests than with multilateral regional security linkages that might stabilize a larger area. NATO membership has unfortunately appeared to represent a panacea that will transcend both national and regional security dilemmas—including those involving Russia. The problem has been that many Central and Eastern European states fear that only those that obtain "full" NATO membership will obtain "full" Article V security guarantees; thus no matter what promises NATO makes in the future, a state's security will not be guaranteed until it is accepted as a "full" member.

The very proposal of NATO membership has already begun to create schisms among political parties within these states. These debates may be particularly detrimental if NATO does not really intend to enlarge membership, thus causing a psychological letdown after a period of "NATO-mania." Such a letdown could provoke an anti–Western backlash. Moreover, U.S. congressional proposals to enlarge NATO may backfire if the U.S. Congress (or parliaments of other countries) refuse to ratify enlargement or else refuse to provide appropriate funding—a possibility which could altogether undermine NATO's credibility.

It is thus not clear whether the promise of NATO membership for selected countries will help to defuse suspicions among states or, on the contrary, exacerbate those suspicions. The NATO Participation Act of 1994 specifies that PfP participants who seek NATO membership must respect "the territorial integrity of their neighbors" in addition to "protecting the rights of all their citizens."[24] But it is not at all clear if border questions and ethnic tensions can be easily resolved in the near future. (Greece and Turkey have yet to resolve their disputes!) If Central or Eastern European states join NATO or the WEU before *nonofficial* revisionist or irredentist claims are truly adjudicated (despite government promises and treaties), there is a possibility that revisionist states and pan-national movements could attempt to use their membership in NATO or the WEU to press for border revisions, or support secessionist movements in neighboring states.[25]

Besides issues regarding territorial integrity, the NATO Participation Act of 1994 also insists states must make "significant progress toward establishing democratic institutions, a free market economy, civilian control of their armed forces, and rule of law."[26] As political oversight of the defense budget and clear division of authority between president and parliament are issues not thoroughly resolved even in developed democracies,[27] it is doubtful that newly independent states can achieve these criteria for NATO membership in the near future. Nor is it clear if it is necessarily in the interests of aspiring NATO members to adopt these rather ideal standards, particularly if a too-rapid expansion of "democracy" and "market liberalism" brings greater political-economic instability. The gains of former communist (if not militant pan-nationalist) parties in almost all of Central and Eastern Europe should signal caution despite popular support for NATO ("NATO-mania") in many of these same states. Gains of former communists in Poland in 1993, followed by the victory of President Aleksandr Kwasniewski in November 1995, are perhaps the most significant in regard to NATO interests. Former communists likewise made gains in Hungary and Bulgaria in 1994. Political risks are also involved despite the newly positive role of former communist parties in undertaking reforms, albeit through *"nomenklatura* privatization."* The danger of political-economic instabilities resulting in an anti–Western coup d'état or the stealing of NATO secrets should be taken into consideration if these states are to be fully integrated into NATO. The nature of civil-military relations in Poland, for example, have remained an obstacle for potential Polish membership in NATO.[28]

In regard to civil-military relations, the prospects of NATO membership may be manipulated (with positive or negative implications) by parties in power seeking to remain in power, to break up opposition movements, or to keep rivals out of key ministries. Such actions would be contrary to NATO's expressed support for the "democratic" process. The mere prospect of NATO membership could be politically destabilizing in countries with significant anti–NATO factions; failure of a pro-NATO ruling coalition to obtain Alliance membership as promised could help bring that coalition down. Concurrently, human rights abuses in Turkey could bring charges of "double standards" by states who might not be admitted on grounds of human rights violations, poor civil-military relations, or other ideological concerns. Slovak Prime Minister Vladimir Meciar argued that the U.S. congressional support for Hungarian membership in NATO but opposition to admission for Slovakia raised a "double standard," in view of Hungary's "nationalistic policies" and "interference in the internal affairs of neighboring countries."[29]

Popular calls for a NATO "without nuclear weapons or troops" appear utopian, and hence would be politically risky if supporters of enlargement ultimately become disillusioned with NATO's promises or the public rejects membership. NATO's refusal in 1995 to state clearly that it will definitely not deploy nuclear weapons on the territory of member states has raised public anxiety. In Hungary, more than forty civic organizations issued a statement demanding that the Hungarian leadership make clear its opposition to deployment of nuclear weapons should Hungary ultimately become a member of NATO. On the other hand, Central and East European states may eventually demand the deployment of NATO forces to send a strong signal of commitment.

Also "public referendums" (Spanish membership in 1982 was accompanied by a referendum) could also clash with the secret nature of NATO decision-making and thus risk disillusionment. For example, the Czech Civic Democratic Party of the Prime Minister Vaclav Klaus (part of a minority right-of-center government after the June 1996 parliamentary elections) has apparently staked its political future on NATO's decision by stating that membership is its primary foreign policy goal. The main opposition, the Social Democratic Party (which emerged as the second largest party in June 1996), is in favor of NATO membership but opposes deployments of foreign troops and nuclear weapons; it has called for a national referendum, despite lack of constitutional authority to do so. The reform-communist Left Bloc, the far-left Communist Party of Bohemia and Moravia, and the right-wing Republican party all oppose NATO membership, and they demand a referendum if the Czech Republic is officially offered membership. In June 1996, roughly one–third of Czech citizens supported NATO membership, one–third were against, and one–third undecided. Should a referendum be held, a "no" vote, or a close "yes" vote, could jeopardize the prospects of NATO membership.[30]

Moreover, it is not clear whether all states, including those of the politically divided Visegrad group (Poland, the Czech Republic, Slovakia, and Hungary) can ultimately meet requirements for NATO membership as articulated by the Participation Act of 1994, because of the rather stringent requirements for membership. It may take between five to fifteen years for states to reach NATO standards, as a minimum degree of interoperability is necessary to make NATO security guarantees meaningful. Except perhaps for Romania, the force readiness, technology, command structures, and training of most Central and Eastern European states are not at all up to NATO standards, and defense spending has been cut to roughly one–half of 1989 expenditures.[31] Poland has cut defense spending by 44 percent since 1987; Hungary has cut by 60 percent since 1988. The force capabilities of most former Warsaw Pact states are obsolete, and these countries lack the infrastructure to develop high-tech weaponry. Depending upon priorities, upgrading to NATO standards may require Central European states to increase defense spending by as much as 60 percent overall, from roughly 2.2 percent of GDP to 3.6 percent.[32] While general public opinion in Eastern Europe may look favorably to NATO, a July 1996 opinion poll stated that only 23 percent of Poles would reduce public expenditure in other areas in order to enter; only 9 percent of Hungarians, 8 percent of Czechs, and 7 percent of Slovaks approve of the using of public funds to bring their armies up to NATO standards.[33] In October 1996 NATO expressed concern over Czech plans to reduce defense expenditures.

Despite good intent and without Russian pressure, some states may thus be inadvertently alienated by the PfP process. Hungary, for example, was unable to participate in "Cooperative Bridge 94" manoeuvers in Poland—because of the expense. Russia did participate in the June 1996 PfP exercises in Lvov, but only because Washington paid $40,000 in transportation costs. Russia thereafter advised that it would not to participate in the August 1996 PfP exercises in Camp Lejeune, North Carolina, ostensibly because the finance ministry had not distributed the necessary funds to the defense ministry.[34] Certain countries may accordingly be unable to meet PfP standards and commitments and thus not be considered for NATO/WEU membership despite their intent to join. U.S. financial assistance to the PfP member states may furthermore be regarded by Moscow as a means to subsidize ultimate NATO membership.

On the other hand, if it is ultimately determined that NATO membership for a particular state is "absolutely vital" to U.S. national security interests, then Washington may be forced to overlook its own criteria for membership in a particular case. For example, even though Slovakia might not meet all the political requirements for NATO membership (due to poor civil-military relations, lack of progress on market liberalization and democratic reforms, and continued problems with borders or ethnic minorities), Bratislava may still considered for NATO membership (along with the Czech Republic, Poland, and Hungary) for two reasons. The first is that the significant Hungarian minority in Slovakia would otherwise make it difficult to accept Hungary into NATO, as Hungarians in Slovakia could provoke a political crisis to obtain support from Budapest. The second reason would be to fill the geostrategic gap between these countries, a factor (which has been denied as relevant by Washington) that would, were Slovakia not admitted, raise questions of NATO's ultimate intent for other states not invited to join. (NATO could, however, claim that its purpose in inviting a new member was to help the transformation to democracy. That, to a certain extent, appeared to be the case in regard to Spanish membership in 1982, but it is more doubtful in the cases of Portugal, Greece, and Turkey, each of which have had military dictatorships while NATO members.)

THE FORMER NEUTRAL STATES

American public debate over NATO enlargement has rarely entertained the possibility of Austrian, Swedish, Swiss, Irish, or, more provocatively, Finnish membership. There are significant public discussions in each of these states, which are presently adjusting to membership in the EU (except Switzerland) after having maintained a neutral status during the Cold War. Austria, Finland, and Sweden appear very interested in a close relationship with NATO; Switzerland and Ireland appear less inclined.[35]

Interestingly, Switzerland (which is not a member of the UN) joined the PfP in December 1996 after forging a commercial agreement with NATO's Maintenance and Supply Agency. At the same time, a Swiss application for membership appears dubious: Swiss Foreign Minister Flavio Cotti has stated that Switzerland will remain faithful to its principle of armed neutrality. Ireland bases its neutrality on a desire not to be caught up in Britain's wars; it has feared that participation in the PfP could lead Irish forces to be placed under a British command within NATO. At the same time, public opinion polls have leaned to Irish participation in PfP as well as in the NATO-led SFOR.

According to June–July 1996 public opinion polls, most Austrians continue to support "neutrality," but many also say that Austrian membership in the EU has increasingly made the concept obsolete. (The Soviet Union had demanded that Austria place a neutrality clause in its constitution in 1955 as a condition for withdrawing Soviet forces.) In February 1995, one month after Austria joined the EU, 70 percent were pro-neutrality, 16 percent were pro-NATO, and 12 percent were undecided. In June–July 1996, 63 percent continued to prefer neutrality over NATO membership, 18 percent were pro-NATO, and 21 percent were undecided.[36] The ruling coalition government (aligning the Social Democratic Party and the People's Party) possesses conflicting views on the subject; the right wing opposition Freedom Party supports NATO membership, however. It is possible that Austrian views of NATO will shift, however, once its population adjusts itself to EU membership. (Moscow's threats to Vienna could shift public opinion as well.)

Austria, Sweden, and Finland have each kept the door open to all security forums, including the OSCE and EU/WEU; each has participated in PfP, but their governments have been reluctant to express publicly the extent of their interest in joining NATO, in part due to their formerly neutral status, as well as to apparent lack of public support. In April 1996 the Finnish and Swedish foreign ministers proposed the concept of a EU peace project under the mandates of the UN and OSCE.[37]

In the same month, Finland proposed "consultation in greater depth with NATO" but also affirmed that NATO-Finnish discussions would not imply a change in its non-aligned status. The Finnish prime minister, Paavo Lipponen, warned against "loose talk" about the prospects of NATO membership; Finnish officials argue that Finnish membership in NATO would further isolate the Baltic states. On the other hand, Finland has not entirely excluded the option. Either a revanchist Russia or a more cooperative NATO-Russian relationship could lead Helsinki to seek NATO membership. The dilemma is that "full" Finnish membership could well overextend NATO capabilities in the effort to protect NATO's accordingly lengthened border with Russia. At the same time, due to Finland's close historical relationship with Moscow, Helsinki could be helpful in bringing NATO and Russia closer together, if Moscow does not perceive it as pursuing irredentist claims. In March 1997, in his first public intervention in Finnish domestic affairs, Boris Yeltsin warned Helsinki against affiliating itself with NATO.

Sweden and Austria, however, do not possess common borders with Russia, nor do they belong to former Soviet or czarist Russian spheres of influence and security. Both Sweden and Austria are highly developed countries that have become EU members and observers in the WEU. Both have participated in PfP activities. Both may be more in line with American democratic, economic, and political-military standards than more frequently mentioned Central and Eastern European states.

Austrian and Swedish membership in NATO (on a strictly non-nuclear basis) should not prove as provocative to Moscow as would the "full" NATO membership of front-line states, such as Finland, the Baltic states, and Poland. Membership could, moreover, work to "double contain" Swedish and Austrian influence in the Baltic states, Finland, and northwest Russia, as well as in Central Europe and Ukraine respectively. NATO membership could possibly help curb extreme nationalist movements in Austria. On the other hand, in March 1996 the Russian foreign minister, Primakov, stated that he "especially" appreciated Sweden's neutrality at a time when NATO was considering expansion to Russia's borders.[38] He also warned Austria against joining NATO.

If Austria and Sweden were to join NATO despite Russian pressures, then it must also be assumed that their membership would not in any way overextend NATO capabilities or political will. On the other hand, if Sweden and Austria decline "full" NATO membership, or if they are not accepted by the American Senate as "full" members, NATO assets could still made available to them through ESDI; the question of "full" NATO Article V security guarantees, however, would be left hanging. (Sweden and Finland have thus far justified their stance against NATO membership by arguing that "full" membership would not necessarily make them any more secure. Sweden in particular stressed that NATO enlargement must not repartition Europe.)

It is highly ironic that while states such as Poland, the Czech Republic, Hungary, Romania, and the Baltic states may be among the most interested in joining, NATO itself may actually be reluctant to accept their eventual membership, due to their background in the Warsaw Pact and their continued need for development. NATO interests may, in fact, be better served by the highly developed, politically and economically stable countries of Sweden and Austria, which have been reluctant to enter.

Again, although the formerly "neutral" states of Finland and Sweden (along with NATO members, Norway and Denmark) have pushed for Baltic state membership in the EU and NATO, neither

Finland nor Sweden has publicly pressed for membership themselves.[39] In August 1996, the foreign ministers of Finland, Sweden, Norway, Denmark, and Iceland stated their unwillingness to provide bilateral security guarantees to the Baltic states.[40] At the same time, Nordic state support for Baltic state membership in NATO incriminates these countries in Russian eyes—as an effort to block Russian access to the Baltic and isolate Russia from its military enclave in Kaliningrad.

THE QUESTION OF CONJOINT SECURITY GUARANTEES

In many ways, two factors have thus far blocked the concept of conjoint NATO-Russian security guarantees. The first is NATO's insistence—as illustrated in the September 1995 *Study on NATO Enlargement*—that all new members will be "full" members. Even if "full" membership does not necessarily imply the necessity to deploy nuclear weapons or foreign forces, the concept still means that NATO has exclusive influence over the defense matters of member states. If, on the other hand, NATO spoke of "associate" membership (or else redefined its concept of "full" membership), it would be easier to adopt a framework for conjoint NATO-WEU-Russian security guarantees. (See Chapter 1.) The second factor is that Central and Eastern European states have themselves been opposed to offers of conjoint NATO-WEU-Russian security guarantees. Central European states consequently argue that their security is best handled "within a coalition framework," i.e., within NATO alone.[41]

Polish and Baltic state spokesmen have thus argued that conjoint security guarantees would place their states in a "gray" or "buffer" zone, with negative consequences: Such a situation is viewed (1) as not conducive to internal stability, and (2) as tending to push countries into positions of permanent dissent, as powerful states would attempt to influence the course of their domestic and foreign policies.[42] The Polish prime minister, Wlodzimierz Cimoszewicz, for example, argued against Russian-WEU guarantees as well: "the concept of so-called cross guarantees for Central Europe by Russia and West European countries implies that the division of Europe will be preserved . . . [and that] Central Europe will be kept as a gray zone which will remain an object and not an independent subject of European relations and that the states guaranteeing its security would retain the right to decide on the political future of the region."[43] Moreover, the Lithuanian constitution explicitly forbids joining any post–Soviet Eastern military-political-economic alliance, commonwealth, or area. Vilnius has thus rejected so-called "buffer" or "bridge zone" concepts and also any form of "mixed integration" into both Europe and Eurasia—seeking instead strictly EU and NATO membership.[44]

A similar point of view in opposition to conjoint NATO-Russian security guarantees has been expressed by a Latvian spokesperson, Colonel Juris Dalbins, who argued that the Baltic states must first develop their own self-defense forces (the Baltic Battalion); yet as these self-defense forces are not sufficient to take on a major aggressor, Baltic states should be integrated into wider security structures, the EU, WEU, and NATO. (The Baltic states have generally feared that military cooperation through the Baltic Action Plan may be regarded as a substitute for NATO membership. They worry that they will not be in the first wave of NATO enlargement and thus they must seek out bilateral arrangements.) This viewpoint has opposed "suggestions that NATO should conclude a bilateral treaty with Russia under which both parties would guarantee respect for the integrity, independence and security of the countries lying between the Alliance and Russia. This would mean that in the event of unrest or a threat to peace, NATO and Moscow would be obliged to deal jointly with the crisis. This would place the Baltic states in a questionable buffer zone. It would mean that Russia, alongside the members of a democratic self-defense organization, would be given a kind of *droit de regard* within our region merely by virtue of its might. . . . [The fact that Latvia] "is working towards integration with the West rather than the Commonwealth of Independent States" means that "such a NATO-Russia treaty would unduly complicate the progress of this Western orientation. Moreover, it could require the West to test its resolve against an unpredictable future Russian leadership in an area where NATO has already conceded Russia's right of oversight. This is not to deny that Russia may be NATO's most important security partner—merely to recognize that it is in the interests of this partnership that security uncertainties should not put Russia in the position of being drawn into military intervention with unforeseen consequences."[45]

Despite opposition to NATO-Russian "cross security" guarantees, however, the Baltic states and Poland do recognize that good relations with Russia are fundamental to their security. Although there is an effort to "internationalize" Baltic security to lead EU and NATO states to acknowledge that the Baltic zone is an integral aspect of European security, there has been also been some recognition that while the Baltic states and Poland may be opposed to *bilateral* Baltic-Russian security accords, they may be willing to join a security system in which Russia takes part under a *multilateral* treaty.[46] Moreover, while these states do not want to be part of any post–Soviet East-bloc relationship, they still have recognized the importance of NATO's enhanced relations with Russia and Ukraine, as well as of the NACC, which involves the latter countries. Concurrently, the rise of Polish-Lithuanian-Belarusian tensions has suggested the necessity to look toward Russian, as well as NATO and EU/WEU, security supports. It must *not* be assumed that Moscow will necessarily support Minsk against Warsaw (even if Moscow has attempted to play both sides of the fence). (See Chapter 5.)

Much as Poland and the Baltic states have largely failed to implement a policy of *Ostpolitik* by dealing directly with Moscow and Minsk, so too has Prague, despite its historically pro-Russian position. The Czech Republic and Poland have disagreed over German and Russian intent and to what extent Moscow in particular should play a *legitimate* role in Central and Eastern European security. Poland has been interested in both joining NATO and developing a regional system of security (and in sustaining Ukrainian territorial integrity). The Czech Republic, on the other hand, has been less concerned with establishing regional ties than in building ties with NATO, as if it were isolated from the regional security nexus. For example, both Prague and Warsaw have agreed that Russia should not obtain a special position in the PfP, but the two have disagreed as to whether Russia should be permitted a special relationship with NATO. Perhaps partly because of the dispute between Bonn and Prague over the legal and property rights of former Sudeten Germans in the Czech Republic (Sudeten Germans consider the Benes decrees to be discriminatory), Prague has, to a certain extent, tended to seek out Russian diplomatic support. The Czech defense minister, Antonin Bundys, has accordingly supported Russia's efforts to gain special status in relations with NATO. Russia "has always been an important factor in [maintaining] the Eurasian balance of power and it is [in] the interest of [all of] Europe that Russia continue playing this role."[47] At the same time, however, Prague worries about a NATO-Russian condominium. In November 1996, Czech Prime Minister Josef Zieleniec argued that NATO applicants should be invited to discussions involving the formulation of a NATO-Russian Charter.

The Polish and Czech viewpoints have yet to be coordinated. Czech policy has largely focused on the United States and the EU. Prague has adopted a minimalist approach to membership in the EU (for fear of Germany). Poland has sought a maximalist position (in the hope that EU membership will ultimately bring with it NATO/WEU security guarantees). Prague has worried that if Poland should enter NATO before it does, then the Czech Republic would fall under a German sphere of influence, because Germany would not be counterbalanced by American influence. At the same time, Prague believes it can offset German influence with the help of Britain and France (within the EU/WEU) rather than turn to stronger Russian support, as Slovakia has. (For better or worse, Slovakia has engaged in a policy of *Ostpolitik*, seeking out both Russian and NATO support.)

To a lesser extent than Warsaw, Prague has not worked consistently to foster regional defense and economic coordination in the Visegrad group, which has been called an "artificial" organization despite its original initiation by Czechoslovakia, Hungary, and Poland in 1990–91, before Slovakia became independent and joined (in 1993). The Czech Republic, for example, attempted to stall a Slovak-inspired Central European Free Trade Association, that would join Poland, Hungary, the Czech Republic, Slovenia, and Slovakia.[48] The key point is that "having ruled out regional security cooperation, Prague has only one card to play against its fear of German [or Russian] domination, and that is rapid entry into NATO."[49] By choosing to play only one card, Prague has risked opening regional divisions.

At the same time, fear of German pressure has led Warsaw to reconsider its approach to Moscow. In February 1996, the Polish foreign minister, Dariusz Rosati, argued that Polish membership in NATO would help protect Poland from Germany, thus Warsaw would support a doctrine calling for NATO cooperation with Russia.[50] Perhaps in an attempt to play on Polish fears of Germany, Moscow on 15 March 1996 proposed a security guarantee to Poland; Moscow also suggested the idea of conjoint NATO-Russian guarantees to Poland—which was rejected by Washington.[51]

In summary, Warsaw and Prague have yet to implement a full-fledged *Ostpolitik*. Rather, they apparently assume that they must enter NATO before they can deal with Russia and Belarus. (This seems true despite NATO's admonition that states must work to resolve "irredentist claims" prior to becoming NATO members.) In particular, Prague and Warsaw (with U.S. and EU supports) should work closely through trade enhancement and joint ventures to wean Minsk away from forging too close an alliance with Moscow, and at the same time seek to reassure Moscow that they will not seek to forge an anti–Russian "Baltic–Black Sea" alliance. An example of such cooperation would be the inclusion of Belarus into a Polish-Ukrainian "Brest triangle" (which could be backed by an inter-locking French-German-Polish "Weimar triangle.") Such cooperation could thus permit a "looser" and a more proportional relationship of power among former Soviet-bloc states.

In many ways, each of these states has looked to NATO as a crutch, to avoid dealing with their own neighbors—which include both Russian *and* Germany. Whereas unilateral NATO expansion into Central Europe alone is likely to press Belarus even closer to Russia (and possibly leave the Baltic states and Ukraine in the lurch), Central and Eastern European cooperation (reinforced by an international security regime) would not only counterbalance German and Russian pressures and interests but help mitigate Russian efforts to sustain hegemony over CIS states. In particular, a joint Polish-Czech strategy is crucial for generating diplomatic support for CCS.

From this perspective, in order to counterbalance German and Russian influence, both Prague and Poland have every reason to encourage legitimate and positive Russian participation in a system of Euro-Atlantic cooperative-collective security linked to Central European defenses. An additional factor is that the *Europeanization* of NATO (involving CJTF and ESDI) may increasingly be regarded in both Prague and Warsaw as the *Germanization* of NATO, particularly if the United States takes a more distant approach of "selective interventionism." Even more intensive U.S., EU, and Russian support for the implementation of a new cooperative-collective security regime under the auspices of the OSCE or UN will accordingly be insufficient if it is not supported by the Central and Eastern European states themselves. The Czech Republic and Poland in particular need to take the lead in helping to counterbalance both German and Russian influence in Central and Eastern Europe, particularly as their apparent refusal to forge either a regional system of security or conjoint security agreements with NATO and Russia could make a general NATO-Russian accord all the more difficult to achieve.

THE QUESTION OF "NEW LINES"

In seeking full integration with American or European security structures, Central and Eastern European states have thus far rejected steps toward multilateral and cooperative-collective security in part because no viable and realistic proposals have been offered.

As argued above, Central European states have feared becoming either a "buffer" or a "front line" zone between two blocs, NATO/WEU and Russia/CIS. Moreover, it has been contended that NATO must not differentiate between the "strong" candidates and the "lesser" ones (as suggested by Secretary of State Christopher's statement of 20 March 1996) but must give all states equal opportunity. NATO recognizes that it must therefore keep the door wide open for those who do not enter in the first wave: "It is very important that after the 'strongest candidates' become fully-fledged NATO members, all the rest should be granted official NATO guarantees for eventual membership."[52]

In this view NATO must continue to be open to all Central and Eastern European applicants, but without alienating Moscow. The key questions become: Can NATO incorporate some former Soviet-bloc states but not others? Or can NATO accept only non-former-Soviet-bloc states and still accommodate all those in the former Soviet bloc? In either case, how long can NATO's doors remain open without resulting in a backlash by Russia or other states not included? Will those countries accepted into NATO on the first round seek to block the entrance of states seeking admittance on the second round, assuming there is to be a second round? Will Central European states, if permitted to enter, continue to support American interests within NATO, or could U.S. and Central European interests diverge? Will Western European states, such as France, or states such as Greece and Turkey, continue to support American and NATO interests if Central European states do enter as "full" members, or could their interests diverge? Or can NATO of the sixteen continue to be open to all Central and Eastern European states—plus Russia—through a truly comprehensive cooperative-collective security pact?

On one hand, Central and Eastern European states are rightly concerned about becoming "buffers" between two potentially hostile blocs; on the other, the risks associated with their membership have generally been downplayed. NATO enlargement may draw new, "impermeable" lines in Europe, if NATO invites only Central European states into "full" membership; for example, Finland, the Baltic states, Romania, and Ukraine risk becoming buffers between two blocs, if not objects of secessionist movements or partition. Or, if NATO opts for an even wider enlargement (or continues to promise eventual membership for those states not accepted in the first round), then Finland, the Baltic states, Poland, and Ukraine may all become "front-line states." Both forms of enlargement would risk overextension of NATO capabilities—particularly undesirable at a time of defense cuts— resulting in a significant gap between strategic demands and resources available. There is a real danger that NATO's promises may either be tested by Russia (or other states) or not be fulfilled due to declining resources and political will.

American policy makers, such as Assistant Secretary of State Strobe Talbott, have argued that NATO can enlarge without producing a new partition of Europe or creating new "front line" states.[53] In effect, Talbott has argued that the fears of Poland and other Central European states of becoming "buffers" between NATO and Russia (and the CIS) are understandable. Yet Central European security would also be at risk should these states move toward the "front line" of tensions in a confrontation with Russia, Belarus, or Ukraine.

Critics, however, have replied to the Talbott view by arguing that the formation of a new line (or lines) is largely inevitable. These critics assert that new lines are in actuality already being drawn, as NATO, the EU, and Russia (as well as the UN and OSCE) compete for spheres of influence and security. (An example of such a possible partition was illustrated when, following a Czech decision, under German pressure, to tighten its borders with Slovakia, Bratislava accused Bonn and Prague of forming a new Iron Curtain!) The issue, then, is not whether there should be new lines "but how to prevent those lines from becoming impermeable. And, even if these lines harden, that result might be preferable to a security vacuum that leaves Central and Eastern European states in the wind."[54] Moreover, there is a danger that an inflexible NATO policy itself may help to carve new lines. From this perspective, it would be, of course, best that no lines divide Europe; but *if* new lines cannot be made "permeable," then a new partition of Europe between NATO and Russia might be preferable to "appeasement," in the form of capitulation to Russian expansion into states that are not to be protected by NATO. In brief, according to this argument, should NATO not soon act to fill the "security vacuum" in Central and Eastern Europe, the United States might have to capitulate to Russian expansion and subversion.

The problem with the latter perspective is that it appears to pose a false choice, either "partition" or "capitulation." Granting the argument that new lines are in fact being drawn, it may still be possible to prevent them from becoming "impermeable." This could be accomplished through the implementation of a militarily integrated system of cooperative-collective security, to promote the engagement (as opposed to the exclusion) of Russia in Europe yet concurrently provide the political-military solidarity sufficient to resist pressure from Russia, Germany, Belarus, or other states.

The first step to prevent both the erection of a new Iron Curtain and the possibility of conflict among Eastern European states, is thus to encourage professionalism in the Russian and Central and Eastern European militaries and to implement confidence and security–building measures. The respective militaries of Russia and the Central and Eastern European countries need to be brought into close cooperation with NATO countries, through Partnership for Peace "plus" and the proposed Atlantic Partnership Council. The second step is to encourage regional cooperation among these states so that they do not look to NATO alone for support. The third step is to strengthen the interlocking relations between NATO, the WEU, and Russia with international security regimes such as the UN and OSCE. The final step is to draw Moscow into greater responsibility for global affairs, while making certain that international cooperative-collective security measures provide checks and balances adequate to forestall a revanchist Russia (or any other revisionist state) from taking unilateral advantages. Such a cooperative-collective security arrangement under the mandate of the UN or OSCE and a strengthened Atlantic Partnership Council would link *cooperative security* with aspects of conjoint NATO, WEU, and Russian *collective security*.[55] (See Chapters 1, 10, and 11.)

CHAPTER 4

Fragmentation of the Russian Federation

NATO ENLARGEMENT AND RUSSIAN "DEMOCRACY"

Proponents of NATO enlargement have argued that "dallying" on expansion has permitted Russian hard-liners to become even more aggressive and that "the failure to expand NATO rapidly has seriously undercut democratic forces in Russia."[1] However, the latter argument has no substantial basis.[2] The few Russian observers who have dared to support NATO enlargement to Russia's borders represent a tiny minority—even within liberal, pro-Western Russian political parties, such as the Yabloco and Russia's Choice.[3]

Gregory Yavlinsky, leader of the Yabloco, for example, does not necessarily oppose NATO enlargement (it is not Moscow's business "to dictate to Prague, Warsaw, or Budapest"), but he has warned of its consequences. He argues that NATO's enlargement may provide the pretext for the Russian military-industrial complex to build a new military bloc subsuming Belarus and Ukraine hence provoking a new partition of Europe. He has furthermore warned that Western talk of deploying nuclear weapons in Central Europe appears to forget the lessons of the Cuban Missile Crisis. At the same time, he observes that Russian intervention in Chechnya understandably accelerated the efforts of states to join NATO and to "integrate into whatever."[4]

General Leonti Shevtsov (leader of the Russian contingent in the multinational force implementing the Dayton Accords) has put the issues of NATO enlargement and democracy this way: "NATO has to understand one simple thing: wherever they shove us, we will strike back. And so why should they crawl up to our borders? Here is the classic NATO reply: to reinforce Russian democracy. So I suggest to them: To safeguard the American people, why not let Russia put a few divisions in Mexico, right along the American border? They just roar with laughter."[5] General Shevtsov argues that although NATO spokesmen affirm that the Alliance is only expanding defensively, Russia would still have to make an appropriate response. Such a response would not necessary be conducive to the cooperative system of European security that NATO purportedly advocates.

Rather than giving strength to the democratic factions, NATO enlargement risks the polarization of rival parties and elites, the disaggregation of the Russian Federation, or a revanchist backlash to (ironically) check the feared breakup of Russia. Once NATO announces its decisions, it is highly likely that vying political elites will seek to build political power bases in response to NATO's actions. Some groups would condemn NATO actions but choose very different responses; other groups may support NATO, but with reservations. It is doubtful that a general consensus will be achieved easily.

In Russia, at least forty–three parties have been created. Of these, the Communist Party of the Russian Federation, led by Gennady Zyuganov, gained the most support in the December 1995 parliamentary elections. Next was "Our Home Is Russia," which represents the "national democratic" or "national liberal" party of the Russian prime minister, Victor Chernomyrdin, and which by February 1996 was supporting Boris Yeltsin and his "Party of Power." The Liberal Democratic Party (neither "liberal" nor "democratic," led by revanchist Vladimir Zhirinovsky) became the third-largest party. The fourth-largest party is the Yabloco, a coalition of social democratic parties, led by Yavlinsky, an economist. The Russian Communist Party and the revanchist Liberal Democratic Party are the two most militant opponents of NATO enlargement. Yet the "national democratic" leadership of Yeltsin and Chernomyrdin has likewise opposed *unilateral* NATO enlargement. The divisions among the weak democratic parties thus indicate that it will be difficult to sustain a policy that is pro-Western and pro-NATO enlargement.

As pro-Western political parties are badly divided (and disagree among themselves as to whether or not to support NATO expansion), and as both external and internal factors continue to weaken the Russian state, NATO enlargement may result in unforeseen and unexpected counter-reactions. Moscow's efforts both to counter NATO's power potential and control the rise of independent republics within the Russian Federation itself have tended to overextend Moscow's capabilities. The weakening of central government controls accordingly risks the formation of breakaway "rogue" military republics, particularly Kaliningrad or Murmansk. On the other hand, much like Iraqi leader Saddam Hussein after the Persian Gulf War, the Russian military could adopt a policy of retrenchment and control only the military-industrial complex (thereby letting the rest of the economy go to shambles). From this perspective, to push for NATO's enlargement without Moscow's real input may prove dangerously destabilizing.

The Russians are not fanatically aggressive, but they *are* fanatical defenders of their society and interests.[6] If NATO enlargement and other actions by U.S. allies are perceived by Moscow as either directly or indirectly aimed at weakening, if not breaking up, the CIS or the Russian Federation itself, then a determined defense of Russian interests could well be transformed, in the not-so-distant future, into a *revanchist* backlash intended to regain a global geostrategic presence and counter American pressures and alliances. Judging by the brutal (yet poorly executed) actions of "national-democratic" Russia in Chechnya in 1994–96, it appears extremely unlikely that the Russian Federation will accept its feared disaggregation as gracefully as the Soviet Union accepted the breakup of its empire in 1991, particularly once Moscow is able to rebuild its military capabilities.

THE 1993 *PRONUNCIAMENTO*

The possibility of a breakup of the Russian Federation itself has been greatly exacerbated by the tragic farce played out between President Boris Yeltsin and the Russian parliament (elected in the Gorbachev era) that led to the forceful dissolution of that parliament in September–October 1993. Yeltsin's inability to deal with the duma (Yeltsin's April 1993 referendum gave him a distinct, but not definitive, measure of legitimacy over his rivals) badly divided the Russian leadership and risked the alienation of the Russian military who were forced to choose sides. Yeltsin's repeatedly stated threats after 20 March 1993 to dissolve parliament had been tacitly supported by President Clinton—despite Clinton's opposition to the use of force— and had been countered by parliamentary demands to impeach Yeltsin.

In September 1993, Yeltsin finally ordered the dissolution of parliament. In response, then Vice President Alexandr Rutskoi (former Afghan war "hero") called for a *pronunciamento*, Spanish or Latin American style—an appeal to the armed forces (and general population) to rebel in support of the parliamentary leadership. However, Rutskoi's *pronunciamento* failed. Ironically, his tactics may have actually increased the tendencies of Russia to become what Rutskoi and his supporters opposed: a "banana republic" made up of conflicting regions equipped with tactical and intermediate-range, if not strategic, nuclear weapons, and in which the central state is not capable of sustaining *parity* as a significant global power.

On one hand, it was Yeltsin's own turn toward "shock therapy"—

combined with the intervention in Chechnya—which alienated his former supporters and blocked the path to a general consensus. The parliament Yeltsin dissolved was the same one that had supported him in the August 1991 coup and ratified the abolition of the Soviet Union and the formation of the CIS through the Belovezhskaya accords.[7] On the other, it was also that same parliament that in 1993 passed a budget which—had it been implemented—might have set the country down the road of hyperinflation, raising the government deficit to 25 percent of GNP, and blocking G-7 and IMF assistance.

Despite the latter concern, Yeltsin's decision to crack down on the parliament with force raised critical questions as to Yeltsin's character as a leader and led to charges that he was not in fact in control of the situation—if not outright drunk. Concurrently, Yeltsin's efforts to enforce censorship of prodemocratic papers likewise brought resentment and accusations that he was heading the country back to its czarist and autocratic past. Yeltsin's decision to dissolve the Russian parliament was itself somewhat reminiscent of that of the czarist regime in the period 1905–17: Czar Nicholas II could not find an election formula to form a duma that suited his policies.

Following the first round of the June–July 1996 Russian elections, prodemocratic supporters were largely impelled to accept Yeltsin's "national democracy" or "national liberalism." Prior to the elections, the September–October 1993 crackdown had generally been regarded as a dictatorial act and raised questions as to Yeltsin's own commitment to "democracy." His government had been accused of extreme corruption and personal favoritism to the detriment of the democratic process, such as in the refusal to investigate charges against Defense Minister Grachev. The decision to crush the Chechen independence movement (in addition to the failure of the government to disclose the actual costs of the operation) turned Yeltsin's former supporters against him.

By January 1996, following the parliamentary elections, most pro-Western "democrats" had been ousted from the government. First, the perceived pro-Western foreign minister, Andrei Kozyrev, resigned, as did the liberal deputy finance minister and architect of Russia's privatization program, Anatoly Chubais. (Following the presidential elections, however, Chubais became chief of staff.) Human rights advocate, Sergei Kovalev, who had insisted that Western leaders come to Moscow for the May 1995 summit in an effort to moderate Yeltsin's policies in Chechnya, also resigned from the Presidential Council. Kozyrev (whose resignation had been expected for months) was replaced by the chief of the Foreign Intelligence, Yevgeny Primakov. The latter intended to design a more assertive "Eurasian" strategy against the West, but one ostensibly open to "compromise."

Democrats, who had initially spoken in opposition to Yeltsin in

1994–95, however, began to retreat from their positions, due in part to the fact that Yeltsin's "Party of Power" controlled the state machinery—and to a large extent the Russian media—and thus had the potential to win the elections. Yeltsin likewise promised to wind down the war in Chechnya. By the second round of the presidential elections, however, it was clear that most Russian democrats had begun to regard Yeltsin as the "lesser of evils" against Gennady Zyuganov.

Following the December 1995 parliamentary elections, Communist leader Zyuganov was generally regarded as the second most influential leader in Russia, after Yeltsin. Zyuganov claimed to be an "economic realist," but the Communist Party sought to increase budgetary spending and the money supply, institute price controls, and protect the domestic Russian market—policies which could result in loss of IMF assistance. Zyuganov attempted to assure Western investors that the Communist Party would not curtail privatization efforts if it came to power. Anatoly Chubais, however, warned Western businessmen not to fall for the "classic Communist lie," that there were two Zyuganovs, one for domestic and one for foreign consumption. In addition, Zyuganov emphasized that NATO enlargement would question not only START II but other arms control agreements as well.

An increasingly pan-nationalist Russian Communist Party proposed the formation of a political-military-economic union with all CIS states, and also support for the (estimated at between twenty–two and twenty–five million) Russian ethnic "diaspora." It argued that everything connected with the territory of the former Soviet Union fell within Russia's "vital interests." Although it had been rumored that Zyuganov would not support such a position until a more politically appropriate date, the Communist Party went against his counsel and supported a March 1996 resolution to declare the dissolution of the USSR illegal prior to the June elections.[8] (The Supreme Soviet decision of 12 December 1991 had abrogated the 1922 treaty that formed the USSR.) The Communist Party thereby potentially jeopardized all post–1991 Russian and CIS laws, agreements, and contracts inside and outside the CIS—and helped to undermine general confidence in the Russian government. By attempting to restore the Soviet Union, both Communists and Russian pan-nationalists (the resolution to renounce the Supreme Soviet decision was also supported by Vladimir Zhirinovsky) sought to force Yeltsin to press for deeper CIS integration, through a "union" with Belarus and other CIS states.

The Russian presidential elections were often depicted as battle of "moderate" Russian nationalism against Communist revanchism led by Zyuganov, but in fact Yeltsin had to appeal to Russian pan-nationalism in order to win. Not only did Yeltsin have to gain "democratic" support of such leaders as Gregory Yavlinsky, he also had to win the support of the constituencies of Zhirinovsky and, more importantly, Russian pan-nationalist Alexander Lebed. Former Lieutenant General Lebed appeared to many to represent the strongman who could bring Russia back to its feet. As Lebed attracted 14.52 percent of the vote on the first round of the presidential elections, Yeltsin was fortunate draw him into his camp, saving Yeltsin from almost certain defeat, at the last minute.[9] (Zyuganov may have had a better chance to win the Russian presidential elections had he not made a tactical mistake of failing to break clearly with the Communist past.)

While certainly not regarded as a "democrat," Lebed had been regarded as a pro-capitalist "Pinochet"—despite the fact that he has opposed the growing extremes in wealth, "illegal" privatization, and "the market of bribes." (Lebed has stated that he is a "quasi-democrat," opposed to an elected parliament in a country like Russia.) As a rival of Pavel Grachev (who was forced to step down as a condition of Lebed's joining Yeltsin's team as his Secretary of the Security Council), he was regarded as a "cheap hawk" who could thoroughly modernize the Russian military. Often depicted as less extreme than Zhirinovsky, Lebed advocated in 1995 the use of all means necessary to protect the ethnic Russian diaspora, including the use of force, and warned that NATO enlargement would result in World War III. By 1996, however, Lebed's campaign had changed tone and tactics (partly due to media counsel). He downplayed his Russian pan-nationalism and argued that his main intent was to reform the army and show that Russia was not a threat. In June 1996, rather than opposing NATO enlargement, he stated that if NATO "has sufficient strength and money," then it can expand, but concurrently he warned that the overall costs might reach $250 billion.

The sudden rise of Lebed to power following the first-round elections in June 1996 resulted in a "palace coup" that weeded the old guard from Yeltsin's Security Council. Lebed's short-lived alliance with Yeltsin led to the ouster of Defense Minister Grachev, and a purge of seven generals and other Council members who were reportedly responsible for the war in Chechnya, large-scale corruption, and stalled reforms. Not only did Grachev step down, but so did Aleksandr Korzhakov, Yeltsin's long-time confidant and head of the Presidential Security Services—often depicted as the contemporary equivalent of Rasputin. Claiming that there had been a coup attempt (a claim later retracted), Lebed seized the initiative to restructure Yeltsin's Security Council.

By July 1996, Boris Yeltsin had signed a decree granting Lebed "wide-ranging powers" over domestic and foreign security (overseeing activities of Russia's competing security agencies), defense readiness, military cooperation, and the development of a global information system.[10] Contrary to the old statute, the new Security Council was to concentrate power in the hands of the President and the Council Secretary.[11] This formulation appeared to give whomever played the role of Secretary inordinate power—a fact which could have been particularly dangerous given Yeltsin's heart condition.

Political commentators correctly doubted Lebed's staying power within the Yeltsin government, due to his political inexperience and the ability of Presidential advisor Anatoly Chubais and Prime Minister Chernomyrdin to join forces against him. Lebed's calls for government regulation of the "energy barons" and accusations that the Chernomyrdin government had failed to fund adequately the 1997 military budget put him in conflict with the prime minister. His demand for greater state regulation of finance and his quest for power also put him in conflict with Chubais. Lebed likewise opposed the policy orientation of his hand-picked defense minister, Igor Rodionov.

Most crucially, Lebed's position on Chechnya put him at odds with the powerful Interior Minister, Anatoly Kulikov—seen as most responsible for the war. In many ways, Lebed was granted the task of negotiating an end to the war in Chechnya so as to destroy him politically. If he succeeded in winding-down the war, the government would take the credit, but if Russian interests were damaged, Lebed would take the blame.[12] Lebed attacked Kulikov's poor handling of the conflict, and his failure to foresee a rebel attack on Grozny in August 1996. Lebed's "success" in drawing-down the war, and in obtaining an agreement to establish a treaty of mutual Russian-Chechen relations by the year 2001, brought on a backlash, resulting in his sudden dismissal in October 1996. Both Zyuganov and Zhirinovsky demanded to know whether he had exceeded his authority in negotiating a peace accord. The basis upon which Chechnya was recognized as a subject in international law was questioned. Interior Minister Kulikov counter-accused Lebed of corruption.

Lebed's popularity, his strong public image of trustworthiness and incorruptibility, and his refusal to be a "team player"—plus the fact that he did not hide his presidential aspirations—were regarded as a significant threat to a weak president plagued by illness. In addition, although domestic political factors were more salient, NATO's unprecedented encounter with Lebed just a few days before his dismissal represented the final straw. The Yeltsin leadership could not permit Lebed, with his newly acquired international status, to become the power-broker between NATO and Russia.

Whether Lebed will continue to play a major role in Russian politics (or largely disappear from the scene, as did former vice president Alexandr Rutskoi) remains to be seen. Yeltsin's dismissal of him may well boost Lebed's popular standing in the shortrun, but sustaining a popular following will prove difficult, given strong governmental influence over the Russian media. Accordingly, the Yeltsin presidential victory does not end the continuing risk of political instability; also Yeltsin's poor state of health may, in the not-so-distant future, open a renewed power struggle. The fact that only between approximately 10 and 20 percent of the Russian population in 1995 regarded themselves as benefiting from Yeltsin's policies also does not augur well for his continuing leadership or for those within the present government. The increasingly militant and revanchist Communist Party has not been vanquished; and the rise of both "reds" and "browns" in the Russian Duma has impelled Yeltsin to pursue a more assertive "Eurasianist" policy toward the West. (See Chapter 6.)

REPUBLICS IN THE RUSSIAN FEDERATION: CONFEDERATION, SECESSION, OR REPRESSION?

Contrary to the intentions of those who staged the August 1991 putsch, and much as the opposition of Brezhnev–era hardliners to Gorbachev's reforms actually accelerated the Soviet collapse, the Duma's resistance to Yeltsin's policies has generally strengthened the forces of decentralization and disaggregation. The feud between the executive and legislative branches of the Russian government has made it more and more difficult to reach an appropriate equilibrium between regional needs and those of the central government.

In many ways, Yeltsin himself is to a great extent to blame for strengthening the regions relative to the central government. In his campaign against Gorbachev in 1991, Yeltsin promised each of the Russian regions, republics, provinces, and districts greater independence or sovereignty, as a way to undermine Gorbachev's rule. Yeltsin also looked to the Russian regions and republics to pressure both the first and second parliaments. At the same time, Yeltsin has not granted all that he appeared to promise. Although the constitutional referendum in November 1993 did take place, it was without the full participation of regional units. Moreover, Yeltsin's brutal military intervention in Chechnya was, in part, meant to send a signal to those republics that might overstep their bounds. Russia has increasingly become an unstable mix of a "unitary" and "confederal" government.

In 1991 Russia inherited forty-nine *oblasts* (or regions), sixteen autonomous Soviet Socialist republics (which subsequently dropped the terms "socialist" and "autonomous"), six *krays* (provinces), and ten autonomous *okrugs* (districts). In 1993 Russia possessed twenty–one republics, one autonomous *oblast*, ten autonomous *okrugs*, forty–nine *oblasts*, and six *krays*, plus the cities of Moscow and St. Petersburg. The Russian leadership has consequently faced stronger demands for either independence or greater autonomy from the republics in the Caucasus, particularly Chechnya and Ingushetia, which were placed together under Soviet rule but broke apart in 1992. (Ingushetia is also in a dispute with Georgia over North Ossetia.) Republics along the Volga are also demanding greater autonomy. Tatarstan, Bashkortostan, and Udmurtia have been seeking autonomy, as have Karelia, Komi, and Yakutia (Sakha), among others.

Since 1991 regional governments have accounted for about 50 percent of taxes raised and 70 percent of federal government spending. Only about fifteen of Russia's eighty-nine regions are net contributors to the federal budget, the rest are net recipients. In 1996, for example, the Primorsk region threatened to withhold taxes if Moscow did not pay back-wages and child benefits to its citizens, creating a potentially "explosive" situation.[13] In general, mineral-rich regions (such as gas producers) have done well, as have key centers of trade (such as Moscow). However, some regions have been unable to develop the full potential of their resources, such as Sakhalin and Kamchatka.[14]

Following the August 1991 coup attempt, Yeltsin tried to ensure that local legislation in each of the republics or regions was compatible with the national legislation, by appointing presidential representatives to each locality. This has resulted in "multiple sovereignty." Disputes between the president, the duma, and the presidential and regional representatives of each republic or regional unit have been frequent. In the April 1993 referendum, for example, Yeltsin failed to win a vote of confidence from the majority of voters in ten of the nineteen republics. Whether Yeltsin (or his possible successor) can ultimately forge an acceptable proportional system of representation within the Russian Federation thus remains to be seen.

By November 1993, and following the September–October 1993 *pronunciamento*, Yeltsin demanded that Russia's eighty–eight regions and republics approve a constitution (promulgated in December 1993) that denied these regions the right to secession or to pass laws which contradict those of the central government in Moscow. (Except for Komi and Karelia, the republics had written constitutions that directly contradicted that of the central government.) In general, republics with large Russian populations or limited natural resources or industries are more reluctant to seek independence. Moscow intended (until the crackdown on the Chechen republic) to make separate agreements with each region in order to avoid the formulation of a common policy by the regional "boyars" (and to play each against the other).

An agreement with Tatarstan was reached after three years of negotiation (and Russian threats to cut off Tatarstan's oil supply). The treaty, signed in February 1994, opened the door to a possible compromise, but it could ultimately be opposed by both Russian and Tatar (Kazan) pan-nationalists. (Tatarstan is roughly half Russian and half Kazan.) The previous (1992) Tatar constitution had stated that Tatarstan was a sovereign state, associated with Russia; the February 1994 agreement had it that Tatarstan was "united" with Moscow. Moscow hoped that its treaty with Tatarstan would serve as a model for those with Yakutia (Sakha) and Bashkortostan. The 1994 Russo-Bashkortostan treaty, for example, gave the latter ownership over all resources and oil refineries (but Moscow has regarded the republic as evading taxes).[15]

The issue of republican secession or confederation has been further complicated by the influence or interference of foreign states.[16] Moscow has attempted to block Turkey and Iran from supporting independence movements in the Caucasus (Chechnya) and Central Asia (Tajikistan). Hungary, Turkey, Iran, Kazakhstan, and France have all reached out to forge relations with Tatarstan, an oil-rich republic with claims (dating to before 1552) extending far beyond its present boundaries. The diamond and resource-rich republic of Yakutia (Sakha) has claimed borders of the early nineteenth century, prior to Russian expansion into the region, and it has been eyed by Japanese investors. Republics along the Mongolian border have also demanded greater independence (and may likewise look to Japan). The PRC has made claims to all of "Russian" Buryatia, although Beijing has engaged in border talks with Russia, in accord with its "sweet and sour" strategy.

The states of Sweden, Norway, and Finland have been strong supporters of Baltic independence and have been regarded by Moscow as supporting Komi and Karelia. In essence, the security of the Nordic and Baltic areas is determined by the futures of three very different centers, Murmansk, Kaliningrad, and St. Petersburg. (In general, the Nordic and Baltic states need to sustain a solid working relationship with St. Petersburg to sustain regional stability.) The very real prospects of economic collapse in Kaliningrad and Murmansk, however, raise fears of territories controlled by rogue militaries and mafias.

WAR IN CHECHNYA AND REPUBLICAN SECESSION

Rather than attempting to forge a compromise through a weaker confederal arrangement, Russia opted for brutal military intervention in December 1994 to stop Chechnya from formally seceding from the Federation. Yeltsin's "war party" argued that any concession to Chechnya was likely to exacerbate demands for independence throughout the Russian federation and that Russian troops could not withdraw without producing an internecine blood bath similar to that which took place in Afghanistan. Hard-liners feared that foreign support for secessionist movements could undermine Russia itself.

Moscow's intervention not only was rationalized as a means to block the Chechen secession movement but also to prevent such states as Azerbaijan, Turkey, and Iran from forming ties with the Chechen resistance or other movements inside the Russian Federation, most relevantly Tatarstan.[17] It was also feared that if Chechnya became independent, Dagestan would be cut off. Moscow purportedly signed secret accords with Ankara and Teheran in an effort to prevent these states from siding with the Chechen resistance. Control of a potential Bulgarian-Greek oil pipeline through Chechnya was also at issue.

Somewhat ironically, Russian democrats (who had initially moved away from Yeltsin), the Communist Party, and certain Greater Russians and pan-Slav proponents generally argued that the Caucasus was not of vital Russian interest. While democrats contended that compromise was possible, Alexander Solzhenitsyn argued that Chechnya should be granted its independence (except for the northern region, where there are Russians and Cossacks) but that all Chechens should then be expelled from Russia. Solzhenitsyn argued that this action would ultimately force Chechnya to admit its dependence upon Moscow. Lieutenant General Lebed did not object to the intervention in itself as much as to the poor military tactics used. Adopting the views of the U.S. military following the Vietnam and Persian Gulf wars, Lebed argued that the Russian military should intervene in crises only once clear political-military aims are established, and then with superior force and training. On the other hand, Vladimir Zhirinovsky supported the intervention—with some qualifications in support of negotiations—although he himself had previously stated the Caucasus was not a vital Russian interest.

Contrary to its presumed intent, however, and in addition to alienating foreign Islamic states, the brutal intervention in Chechnya began to alienate Moslems and autonomous republics *within* the Russian Federation itself; it actually *accelerated* fissiparous tendencies in the Russian Federation, due both to the expense of the operation and the internal (if not international) political side effects. In January 1995, regional leaders of Bashkortostan, Karelia, Mari-El, Mordvinia, Tatarstan, Udmurtia, and Chuvashia met to discuss the crisis in Chechnya. In February they formed "Russia's Regions" and appealed to Moscow to respect the principles of federalism and law in an effort to achieve "equality for all members of the Russian federation." In effect, they feared the possibility that a "state of emergency" might ultimately be decreed against them, threatening their status as relatively autonomous actors.[18]

The December 1995 Chechen elections led to the defeat of separatist leader Dzhokhar Dudaev, who then sought to internationalize the conflict by spreading "the fire of war" to neighboring regions. With the escalation of conflict (and hijacking of a ferry in Turkish waters in late

1995), in January 1996 presidential candidate Gregory Yavlinsky called for a peace conference to be held in Moscow. Perhaps to steal some of the thunder from the opposition movement, Russia's deputy foreign minister, Nikolai Afanasievsky, also warned that the continuing conflict in Chechnya could aggravate Russian relations with the Moslem world, making Russia the focal point of so-called "fundamentalist" aggression, which would benefit the West and Japan.

In March 1996 Boris Yeltsin finally offered a "truce," which may have initially been intended to establish a partition of the region.[19] Yeltsin's heavy-handed tactics and escalation of the conflict appeared similar to Richard Nixon's actions during the Vietnam War prior to American withdrawal. Russian forces engaged in a "pacification" program, systematic looting, and the extortion of money for agreement not to raze villages; at the same time, Chechen tactics have involved the seizing of civilian hostages.[20] Unlike the situation in Vietnam, however, Moscow insisted that the intervention be considered an "internal" Russian affair—a position accepted by Washington, to congressional cries of "appeasement."

The rise of Alexander Lebed as Security Council advisor, as noted above, provided Yeltsin a convenient scapegoat. If Lebed could end the crisis, the administration could claim credit; if anything went wrong, Lebed could be blamed. Lebed engaged in talks, calling for a five-year ceasefire followed by a referendum on Chechen independence. Lebed, however, was subsequently dismissed and called a "traitor." Supporters of intervention in Chechnya refused any settlement that would compromise Russia's territorial integrity.

RUSSIA'S DOMESTIC ECONOMIC CRISIS

Russia's industrial recovery was to a great extent hampered by the extent of public and intra-industry debt (money generally loaned by one government enterprise to another). Total wage debt equaled 29.9 trillion rubles ($5.7 billion) at the end of July 1996. The state budget was owed 80 trillion rubles, and barter deals equal about 30 percent of industrial turnover. Investment has fallen by 14 percent and capital flight has exceeded $35 billion, according to First Deputy Prime Minister Oleg Lobov. (As long as ruble inflation continues, it will be difficult to keep capital within the country.) Foreign debt has reached between $120–130 billion; servicing requires $20 billion annually.[21]

Moreover, efforts to balance the budget were not aided by either the war in Chechnya or election-year politics. In early 1996 Anatoly Chubais (prior to his becoming Yeltsin's chief of staff) accused President Yeltsin of an election-year "spending spree" at the risk of the bankrupting the state. The war in Chechnya may have cost as much as

3.5 trillion rubles in 1995. (The first forty-five days may have cost 800 billion rubles.) The Yeltsin government responded that the costs of the war were offset by the liberalization of the price of oil and other reforms that brought in about 15 trillion rubles.[22] Even if true, other vital sectors of the economy lacked significant funding.

The most fundamental danger is that the reform process could generate large-scale structural unemployment that cannot be absorbed in the near-term, thus representing a continuing source for socio-political discontent. The OECD put registered unemployment at 5.7 percent in 1993; 9.0 percent in 1994 (about 800,000); and projected 12 percent for 1995 and 14 percent for 1996. However, these unemployment figures did not count hidden unemployment, which has been covered by such ploys as "holidays without pay" (forced leave) or part-time work schemes. At the same time, the OECD reported that jobs are being found in the "extensive informal sector" (an apparent euphemism for the "black market"). If big bankruptcies of unprofitable or highly subsidized banks and firms begin to affect the overall economy, unemployment could rise to 10–11 million (out of 70 million).[23] The gravity of Russia's general political-economic crisis can, for example, be seen in the fact that the Moscow power company cut off electric power to the command center of the strategic rocket forces, at Odinstvo near Moscow, on 21 September 1994 due to an estimated 50 billion rubles ($20 million) in unpaid bills! (The government subsequently decreed that power could not be cut from military installations!)

Socio-political instability may be further exacerbated by widening gaps in income, in which high, medium, and low-income earners gained in 1985–91 (the Gorbachev years), but whose income dropped by up to half in 1991–92. Total real household wealth declined 86 percent from the end of 1991 to the end of 1992! Moreover, in 1994 income rise outstripped price hikes only for the wealthiest 20 percent.[24] Real income dropped by 8 percent. However, by 1995 the income differential had ostensibly stabilized, with the richest 10 percent earning thirteen times the poorest 10 percent! Thus far, Russia has sought to achieve a widespread ownership of enterprises by the general population, through the distribution of vouchers. But if the general population must sell its newly acquired assets due to a plunge in real income and wealth, ownership may become concentrated in fewer and fewer hands, such as conglomerates and pension funds.[25]

Russian domestic economic interests tend to be oriented toward protectionism, although the "new rich" benefit from an open market. Russian political parties compete for votes of essentially four economic interest groups: (1) groups oriented toward the Russian market seek protection from foreign competition; (2) importers tend to support a free market, as the opening up of new investments and markets has tended to be a source of wealth for the new rich; (3) exporters (who are few in number but have been made powerful, in part to hard-currency gains) support marketization to a certain extent, but also want to protect their privileged position; (4) the military-industrial complex as a whole has lost more than it has gained following the transition to market forces. In general, exporters and the military industrial complex tend to join forces against more free market–oriented importers.[26]

THE MILITARY-INDUSTRIAL COMPLEX

Perhaps the greatest barrier to political-economic reform, is consequently, the military-industrial complex—which has sought to hold onto what remains of its lost status and prestige. Rather than becoming "self-eating," as predicted by Gorbachev-era "new thinkers," the Russian military industrial complex has yet to disintegrate entirely. Arms sold in the Soviet era were often sold at fifty-year concessional terms. But many of the former Soviet client states which bought those arms have been in near-bankruptcy. In an effort to recuperate the former Soviet position, the new Russian arms dealers have often been selling weapons at bargain-basement prices. Russian arms producers are looking towards new markets in Asia (in addition to the PRC) such as Malaysia and South Korea, and to Latin America (such as Colombia). A report distributed to Congress stated that the United States could lose up to $10 billion due to Russian competition in this field—leading Congress to take a tough line with Moscow.[27]

On the other hand, Moscow has protested American efforts to gain supremacy in the world arms trade. In the period 1991–94, the United States accounted for 56 percent of the value of all arms sales agreements. Even though the overall value of U.S. arms sales dropped, Western Europe accounted for 32 percent, Russia only 6 percent, and China 1 percent (even granted that Russian arms sales increased substantially in 1994, partly due to significant arms sales to the PRC). Only the United States and France registered a significant increase in arms sales in the period from 1987–90 to 1991–94 partly due to arms sales to Taiwan and South Korea. China registered the largest losses, with a 81 percent decline; the UK declined 77 percent; Russia 62 percent, and North Korea 57 percent. Iraq, Cuba, Afghanistan, Syria, Angola, and India (all traditional Soviet/Russian client states) made significant cuts in arms purchases. Arms sales by themselves do not tell the whole picture: Moscow has argued that a significant "brain drain" in the arms industry has occurred, weakening Russian capabilities and spreading dual-use and military technology throughout much of the world. Furthermore, as top scientists have been lured away by high salaries, some countries have been able to develop similar products and thus have no need to purchase Russian exports![28]

Whereas a thorough economic reform in Russia would require the shutting down of giant military industrial complexes, this could take place only with the significant liability of an increase of at least 15 percent in unemployment. Moreover, a significant proportion of the Russian voting population depends directly or indirectly on the military-industrial complex; this fact militates against relatively profound reforms. The military-industrial complex has opposed ruble convertibility in particular, as a convertible ruble would greatly augment the *real* costs of defense production. Russian hard-liners have regarded Western emphasis on ruble convertibility as another way to pressure, if not weaken or break up, the Russian military-industrial complex. Moscow furthermore fears that NATO enlargement into Central and Eastern Europe will cut arms sales to traditional Soviet clients as NATO attempts to make all equipment "interoperable." The fact that Bill Clinton reversed George Bush's freeze on arms sales to Central Europe has tended to exacerbate American, European, and Russian rivalry for arms sales in the region. (See Chapter 1.)

ANOTHER COUP D'ETAT? OR MORE OF THE SAME?

Since the August 1991 putsch attempt, and then again following the September crackdown on the Russian parliament and Alexander Rutskoi's *pronunciamento*, legitimate fears have been raised as to the stability of the new Russia, as to whether it will remain willing to resolve international and domestic disputes by democratic compromise. In September–October 1993 Moscow cracked down on a recalcitrant Russian parliament. The military was reluctant to act unless Yeltsin made concessions in regard to the "threat" of NATO enlargement and also to greater central government support for military interests.

On 14 September 1994 it was reported that Yeltsin had created a ring of elite military units around Moscow that might be used to protect the government from revolts by dissatisfied units which had returned from East Germany and the Baltic states. (Yeltsin's guard has also been used in disputes with Russian mafias.) A new Department of Military Politics was also created, to handle the concerns of a newly politicized military. In general, promotion based on loyalty to Yeltsin or Grachev (prior to the latter's dismissal) had angered army officers. In addition, army officers demanded an augmentation in defense expenditure, compulsory military service, improvement of social benefits for military personnel, as well as censorship of severe press critiques of the military. At the same time, the Russian government was purportedly spending 1.5 times as much as had the Soviet-era government on interior troops—in order to prevent mass unrest.[29]

Following the removal of General Grachev, Lebed protested the 1997 budget plan of 101 trillion rubles ($20 billion), which was far short of the 260 trillion rubles requested by the defense ministry. Defense spending was estimated at around 80 trillion rubles ($17 billion) in 1996, or only 10 percent of the U.S. level.[30] (The Russian army now has about 1.5 million troops, as compared to 4.5 million in the Soviet army.) Lebed's concern arose from the real possibility of rebellion within the armed forces. In August 1996, Lev Rokhlin, chairman of the State Duma Defense Committee, warned that deteriorating conditions in the military had created an "explosive situation" in which more and more servicemen were expressing open discontent, leading to the formation of strike committees. The military was owed some 15 trillion rubles ($2.8 billion) from the federal government. There continued to be a considerable shortfall in housing: more than 150,000 officers, noncommissioned officers, and warrant officers were on waiting lists for housing.[31]

After the August 1991 coup attempt, Russian intelligence had predicted that the next coup would be sparked by officer's wives ("engines of disobedience"!) who were dissatisfied with living in communal apartments and barracks and who would subsequently urge their husbands to rebel.[32] By 1995–96, women at the 472nd Air Fighter Command in Kursk had, in fact, formed human chains on runways to protest their husbands' wage arrears, equal to 6 billion rubles ($1.2 million). At the 26th Submarine Division of the Pacific Fleet sailors' wives tried to prevent submarines from going to sea, because of nonpayment of allowances. Wives of servicemen also picketed a landing strip in Murmansk, because the pilots had not been paid. The wives of Baltic Fleet sailors attempted to block the road from Kaliningrad, in protest of wage arrears.[33] (It is a disquieting fact that strikes by women had helped spark the 1904–05 Russian revolution!)

The army is consequently in a dangerous state of decay. The army has been riven with internal political discord and lack of discipline, as competing factions seek to influence enlisted men. Local military elites have begun to form links with regional mafias. All these factors lead to calls for a "strongman"—as the new "democracy" appears totally corruptible.[34] Defense Minister Igor Rodionov has stated that it would be "difficult but not impossible" to transform the Russian military into an all-professional force by 2000, given the "necessary economic conditions." Rodionov accordingly dismissed Western promises that the "colossal forces" being devoted to NATO enlargement did not threaten Russia as "just words. . . . We must draw conclusions from history."[35] The "threat" of NATO enlargement accordingly represents a possible rallying point on which to galvanize the Russian army and the general population to action to restore the motherland.

CHAPTER 5

The Splintering of the Soviet Empire

RUSSIAN EFFORTS TO CONTROL THE CIS

Essentially two interrelated factors pushed the United States into closer interaction with Moscow from 1991 to 1994. The first priority was to control the spread of nuclear weaponry (see Chapter 7). The second was to forestall potential conflict among the newly independent states and former Soviet republics. As many disputes within the former Soviet empire and Eastern Europe are still related to Soviet-imposed boundaries and ethnic manoeuvering, the collapse of that empire has resulted in the creation of both Russian and non-Russian ethnic diasporas and has released latent irredentist claims by emerging states or political factions. Between twenty–two and twenty–five million ethnic Russians (not including up to another twenty–five million members of Russified or Sovietized ethnic groups) have been left in fourteen non-Russian countries; more than eighteen million citizens of fourteen other countries were left outside their respective homelands. More than seventeen million people were left without statehood.[1] Over 204 ethno-territorial conflicts have been sparked in the area of the former Soviet Union alone.[2]

In addition to attempting to retrieve nuclear weapons dispersed throughout its former empire (aided by U.S. pressure and promises of financial assistance), Moscow has sought to bring each former Soviet republic into a new defense and economic interrelationship. In late 1992 Moscow began to consider an "enlightened post–imperial integrationist course" in its relations with the former Soviet bloc—with Russia at the head of the CIS. Russia argued that its position of *primacy* over the former Soviet Union should obtain international legitimacy due to the country's key military and security role. Conjoint U.S.-Russian policy, intended to ameliorate the risks of conflict within the Commonwealth of Independent States, accordingly meant (1) legitimizing a Russian monopoly over nuclear weapons; (2) tacit acceptance of Russian *primacy*, if not *hegemony* or *dominance*, over the CIS (but with Ukraine in a special category); and (3) acceptance of Russia as the replacement for the Soviet Union as a permanent member of the UN Security Council.

By the spring of 1993, however, Russian pressures on former Soviet bloc states were beginning to be regarded as permitting Russia to reassert its traditional *hegemony* over the Eurasian continent. Joint U.S.-Russian executive pressure on former Soviet bloc states led to congressional accusations that the Bush administration, and subsequently the Clinton administration, were too soft on Moscow. Not so ironically, the "Russia-first" strategy appeared tacitly to support Russian efforts to reestablish *hegemony*, if not *dominance*.

On the other hand, each of the former Soviet republics has to a certain extent resisted Moscow and has attempted to forge its own, more independent foreign, economic, and military policy. Each CIS state has had to grapple with divergent territorial claims, ethnic and national disputes, and ecological crises. In essence, the degree to which CIS states will be able to sustain a relative independence from Moscow will be determined not only by intrinsic Russian political-economic capabilities but also by Moscow's perceptions of potential internal and external "threats." Russian interaction with NATO, the EU/WEU, China, and Japan, as well as with the CIS states themselves, will affect whether Moscow takes an increasingly "hard" or "soft" stance in regard to the CIS and the "near abroad." These relations will also influence Moscow's decision to take either a tougher or more conciliatory stance toward the major powers, particularly the United States. Russian interactions with NATO and other key CIS states will also largely determine whether the new lines presently being formed in Europe will prove "permeable" or "impermeable." At the same time, the nature and extent of U.S. and G-7 aid will influence—but not necessarily determine—whether Russia and the CIS states can establish a more or less proportional relationship.

UKRAINE, RUSSIA, AND THE CRIMEA

Historical Russian-Ukrainian animosities (largely dating from the 1654 Pereiaslav agreement seen as leading to the collapse of Ukrainian autonomy), plus decades of despicable, totalitarian misrule, have created a gulf between the Ukraine and Russia that will prove difficult to bridge, despite constant allusions to a common Slavic heritage. Stalin's division of Polish territory between Belarus and Ukraine laid a basis for irredentist claims should questions regarding border demarcation not be entirely resolved or if political-economic instability reopens latent tensions. Ukrainian efforts to establish political-economic and military independence from Russia in particular have not been well received by Moscow. Russia fears that Ukraine has been working to forge a "Baltic–Black Sea alliance" intended to isolate Russia by means of a "double buffer zone."

As Moscow began to remove nuclear weapons from the CIS states— with the collaboration of Washington—it began to be feared that Russia was attempting to reassert hegemony over the former Soviet Union. Ukrainians in particular worried that Moscow might be trying to bring a pro-Russian elite to power in Kiev before a truly national identity had time to grow in Ukraine. Concurrently, members of Kyiv's parliament, the Rada, suspected that Washington had sided with Russian interests and therefore initially attempted to stall returning or destroying nuclear weapons and also ratifying the NPT.

In early September 1993, at the Ukrainian resort of Massandra, Moscow augmented pressure on Kiev, such as by threatening to raise energy prices to world market levels. In effect, Russia threatened war, and possibly a preemptive strike, if the Ukraine did not sell part of its Black Sea Fleet in return for cancellation of the oil debt to Russia, and send its nuclear weapons back to Moscow in exchange for nuclear fuel. By January 1994, however, Ukraine agreed to drop its claims to nuclear weapons and signed a tripartite nuclear disarmament agreement with the United States and Russia. (See Chapter 7.)

Russian demands to continue use of the naval base at Sevastopol—as well as Russian threats to retake the Crimea—were particularly contentious. After several years of threats and counter-threats, Kyiv and Moscow appeared to move to a compromise over the remaining forces of the Black Sea Fleet and Russian basing rights. According to the June 1995 agreement, the two states were to split the fleet in half but Moscow was to purchase most of the Ukrainian part (acquiring 82 percent). Russia was to use the base at Sevastopol and pay rent in energy supplies; Ukraine was to use part of the base for its smaller fleet.[3] Ukraine was to have gained ships and bases but few officers, as the latter have tended to desire the higher Russian salaries.

In February 1996, Ukraine refused to sign the Tashkent Treaty on a CIS military alliance. In April, an Ukrainian-Russian Friendship Treaty was once again postponed, due to continued disputes over the Black Sea Fleet and Russian basing rights, but also because of significant Ukrainian opposition to the Russian-Belarusian "union." Nationalists argued that an agreement over the Black Sea Fleet would permit Russia to retain its hegemony over the entire Black Sea region.

Moscow would thus retain its naval power projection vis-à-vis Ukraine, if not *against* states such as NATO-member Turkey. In June 1996 the Ukrainian parliament voted to ban all foreign military bases (Russia has refused to withdraw all land forces from Ukrainian territory) but left a period in which the Russian fleet could remain; in July the Ukrainian foreign ministry declared that Russia could not use Sevastopol as a base for its fleet but would have to find other options.[4]

Interestingly, however, despite the dispute over basing rights, Russia appeared to accept Ukrainian steps to consolidate control over the Crimean secession movement. In March 1995, following a May 1994 vote of the Crimean parliament (the "Pentagon") to restore the May 1992 constitution, Ukraine moved to stifle Crimean secession efforts. Despite the involvement of ethnic Russians in the Crimean independence movement, which demanded that Kyiv return the Crimea to Moscow (given by Khrushchev in 1954), this Ukrainian action was apparently taken with the tacit acceptance of Moscow. As the May 1992 Crimean constitution was regarded as a statement of secession, both Moscow and Kyiv may have sought to stifle the potential "demonstration effect" of Crimean independence upon similar movements in both Russia and Ukraine (particularly Tatar claims to sovereignty within the Russian Federation and in the Crimea). Furthermore, as the Yeltsin regime has intended to reintegrate Ukraine into the CIS, Moscow may have wanted to show solidarity with Kyiv rather than to display support for the Russian ethnic diaspora that "greater Russian" or pan-national Russian chauvinists (such as Alexander Lebed) have demanded.

From this perspective, Ukraine's attempts to balance its relations between the West and the East are primarily an effort to counter excessive Russian influence. At the same time, it is not clear in which direction Ukraine is drifting. Alienation in the armed forces is widespread. Out of roughly a thousand officers interviewed in June 1996, some 57 percent believed that the army cannot not defend the state; and 74 percent see no real reform of the army. Some 41 percent seek to sustain Ukraine's non-aligned status, while 12 percent want NATO membership. Only 8 percent believe Kyiv should have signed the Tashkent Collective Security Pact, while 37 percent are not opposed to setting up a Russian-Ukrainian-Belarusian security pact.[5]

In February 1997 in a significant speech, Ukrainian President Leonid Kuchma blamed Russia for the failure to sign a Treaty of Friendship, and stated that Russia treats Ukraine as if it were still within its sphere of influence.[6] That same month, the Ukrainian parliament failed to pass the "zero agreement" (signed by the Russian and Ukrainian prime ministers in 1994) that was to divide Ukrainian and Russian debts and assets, including claims to former Soviet gold, hard currency, and property. (The Rada wanted detailed information on Soviet assets and debts at the time when the USSR broke apart.)[7] The issue of the Black Sea fleet had yet to be resolved; in addition, Kyiv declared that it would unilaterally delimit the Ukrainian border—if Moscow does not soon work cooperatively to resolve border disputes.

Likewise, in February 1997, Ukraine conditioned its support for NATO enlargement and continued to oppose the deployment of nuclear weapons on the territory of new NATO members. Foreign Minister Hennadii Udovenko feared that a NATO-Russian Charter might lead the United States to accept Russian hegemony over Ukraine in exchange for NATO enlargement into Central Europe. Kyiv stated its apprehension that the proposed NATO-Ukrainian agreement would not offer any legally binding guarantees going beyond mere consultations and international assurances.[8]

POLAND-BELARUS-UKRAINE

Since 1991, the Polish government has sought to establish positive diplomatic relations with both Belarus and Ukraine, as an effort to wean these states away from Russian influence. At the same time, Warsaw has tilted more toward Ukraine than Belarus. This has been true despite potential irredentist claims upon both Belarusian and Ukrainian territories, based on the 1921 Polish-Soviet Treaty of Riga and eighteenth century claims to "historic Poland." (Warsaw was the first capital officially to recognize Kyiv, in December 1991.) About 300,000 Belarusians live in Poland, and 418,000 Poles live in Belarus. Poland could lay claim to Hrodna, but both sides have thus far sought to allay tensions. Concurrently, five million Russians exert strong political influence in Belarus.[9] For its part, Warsaw has realized that to make irredentist claims could also conjure up Bonn's claims to eastern territories (including Silesia and Pomerania) granted by Stalin to Poland in the aftermath of World War II. (See Chapter 3.)

Ukraine has considered Poland to be a "special strategic partner." In June 1996 Poland and Ukraine signed a bilateral agreement stating that Kyiv would not oppose Warsaw's membership in NATO. (But the Ukrainian prime minister declared that Kyiv could not accept the deployment of nuclear weapons in Poland.) Ukraine also attempted to manipulate its relationship with Poland so as to back its ultimate quest for EU membership, as well as "associated membership" with NATO—despite Kyiv's own recognition that such a status in NATO does not yet exist (as it does in the WEU). By proposing "associated" NATO membership Kyiv may have been testing NATO's reaction (in addition to playing pro and anti–NATO factions against each other in the foreign ministry).[10] (See also the discussion above.)

Although both Poland and Belarus have sustained claims on Lithuania, Warsaw has largely supported Lithuania against a generally pro-Russian Belarus after the 1991 breakup of the Soviet empire.[11] In February 1995, Belarus and Lithuania did, however, finally sign an agreement "On Good Neighborly and Friendly Relations." A March 1996 Belarus-Russian agreement to forge a closer Russian-Belarus "community" or "union," on the other hand, raised fears of a Russian effort to pressure both Poland and Lithuania, as well as Latvia and Estonia.

While Polish-Ukrainian relations appeared to be positive, Belarusian-Ukrainian relations were described as "not satisfactory" by Prime Minister Mikhail Chyhir of Belarus in December 1995. Trade between Belarus and Ukraine dropped from $1.16 billion in 1992 to a mere $322 million in 1994. From a geostrategic perspective, the tighter military relations between Belarus and Russia become, the worse relations between Belarus and Ukraine may become. (Russian Defense Minister Grachev signed agreements with Belarus that called for joint regional forces and for Russian use of bases in Belarus. Russia retains between twenty–five to thirty thousand troops in Belarus.)

On 20 July 1996, the Polish, Ukrainian, and Belarusian foreign ministers met in Brest to discuss the prospects of regional cooperation. In addition to issues concerning border controls and illegal immigration, one idea, proposed by the Polish foreign minister, Dariusz Rosatti, was to include the Brest *oblast* of Belarus in a "Bug" Euroregion, forming a "Brest triangle" that would seek to integrate Belarus into a Central European association. As Belarusian participation would be supported by Western investment (perhaps involving the "Weimar triangle" of Germany, France, and Poland), the hope was to wean Belarus away from too close a relationship with Moscow and provide some support for an increasingly isolated Minsk.[12] However, there is no reason to assume that Russia will give total support to Belarus; as argued below, Russian-Belarusian relations are not as tight as often claimed.

RUSSIA AND BELARUS

Despite the signing of a Russian-Belarusian "union" in March 1996, not all tensions between Moscow and Minsk have dissipated. Although Minsk has become more open to a strategic alliance with Moscow than has Kyiv, a close Russian-Belarusian alliance cannot be a foregone conclusion—particularly if Belarus receives the proper enticements to gradually wean it away from Moscow. Significant elements of the domestic opposition continue to oppose too close an alliance with Moscow and continue to propose a neutral Baltic–Black Sea confederation, with Minsk as the capital.

For its part, Moscow has vehemently opposed any proposals that favor a "Baltic–Black Sea alliance," as a form of "encirclement." Moscow has remained suspicious of the perceived efforts of such states as Poland to draw both Belarus and Ukraine away from the Russian orbit. In February 1996, for example, Moscow pressured Belarus, Poland, and Lithuania to provide a secure route to Kaliningrad—in part to check Polish and Baltic state efforts to join NATO.[13] In March 1996, in part under "red" and "brown" pressure to restore the former Soviet Union, as well as in response to the "threat" of NATO enlargement, President Yeltsin worked to forge a Russian-Belarusian "community" or "union" and planned to work out similar accords with Kazakhstan and Kirgystan. The Russian-Belarusian agreement (signed 2 April 1996) was in part based upon the so-called "zero agreement," whereby Russia ostensibly waived roughly $900 million for gas supplies and credits, and Belarus in turn canceled Russian claims to nuclear weapons removed from Belarusian territory. (Russian critics of the deal argue, however, that Belarus still has to pay significant debts to Moscow.)

In general, Moscow has tended to look upon Minsk as a province and not a capital. Belarus, for example, is heavily dependent upon Russia for petroleum, and Russia is its major market for trucks. From a geostrategic perspective, Belarus has become increasingly important to Russia, particularly as Russia must move out of forward-deployed positions in the Baltic states. Russian submarines have generally relocated to the Kola peninsula, as the Paldiski nuclear submarine station in Estonia is to be demolished. Moscow will, however, continue to operate its early warning system in Latvia until the year 2000, when a new system is to be completed in Belarus. The Russian defense ministry has accordingly insisted that the early warning system represents a "vital" national interest that must be backed by a closer Belarus-Russian strategic pact.[14] (The key question—who is to pay the costs of a CIS air defense system—has, however, yet to be answered.)

At the same time, the fact that Minsk still has some relative autonomy in respect to Moscow is illustrated in Belarus becoming the twenty–fourth country to join the PfP initiative, in February 1995. Belarus joined the PfP *after* the Russian refusal to join the PfP Individual Partnership (in December 1994) and *prior to* the Russian promise (at the May 1995 U.S.-Russian summit) to reconsider the Individual Partnership. In December 1996, Minsk supported the NACC process, and requested a special relationship with NATO.

Belarus, much like Ukraine, has also hesitated on the transfer of nuclear weapons to Moscow. American actions may have inadvertently caused Belarus to move closer to Russia. Belarus had agreed to turn its nuclear weapons over to Russia as part of an agreement with the United States, but it received only $75.3 million in aid from

Washington. This fact helped to strengthen the arguments of anti–reform elements in Belarus. Washington's miserliness was grist for those in Minsk who complained that the West was untrustworthy. In an effort to gain greater U.S. assistance, Belarus threatened to return to a reconstituted Russian empire.[15]

Moreover, Moscow's claim to rule its neighbors may be exaggerated at least from an economic standpoint.[16] Although Belarus and Russia negotiated a customs union with a single administration, and had agreed to previous plans to implement common economic policies in 1993, Russia rejected the option of monetary union in April 1995. Russia did not want to bear the burden of the Belarusian economy, which had an inflation rate running around 50 percent a month in 1994. As Yeltsin put it, "If we do not reform at the same pace, there will be no integration."[17] In turn, Belarus did not want to be dependent upon Russian administrative and financial whims. The two sides, for example, continued to dispute over the alleged smuggling of contraband from Belarus to Russia.

Despite efforts to form a largely unimplemented Russian-Belarusian "union," the Russian military presence, devastating ecological damage, disclosures that the Russian military were to be granted free rent, plus the facts that the early warning system would require extensive electricity and would become a target in case of war, all led to significant popular protest in Belarus. The Russian military presence was accordingly regarded as a threat to Belarusian sovereignty.

Russian hard-liners subsequently began to accuse Washington of attempting to break up the Russo-Belarusian alliance. Viktor Ilyukin, a deputy of the duma, charged the CIA with attempting to alienate Belarus from Moscow. At the same time, opposition Belarusian politicians called for a campaign to impeach President Aleksandr Lukashenko, who was accused backtracking on reforms and of seeking a personal dictatorship. Not surprisingly, Lukashenko then banned political rallies until the winter of 1996 (forcing two opposition leaders of the Belarusian Popular Front to seek political asylum in the United States). Lukashenko also attempted to rally collective farm workers to his side. Due to his conflict with the Belarusian parliament, the unpredictable Belarusian president (despite his ostensibly pro-Russian stance) did not obtain strong support from the Yeltsin government. Moscow appeared to be looking for a way to mediate between Lukashenko's dictatorial tendencies and the demands of the Belarusian parliament. The November 1996 referendum, however, gave Lukashenko sweeping powers and allowed him to dissolve the parliament. (Russia and China have been the only two countries to recognize officially the government after the referendum.) Belarusian society appears to be militarizing as Lukashenko seeks to protect his power base from internal and external "enemies": the army reportedly increased from 70–80,000 in 1995 to 113,000 in February 1997.

Yeltsin and Lukashenko have firmly stated their opposition to NATO enlargement; yet both have also affirmed that Russian-Belarusian "unification" is not aimed against NATO. Accordingly, in March 1997, Lukashenko called for NATO-Belarus talks—particularly as Washington (and the EU) had significantly downgraded relations with Minsk. (Washington had suspended $40 million in aid on account of "human rights" violations.) At the same time, as political-military and economic relations between Russia and Belarus are not as tight as often assumed, there is no reason to assume that Moscow will necessarily provide Minsk its full support. Belarus may find itself increasingly isolated, particularly if NATO, Russia, and Ukraine do reach joint agreements. A new April 1997 draft on a Moscow-Minsk "union" did not go far enough in the eyes of Lukashenko.

At the same time, however, the push for NATO enlargement may precipitously press Moscow and Minsk together into an unwieldy relationship—assuming a NATO-Russian Charter fails to materialize. Belarus may also seek to block NATO enlargement—as well as NATO-Russian-Ukrainian accords. If Belarus cannot be given incentives to wean it toward a more neutral stance (for example, involving the formation of the Polish-Ukrainian-Belarus "Brest triangle"), there is a real danger that Minsk may play a geostrategic role similar to that of East Germany in regard to the Soviet Union during the Cold War, but in circumstances that are far more unstable. That is, Minsk may attempt to play Moscow and Washington against each other, while at the same time accusing Vilnius, Warsaw, and Prague of becoming "centers of actions aimed against Belarus."[18]

RUSSIA AND KAZAKHSTAN

In December 1991, Russia, Belarus, and Ukraine met at Minsk to establish the Commonwealth of Independent States, which was depicted as a "Union of Slavic Countries." The fact that Kazakhstan was not invited created suspicion that Russia had ulterior motives in not welcoming the largest Central Asian country into a new relationship. Rather than attempting to obtain greater independence from Moscow, however, Kazakhstan has generally sought closer integration, by interlocking itself with republics in the Russian Federation itself.

Somewhat ironically, Kazakhstan quickly became more supportive of the concept of an integrated, Russian-led CIS than did Slavic Ukraine, which pictured the CIS as a "civilized way of divorce." At the same time, Almaty (the former Alma-Ata) sought assurance that

Russia did in fact support Kazakh interests and that Russia did not intend to slice off the ethnically Russian northern tier of Kazakhstan, as demanded by such pan-nationalists as Alexander Solzhenitsyn, among others. Kazakh leader Nursultan Nazarbayev moved by August 1992 to forge an alliance with Tatarstan and Bashkortost (both inside the Russian Federation) in an effort to keep Kazakhstan interlocked with the Russian Federation.[19] While Moscow could threaten to support ethnic Russians inside Kazakhstan, Almaty could counter-threaten to support pro-Kazakh Central Asian republics inside the Russian Federation itself.

On one hand, Kazakhstan has attempted to secure itself by tying itself to Russian interests; on the other hand, it has looked to the United States for security "guarantees." The promise of U.S.-Russian security "assurances" following Kazakhstan's nuclear disarmament did not prevent President Nazarbayev from stating that large-scale Western investment in his country would be protected by the West. Secretary of State James Baker subsequently stated in 1992 that the United States did not offer any "hard" security guarantees to Kazakhstan, only the "soft" assurances promised by the NPT and the OSCE. (See also Chapter 7.)

Another factor is that Kazakhstan has opposed pan-Islamic and pan-Turk movements as well as Chinese irredentist claims to "East Turkestan"; Almaty has accordingly sought closer ties with Russia, particularly in regard to Nazarbayev's calls for a "Eurasian Union." At the same time, in an effort to straddle both sides of the fence, Kazakhstan has sought to improve border and defense relations with the PRC, by refusing to recognize Taiwan or support Tibet. Although Kazakhstan opposed Chinese nuclear testing in the 1990s, for example, it also sought China's cooperation in redeveloping the ancient trade route known as the Silk Road.

In January 1995, despite potential Russian threats to northern Kazakh territory and genetic horrors created by the years of Russian nuclear testing on Kazakh territory, Kazakhstan agreed to form joint armed forces with Russia by the end of 1995. Moreover, and despite its initial opposition, Almaty agreed to dual citizenship rights for Russians living in Kazakhstan; also, Russia and Kazakhstan agreed to a joint policy in regard to Azerbaijan and the Caspian Sea. By March 1996, however, relations between Kazakhs, Chechens, and Russian nationalists were tense, aggravated by Kazakh threats to ban the Communist Party following the March resolution declaring the 1991 dissolution of the Soviet Union "illegal."[20]

KAZAKHSTAN AND OTHER CENTRAL ASIAN COUNTRIES

Kazakhstan has unsuccessfully looked to forge a new regional bloc with Uzbekistan and Kirgystan. At the same time, Ukraine has been extending ties with Turkey in particular, but also other Central Asian states, including Pakistan, the rival of Russian-backed India. These steps are partly an effort to counterbalance Russian hegemony over Black Sea states.[21] Kyiv, for example, has sought to construct a pipeline through Turkey, Iran, and Azerbaijan, as a way to avoid dependence upon Moscow. Kazakhstan and other Central Asian republics, while apprehensive about pan-Islamic propaganda supported by Iran, are also wary of pan-Turkish goals. These states do not want to alienate Russia (or China) by being perceived as supporting pan-Turk interests. At the May 1992 Tashkent summit, all Central Asian states, plus Armenia, for example, assured Moscow of their support for Russian leadership. Moscow has thus far played the role as "hegemonic balancer" among the rival Central Asian states.

In effect, Kazakhstan and Uzbekistan are in regional competition for hegemony over the Central Asian states. This has raised fears of either a Kazakh or Uzbek "mini-imperialism," which makes the prospects for regional cooperation look rather bleak. Uzbekistan is confronted with both internal and external ethnic tensions, a factor that has led it to spread its interior forces into almost every region of the country. "Islamic" north Tajikistan is pro-Uzbek; the south is pro-Russian. In January 1996, Russian Foreign Minister Primakov stated that if Russia withdraws from Tajikistan, "then the wave of destabilization will cover Central Asia."

Turkmenistan, in particular, is fearful of Iranian and Afghan influence, but it, like Kirgystan, is also fearful of Uzbekistan. Turkmenistan has accordingly sought closer ties with both Iran and Turkey, while it has sought to counterbalance these relations by a close relationship with Russia. In many ways, Central Asian states may be vying with each other to establish a special relationship with Moscow in order to counter the regional ambitions of their neighbors.[22] Uzbekistan, which is the least willing to establish close political-military ties with Russia appears, however, to vacillate between support for Russia's "leading role" in the region and statements that Russia should recognize Uzbekistan as an "equal partner."[23]

In March 1997, Kazakh president Nursultan Nazarbayev warned that haste in NATO enlargement puts Russian democrats in a tough position, and that NATO enlargement should not encroach upon Russian interests. His remarks came just before NATO Secretary-General Solana went on a tour of Central Asian capitals to discuss PfP activities—an event criticized by Moscow as an effort to undermine Russian influence in the CIS.

RUSSIA AND THE CIS: PRIMACY, HEGEMONY, OR CREEPING DOMINANCE?

Russian strategists appear divided over how to deal with the rest of the states in the CIS and how to balance the interests of Russia with those of the rest of the members. Boris Yeltsin has appeared to be seeking "deeper integration" leading to "confederation." The Communist Party has demanded a more unitary system, similar to the former Soviet Union. By April 1996, essentially three alliances within the CIS had been formed: the Central Asian Union; the Union of the Four (Russia, Belarus, Kirgystan, and Kazakhstan); and the Union of the Two (Belarus and Russia.) Concurrently, Russia has additionally attempted to draw Kazakhstan, Belarus, (plus Tajikistan, Turkmenistan, Kirgystan, Kazakhstan) with it into closer relations with China. This effort is also designed to isolate Ukraine and pressure it to move closer to the CIS.

The official view is that Russia represents the only "locomotive" capable of pulling the CIS states together in strategic, political, and economic terms. At the same time, however, Moscow appears to realize that a traditional imperialist policy cannot be sustained. On one hand, Moscow has attempted to reintegrate the economies of the CIS states, often by threats of economic blockade or force. On the other hand, Moscow may be reluctant to go too far with economic integration, perceiving, for example, monetary integration as too great a strain on Russian finances. Russia made it clear that it would not subsidize Belarusian budget deficits; Moscow has also opposed the entry of Tajikistan into the ruble currency zone. Russian calls for the transformation of the CIS into a European Union–type organization thus do not appear feasible for the foreseeable future.

Yet as Russia has attempted to forge a Russian-Belarus-Kazakh alliance to pressure Ukraine into accepting a more "cooperative" relationship with the CIS, the latter generally suspects that the Moscow's intention is not really *primacy* but tight *hegemony*—if not *dominance*. Kyiv has argued that it will participate in the CIS as an equal in a loose *confederation* but will not accept Russian *hegemony*—if it can help it.

While Moscow appears to be seeking Russian *hegemony* over the CIS, there exist three other possibilities. The first is a Russian-*dominated* CIS (the view supported by revanchists); the second is the breakup of the CIS itself; the third is that Russia ultimately respects the other CIS states as "equals." In an ironic way, the first and second possibilities are interrelated. Russian revanchists argue for a strong, Russian-dominated CIS that will prevent the breakup not only of the CIS but also the Russian Federation. Pan-Russians seek to link up with ethnic Russians in CIS states so as to subordinate these states to Russia.

But the very actions of hard-liners (including the August 1991 coup attempt and Alexander Rutskoi's September–October 1993 *pronunciamento*) have tended to exacerbate the forces that could dismember both the CIS and the Russian Federation. This fact gives the second possibility—of a break-up of the CIS, if not the Russian Federation itself—greater credence.

Communist and pan-nationalist calls in the duma to renounce the 1991 Belovezhskaya Accords which created the CIS and the 12 December 1991 decision of the Supreme Soviet decision to abrogate the 1922 treaty forming the USSR represent a potentially destabilizing effort to delegitimize all post–1991 reforms and laws.[24] These efforts were accordingly criticized by Foreign Minister Primakov as (1) undermining Russia's reputation as a reliable international partner; (2) denying sovereignty to the new republics; (3) torpedoing government efforts to reintegrate the CIS; and (4) strengthening pro-NATO opinion in Eastern Europe. Ukrainian president Leonid Kuchma has stated that although the duma resolution was non-binding it posed a "threat" to Ukraine and "placed a mine under the CIS."[25] Kazakhstan and other CIS states also condemned the vote.

The third perspective argues that Russia should treat the other CIS states as "equals." This perspective has charged that the CIS administrative bodies, such as the interstate economic committee, formed in October 1994, have begun to migrate away from Minsk (where they are supposed to be) and toward Moscow. None of the CIS administrative organs have been headed by representatives of Ukraine or any other former Soviet republic. In effect, they have remained moribund because of Moscow's desire "to play an openly dominant role in them. . . . [Russia has refused to] recognize in practice the equality of all the former Soviet republics and acknowledge a readiness to make significant concessions to weaker partners. . . . Specifically this means that Russia [recognize] the principle of rotation and [abandon] attempts to subordinate any CIS body to itself."[26]

This third option appears utopian at present. Among other things, significant Russian disputes with Ukraine have prevented a more proportionate distribution of power among the CIS states from developing, since Moscow refuses to treat Kyiv as an "equal." Considering Russia's relative assets in the defense and economic areas, a more proportional approach can become feasible only in more politically and economically secure conditions. At the same time, any return to anything like the USSR is also illusory; a confederation (much like that of the present EU) based mainly on economic and cultural ties, not military activities, has been depicted as the most plausible option by international affairs experts of the Council on

Foreign and Defense Policy in Moscow.[27] This more "realistic"
possibility depends upon the establishment of a non-threatening
relationship between Russia, the United States, the EU, China, and
Japan—as well as the nature of trade and assistance resulting.

It thus remains to be seen whether Russia and the other newly
independent states will continue to work out their disputes through
"democratic compromise" or whether Russia will move toward a
tighter *hegemony* of the CIS, in a step-by-step fashion. At present,
Russia really has neither the capacity nor the will to dominate once
again the former parts of the Soviet Union. In many ways, it is more
concerned with maintaining central government controls over the
Russian Federation itself. (See Chapter 4.) While Russia will continue
to press for *hegemony* (if not *dominance* in certain regions), it may still
be possible to dampen that drive in areas that are of perceived "vital"
interests to the United States and Europe. Rather than threatening
Russia with NATO's unilateral expansion—which may tacitly link
NATO to the "Baltic–Black Sea alliance" and result in a destabilizing
counter-reaction—it would be best to establish global security and
economic conditions that would permit Russia actually to relax controls
over the CIS. The effort to dampen the Russian drive for hegemony
would accordingly entail a non-threatening and non-encircling
approach to the security of Central and Eastern Europe and the CIS, by
means of an international cooperative-collective security regime. (See
Chapters 10 and 11.)

KEEPING RUSSIA AND THE CIS ON A TREADMILL

Related to the costs of global stability are the costs of sustaining the
political and economic stability of Russia and the CIS. On one hand,
not to assist Russia's transition to democratic liberalism risks either
the breakup of the Russian Federation itself or a revanchist backlash.
On the other hand, Western aid and assistance could help to rebuild
Russian military, technological, and economic capabilities—and
permit it to reassert its hegemony or dominance over the CIS.

Ironically, the breakup of the Soviet Union destroyed the
possibility of a single integrated market, which would have allowed
greater economies of scale for CIS firms, in addition to providing
greater incentives for Western multinational corporate investment. Yet
as Russia sees itself as the only state still capable of rebuilding a
modicum of the former Soviet economy, it hopes to take the lead in key
aspects of market-oriented reform efforts and what has been dubbed
"*nomenklatura* privatization" among the CIS states. In attracting
Western capital and assistance from the majority of the G-7 countries,
Moscow claims that it is only seeking *primacy* over the CIS. Yet,

ironically, should Russia be able to "out-reform" the other CIS republics, it will be able to sustain its hegemonic position.[28]

At present, however, American and G-7 policy appears to be to keep Russia (and the CIS) on a treadmill, not permitting sufficient aid or assistance to actually stabilize the Eurasian region. Yet it is the essential argument of this book that aid and assistance must accompany a general political-military entente. A Russia—that is domestically stable and strategically secure—will be a far more willing partner and a more cooperative member of the CIS than a Russia that fears domestic instability and foreign "encirclement."

In many ways, the new Russia has been regarded as a public charge, one that requires a more activist approach on the part of the IMF and World Bank, among other international lending and financial institutions. Indeed, as President Clinton stated on 1 April 1993, "If Russia's reforms turn sour, if it reverts to authoritarianism or disintegrates into chaos, the world cannot afford the strife of a former Yugoslavia replicated in a nation as big as Russia."[29] Yet, Boris Yeltsin's own warnings, intended to augment foreign assistance—that "general unrest" could lead to a renewed "cold or hot war" or a return to totalitarian rule, if the West and Japan do not more substantially assist the Russian economy—have not inspired long-term confidence.

The April 1993 G-7 summit in Tokyo pledged $43.4 billion in a multilateral aid package that included $15 billion in official debt rescheduling offered by the Paris Club. The offer largely represented a repackaging of previous agreements, which included the $24 billion originally promised by the IMF in mid-1992. Most of the aid was to be conditioned on Russian progress toward market-oriented reforms and ruble convertibility. President Clinton and the G-7 then began to urge the IMF and the World Bank to take a softer approach (instead of waiting for Russia to establish a track record of financial discipline before releasing aid), in fear that the IMF's "shock therapy" would generate greater social and political instability. In June 1994 the Paris Club rescheduled another $7 billion. However, Russian officials sought a more sweeping arrangement (basing their claims in part on the massive investment Germany had made in Central and Eastern European countries).

In April 1995 Russia was to obtain $1 billion out of a promised $6.4 billion promised to help stabilize the ruble. Despite the exorbitant costs of the war in Chechnya—in addition to the fact that Moscow could pay back only $4 billion out of the $15 billion it owed in outstanding international debts in 1995—the IMF judged the level of Russian government spending and inflation to be acceptable. The 1995 Russian government budget passed 289 votes to eighty–one, thus permitting the first $1 billion installment of the $6.4 billion standby loan from the IMF. In March 1996 the IMF approved a $10.1 billion loan, but only after Russia agreed not to raise import barriers and promised to resume imports of American poultry![30]

As the combined budget deficit of the EU has represented roughly 5.6 percent of GDP, European states have been reluctant to increase either aid or imports. Aid to former Soviet states has become more problematic for Germany, France, and Britain. Germany is faced with the grossly underestimated costs of unification (see Chapter 2), while France and particularly Britain confront rising debt-to-GDP ratios. At the same time, however, both France and Germany promised to grant Russia greater credits or investment—perhaps not coincidentally in the same week in February 1996 that Boris Yeltsin announced his candidacy for president. The French foreign minister, Alain Juppé, and French industrialists announced a major investment "donation"; German leader Helmet Kohl likewise reconfirmed German support of a $1.5 billion grant for Russia. (Germany holds at least 46 percent of Russia's $40 billion debt to the Paris Club. Total Russian foreign debt has been estimated to be as high as $120–130 billion. See previous Chapter 4.)

States such as Japan, South Korea, and Taiwan have large surpluses but are generally reluctant to risk investments in unstable conditions. Japan in particular has wanted a return of the Kurile Islands in exchange for greater Japanese aid to Russia. Tokyo offered some $8 billion in late 1992 to former Soviet Central Asian republics, ostensibly to check the rise of pan-Islamic movements which might destabilize oil supplies for Japan. Although there are indications that Japanese aid to Russia may no longer be made conditional upon a return of the Kurile Islands (see Chapter 6), Tokyo has generally preferred to invest in China than in Russia, partly to dampen China's drive for regional hegemony and help prevent its potential disaggregation. In essence, significantly more international investment has gone to the communist China than to Russia and the CIS, or even to Central Europe.[31]

AMERICAN ASSISTANCE

The effects of the Cold War have not only helped to bankrupt the old USSR and the new Russia but have weakened the political and financial ability of the Western countries to provide significant assistance to countries and regions that desperately need aid. After the buildup of Cold War debt, Congress would be hard-pressed to find funds—even if the political will to do so were available. Roughly 50 percent of the U.S. budget comprises sacrosanct entitlement programs; 14 percent goes to pay back-interest on the national debt (a figure that could rise to equal defense spending); 17 percent goes to discretionary domestic programs, which include pork-barrel projects; roughly 17 percent goes to defense spending; and the remaining 2 percent goes to foreign aid.[32] From 1991 to 1994 the United States delivered roughly $3.5 billion in aid to the former Soviet Union: the U.S. Agency for International Development (AID) provided roughly $1.2 billion; the Export-Import Bank provided $300 million for former Soviet republics; the Energy Department gave $121 million, largely for conversion of nuclear facilities; and the U.S. Information Agency contributed $120 million to help develop independent news services.[33]

American policy, however, has tended to lack focus and coordination. On one hand, U.S. assistance has often been criticized for assisting the old *nomenklatura* and state-controlled firms to stay alive. On the other, aid has also been criticized as self-serving, providing salaries for consultants with no experience in Russia or by tailoring assistance largely to suit the U.S. agricultural industry (such as poultry products). Concurrently, American aid has taken an anti–Russian direction. Up until 1996, roughly 55 percent of all U.S. aid going to the former Soviet Union went to Russia. Republican Party leaders then counter-proposed that 67 percent of all aid should go to non-Russian republics. Republicans argued that the reduction of U.S. aid would be offset by trade enhancement legislation. Congressional justification for the change in aid policy appeared to be blatantly anti–Russian. It ignored the fact that Ukraine, for example, had postponed most key market-oriented reforms—in contrast to Russian progress in reform. By 1996, following Republican demands, Ukraine became the third–greatest recipient of U.S. aid, following Israel and Egypt; Russia moved from third into fourth place.[34]

Moreover, the nature of aid provided may result more from inner bureaucratic imperatives than real needs. The U.S. Treasury Department had initially pushed a policy of "shock therapy" tempered by greater U.S. aid and soft loans. Concurrently, National Security Advisor Anthony Lake promoted a policy of democratic liberalism, which put the Clinton administration in a difficult position, in the sense that Yeltsin was not perceived as the perfect embodiment of a "democratic" leader by much of the Russian population.[35] The U.S. General Accounting Office argued that U.S. bilateral assistance to the former USSR was not being coordinated at all under the October 1992 "Freedom for Russia and Emerging Eurasian Democracies and Open Markets Act." The program, orchestrated by the National Security Council Policy Steering Group and chaired by Deputy Secretary of State Strobe Talbott, has had little influence or authority to direct worldwide programs such as the Export-Import Bank, Overseas Private Investment Corporation, Department of Agriculture, or Department of Defense. In addition, there have been disputes with other government agencies, such as AID, and programs run by the cabinet, such as the 1993 Gore-Chernomyrdin Commission.[36]

Washington has also been reluctant to consider proposals to assist industries that are either vital to the Russian military-industrial complex or could become competitors with U.S. or allied industries. Concurrently, Moscow has insisted that high-technology transfer represents one of the key bases for a close, long-term relationship. Washington, for example, has attempted to block Moscow from acquiring supercomputers capable of nuclear design and testing; yet in February 1997, Russia was able to acquire several advanced IBM systems through a European middleman.

One concern is that if the United States does attempt to draw Russia into NATO, the Russians could learn NATO military expertise that could advance its own military-technological capabilities. Moscow has opposed sharing its own military technology and operational techniques with Washington, because it fears that NATO could acquire Russian military secrets (and a view of Russian weaknesses). In addition to ineffective coordination, aid in dismantling nuclear weapons programs has been criticized for not disassembling the actual warheads, even though aircraft, missiles, silos, military industries, and submarines are being dismantled or reconverted.

Concurrently, Russian critics have charged that U.S. aid has represented a "carrot" to buy a pro-Western policy—including NATO enlargement. Yeltsin's hard-line critics believed that pro-Western advisor Anatoly Chubais (who did not give Yeltsin his total support) was chosen as head of the presidential staff under orders from the IMF, U.S. multinational corporations, and Washington. It was alleged that Vice President Al Gore sent a "secret memorandum" to Yeltsin in 1996 urging that Russia return to a tough monetarist course, suggesting that if Chubais stayed, he would be able to persuade American financial institutions to buy into Russia's debt, thus making possible up to $7–12 billion in investments.[37] (Despite apparently strong backing from Washington to secure his position, however, Chubais, along with Yeltsin and Chernomyrdin, spoke out against NATO enlargement, in early 1997.)

Total American investment in Russia, however, only amounted to $2.5 billion in mid-1996 (roughly one–third of all direct foreign investment). The Gore-Chernomyrdin talks in 1996 did promise up to $12 billion in significant investments, largely in the oil and gas industries. Yet these proposed investments have been made largely contingent upon changes in Russian monetary policy, legal codes, property rights, and other market-oriented legislation. Unless investments are U.S. government–subsidized or their risks are guaranteed, it is doubtful that Russia can attract significant financial investment. This is particularly true if Russian politicians continue to warn of political instability, civil war, dictatorship, mafia actions, or threaten to retaliate against American and German firms should NATO enlarge (as former Security Council Advisor Lebed allegedly did, although he subsequently denied it).[38]

The key issues really revolve around fiscal responsibility and the lack of a sound investment climate. International portfolio managers now tend to diversify investments throughout Central and Eastern Europe and Russia, so as to not risk too great an investment in any one country. Moreover, major investment firms are reluctant to place money in small entrepreneurial firms which provide meager returns; but these are perhaps the best outlets for investors in terms of overall Russian and CIS development. In general, private capital is not looking to invest in Russia or the former Soviet bloc due to the lack of ruble convertibility, as well as the lack of uniform investment and taxation policies—not to forget mafia criminality. (As many as 75 percent of private companies may be paying protection money to mafia organizations.) Ironically, the rise of the post–Soviet mafia—which threatens American and world interests through the illicit sale of arms and military technology (including nuclear materiel), tax fraud, insurance scams, and drug trafficking—has forced Washington to look toward greater cooperation with a largely ineffective Russian government![39]

The right to own land, for example, needs to be defined strictly by law, and the value of vouchers for purchase of industries needs to be specified clearly. The allowable percentage of foreign ownership (whether firms can be 100 percent–owned by foreigners or not) likewise needs to be worked out. Emerging Russian entrepreneurs have generally had more problems receiving credit and gaining access to commercial real estate and marketing channels than have state-owned or privatized businesses. Moreover, the privatization itself may not be of the kind expected by the United States. Factory owners at all experienced in marketing have been known to abscond with funds; privatization of government enterprises can be a trick to absolve the Russian or CIS governments of bankruptcy claims.

Disputes between various levels of local and regional governments within the Russian Federation have likewise weakened prospects for strong U.S. or European support. Regional units have attempted to claim that their laws on and controls over national resources take precedence over those of the central Russian government. Localities have opted for greater tax exemptions and subsidies, more favorable revenue sharing, and increased autonomy in foreign trade regulation. Differing degrees of subsidization have led to large price differentials and to internal trade barriers. The widening income gap between regions may result in a neo-medieval pattern of highly disparate wealth—as opposed to a new federalism that would work to balance central government and regional concerns. These factors consequently exacerbate fissiparous tendencies within the Russian Federation.

In part because the collapse of the Soviet Union broke up a potentially integrated market, and because of problems relating to property laws and taxation, multinational corporations may not wish to take risks in the CIS states or Russia; they may look instead to "liberal" states in Southeast Asia or Latin America. On the other hand, the introduction of "free economic zones" in Russia and Belarus (similar to those in the PRC), plus the proposed development of Arctic transit routes, could—in the long run—entice foreign investment to aid the development of the Russian North by linking Russia with Nordic states, the Asian Pacific, as well as Alaska.[38]

In the meanwhile, the consequences of a general "stagflation" in Europe and a depression in post–Soviet Eurasia have made prospects bleak for aid, not only to the new Russia but also other areas of the world in desperate need. The signing of the Uruguay Round of the General Agreement on Tariffs and Trade (GATT) and the formation of the World Trade Organization (WTO)—combined with efforts to integrate the European Union—could help boost world income by about $100–200 billion, partly by slashing state subsidies to noncompetitive enterprises. On the other hand, protectionist demands have weakened the interest of G-7 countries in lowering tax barriers to Central and Eastern Europe and the CIS states, and in ultimately drawing the new Russia into the WTO. *The danger is that any significant crash in the global financial markets would only exacerbate the severe depression already confronting Russia and the CIS and weaken the prospects of a positive political and economic recovery.* While it is imperative the United States, Europe, and Japan formulate a concerted approach designed ultimately to integrate Russia into the WTO, OECD, the EU, and the G-7 (even if only in terms of associate membership so as to help boost Moscow's political-economic influence and status), it is not absolutely certain that these three centers of power and financial influence can press Russia in a positive "democratic" direction or check its efforts to reassert its hegemony over the CIS as a whole. (See Chapter 9.)

CHAPTER 6

Russia and Eurasia

RUSSIAN GLOBAL STRATEGY

Russian strategists appear to be moving away from a pro-Western orientation and toward a Eurasian approach, although Russian pan-nationalists remain skeptical of both. In general, the pro-Western orientation has opposed too great a cooperation with the East and has preferred to keep Russian relations as open as possible with the United States and Europe. This group has wanted to keep the door open to Western trade and investment and believes that the PRC in particular possesses geostrategic and political-economic interests that could ultimately clash with those of Russia.

Eurasianists, however, have argued that Moscow should play an important role in the East and that Russia could use its eastern policies to pressure the West (and Japan) to accept more closely Russia's interests and needs—in part to counterbalance the loss of the Soviet position in regard to Central and Eastern Europe. In many ways, the keystone to Moscow's control over its Far East is its control over the Kurile Islands; it is feared that the total loss of the Kuriles would open the Russian Far East to Japanese and Chinese rivalry. Moreover, Eurasianists fear that Russia would lose its ability to project submarine-launched-ballistic-missiles (SLBMs) into the Pacific. By developing closer relations with states such as China, India, Iran, and Iraq, Eurasian strategists argue, Moscow can pressure Japanese policy and attempt to deflect potentially anti–Russian political movements and alliances away from the Russian Federation's soft underbelly—in addition to countering U.S. global strategy.

For their part, Russian pan-nationalists are wary of close ties to the

PRC. This group has been particularly worried about burgeoning Chinese political and economic (and sheer demographic) influence in the Far East. Russian pan-nationalists have also opposed closer military-technological trade and arms sales (such as of the Su–27 "Flanker" fighter aircraft) with China that could ultimately backfire against Russian interests. This group hopes to link together the Russian diaspora in the non-Russian republics and ultimately restore Russian hegemony over all Eurasian powers.

Thus far, the Eurasianists appear to have won out over the pro-Western and pan-nationalist strategies. Evidence is that a close relationship seems to suit both the Russian and Chinese leaderships, for the time being. Steps toward a closer Russian-Chinese relationship were outlined in March 1992 in a policy paper by Yeltsin's former political advisor, Sergei Stankevich. Such steps were not really implemented until late 1992 and 1993, when Russian hard-liners began to challenge the perceived "infantile pro-American" approach of Andrei Kozyrev.[1] In effect, since late 1992 and early 1993 Yeltsin has tightened the Russian-PRC relationship and sought closer relations with India and Iran, among other states. The fact that both Russia and the PRC in particular would most likely benefit (at least in economic and financial terms) from good relations with the West more than with each other has not prevented them from moving closer. Beijing may use its relationship with Russia as strategic leverage to "give Americans a warning" and as a means "to soften U.S. policy," while Moscow hopes "to speak at ease" with a more reliable China.[2]

Contrary to hopes that the world-wide "victory" of democratic ideals would permit a "democratic" Russia and a democratic United States to forge an alliance of democratic states (including the EU, Japan, and such states as "democratic" India) *against* the last major bastion of Communist totalitarianism, the People's Republic of China, Moscow and Beijing have appeared to be moving into a closer collaboration. Yeltsin's links with the PRC have in many ways become stronger than those established by the Soviet regime, despite Yeltsin's multiparty "democratic" and "anticommunist" domestic policy.[3] While the two states may not necessarily forge a full-scale military alliance, they could at least tacitly agree to pursue their geostrategic interests against the United States, the EU, and Japan rather than against each other.

Russia and the United States have thus, perhaps ironically, begun to compete for the PRC's military and economic allegiance—much as they did during the Cold War. The key difference is that Russia is now playing its own version of the "China card," through the sale of sophisticated weaponry, plus nuclear and "dual-use" technology. In addition to weapons profiteering, this strategy appears to represent a sophisticated gambit designed to pressure U.S. policy and force a compromise over NATO enlargement, among other issues. Russia's efforts to reassert its Eurasian interests are also intended to gain international recognition and legitimacy for its role in the "near" and "middle" abroad and its stature as a global power—the "far abroad."

Russia's efforts to play the China card, however, represent a risky strategy that could backfire against Russian and American (and also Japanese) interests. The previous Sino-Soviet alliance grew out of tensions surrounding the division of Korea, and U.S. support for Japan and Taiwan, culminating in the Korean War. The present Sino-Russian entente has thus far permitted Beijing to engage in an increasingly assertive strategy towards Taiwan, with many parallels to the 1957–58 Quemoy and Matsu crises. Closer Sino-Russian collaboration may also affect North Korean calculations. As compared to the Sino-Soviet relationship in the 1950s, the PRC is no longer a junior partner. Beijing now possesses an improved and much more powerful political-economic, naval, intercontinental ballistic missile, and nuclear capability.

By tacitly assisting Beijing's foreign policy goals, Moscow's Eurasian strategy jeopardizes the U.S.-Japanese alliance between American military might and consumerism, and Japanese dual-use high-technology and finance—to the detriment of Russian interests. The concern is that behind-the-scenes support of Chinese claims (even if Russia itself prefers a "peaceful resolution" of the crisis between Taiwan and the PRC) could backfire against Moscow itself (as well as Washington). Playing the China/Eurasian card could, most dangerously, provoke a Japanese counter-reaction. Even if Beijing and Tokyo do not clash directly, the latter could opt for greater political and nuclear independence.

On the one hand, Russia is not certain it can trust either NATO or the PRC; however, Moscow may believe that it can gain a temporary advantage by dealing with both simultaneously. By supporting the PRC only to a certain extent, it may hope to pressure NATO into a compromise.[4] At the same time, however, if the Russian Federation cannot reach a close entente with both NATO and Japan, it may well opt for a full-fledged Eurasian alliance. If it *also* fails to formulate a close Eurasian alliance, it may find itself confronted with the prospects of "encirclement" and the choice of implosion or war.

RUSSIA, TURKEY, GREECE, AND IRAN

The collapse of the Soviet Union promised to open much of Central Asia to Turkish influence; on the other hand, Turkey is itself in effect counter-encircled "360 degrees," externally and internally by conflict. Initially, Russia, Armenia, and Greece, among other states, tended to regard Turkey as using its membership in NATO to strengthen its position in the Aegean, the Caucasus, and Central Asia. However, Turkey has not been able to make significant strides in Uzbekistan, Turkmenistan, or Kirgystan, and Kazakhstan has been reluctant to move too close to Turkey, due to Russian influence and pressure.

Internally, Ankara has been at war since at least 1984 with the Kurdish Workers Party (PKK), a secessionist movement. Turkey's Kemalist, secular government has also been contending with a growing Islamic movement since 1987. The Islamic Refah Partisi (Welfare Party) tripled its electorate between 1987 and 1995, from seven percent to twenty–one percent, and then captured the prime ministership in 1996 as part of a coalition government (Necmettin Erbakan becoming the prime minister). Prior to taking control of the government, the Refah Partisi program showed itself to be against the U.S.-led force that was providing shelter for Iraqi Kurds, and to be against military ties with Israel and for closer relations with the Palestinian Hamas. (The Refah Partisi initially opposed the Israeli-Turkish military training pact, for example, yet it subsequently renewed it.) While it may ultimately curb its pro-Islamic orientation (in part due to threats against Islamic anti–secularism from the military), the Refah Partisi has threatened to pull out of NATO, or not support NATO enlargement, if the latter pursues "anti–Islamic policies." (Secular Turkish nationalists have also opposed NATO enlargement. See below.) In essence, the new government initially sought to re-equilibrate Turkish policy toward Iran and Iraq (as well as Libya!) in order to address its isolation from the Islamic world—after having lost some $20–30 billion in trade with Iraq following the UN embargo.

Externally, Ankara is concerned about conflict over the former Yugoslavia (with ties to Bosnia and Albania); and between Azerbaijan and Armenia over Nagorno-Karabakh; to the south, the Persian Gulf War cut off Turkish trade with Baghdad and further exposed Turkey to PKK terrorist strikes. (U.S. efforts to set up Operation Safe Haven for the anti–Iraqi Kurds did not prevent anti–Turkish Kurdish groups from crossing the border.) Efforts to control PKK terrorism resulted in Turkish military intervention in northern Iraq in mid-March 1995, moving forty kilometers into Iraqi territory with thirty to thirty–five thousand troops—purportedly the largest Turkish operation since its intervention in Cyprus in 1974.

Turkish actions (which followed the signing of an EU-Turkish customs union, which still needed ratification by the European parliament), appeared to jeopardize its relations with the EU. Turkey had applied for EU membership in April 1987, but its application had stalled in December 1989, due partly to fears of Turkish immigration and on the grounds of human rights abuses, and the general repression of Kurdish rights. (Ankara had jailed Kurdish parliamentarians, for example, in December 1994.) A customs union with the EU was finally worked out in 1995, becoming effective January 1996.[5] Turkey has threatened to veto NATO enlargement into Central Europe, if it does not obtain EU membership. The dilemma is that Ankara does not appear to have any interest in backing Central European state membership in NATO—if the EU/WEU does not reciprocate.

Issues involving the Black Sea Fleet also affect Turkey. Ankara cannot ignore tensions between Kyiv and Moscow over that force. Russian-Turkish conflict over the Bosphorus and the Dardenelles was resumed in December 1994 when Ankara augmented security and safety regulations in the Straits. These actions were regarded by Moscow as an effort to block the transport of Caspian Sea oil and as a violation of the 1936 Montreux Convention.[6]

Intra-NATO conflict between Greece and Turkey is just as significant. Greek-Turkish relations do not appear to be improving in regard to disputes over Cyprus, Thrace, or access to Aegean resources. In June 1995 the Greek parliament ratified the 1972 UN Law of the Sea Convention, which authorizes Greek territorial waters in the Aegean to extend out to twelve nautical miles—provoking a potential conflict with Turkey, *if* enforced. From this perspective, a major schism between NATO and EU/WEU could occur if the dispute between Greece (a member of NATO and of the WEU) and Turkey (a member of NATO but a non-voting associate member of the WEU) begins to intensify. In the war in former Yugoslavia, Greece supported Serbia; while Turkey favored Bosnian Moslems and forged an alliance with Tirana to counter Serb threats to Kosovo and Greek influence in southern Albania. Concurrently, Athens has tended to look to Moscow for diplomatic support against Turkish (if not American) pressures. In 1997, Russian sales of S-300 surface-to-air anti–missile systems to the Greek region of Cyprus sparked new tensions.

On the one hand, drawing Turkey into Europe may help to check a seemingly burgeoning anti–Western pan-Islamic movement and help find a confederal solution to the Kurdish question, but only if EU finance becomes more readily available and OSCE diplomatic and political intervention becomes more acceptable. Turkey could participate in WEU military-decision-making (so as to counterbalance Greek influence). On the other hand, drawing Turkey into a "greater West" will need to be balanced by limiting the potential for direct or indirect Russo-Turkish conflict in Central Asia. The United States and EU, however, may be doing too little and too late.

Whereas Turkey had been regarded by the United States as pro-Western and a secular bastion against pan-Islamic movements (prior to the rise of a pro-Islamic government in 1996), Russia has tended to regard Iran as the lesser of two evils for the reason that Turkish claims to Central Asia have become worrisome. Iran and Russia also possess a common interest in keeping Azerbaijan weak and divided for fear that a united, oil-rich Azerbaijan might spark new secessionist or pan-Islamic movements in Central Asia but also claim oil-rich territories (or resources of the Caspian sea) now claimed by either Russia or Iran. (The Soviet Union and Iran had signed a formal agreement defining their zones of influence in the Caspian Sea.)

Russia and Turkey have likewise been battling over rival pipeline plans to transport oil from both Kazakhstan and Azerbaijan through highly unstable regions to world markets. Turkey has sought to build an oil pipeline from Central Asia to Turkey that would pass through the Caspian Sea, possibly including Armenia (the western option) assuming Ankara can ultimately help forge a compromise over Nagorno-Karabakh. Russia, however, has sought a "northern," Bulgarian-Greek route to the Mediterranean that could pass through Chechnya. Additional tension has resulted from a change in the U.S. position, which had originally given exclusive support to the route through Russia. Washington began to look toward Ankara, but it also began to back commercially viable multiple pipelines, including the Russian option—assuming financing became available. According to Russian views, the United States was most concerned that Russia should not be permitted to route a pipeline through Iran. Russia may have threatened to do so in order to gain tacit U.S. support for its intervention in Chechnya.[7]

Teheran, like Moscow, has been concerned with the rise of Azerbaijan as a oil rich state. Teheran has denounced Azeri claims to the Caspian Sea as illegal. The Russians have made thinly veiled threats (in addition to generally supporting Armenian claims against Azerbaijan) to impel Baku into accepting "an economic option that takes into consideration its political and long-term viability."[8] Both Russia and Iran fear that Azeri financial capabilities will undermine both Russian control over Central Asia and Iranian control over roughly twenty million Azeris.

Russia has attempted to convince Kazakhstan to support its side on the Caspian Sea dispute so as to isolate Azerbaijan in the CIS. Russia is already considered to be playing hegemonic, "divide and rule" tactics vis-à-vis Georgia and its secessionist movements in Abkhazia and Southern Ossetia. Moscow's reasons would be in part to block these states from forming political-economic and military ties with Azerbaijan, Turkey, or other states, in order to "stabilize" the region and protect Russian oil interests. Russia has concurrently established military bases near the Turkish border in both Armenia and Georgia, and it has tacitly supported the PKK (which has held rallies in

Moscow), to check the expansion of Turkish influence. Moscow has thus hoped to block potential strategic-economic linkages among Ukraine, Azerbaijan, Turkey, and Pakistan; it has also sought to block Ukrainian ties to Iran. (While Russia has established military bases in Armenia and Georgia, the United States has also deployed naval units in the Black Sea and has taken steps toward U.S.-Georgia military cooperation, in part to protect the Baku-Bitumi oil pipeline. In addition, pro-Russian factions have accused Ukraine of offering NATO basing rights on the Crimea, charges denied by Kyiv.)

Russian actions in Chechnya are a response to events in the Caucasus in general. In regard to the Caucasus and Caspian Sea, Moscow fears a new *cordon sanitaire* in which "forces potentially hostile to Russia would gain opportunities to control the principal transport arteries used for Russia's imports and exports, something that, in view of the dependence of entire economic branches and regions of Russia on exports of raw materials and imports of food and other goods, could prove to be a very effective level of pressure on Russia's leadership."[9]

In essence, Moscow has particularly sought to counter pan-Turkish influence in Central Asia. As it sees Iran as a lesser evil, it generally seeks to play Iran against Turkey, although Moscow does not want to alienate the latter. Concurrently, Moscow has hoped to deflect Iranian interests into the Persian Gulf, away from Russia's soft Central Asian underbelly. On the one hand, Russia has remained Turkey's largest trading partner, and Ankara has generally tried not to offend Moscow. On the other hand, Russia has continued to be guided by an analogy to its geohistorical "Crimean War" syndrome: fears of NATO's capability to block the Straits and enter the Black Sea.

IRAN

Since May 1995, Washington has been stepping up efforts to isolate the Islamic Republic by attempting to check its support by Russia and the PRC, as well as that of European and American firms—by means of an economic embargo. American steps to isolate Iran result in part from the CIA estimate that Teheran may acquire an atomic weapons capability over the next five to ten years, and also from Iranian-backed efforts to break up an Israeli-Palestinian-Syrian rapprochement. Teheran has also opposed NATO enlargement, arguing that it would not help peace in either Europe or Central Asia. U.S. efforts to block sales of Russian technology have been based on calculations that Russian (and Chinese) assistance may indirectly assist Iranian nuclear efforts and that Russia will not put significant proliferation restrictions on the Iranian nuclear program.[10]

Ironically, U.S. efforts to embargo Iran may also stem from an effort to contain Iranian claims to the Shi'ia population in Iraq as well as to Shi'ia holy places—plus oil-rich Iraqi territory near Basra. (The defeat of Iraq having opened a "strategic void" in the region, Iran has had numerous border clashes with Iraqi forces since the Persian Gulf War.) In addition, Iran has bought Russian diesel submarines with mine laying capabilities and has begun a military buildup on Gulf islands close to the Strait of Hormuz. From its perspective, Moscow has argued that Washington's focus on Iran is intended to "drown out" Israel's nuclear program. Foreign Minister Primakov has denied allegations that Iran obtained four Soviet-designed nuclear warheads from Kazakhstan. American policy has thus developed into a "dual containment" of Iraq and Iran—a policy that has not been accepted by Russia, the PRC, the EU, or even states like Turkey, a NATO member.

Continuing tensions in the Middle East and Persian Gulf have caused real concern that an Israeli-Palestinian (and Syrian) rapprochement may be undermined by both Israeli and Palestinian extremist groups. (Former Israeli prime minister Yitzhak Rabin, who sought out compromise with Yassar Arafat, was assassinated by a militant Israeli. Hamas, the strongest Palestinian group opposing Arafat's "capitulation" to Israel, has engaged in terrorist attacks since the beginning of 1996.) Iran has been the primary supporter of such pan-Islamic movements, Hezbollah and Hamas. At the same time, anti–Western Islamic movements have also been given strong support by Saudi Arabia (apparently through difficult-to-control private sources). Although Saudi Arabia (and Pakistan) have continued to fund the Sunni pan-Islamic revolution in Afghanistan (the Taliban movement) since the withdrawal of Soviet forces, Saudi public funding for other Islamic groups (which have sought to undermine Egypt, Tunisia, and Algeria) has been curtailed.[11] Private donations from pro-Muslim groups in the United States have also provided aid to Hamas.

In addition to the pan-Shi'ia, pan-Islamic movement in Iran, pan-Islamic movements (of differing factions) have been on the rise. Sudan, Pakistan, and Saudi Arabia have directly or indirectly supported pan-Islamic revolutions in Egypt, Algeria, and the continuing conflict in Afghanistan, Bosnia, Tunisia, and Morocco. Turkey, Iran, and Saudi Arabia each sought credit for "supporting" Bosnian Moslems (in part in an effort to prevent any one state from gaining a monopoly of influence). Pan-Islamic groups trained by Pakistan and the CIA to fight the Soviet Union in Afghanistan may have had links to the 1993 bombing of the World Trade Center in Manhattan. In mid-1995, Sudan was accused of supporting an assassination attempt against Egyptian president Hosni Mubarek. Despite Beijing's repression of ethnic Turkic Uighur Sunni Moslem groups, Sudanese Sunni Islamic leader Hassan El-Tourabi has stated his conviction that the combined rise of China and the Islamic "renaissance" together represent the key factors that will undermine Western and Russian "hegemony."[12]

NATO's quest for a rapprochement with states in l'espace euro-méditerranéen has additionally raised a new security concern from the Russian perspective. Egypt, Tunisia, Morocco, and Israel have all been approached by NATO to establish closer relations. Although NATO's effort is mostly directed against "pan-Islamic" movements, Russia could interpret its actions as a means to isolate Russian interests in the Mediterranean, but only if Russia and NATO can not forge a close entente. Egypt, however, fears that too close a relationship with NATO and Israel may fan, not dampen, pan-Islamic movements. Algeria was not included in the rapprochement with NATO in order not to undermine the government further.

Egypt is the pivotal state in the region. An anti–Western, pan-Islamic regime could uproot the Camp David Accords, which have helped to guarantee the peace with Israel. Unemployment in Egypt has been hovering at 17 percent; 50 percent of the population is illiterate; and the population is expected to rise from sixty million to 104 million by 2025. Moreover, discontentment in the army may threaten the regime at a time when the U.S. Congress has threatened to cut the U.S. AID package of $2.1 billion per year. (Fifty–six percent of U.S. funds goes to the Egyptian military budget. AID has put $35 billion into Egypt over the past seventeen years.)[13]

RUSSIA, INDIA, AND CHINA

The Soviet withdrawal from Afghanistan in 1988–89 and the fall of the pro-Soviet Najibullah government in April 1992 represented the first steps toward the near-total collapse of Soviet/Russian influence in the region. The continuing internecine civil war in Afghanistan reflected not only the rival interests of the divergent factions of the Afghan resistance but also the policy differences among the states that most supported that resistance: Pakistan, Iran, Saudi Arabia, China, and the United States. By September–October 1996, the militant Taliban, backed by Pakistan, Saudi Arabia, and (tacitly) the United States, moved into Kabul—raising fears of a pan-Islamic encirclement in India, Russia, and the CIS states. (Washington has tended to see the Sunni Taliban as a counter to pan-Shi'ite Iran.)

Efforts to keep pan-Islamic movements or militant anti–Russian nationalist or independence movements from spreading into Uzbekistan and other Central Asian states have led Moscow toward a closer entente with both Beijing and New Delhi. (The latter two countries settled their border disputes in September 1993). Having lost in Afghanistan, the Russians fear the "domino effect." Russia has intervened in the civil war in Tajikistan; the Tajik opposition regrouped in Afghanistan. Russia has been accused of engaging in cross-border attacks.[14] The new Russia may well intervene in Uzbekistan, if it deems intervention necessary. Both India and Russia fear that a militant Uzbekistan (possibly in rivalry with Kazakhstan) would have a destabilizing effect in Central Asia. (See Chapter 5.)

On his visit to India in February 1993, Boris Yeltsin envisioned the prospect of India, China, and Russia forming a "bridge of stability" in Central Asia (a bridge which may also include Iran). In addition, Russian aerospace sales to New Delhi have raised American concerns that Russia is breaking its informal agreement to abide by the Missile Technology Control Regime.[15] American efforts to block those sales (actions regarded as tacit support for Pakistan) may have helped to alienate Indian leadership. Concurrently, however, Washington has been attempting to mend fences with New Delhi through military technology sales and naval cooperation.

Prior to the breakup of the Soviet Union, Moscow's support for India had been regarded by Beijing as an effort to "counter-encircle" China, which holds as much as 20 percent of Kashmir, and to break China's alliance with Pakistan. The latter holds about 35 percent of Kashmir while India holds roughly 45 percent. However, as Beijing has been suspicious of the intentions of newly independent states such as Afghanistan, Mongolia, and Kazakhstan, and as it fears the possibility of pan-Turk and pan-Mongolian agitation, it has looked toward a rapprochement with Russia and India. China and India have thus moved to reduce troop levels along their 2,500 mile border; and in December 1996, New Delhi announced that it would cease development of its Agni intermediate range ballistic missile project capable of striking Chinese territory, as a signal of reconciliation with Beijing.

Russia, Kazakhstan, Kirgystan, and Tajikistan have all engaged with the PRC in confidence-building measures on their borders. In early 1994, China and Kazakhstan agreed to reconcile their border disputes, but official agreements cannot always contain political, economic, and social pressures. This is particularly evident as Beijing has sent mixed signals as to its ultimate intentions. For example, Kazakhstan remains suspicious of Chinese claims to its territory (including Almaty) and has thus looked to Russia for protection. Both Russia and China continue to fear Japanese political-economic influence in Siberia and Mongolia; at the same time, Russia is concerned with the burgeoning Chinese demographic and economic pressure in the region, including illicit cross-border trafficking. Russia and China also have a common interest in countering tacit Japanese support for Russian Far Eastern autonomy or independence movements (through "yen diplomacy"). The PRC has accordingly sought at least tacit Russian and Indian support for its repression of secessionist movements in Tibet, Xinjiang, and Inner Mongolia, and for the continuing co-optation and repression of the Chinese democracy movement. This appears to be a trade-off for Chinese acceptance of India's repression of Kashmiri independence.

Accordingly, in February 1993 Yeltsin strongly affirmed that "truth was on the side" of India in Kashmir. The Indian state (which contains 110 million Moslems or roughly 12 percent of the population) increasingly sees itself "encircled" by pan-Islamic movements in Pakistan, Afghanistan, and to a certain extent, Iran. Russia and India may fear the rise of a Ukrainian-Turkish-Pakistani-Chinese connection, particularly as Beijing has purportedly supplied Islamabad with nuclear and ballistic missile technology. Such an encircling alliance could come about under the assumption that Moscow cannot wean China and Ukraine closer to Russia. (See also Chapter 5.)

Hindu chauvinist movements consequently appear on the rise: in March 1995, Hindu chauvinists of the Shiv Sena and Bharata Janata parties won 138 seats in the regional election of the richest Indian state Maharastra (which includes Bombay). The ruling Congress Party won only eighty–six seats. Four years after the December 1992 attack on the Ayodya mosque, tensions between India and Pakistan over Kashmir have continued to intensify, with the burning of the town of Charar-I-Sharief in Kashmir in March 1995, an action blamed on the Indian army by the Kashmiris and on the Islamic resistance by New Delhi.[16] However, in 1996 the Bharata Janata party was unable to hold together a coalition government in the national parliament.

If no compromise can be reached, Indo-Pakistani tensions risk the first war between two nuclear powers—not counting the significant Sino-Soviet border clashes in 1969. In the "world's loftiest battleground," India and Pakistan have spent billions of dollars along the Siachen Glacier that divides the Indian from the Pakistani sector of Kashmir. Moreover, conflict between India and Pakistan could well draw in regional and major powers. (In September 1996, both India and Pakistan refused to sign the Comprehensive Test Ban Treaty.) An Indo-Pakistani war, or the threat of Indian disaggregation, could well bring Russia to support its Indian ally—an alliance apparently reconfirmed by Yeltsin's February 1993 visit to New Delhi.[17] On the other hand, the threatened disintegration of Pakistan may or may not draw in Beijing.

THE FAR EAST

Post–Cold War U.S.-Japanese tensions have manifested themselves in a propaganda war. Fifty years after the end of World War II, Americans criticized violations of American and Chinese prisoner rights during World War II (including biological warfare experiments on U.S. prisoners of war). In retaliation, the Japanese have condemned the U.S. atomic bombings of Hiroshima and Nagasaki.

The end of the Cold War shook up Japanese domestic stability—in 1989 the Japanese Liberal Democratic Party lost its majority in the upper house. Revelations that CIA funding helped to keep the Japanese Liberal Party in power during the Cold War (plus an alleged CIA role in auto trade negotiations in spring 1995) did not help Japanese-American relations (or the Japanese Liberal Party). In addition, American efforts to force open Japanese markets created resentment. Japan has largely protected its domestic market and has sought new foreign markets and direct investment opportunities for its burgeoning yen surplus. Japan's GNP in 1995 represented roughly 85 percent of the U.S. GNP—up from a mere 6 percent in 1955! Tokyo did, however, finally agree to a "partial" opening of the rice market, as part of an agreement reached in the World Trade Organization.

In September 1995, a rape by U.S. servicemen of an elementary-school girl on Okinawa raised significant protests and questions about the legitimacy of the U.S.-Japanese alliance, which subsequently forced the United States to relocate its forces within Japan. The Pentagon reassured Asian states that the United States would sustain 100,000 troops in Asia, 47,000 in Japan and 37,000 in South Korea, but it announced that it would shift troops away from the strategically-located position on Okinawa. Tokyo agreed to provide logistical support to U.S. troops in peacetime; at the same time Japan is to study the deployment of Japanese troops alongside U.S. forces.

As in Europe, U.S. calls for "responsibility sharing" have fueled tensions with the Japanese. Tokyo has referred to the U.S.-Japanese strategic partnership as "taxation without representation." Japan has been concerned that U.S. retrenchment from "superpower" status will impel it to take more decisive leadership in defending its own security concerns in any conflict with its regional neighbors. While Japan remains dependent upon the U.S. nuclear and naval deterrent, Tokyo has begun to develop into a military power, capable of extending its naval capabilities a thousand nautical miles—if not to the Persian Gulf—to guard its supplies of oil, natural gas, and raw materials that pass through the South China Sea. At the same time, however, Tokyo faces its own domestic political and economic crises, which involve political corruption and a "Japanese-style recession."

Moreover, Japan, much like Germany, has in part been unable to expand its security role, due to its own historical and legal legacy, and as it is not yet a member of the UN Security Council. Japanese policy is further complicated by the fact that Tokyo, Moscow, and Beijing have yet to sign a peace treaty formally ending World War II. Japan, however, did commit itself to participate in UN peacekeeping missions in Cambodia, Mozambique, Rwanda, and (after considerable parliamentary debate) the Golan Heights, in September 1995.

After its initial reluctance to join in the U.S.-led coalition in the "forty-day" war versus Iraq in 1990, Tokyo finally decided to send mine sweepers into the Persian Gulf to defend its shipping interests. Not only has it been necessary for Japan and West Germany to finance the U.S. debt debacle (as well as provide significant financial support for the U.S.-led coalition against Iraq in 1991), but the Pentagon found itself in the precarious and embarrassing position of being partially dependent upon high-quality Japanese semiconductors and other strategic high-technology items.

The Japanese have continued to fear the Russian military presence and military-technological modernization in the Sea of Okhotsk and pressure on the Northern Territories (Kurile Islands); thus they have not yet opted to abandon their alliance with the United States. At the same time, they have gradually shifted their policy away from an overtly anti–Russian position, particularly once both North Korea and the PRC began to be perceived as potential threats.

From 1991 to 1993, Tokyo was reticent to provide greater financial assistance to Moscow, largely due to its stated fear of Russian conventional, naval, and nuclear forces in the Far East. Many of these naval forces had been moved out of the Black Sea due to tensions with Ukraine, in a geostrategic shift in military forces that augmented pressure on Tokyo. Mikhail Gorbachev had failed to make a deal through an offer of a Soviet-American-Japanese alliance. Boris Yeltsin has yet to forge a deal, although a trade of at least two of the Kurile Islands for up to $30 billion in Japanese investment had been suggested. Yeltsin has had greater difficulty in forging any kind of compromise with Tokyo since the September–October 1993 crackdown on the Russian parliament and the consequent need to consolidate the Russian military. (Prior to Gorbachev's fall, Yeltsin, as president of Russia in 1990, had opposed "concessions" that Gorbachev had been offering Tokyo.) The Russian military has thus far opposed any concessions which might weaken its geostrategic outreach into the Pacific and control over the Far East.

Tensions in the region were made evident from the Russian sinking of a Japanese fishing boat on 4 October 1994. Moscow complained that seven hundred vessels (most of them Japanese) violated Russian territorial waters in the Far East in 1994. Japan has been reluctant to sign a fisheries treaty with Russia, because it fears even implicitly acknowledging Russian sovereignty over the disputed Northern Territories).[18] Concurrently, Russia has yet to be accepted into the Asia-Pacific Economic Cooperation regime (APEC) in which it hopes to influence regional policies.

Russo-Japanese relations also been tense because of alleged Russian links to the Aum Shinrikio cult, accused of acts of assassination and terrorism, including the explosion of poison Sarin gas in the Tokyo subway in March 1995. The sect leader had high-level contacts with Russian political and military leaders, who purportedly provided special military training for his sect by former KGB and Spetnaz (special forces) personnel.[19] Aum allegedly looked to U.S. suppliers of weaponry as well.

While the Japanese have been concerned about the prospects of a "great depression" in the former USSR, they have been just as worried (if not more so) about the prospects for political and economic instability in the PRC. Prior to 1994, Japan had argued that Washington's security and economic outlook had become too "Eurocentric." In contrast, Tokyo preferred a policy of accommodating, rather than confronting, the PRC. The Japanese response to burgeoning Chinese military power and the post–Tiananmen Square repression had accordingly been to influence Chinese behavior through increased economic assistance and diplomatic support. After Tiananmen Square, Japan was the first country to resume aid—in contrast to American reluctance. Tokyo's hope was to dampen or contain Chinese claims to regional hegemony by increasing Japanese trade, aid, and investment.

However, despite the quick return of Japanese financial assistance after Tiananmen Square, it was clear that Japan and China had issues to resolve, such as the Senkaku Islands and Japanese war reparations. (These issues have continued to inflame Chinese pan-nationalists in both the PRC and in Taiwan.) In 1994, two Japanese prime ministers, Morihoro Hosokawa and Tsutomu Hata, began to take a tougher public position on Chinese nuclear testing and military modernization. Japan suspended $75 million in grant assistance in 1995 to protest Chinese nuclear testing.[20] Tokyo scrambled fighter jets to counter a violation of Japanese airspace by Chinese jets in the fall of 1995. Japan also took a tougher stance in regard to regional Chinese claims, particularly in regard to the Senkaku Islands. (Beijing had reaffirmed its claims to the latter in 1992; Tokyo decided to extend formally its exclusive economic zone to the area, to counter Chinese claims, in early 1996.[21]) Japanese-American discussions on theater ballistic missile defenses (officially in response to North Korean threat) were met by Chinese threats to deploy multiple-warhead missiles against Japan in 1995. In 1996, Japan also protested Chinese missile testing off the coast of Taiwan.

The change in Japanese policy came as Tokyo began to move away from a strictly anti–Soviet, anti–Russian approach—despite the issues that continued to divide Moscow and Tokyo as outlined above. In 1993

Tokyo declared that Russia had cut its troop presence in the Far East by 50 percent. In April 1993, Japan (with U.S. and G-7 backing) began to "delink" demands that Russia return all four Kurile Islands to receive Japanese financial assistance. Moscow stressed trade and aid; Japan emphasized the need for progress on political and legal issues involving investment, as well as the ultimate return of the islands. In September 1994, Japan quietly sought to improve security ties with Russia. Japan's Maritime Safety Agency conducted joint rescue exercises with Russia. In November 1994, a trilateral U.S.-Russian-Japanese conference was held dealing with Northeast Asian security issues, and in January 1995 the head of the Japanese Defense Agency visited Moscow. Moscow and Tokyo were to discuss a formal end to World War II sometime after the 1996 Russian presidential election. (Tokyo and Beijing have yet to resolve the issue of World War II reparations and "war crimes.")

For its part, Moscow has been concerned with Japanese political-economic influence in Russian Siberia and Sakhalin Island. It fears that the return of the Kuriles would set a precedent for independence movements throughout the Russian Far East and would open the door to other territorial claims, particularly those of the PRC. By January 1996, Russian Foreign Minister Primakov suggested that Moscow and Tokyo develop closer relations and "leave the settling of the territorial problem for future generations;" a Japanese foreign ministry spokesperson replied, however, that Primakov's suggestion was "unacceptable."[22]

Despite this apparent setback, the general shift in Japanese policy has been based, in part, on concerns that Chinese policies "might be heading in the wrong direction" in the words of Prime Minister Ryutaro Hashimoto (in March 1996).[23] The danger is that the PRC itself, like the former USSR, may be on the verge of either disaggregation (as a result of independence movements in Tibet, Xinjiang, Inner Mongolia, and southern China) or on the verge of assertive expansion, or both. The nationwide repression of the Chinese democracy movement after the events of May–June 1989 (coupled with a previous crackdown in Tibet in 1989) was intended to squash both "democratic" and secessionist movements. Even following Tiananmen Square, the Chinese elite (correctly) believed that they could play upon intra-West and U.S.-Soviet/Russian rivalry to gain much-needed American, European, and Japanese (if not Russian) finance, investment, and technology.[24]

Beijing may well have played its cards right vis-à-vis a maladroit U.S. policy that forced President Clinton in mid-1994 to drop the linkage between most-favored-nation (MFN) status and a certified improvement in China's human rights record. Chinese threats to give greater diplomatic support to North Korea, fears that Chinese

economic collapse might result in millions of refugees, and also
military pressures on Taiwan, helped to alter Clinton's supposedly
tough stance. Dropping the human rights linkage to MFN, the Clinton
administration intended to pressure the Chinese on trade and
copyright violations by means of its membership in GATT—renamed
the World Trade Organization. In April 1995, the EU also stated the
PRC must widen its markets before Beijing is permitted to join the
World Trade Organization.

The gradual American retrenchment from Asia since the Vietnam
War has in many ways raised tensions among Japan, Russia, and
China. Washington normalized ties with Hanoi in January 1995 (but
did not give full diplomatic recognition). Hanoi has sought a U.S.
rapprochement (without war reparation demands), in part by offering
to open Cam Ranh Bay as a free trading port. Hanoi agreed to let
Russia use naval facilities in Cam Ranh Bay until 2004, and the U.S.
Navy could also use it once relations were fully normalized. As the
Vietnamese regard the Russians as "Americans without dollars,"
Hanoi has welcomed American steps toward normalization. In
addition, Hanoi joined ASEAN in July 1995 (but without firm
guarantees that ASEAN will back Hanoi against Beijing). U.S. steps
toward Vietnam could at least offer a way to counterbalance the
influence of the PRC (as well as that of Japan and Taiwan). The
rapprochement with Vietnam provides an alternative country for
investment in potential competition with the PRC. By working closely
with Moscow, Washington could attempt to contain Beijing's more
assertive claims in the region.[25] At the same time, however, Russian
dialogue with ASEAN and support for its drive to establish a nuclear-
free zone in Southeast Asia (aimed primarily at the PRC) were at odds
with U.S. efforts to protect transit rights for its naval ships through
Indonesian territorial waters. (U.S. policy is not to affirm or deny the
presence of nuclear weapons aboard its naval vessels.) The United
States and United Kingdom saw the pact as a declaration of no-first
use of nuclear weapons. China and the United States both objected to
its support for the extension of territorial rights to two hundred
nautical miles. Washington accordingly refused to join the Asian
nuclear weapons–free zone signed by ASEAN in December 1995.[26]

Importantly, Japanese financial support for UN peacekeeping forces
in Cambodia (at an overall cost of $3 billion) helped return the latter
to its traditional position as a "buffer" state between Thailand, China,
and Vietnam. At the same time, however, the present monarchist
Cambodian government of Prince Sihanouk has tilted toward Vietnam
rather than toward China, which enraged the not entirely contained
Khmer Rouge. UN operations had been difficult (with substantial
levels of corruption) and will be judged as successful only once the

Khmer Rouge is marginalized. Japanese support for UN activities in Cambodia also represented a step in Tokyo's quest to become a member of the UN Security Council. (See Chapter 10.)

It is perhaps ironic that both Russia and China fear that the United States will no longer be able to "double contain" Japanese military capabilities. In addition, American military retrenchment (for example, U.S. withdrawal from bases in the Philippines), Chinese claims in the South China Sea and to Taiwan, tensions between North and South Korea, trade tensions with Washington, and perceived threats in Asia from either Russia, China, or the two Koreas have all begun to exacerbate Japanese and Chinese rivalry in the region. Japanese–South Korean tensions over the Takeshima/Tokdo islands resurfaced following Tokyo's claim to a two-hundred nautical-mile exclusive economic zone with the signing of the 1972 Law of the Sea Convention. The Senkaku Islands are also disputed, between Japan, China—and Taiwan. Following the Soviet collapse, Japanese military spending (with pressure by the U.S. for "responsibility sharing") became the second-largest in the world, even though both Beijing and Moscow publicly underestimate their defense spending by a considerable portion (by as much as 50 percent.)

American and Russian political-military retrenchment (and a relative buildup of Chinese and Japanese military capabilities) has also raised the prospect of a nuclear North Korea. The latter scenario is particularly plausible if concerted pressures by the United States, Japan and Russia (ideally with Beijing's backing as well) cannot stop North Korea from developing an independent nuclear deterrent. In April 1996 North Korea made incursions into the Demilitarized Zone. In addition, Pyongygang tested its Nodong-1 missile capable of hitting anywhere in South Korea; it can also strike Japan and the U.S. military bases at Okinawa (formerly) and Guam.[27] North Korean threats to leave the NPT regime have produced U.S. offers of finance, peaceful nuclear assistance, and ultimately diplomatic recognition. North Korea believes that the 21 October 1994 Geneva accord will permit it to escape unification along the German model in return for freezing its nuclear program before 1999.[28] North Korea has thus hoped to use its potential nuclear capability as strategic leverage to draw the United States closer, and break the U.S.-South Korean alliance, if possible. Accordingly, if not correctly managed, the Korean peninsula could add more sparks to the arms and naval rivalry in the region, due both to isolation of the North and to South Korea's efforts to block the signing of a peace treaty between Washington and Pyongygang leading to the recognition of the Kim Jong Il regime. (Both Russia and China have recognized South Korea, largely to the exclusion of the isolated North.) Both North and South Korea are significant exporters of arms and military technology, and South Korea is already a major economic competitor of Japan. South Korea has not been making strong efforts to reconcile itself with the son of Kim Il Sung (seen as perpetuating the first communist "dynasty"). At the same time, the possibility of Korean unification itself raises concerns: without a concerted Asian policy, a newly unified Korea could shift the regional equilibrium and be perceived as a "threat" to both Japanese and Chinese strategic and economic interests.

CHINA AND RUSSIA

Despite substantial efforts to establish a Sino-Russian entente, the Chinese have remained suspicious of long-term Russian ambitions in the Far East and Central Asia. Even after the withdrawal of Soviet and Vietnamese troops from Afghanistan and Cambodia, respectively, and a reduction of forces along the Sino-Soviet and Mongolian borders, the Chinese view the new Russian "democracy" with suspicion. Beijing is particularly concerned with the rise of potentially anti–Chinese "Greater Russian" and pan-Slav movements in Russia. (These movements had largely been contained by the Soviet Communist Party.) At the same time, Russia is concerned with the burgeoning Chinese political-economic and demographic presence in the Russian Far East—an economically depressed area where the eight million ethnic Russian population is diminishing relatively and faces a hundred million Chinese in Manchuria.)

The April 1996 confidence-building agreements between Russia, China, Tajikistan, Kirgystan, and Kazakhstan were intended to resolve border issues, set up Russian-Kazakh joint ventures, and settle the Caspian Sea pipeline. However, it did not settle questions involving the status of the Caspian Sea or ownership of its resources, nor did discussions deal substantially with the rights of ethnic Russians in Kazakhstan.[29] From the Chinese perspective, the agreement is also designed to curb Uighur-Moslem separatism, and it was accompanied by a crackdown and clashes with Uighur separatists in Xinjiang province. The June 1996 Russia-PRC-Mongolian and July 1996 Russo-Chinese agreements likewise sought to define border and trade issues. At the same time, Sino-Russian efforts to define borders met a new stumbling block. The governor of the Primorsk Kray has sought a constitutional review of the 1991 Soviet-Chinese border agreement, arguing that the deal gives land of crucial economic and strategic importance to Russia away to the PRC.

As the new "national-democratic" Russia has strengthened its general entente with communist Beijing (despite mutual suspicions), both states may also be moving toward an increasingly assertive

Eurasian strategy, either separately or in collusion. In accord with its new "democratic" ideology, Moscow had, at least initially, sought closer relations with Taiwan in 1991–92; however, the development of close ties between Moscow and Taipei was largely blocked by Beijing, which feared a U.S.-Russian-Japanese-Taiwanese "encirclement." It furthermore seems increasingly unlikely that the new Russia will abandon its "two-faced" Eurasianist strategy with Beijing unless Russian relations suddenly improve with the United States and Japan. It appears more likely that Moscow will seek even closer cooperation with Beijing, despite the evident tensions.

Beijing has opposed what it perceives as the rise of pan-Mongolian movements both outside and inside its borders. The collapse of the Soviet Union freed not only Eastern European and Central Asian states but also Mongolia, which has looked largely to Japan for support. In the effort to counter pan-Mongolian claims in Inner Mongolia and Xinjiang province following the rise of an independent Ulan Bator, the Chinese leadership reportedly claimed "all of the Mongolias"— which includes Mongolians in Russian Buryatia. In addition to a common policy toward Central Asian pan-Turkic and independence movements, Russia and China may seek to implement a common strategy against perceived pan-Mongolianism. One cannot rule out a Sino-Russian condominium over Ulan Bator, in an effort to block Japanese influence in the region.

Moscow has attempted to assuage the Chinese leadership largely through arms and high-technology sales since the August 1991 putsch. Yeltsin's government upheld Gorbachev's decision to sell Su-27 "Flanker" fighter jets plus S300 surface-to-air missiles to China. By 1996, Beijing was also to buy licenses to produce Su-27s (which have the range to reach the Spratly Islands from the Paracels) and may purchase more advanced Su-30s. Beijing also obtained four Kilo-class diesel submarines, and a limited number T-72 tanks. The Su-27 deal included an understanding that the planes would not be used against Russia. China has currently bought roughly 20 percent of its arms from Russia. (Moscow, however, has yet to offer Beijing its more advanced Su-35 jet or MiG-31 interceptors.[30]) At the same time, Moscow has realized that it has been upsetting East Asian countries as well as the United States by its military cooperation with the PRC. (In response, Taiwan, Indonesia, Malaysia, and Singapore have bought advanced weaponry, to counter Chinese capabilities. Taiwan, in particular, purchased 150 U.S. F-16s and French Mirage 2000s, among other weapons systems.)

Russia, Ukraine, and Belarus have each considered selling excess military surplus to China. Although Ukrainian efforts to sell the PRC (or India) an aircraft carrier were reportedly dropped under Japanese mediation, the PRC has attempted to play the former Soviet states against each other. For example, in exchange for Ukrainian recognition of Chinese claims to Taiwan, Beijing recognized Ukraine and its control over the Crimea. A potential Ukrainian-PRC alliance (linked to Turkey and Pakistan) would accordingly be perceived by Moscow as a new "encirclement"—if Moscow cannot head off such an alliance by drawing Kyiv or Beijing into a Eurasian entente, and assuming Ukraine itself does not splinter into pieces.

CHINESE CLAIMS AND POWER POTENTIAL

The effort of the People's Republic of China to pursue its "four modernization" program with its own "independent" policy of flexible response, a burgeoning navy and capacity for regional intervention, as well as an economy projected to outstrip Russia and (perhaps) Japan in GNP around the year 2010, all represent a long-term effort to achieve "superpower" status by the mid-twenty–first century. Chinese pan-nationalists call for a "greater Chinese economic sphere" that would include the PRC, Taiwan, Hong Kong, Singapore, Malaysia, Thailand, Cambodia, Vietnam, and the Philippines. Chinese pan-nationalists seek to either co-opt or repress the "fifth modernization"—the Chinese "democracy" movement—in the effort to achieve a greater China.

At the same time, however, the Chinese ability to create such a sphere may be greatly overrated, particularly as promises of Chinese growth may be exaggerated. Chinese industrial output may be overestimated by as much as 30 percent (roughly $70 billion) due to intra-industry borrowing and debt-leveraging among medium and large state-owned firms, a practice known as "triangular debt." This fact implies a prospect of greater political-socio-economic instability, as China is increasingly confronted with the choice of stagflation or further privatization. Although the private sector has gained considerable ground and now employs a hundred million people, the debt-ridden public sector also employs one hundred million people, who in turn support families containing several hundred million more.[31] The majority of China's remaining state-run factories are located in the northeast and are subsidized by taxes from the booming south. Radical reform of the state sector (without providing a bridge to employment in the more efficient private sector) thus risks significant socio-political instability, particularly as the competition of more efficient private firms impels the state sector to tighten its budget.

Moreover, Beijing perceives energy resources as key to its growth and domestic stability. At present, imported oil makes up some 17 percent of China's energy consumption, and it may become a net importer of roughly 1.2 million barrels per day by the year 2000. In part due to its increasing oil demand, Beijing has claimed the Spratly Island group in the South China Sea, involving a possible conflict over oil and naval transit rights with the Philippines, Malaysia, Vietnam, Brunei, and Taiwan, if not with Japan and the United States. (Approximately 70 percent of Japanese oil passes through the South China Sea.) Beijing has accordingly developed a rapid-deployment force for intervention in regional disputes and is to build three naval bases on its eastern seaboard by 1998. At the same time, it would need foreign capital and technology to exploit these petroleum reserves.[32] In 1995, Qiao Shi, chair of the National People's Congress, restated Chinese claims to the Spratly Islands. While China has regarded its actions in regard to the Spratlys as a rightful counter to historical injustice and the encroachment of foreign powers, Manila, for example, has regarded Beijing's strategy as a hegemonic "sweet and sour" approach. The latter strategy aims at steady expansion into the region while simultaneously pursuing bilateral peace talks with individual states, talks that are in reality designed to "divide and rule" the rival claimants.[33]

The dilemma is that the Chinese Communist Party (and the PLA) has yet to renounce its claims to reunify with Taiwan by force, whereas Taipei has at least appeared to drop its own reunification aim—the goal of "recovering the mainland"—in the August 1993 Kuomintang 14th party congress.[34] Beijing has thus continued to demand a "one country–two systems" approach to the Taiwan question and has threatened to use force if necessary. Beijing has sold nuclear technology, missiles or arms to Saudi Arabia, Pakistan, and Iran—in rivalry with U.S. and Japanese interests and as a means to isolate Taiwan. Former Chinese leader Deng Xiaoping had stated five conditions that could provoke a military attack against Taiwan: a Taiwanese nuclear capability; a Taiwan-Russian entente; an outbreak of extreme political disorder on Taiwan; a declaration of Taiwanese independence; and a rejection of reunification talks "for a long time."[35] Rightfully or not, China strongly protested the "unofficial" visit of Taiwanese president Lee Teng-hui to Washington in June 1995 as representing a step toward Taiwanese independence. The death of Deng Xiaoping in February 1997 may not result in a power struggle (as China's political leadership has largely been able to sort itself out since the 1989 Tiananmen repression and during the last several years of Deng's illness); at the same time, following the Chinese military's general reluctance to intervene and repress the peaceful, nation-wide student protest in 1989, the communist leadership under Jiang Zemin and Prime Minister Li Peng may find itself increasingly dependent upon the PLA for support. The latter is responsible for both internal and external security, and continues to demand unification with Taiwan.

The danger is that domestic instability in the PRC itself (Tibet, Xinjiang, the potential for popular protest in Hong Kong after it returns to the mainland in mid-1997, coupled with the general legitimacy crisis facing the Chinese Communist Party) could result in demands to eliminate the Taiwanese political, economic, ideological, and military "threat." Moreover, as the Chinese Communist Party attempts to sustain its legitimacy and political controls over rebellious provinces, it is possible that Beijing could ultimately choose a more assertive policy and more forceful efforts to achieve a "Greater China"—partly as a means to co-opt domestic dissent.

On the other hand, Beijing may continue to bide its time, and it may not reach out as far as Taiwan. China's more assertive policy may thus be designed to secure oil fields in the Spratly Island area and assert regional hegemony step-by-step, if not attempt to break up ASEAN. China is capable of a blockade of Taiwan but it is thus more likely to engage in economic pressure and selective military harassment.[36] Chinese missile testing off the shores of Taiwan in August 1995, and again in February–March 1996 prior to the 23 March Taiwanese presidential elections (landing three unarmed missiles near Taiwanese port cities and causing the Heng Seng stock index to drop 7.3 percent) represent threats to place long-term pressure on Taiwan. (During the crisis, Beijing deployed 150,000 troops in Fujian province across the straits, as a means to pressure Taiwan, perhaps much as Beijing pressured Hanoi by placing troops on Vietnam's northern borders after the Sino-Vietnamese clash in 1978–79).

Chinese pressure on Taiwan was intended to check gains of the Taiwanese independence movement before the March 1996 elections. The danger is that so assertive a policy may ultimately backfire, making the independence movement even more adamant, while raising new tensions with Japan, Russia, and China. Beijing's actions could either push Japan and the United States into a closer defense relationship and thus strengthen the Taiwan Relations Act of 1979, or else impel Tokyo to develop an independent political-military stance in fear of an American turn toward "selective interventionism." From the Beijing's own standpoint, Chinese actions could backfire, and thus undermine the U.S. "double containment" of Japan, particularly if Tokyo loses confidence in the American will to protect its sea lines of communication and its supply of oil.

Beijing may, however, still assume that the United States will move toward "isolationism" rather than back its former enemy, Tokyo. Beijing may also believe that Washington will ultimately "appease" Chinese regional ambitions, particularly after the United States gave up its bases in the Philippines—and particularly if Beijing can bring

Moscow to its support. Granting MFN status year after year may also be regarded by Beijing as an act of appeasement; cutting it off may be regarded as an act of war. Withdrawing MFN status would cause Chinese goods to rise in price from eight to forty percent on the U.S. market. But the withdrawal of MFN is more likely to hurt Taiwanese, Hong Kong, and South Korean investment in the PRC. In addition, in regard to Taiwan, Washington has neither affirmed nor denied its pledge to support Taiwan in the long run, but it did send two aircraft carriers, USS *Independence* and USS *Nimitz*, to the region in March 1996. Following the election of Lee Teng-hui as president of Taiwan, Beijing promised negotiations over the future of the island—the "sweet" part of China's generally "sour" approach. (Beijing had stopped talks with Taipei after Lee's visit to the United States.)

Chinese nuclear testing has also been indicative of China's more assertive strategy and has put the United States, Russia, and Japan on guard. In a nuclear explosion that appeared to be timed as a reaction to Japan's largest military exercises since World War II (September–October 1993), China ended its informal moratorium on nuclear testing. Japanese military exercises involved ninety thousand servicemen and hundreds of warships and aircraft in and around Japan (raising North Korean, Russian, as well as Chinese, concerns); American units also participated.

The next Chinese break of the informal test ban came just two weeks after President Clinton renewed Chinese MFN status, in June 1994; another test came just after the indefinite extension of the NPT in May 1995. The NPT has generally been regarded by Beijing as an aspect of a U.S.-Russian condominium or joint "hegemony" intended to deny China recourse to a nuclear deterrent. Chinese nuclear testing may also signal a willingness to defend North Korea and other Chinese interests. Moreover, in May 1995 (according to Tokyo), China tested a Dong Feng ICBM with a range of eighth thousand kilometers—far enough to hit the west coast of the United States. Beijing may also may be on the way to developing land and submarine-based missiles with multiple warheads. (China did, however, promise to commit itself to the comprehensive nuclear test ban in 1996.)

On 25 March 1997, Vice President Al Gore led the first significant high level mission to China since the 1989 Tiananmen repression. By offering significant trade and investment deals, and by downplaying issues concerning human rights, the Clinton Administration has hoped that its policy of "constructive engagement" will yield a more positive Sino-American relationship. Not-so-inadvertently, however, the Gore visit to Beijing, and his meeting with Li Peng, came on the heels of the Clinton-Yeltsin summit (and its "agreement to disagree"), which, in effect, threatened NATO enlargement into Central Europe. From

Moscow's perspective, these two nearly simultaneous events may well foretell of an attempt to draw the PRC back into an American sphere of security and influence, at the same time that the United States would potentially isolate Russia in Central Europe—once again raising the specter of "encirclement." Concurrently, from Beijing's perspective, the high level American visit permits China to play American against Russian interests, so that Beijing can expand its spheres of influence and security throughout the Asian-Pacific region. Rather than working *with* the Russians so as to "double contain" China, Washington thus appears to be initiating a new cycle of competition *against* Moscow so as to obtain Beijing's geostrategic and political-economic allegiance.

In conclusion, it is important to point out that despite Russia's tilt toward a Eurasian strategy, Washington still needs Moscow's cooperation in regard to North Korea, India, Iraq, and Iran. Even a NATO-Russian entente will not hold for long—if the United States, Europe, and Russia cannot coordinate strategy in regard to the PRC and other potentially anti–Western powers. The United States and Russia ultimately need to develop a more cooperative policy in regard to the last major communist bastion, the People's Republic of China, in order to prevent the latter from thoroughly manipulating U.S., European, Japanese, *and* Russian interests, and to prevent the potential formation of alternative anti–Western (and anti–Russian) alliance systems. Such an entente (forged by means of a compromise over NATO enlargement in Central Europe and a joint U.S-Russian-Japanese protectorate over the Kurile Islands) would not seek to isolate the PRC but attempt to engage it by helping to provide for its energy and resource needs and by reducing tensions in the South China Sea, through confidence and security–building measures. These steps could possibly lead to a solution which brings Beijing and Taipei into a closer confederation, but banning the presence of PLA forces on Taiwan.

CHAPTER 7

Jeopardizing Arms Reductions

NATO ENLARGEMENT AND RUSSIAN NUCLEAR THREATS

Ambassador Paul H. Nitze has argued, "With the vulnerability of Russia's new democracy, pushing for NATO enlargement will likely exacerbate the existing, destructive internal pressures. A wrong move on our part could easily backfire, triggering a rise to power by Russia's nationalists, sidetracking START II and possibly unraveling other arms agreements—without which NATO will find itself back in a Cold War environment. It is far better to act on the belief that Russian nationalists are growing in political power and be wrong by curtailing NATO expansion, than it is to risk European instability in the face of new confrontation with Moscow. . . . Our long-term objective should be to promote the engagement not the exclusion of Russia in Europe."[1] If proposals for NATO enlargement (or for a cooperative-collective security regime) are not fully negotiated with Russia, Ukraine, and lesser powers, the START II agreement, the 1987 INF Treaty, the 1967 ABM treaty, as well as the 1990 CFE treaty, could all be jeopardized.

In particular, the public discussion of deploying NATO nuclear weapons in Poland and the Czech Republic was denounced by Moscow as a potential violation of the CFE treaty and the INF accord. The fact that the September 1995 *Study on NATO Enlargement* did not absolutely preclude the possibility that new NATO members might accept forward-deployed foreign forces or nuclear weapons, or that they might ultimately acquire the training and infrastructure required for such deployments, led to an acrimonious debate within Central Europe (see Chapter 3) and counterthreats by Moscow.[2] Here, Alliance doctrine appears to be at fault. NATO refuses any non-member any form of *droit de regard* over the deployment of nuclear weapons, seeking to keep its options "open." On one hand, this leads to Russian suspicions as to NATO's ultimate intent; on the other, it causes Russia to entertain worst-case countermeasures based on the assumption that NATO will ultimately deploy such weaponry. Moreover, even a "defensive" stance to sustain credibility for Article V security guarantees for Central European states may, in fact, require a significant offensive capability.

Russian leaders consequently threatened a forward deployment of tactical nuclear weapons, if not a redeployment of intermediate-range systems in Belarus, Kaliningrad, and on Russian Baltic Fleet warships, if NATO did expand. In October 1995, it was rumored that the new Russian military doctrine might counter the acceptance of Central European states into NATO by the immediate reoccupation of the Baltic states. In November, General Grachev warned that NATO enlargement would impel Russia to look towards the CIS, the Far East, and the Middle East for new allies. In January 1996, Grachev warned that Russia would have to reexamine its views on the role of tactical nuclear weapons and its treaty obligations in the military sphere. The Russian elite believe that U.S. nuclear policy, and the structure of U.S. forces as outlined in the 1994 Nuclear Posture Review, for example, are designed to achieve and sustain strategic-nuclear superiority over Russia. Russian suspicions have stalled parliamentary ratification of START II and may impel modifications in the treaty.[3] (In March 1997, Washington did propose significant cuts for START III. See below.)

In addition, Russia has continued to take steps to reach for geostrategic parity with the United States, even from a position of relative weakness. Foreign Minister Primakov has, for example, sought to strengthen relations with Cuba and other Latin American states. In October 1995, Russia took significant steps to revive oil and sugar trade, support Cuba's nuclear energy program, and enhance military-technological ties with the Castro regime. The Russian military believe that their electronic monitoring station at Lourdes, which permits Moscow to monitor NASA and the eastern seaboard, constitutes "parity" with the U.S. ability to eavesdrop on Russian affairs. The Russian military accordingly hope to sustain the *threat* to redeploy ballistic missiles as a counter to NATO's encroachment upon Russian spheres of influence and security—despite Helms-Burton legislation that has threatened to cut off U.S. assistance to states that trade with or invest in Cuba.[4]

The January 1996 change in government personnel did not greatly change Russian policy. In July 1996, the new defense minister, Igor Rodionov (who replaced Pavel Grachev) indicated that Russian military strategy toward NATO enlargement had not changed significantly; NATO expansion "would dangerously alter the strategic military balance in Europe." Rodionov argued that NATO enlargement into Central Europe would expand NATO territory 750 kilometers to the West, a fact which would significantly reduce the early warning time for response by Russia's anti–missile systems. Alliance forces would also grow dramatically, implying expanded operational possibilities. NATO would acquire 280 airbases of differing categories, and thus would be able to upgrade airstrike capabilities, as NATO's tactical aircraft could reach Western areas of Russia, including Smolensk, Kursk, and Bryansk. NATO would able to take over Poland's strategic ports, thus resulting in the capability to close off completely Russia's Baltic fleet. NATO could likewise utilize and upgrade Central European infrastructure and resources which would permit the "secret tactical deployment of forces in under 30 days." Most crucially, by expanding to the Russian and Belarusian border, NATO's tactical nuclear weapons would become strategic.[5]

As Alexander Lebed put it at his (7 October 1996) one-day encounter with NATO Secretary-General Javier Solana in Brussels, should NATO not give priority to NATO-Russian relations, the Russian duma would probably question the whole context of arms control, in the belief "that NATO enlargement will lead to enormous changes in the strategic climate and therefore it will not be possible to ratify the START II treaty. And we're also worried about all the other treaties which have already been agreed on. . . . We need to have either an agreement or a treaty which would be very specific in terms of its legal implications . . . and START I and START II would be signed in that context along with the treaty on the elimination of chemical weapons and several other treaties as well."[6]

From the Russian perspective, the prospect that even if new NATO members do not have to belong to NATO's integrated military command is not entirely re-assuring, the attitude of Central European states appears to be to demand "full-fledged" membership. After the publication of the September 1995 *Study on NATO Enlargement*, both Warsaw and Prague endorsed the possibility of NATO deploying nuclear weapons and stated their intent to share fully in Alliance responsibilities, thus confirming Russian suspicions.[7] In June 1996, German defense minister Volker Rühe stated that NATO did not plan to station nuclear weapons or foreign forces in new members when it expanded, but new members would have to be "integrated militarily" and possess the same rights and duties as other members.[8] (The view that NATO should keep its options open had been affirmed by Defense Secretary Wiiliam Perry, who declared in 1996 that Russia has yet to reduce or remove its tactical nuclear weapons from the western regions of Russia as Moscow had previously promised in informal agreements.)

Former Soviet leader Mikhail Gorbachev has questioned why there are "investigations under way on the territories of prospective NATO members to determine how and where to best station new military structures"—if NATO's intent is truly peaceful. Gorbachev further argues that "along the perimeter of Russia . . . 'security knots' are being woven in which there is no room for Russia. Nothing could be more effective in reviving the Russian complex of being 'surrounded.'"[9]

Just as significantly, keeping NATO's nuclear options open could well alienate Kyiv, which has categorically opposed deployment of nuclear weapons anywhere near Ukrainian borders. Such a development would complicate peace negotiations in Europe and threaten the improvement of relations with Russia. Ukraine has feared that it would become a "buffer zone" between two military groupings, which would force Ukraine to choose sides.[10] Enlargement (if not counterbalanced with NATO-Russian, NATO-Ukrainian ententes) could lead Kyiv to look more closely to an alliance with Poland, and could simultaneously strengthen pro-Russian factions in the Ukrainian military. An alienated Kyiv could retain (or produce) a limited nuclear capability, undermining the January 1994 trilateral U.S.-Russian-Ukraine treaty on Ukrainian nuclear disarmament. Kyiv could either point nuclear weapons "all azimuths" or else threaten to draw NATO into support by the early use of such weaponry—a strategy similar to the French strategic concept of a nuclear "triggering link." Ukraine could also look for an alliance with China, which would exacerbate Russian fears of "encirclement," in a scenario where Sino-Russian relations deteriorate and Russia cannot pressure Ukraine or other CIS states into a "Eurasian" alliance with the PRC. As Kyiv is pivotal in the new European equilibrium, for it to choose between NATO or Russia (or even China) could undermine the post–Cold War peace. (On the other hand, Ukraine could also break up under pressure from both pro-Western and pro-Russian internal factions, which could provoke a new regional crisis and threats of partition.)

NUCLEAR ARMS REDUCTIONS

Following Soviet collapse, Washington was concerned that as long as there was continued instability within either the Russian Federation or the newly independent former Soviet republics it would be questionable how long any particular leadership would be in effective control. Political instability raised doubts as to whether any new government would abide by previous arms control treaties and agreements. It also raised renewed questions as to precisely who had effective control over strategic and tactical nuclear weapons, or ballistic missiles.[11] Deep political divisions could furthermore force the military to take sides, taking their capabilities with them.

Moreover, there was no need *further* to antagonize—if not totally destabilize—Moscow by permitting a potentially rival state to retain its nuclear weaponry. Out of the fifteen newly independent republics, four (Russia, Ukraine, Kazakhstan, and Belarus) continued to possess significant nuclear and conventional forces. This fact initially brought both Washington and Moscow together in a common cause. Granting Russia a monopoly over the control of nuclear weapons appeared to represent the lesser of evils and to be essential to forestalling Ukraine, Kazakhstan, and Belarus from making good on their implied or overt threats to retain independent nuclear weapons capabilities. At the same time, initial Russian promises of nuclear power-sharing (involving a joint CIS command or dual-key controls over nuclear weaponry among CIS states) were ruled out by Moscow in favor of a Russian monopoly over the nuclear deterrent. The dissolution of the CIS military command in June 1993 then gave Russia de facto operational control over nuclear weaponry, thus ending the myth of a CIS finger over dual-key nuclear systems. At the same time, U.S. policy permitted Russia to establish *primacy* if not *hegemony* over the former nuclear-weapons states within the CIS.

Although a number of American analysts had supported a Ukrainian nuclear deterrent, in particular to counter a potential Russian threat as a "well-managed" spread of nuclear weapons capabilities, the argument ignored the fact that nuclear weapons in Kyiv's hands would be destabilizing.[12] First, even if they did not necessarily invite preemption by Moscow (and assuming that Kyiv possessed the financial ability to keep them safe and in working condition), such weaponry would risk the breakdown of the START II treaty—Moscow would prepare for the worst. Second, although it is doubtful that Ukraine would adopt an all-azimuth strategy, it could still adopt a neo-Gaullist approach and seek a "triggering link" to the U.S. or European nuclear deterrents. Such a strategy would involve an effort to draw the United States or Europe into a struggle against Russia (or Belarus) by threatening early use of atomic weaponry. Kyiv could also threaten nuclear weapons against lesser regional actors, such as Slovakia, Hungary, or, more likely, Romania, who have territorial or irredentist claims against Ukraine.

In addition to attempting to eliminate non-Russian nuclear weaponry (and thereby limit proliferation from CIS states other than Russia), conjoint U.S.-Russian pressure was also intended to make certain that each state would abide by the 1990 Conventional Forces in Europe Treaty and enter the 1967 Nuclear Non-Proliferation Treaty as non-nuclear powers. U.S.-Soviet pressure consequently led Belarus and Kazakhstan to eliminate nuclear weaponry from their territory. It also brought the January 1994 trilateral U.S.-Russian-Ukrainian agreement to eliminate nuclear weapons from Ukraine. The latter pact moved well ahead of schedule in eliminating nuclear weapons from Ukraine by 1996—as opposed to the year 2001.

Kazakhstan, in particular, was accused of lax controls over its nuclear material and of providing Iran with tactical nuclear weapons—a charge denied by both Moscow and Almaty. In fear of nuclear proliferation, Washington engaged in Project Sapphire. In November 1994, it secretly transported more than 1,300 pounds of poorly guarded weapons-grade material (equivalent to twenty nuclear warheads) from a nuclear facility at Ust-Kamenogorsk back to U.S. territory—at the cost of tens of million dollars, and with the approval of Moscow. This action was deemed a "landmark event" in President Clinton's non-proliferation strategy.

As of mid-March 1995, over 1,300 warheads in Belarus, Ukraine, and Kazakhstan had been deactivated and over a thousand had been returned to Russia. By the end of 1995, Ukraine had removed roughly 75 percent of its warheads which left less than a thousand to be removed by 1996—well before the deadline. Kazakhstan still had six hundred nuclear warheads, reduced from 1,410. Belarus had thirty–six reduced from eighty–one. Russia itself has retained 7,074 warheads.[13]

By May 1995, 350 warheads had been transported out of the Ukraine (with something over a thousand remaining). Seven hundred air-launched cruise missiles had been deactivated, of which 360 went to Russia and 340 were awaiting transport. Despite resistance and setbacks, Ukraine was said to have become a nuclear-free state on 1 June 1996, after eliminating 130 SS-19s and forty–six SS-24s.[14] In September 1996, Kazakhstan tore down its remaining one hundred ballistic silos. In November 1996, Belarus removed the last fourteen of its eighty-eight SS–25s. Minsk had stalled on removing these systems, ostensibly due to lack of finance; it also cited the "threat" of NATO enlargement as reason to hold onto nuclear weaponry, even though its nuclear systems were under Russian command.[15] By the end of 1996, all three states were said to have totally removed their weaponry. (At the same time, Kyiv retains the technological and industrial capacity to rebuild its nuclear capacity sometime in the future, if it so desires.)

The U.S.-Russian-Ukrainian trilateral agreement to eliminate nuclear weapons was based upon conjoint *security assurances*, granted by the United States and Russia, once Ukraine signed the NPT. The NPT provides "soft" security assurances, in which any threats of conflict will be taken to the UN Security Council, but it does not provide formal, "hard" *security guarantees* similar to those provided for a member of the NATO alliance. The fact that Russia took the place of the Soviet Union on the UN Security Council evidently did not reassure Ukraine. Kyiv continued to fear Russian claims to the Crimea and pressure on sections of the eastern Ukraine, such as the coal-rich Donbass region. Ukraine consequently welcomed the French-initiated Stabilization Pact on Eastern European security in 1993–95. At the December 1994 OSCE summit, Ukrainian President Leonid Kuchma also welcomed OSCE principles, which recognized the inviolability of borders. Moreover, Kuchma argued that by signing the NPT Ukraine would obtain "guarantees" for its security and territorial integrity. In addition to the UK and France (which engaged in a separate accord), China granted security supports to Ukraine, officially in the context of the NPT (of which Beijing is a member). Kuchma added that the PRC "has now acceded to the guarantees of [Ukrainian] security."[16]

The French and Chinese accords raised questions, in that these pacts could eventually open the door to the possible formation of French/EU or Chinese alliances with Ukraine. It is certain, for example, that the PRC and Ukraine have been moving toward closer military cooperation since November 1992. Although no major weapons transfers have yet been reported, both Russia and Ukraine have been accused of supplying SS-18 missile technology to the PRC; but these alleged transfers may have been made by mafia groups with military links.[17] At the same time, U.S. officials have indicated that the tripartite security pact did involve several secret provisions—which might have led Kyiv to support the disarmament pact despite Russian threats.[18] In many ways, the January 1994 Trilateral Agreement has represented the keystone of post–Cold War U.S.-Russian cooperation. The collapse of this accord could mean the collapse of the post–Cold War peace.

In effect, with its monopoly of nuclear weapons, Moscow gained political-military *primacy* (if not aspects of *hegemony*) over former Soviet states. At the same time, however, Moscow has argued that it has been losing its position of nuclear-strategic *parity* with the United States. Consequently, U.S.-Russian negotiations to reduce nuclear weapons appeared to have stalled since 1994. At the May 1995 summit, presidents Yeltsin and Clinton declared that they would attempt to gain legislative acceptance of START II and then move on to START III. The May 1995 U.S.-Russian summit also promised mutual inspections and data exchanges. Washington and Moscow had pledged under START II to reduce nuclear warheads to roughly 3,000-3,500 by the year 2003, which included a 1,700-1,750 sublimit on SLBM warheads and a ban on land-based multiple independently targetable reentry vehicles (MIRVs) after 1 January 2003. Boris Yeltsin hoped to cut the number of strategic warheads in half—to about 1,500—if the United States would sign a START III accord. American analysts argued that budgetary cutbacks should bring Russia to a level of less than 3,500 nuclear weapons by 2005, whether or not Russia ratifies START II. Russia has moved toward development of a single-warhead

Topol ICBM, but it has made slower progress toward the development of a new submarine-launched missile.[19] In the meantime, Russia may demand that it keep all 170 SS-19s as single-warhead missiles in silos. (The START II agreement permitted Russia to retain only 105 SS-19s.)[20] (Concurrently, hard-liners have threatened to retain Moscow's MIRV capability, if U.S.-Russian relations deteriorate.)

As little progress had transpired by January 1996, however, American critics charged that Russia was backtracking on its agreement. They charged that Russia had refused to implement the "Joint Statement on the Transparency and Irreversibility of the Process of Reducing Nuclear Weapons"; that Russia was not implementing a 1994 agreement to cease producing plutonium; that the 1992 U.S.-Russia deal in which the United States would provide $12 billion for five hundred metric tons of scrapped nuclear arms was in jeopardy; and that the United States was not certain of the location of the enriched material.[21] Clinton administration supporters hoped that high level involvement could get the agreement back on track. (In April 1996, Yeltsin indicated that he would give Clinton information on the secret military command complex being built in the Ural mountains.)

On the negative side, the Russian parliament had yet to ratify the START II agreement. First, Russian acceptance of START II was made contingent on Ukraine signing the Nuclear Non-Proliferation Treaty. Second, the parliamentary elections (held in December 1995) and then the June 1996 presidential campaign also stalled progress. The new defense minister, Rodionov, declared opposition to START II. (Unlike the U.S. governmental system, in which only the Senate votes on such a treaty, both the State Duma and the Federal Assembly must agree.) In general, the opposition in the Russian parliament (particularly in the duma) has argued that the military-strategic equilibrium has changed since the conclusion of START II. Duma representatives believe that the treaty betrays the national interest and regard it as a serious unilateral concession to the United States. Opponents of the treaty do not want to be seen as giving up the strongest leg of the nation's nuclear deterrent—land-based ICBMs with MIRVed missiles—without renegotiation. The duma has argued that land-based MIRVed missiles cost roughly a tenth of single-warhead missiles and that Russia cannot afford to modernize old nuclear weapons systems. The duma estimates that it may cost Russia as much as $40–50 billion to dismantle the old missiles and build missiles with single warheads. It has furthermore been argued that Russia cannot ratify START II, since only 40 percent of the implementation costs of START I have been met.

Related to this concern is the disarray of Russian military. The parliament has argued that nuclear weapons represent Russia's only deterrent, particularly with the military having performed so poorly in Chechnya. Moreover, the START II treaty has been regarded as giving Washington a further advantage in sea-based MIRVed systems, which have generally been the weakest aspect of the Russian nuclear deterrent. The September 1995 use of Tomahawk cruise missiles by NATO on Bosnian Serb positions resulted in non-binding demands by the Russian parliament to suspend the NATO-Russian Individual Partnership agreement signed in May 1995. The use of high-tech cruise missiles (originally designed for use against Soviet mobile missile defenses) appeared to be a *qualitative* escalation of the Yugoslav conflict, from the perspective of Russian hard-liners. The use of such weaponry reinforced the view that Moscow needed to achieve nuclear-strategic *parity* with Washington. As many parliamentarians do not want to be seen as kowtowing to the latter (by easily accepting NATO enlargement into former Soviet or czarist spheres of security and influence), they are instead willing to risk a potentially destabilizing arms race. Hard-liners were particularly upset with reports that the Yeltsin administration may have been willing to give up the "principle of military-strategic parity with the United States."[22]

Moreover, in March 1996, Russian opponents of NATO enlargement threatened to deploy, on the western borders, nuclear air and sea-defense systems, including IRBM systems, such as the SS-20, banned by the 1987 INF pact. Although it has been argued that Russia does not possess the finances to break out of the START II agreement, its opponents argue that Russia can extend the life of the SS-19 and maintain cheaper (but destabilizing) multiple warhead systems rather than deploying single warheads as specified by START II.[23]

Parliamentary supporters of START II—who do not appear to have a solid majority in the duma—argue that the United States can rapidly outbuild Russia and can deploy as many as eight thousand warheads, while Russia can sustain only about 3,500. Proponents argue that speedy ratification will thus be cheaper and less provocative in the long term. Most likely, Moscow will act as if the START II agreement has been ratified. It may, however, stall on its implementation due to the expense—that is, unless more militant factions come to power. In September 1996, duma Defense Committee chair Lev Rokhlin stated that it was in the Russian interest to sign the treaty but the duma was unlikely to ratify it.[24]

Although the U.S. Congress did approve START II on 26 January 1996, it likewise threatened not to abide by START II guidelines. Congress has generally perceived Russia to be rebuilding the Soviet empire or attempting to block the efforts of independent Central European states to join NATO. Apparent efforts to force Belarus, Kazakhstan, and Ukraine into the CIS and brutal Russian actions in the "near abroad" have angered American senators. Russian efforts to integrate former Soviet-bloc states into the CIS have not entirely precluded to threats of a preemptive strike against former Soviet-bloc republics—particularly Ukraine—to impel these states into a military or economic union.[25]

The November 1993 Russian defense doctrine dropped the old Soviet pretense (as promised by the Brezhnev-era doctrine) of "no first use" of nuclear weapons. Although the new defense doctrine stated that the threat of global conventional or nuclear war had abated, it warned that Russia could use nuclear weapons against states that do not sign the NPT. This threat was designed to impel Ukraine and other states to sign the agreement. Russia has also reserved the right to use nuclear weapons against non-nuclear states if they are allied, or have signed an agreement, with a nuclear state. A refusal to adopt a "no-first use" position was reaffirmed in February 1997 in an new policy draft.

At the March 1997 summit, presidents Clinton and Yeltsin agreed to asymmetrical reductions in the Russian favor for START III, involving a ceiling of 2,000–2,500 nuclear warheads on long range missiles by the year 2007. Such a pact could eliminate the need for Russia to rebuild its single warhead missile force to catch up with U.S. capabilities— assuming the issue of NATO enlargement does not become a stumbling block in the negotiations, and that the Russian parliament ratifies the START II accord before moving onto to START III. Likewise the U.S. Congress will need to accept a protocol to accept adjustments to the START II treaty, so that it can simultaneously begin to consider START III. The latter will also seek to limit submarine-launched cruise missiles and tactical nuclear weapons, among other weapons systems.

BALLISTIC MISSILE DEFENSE SYSTEMS

Related to Russian fears of the American nuclear posture are American threats to leave the ABM treaty. The Congress has threatened to develop a ballistic missile defense (BMD) system that would cover the extensive sections of the United States. Although the American intent is ostensibly to protect itself against missile attacks from "rogue" states, Moscow may well regard such an all-encompassing system as a means to shield the United States following a first-strike assault against Russia. Moreover, American efforts to improve the Patriot ABM system and forward-deploy advanced land and sea-based "theater" high-altitude antimissile systems have also been regarded by some as a shield, possibly permitting the United States to launch a first strike. U.S. Congressional supporters of anti-missile defenses may seek to block a START III accord, if the Clinton administration makes too many concessions to Moscow on BMD systems.

The focus of ballistic missile defenses has shifted from the media hype and outer-space "Star Wars" systems of the Reagan administration to a more realistic focus on theater defenses. By the turn of the millennium, about twenty countries could have ballistic missile capabilities, possibly armed with chemical and biological, if not nuclear, warheads. Both the Senate and House have proposed legislation that would develop both theater missile defenses as well as BMD systems designed to protect several regions of the United States, by the year 2003—the very year in which START II is to complete cuts in Russian and American strategic warheads. Congress has authorized $3.6 billion for BMD research and development, $750 million more than the Clinton administration requested; $450 million of these funds were directed toward a BMD system to be in place by the year 2003; Russian observers have argued that the deadline is intended to give the United States superiority, as Russian ICBM capabilities continue to diminish. The provision mandating deployment of a BMD system by 2003 was cut out of the February 1996 Defense Authorization Bill, but Congress sought to introduce it in separate legislation.[26]

Those who support the development of nationwide BMD systems argue that the theory of "mutually assured destruction" (mutual deterrence or dissuasion) will work against a rationale actor but not against a "kamikaze" state, a state willing to take significant risks, involving nuclear blackmail. It is also argued that mutually assured destruction likewise cannot defend against accidental launch or miscalculations. On the other hand, no BMD system can guard against foreign-supported terrorism inside a state's borders. Nor can a BMD system guard against low-flying cruise missiles or ballistic missiles with a flattened trajectory. There is considerable irony in the fact that the Congress appears more interested in breaking out of the ABM treaty than do U.S. allies or Russia. After all, Russia, Europe, and Japan are more directly threatened by these new "ballistic missile states" than is the United States. Furthermore, both the UK and France oppose breaking out of the ABM treaty, on the grounds that the counter-deployment of a Russian BMD system (combined with a new nuclear weapons race) would render their own essentially second-strike nuclear capabilities obsolete. Third, those who advocate a nationwide ABM system must believe that it is feasible; they must also assume that the United States can *achieve and sustain an unchallengeable military-technological preeminence*—an assumption which may not prove viable, given the global spread of military and "dual use" technology as well as of satellite and communications technology. Finally, not only would Russia then seek to develop a BMD system, but the PRC would also be encouraged to do so.

In their May 1995 summit, presidents Clinton and Yeltsin stated that they would continue negotiations to resolve the issues relating to U.S. advocacy of theater missile defenses in the context of the ABM treaty, which limits the number and nature of ballistic missile defenses. Moscow argued that new upgraded American defenses (even for short-range theater purposes) could represent a violation of the ABM system, particularly if they are forward-deployed overseas. Russian concerns involved the February 1995 statement of intent by the United States, France, Germany, and Italy (the UK and Netherlands might join) to develop a medium extended-range air defense system which would replace the Hawk Air defense system and perhaps the Patriot. This new system is intended to protect forces from attack by aircraft and ballistic missiles by 2005. Largely in response to North Korean and Chinese missile programs in 1995, Japan and the United States have also looked to create a theater missile defense system.

Part of the problem results from the definition of the threshold between "theater" and "tactical" systems, particularly if deployed forward and in large numbers. A partial compromise was worked out over new BMD systems in September 1996. The first stage addressed shorter-range BMD; the second stage of the agreement is to deal with high-velocity systems. Systems that could intercept with a velocity greater than five kilometers per second or at a range of more than 3,500 kilometers would violate the treaty; yet missiles traveling at less than three kilometers per second would not. The agreement thus permits Washington and Moscow to develop a tactical defense against short range ballistic missiles. Furthermore, Washington and Moscow took part in the first-ever joint, coordinated tactical antimissile exercises, begun 4 June 1996 at the Falcon Air Force base in Colorado. [27]

Despite the compromise (and to counter the long-term implications of the U.S. initiative), in January 1996 the CIS heads of state unanimously approved the creation of a mutual air defense system, to commence April 1st. (This action followed a 25 November 1995 meeting at Sochi, which represented a step toward a full-fledged CIS security system.) The system was to include most CIS states, except Azerbaijan, Moldova, and Turkmenistan; Ukraine may seek technical assistance, but not join. Air defenses were to be installed in Georgia, Kirgystan, and Tajikistan, and upgraded in Armenia, Kazakhstan, and Uzbekistan. In March 1996, concurrent with Russian-Belarusian steps toward "union," Defense Minister Grachev emphasized the need to coordinate CIS defense policies, particularly in regard to NATO enlargement. As part of the effort to draw in Belarus, this new air defense system could be a step toward the formation of a new CIS defense bloc. (Minsk and Moscow, however, continue to haggle over who is to pay for the system.) Although Kyiv and Moscow remained divided over the CIS air defense system—in addition to basing rights for the Russian Black Sea Fleet in the Crimea—the two states did sign protocols for the joint use of outer space and a joint policy in regard to the CFE treaty; also they agreed to jointly finance together a BMD system. Russia also agreed to purchase Ukrainian SS-19s and strategic bombers.

THE CFE TREATY

The CFE treaty is regarded as the prime example of "cooperative security" by the Department of Defense. Concurrently, conventional weaponry represents only one dimension of the strategic military equation. The proposed expansion of NATO risks upsetting the entire military-technological aspects of the NATO-Russian relationship, as indicated in Defense Minister Rodionov's remarks quoted earlier in this chapter, and assuming that no compromise is reached.

The collapse of the Warsaw Pact has, on the positive side, resulted in significantly reduced forward deployments; on the negative side, however both northeastern and southeastern Europe face greater risks and shorter warning times. Ironically, while the Central Front does not pose an immediate threat, the Baltic Sea, as well as the Black Sea, the Caucasus, and Caspian Sea areas have become potentially explosive. Norway and Turkey had in 1990 insisted on the creation of CFE flank zones to prevent Moscow from redeploying troops; but the collapse of the Soviet Union has radically altered the balance of national forces in each region.

In the north, this fact has raised questions as to whether or not NATO would be prepared to defend the Baltic states and Finland, or even more to the point, Norway, a NATO member.[28] In essence, the loss of ports on the Black and Baltic seas has enhanced the importance of Russian bases on the Kola Peninsula and on Sakhalin Island (in the Sea of Okhotsk), even if the fleet has been downsized. Moreover, the highly unstable nature of the Russian military on the Kola Peninsula (and in Kaliningrad) raises concerns for Baltic littoral states. In the south, tensions between Greece and Turkey, have raised questions about NATO support to either state. Questions have also been raised as to the reliability of either Greece and Turkey in support of U.S. or NATO policies. Concurrently, Russian-Ukrainian tensions over the Black Sea fleet have yet to be resolved.

Even on the Central Front, Belarus, continues to eye its neighbors with suspicion, and this region could see a major confrontation should NATO enlarge into Central Europe without an explicit U.S.-Russian agreement. Russian political leaders have generally remained skeptical about any real "transformation" of the Atlantic Alliance, despite the creation of the NACC and the PfP. NATO enlargement could consequently undermine the concept of "universal collective security" and the process of "pan-European stability and security." Concurrently, Belarus itself may seek to block a NATO-Russian agreement—precisely in fear of a NATO-Russian condominium.

From the Russian perspective, NATO gained a significant advantage in conventional weaponry with the break up of the Soviet bloc, such as by absorbing East German forces. In 1996, NATO was seen to have a three-to-one ratio over the conventional forces of Russia. Unless the CFE treaty is substantially revised (as has been proposed by Washington in February 1997, see below), NATO is likely to have a four-to-one advantage, as well as an edge in other weapons systems, particularly if the Alliance is enlarged. Moreover, the issue is not merely quantitative; "the ratio of military forces and material will be radically different, guaranteeing NATO a position of military superiority."[29] Moscow has accordingly demanded certain "modifications" of the Gorbachev-era CFE treaty to meet post–Soviet security concerns, particularly in regard to deployments in the southeastern and northeastern flanks.[30] Prior to resigning as foreign minister, Andrei Kozyrev had warned against "horse trading"—in reference to deals over the CFE in exchange for NATO expansion.[31]

Russia has destroyed less than one-quarter of the 6,331 tanks, and only half of the 1,988 armored vehicles, it promised to in 1990. Officially, Moscow wanted to extend the deadline to 1998, but according to ITAR-TASS, the Russian defense ministry believed that Gorbachev's unilateral "political commitment" (made in Vienna in July 1991) to destroy tanks and armored vehicles beyond the Urals by 1995 was no longer in its strategic or economic interests. Uzbekistan, Kazakhstan, and Turkmenistan also missed the end-of-the-year deadline to destroy Soviet-era military equipment. In addition, Belarus momentarily suspended its CFE-mandated weapons destruction program in February 1995, citing the excessive cost.[32] On the other hand, Russia did plan to destroy equipment west of the Urals in accord with the CFE treaty by November 1995, despite financial shortfalls.[33]

With growing tensions in its southern flank, Moscow has intended to deploy greater numbers of forces in the Black Sea and Caucasus region, not only to deal with the crisis in Chechnya but also to pressure other states in the region. Russia has established several military bases in Armenia and Georgia along the Turkish border. In response, Kyiv has stated its interest in building up its forces in the Odessa military district, likewise in violation of the CFE agreement.[34] In June 1996, Kyiv and Moscow reached a compromise, however, in which CFE flank restrictions were reduced in the Odessa *oblast*. Concurrently, Moscow warned Washington about its naval presence in the Black Sea and expressed concerns with close U.S. military ties over Albania and

Georgia. U.S.-Georgian military cooperation, for example, has been seen as protecting the Baku-Bitumi oil pipeline. Moscow has likewise been concerned with alleged U.S.-Ukrainian negotiations involving the use of Crimean bases by U.S. or NATO naval forces.

Washington has hoped to restrict Russian troops and military equipment in the Caucasus. Such forces could potentially threaten Turkey, at a time when Greek-Turkish relations have come close to confrontation, with Greece and Turkey engaging in an arms race. By a practice known as "cascading," the CFE treaty has permitted the transfer of forces away from the Central European theater and toward more peripheral regions, such as southeastern Europe.[35] NATO has attempted to sustain a rough "parity" between the two sides. Turkish arms demands, however, are perhaps exacerbated by the fact that it is totally "encircled" by tensions. (See Chapter 6.)

In the north, Russian security concerns pressures are not related to the ethnic Russian diaspora alone but also to geostrategic, political-economic, and military security concerns. Military retrenchment from the Black Sea and the Baltic states has increased the value of secure transit rights to Kaliningrad. Retrenchment has also enhanced the importance of nuclear bases on the Kola Peninsula, which would place pressure on the Baltic states, as well as Sweden, Finland, and Norway. (Nordic airspace, by the way, is the transit route for U.S. penetrating bombers and air-launched cruise missiles, or ALCMs.) Military retrenchment in the West has also put additional pressures in the Far East, such as in the Sea of Okhotsk, which in turn places pressure on Japan. Former Russian defense minister Grachev consequently sought a revision of the CFE treaty for the Northern (formerly Leningrad) district, to counter Nordic support for the Baltic battalion and also the "threats" of Poland (and the Baltic states) entering NATO.

Additionally, NATO exercises ("Battle Griffin") along the three-hundred-kilometer Norwegian-Russian border in March 1996 raised suspicions, particularly as Norway had unilaterally restricted NATO activities near the border during the Cold War. Russian observers argued that NATO's actions in Norway were intended to (1) test Russian reactions to future NATO enlargement toward its borders; (2) achieve a capability to deploy forces swiftly to the northeast; and (3) assume a position to threaten the Kola Peninsula and Murmansk.[36] American officials downplayed the exercises as not a provocation to Russia. Concurrently, Moscow made several positive agreements with Norway in March 1996, despite NATO exercises. (Norway and Russia, for example, have been engaged in cleaning up former Soviet nuclear waste sites in the Nordic region.)

Nordic states have thus far opposed any alteration of the status quo, but at the same time, these states have been concerned with strategic uncertainties in the northern region, particularly in regard to Kaliningrad and Murmansk. The Swedish and Finnish decision (in response to Russian threats) to join the EU (and to look toward NATO membership by participating in the PfP) was at least in part for strategic purposes.[37] However, Helsinki has remained open to cooperation with Russia; in May 1996 Finland agreed to the purchase Russian S300 antimissile systems (somewhat similar to the American Patriot) system and discussed other security issues.[38]

Following the Vienna Review Conference for Conventional Forces in Europe in June 1996, the CFE flank zone changed. Russia has until 31 May 1999 to comply with flank limitations (which it had been violating since November 1995). By shrinking the flank zones, the agreement (to be sent for ratification by all CFE signatories by 15 December 1996) would permit Russia to deploy more heavy weapons along its northern and southern borders than was permitted under the original terms.[39] The Baltic states, among others, however, have opposed the compromise in that it permits Russia to deploy an extra six hundred tanks in the northern Pskov *oblast* (ostensibly to counter Baltic state territorial claims in the region); these states thus have demanded antitank missiles, as well as some form of security guarantee (i.e., NATO membership), to compensate for Russia's gains. Without some sort of offsetting arrangement, the revised CFE agreement might fail to be ratified by national legislatures.

Failure to reach compromise proposals could jeopardize ratification of the START II accord by Russia and delay economic assistance, including Nunn-Lugar funding for nuclear weapons conversion.[40] In February 1997, Washington did offer a possible compromise with Moscow. Ceilings on the number of weapons would apply to individual countries, and not to blocs as in the 1990 agreement. There would be a national ceiling for tanks, helicopters, and combat aircraft deployed. NATO would promise to accept territorial zone limits that would prevent any massing of allied forces, particularly in front-line areas. At the same time, NATO and Russia had yet to reach an agreement in regard to the possible deployment of nuclear weapons or advanced military infrastructure upon the territory of new NATO member states. (Washington counter-accused Moscow of retaining large numbers of tactical nuclear weapons in western areas of Russia, weapons which were to have been eliminated by informal agreements made in the early 1990s). American proposals also advocated the modernization of armaments—a position that might not be entirely acceptable to Moscow, even with reduced numerical ceilings.[41]

A possible collapse of the CFE treaty—combined with the evident deterioration of the Russian army—could additionally result in a greater Russian reliance on MIRVed ICBMs and IRBMs.

THE QUESTION OF ARTICLE V SECURITY GUARANTEES

It is no secret that the primary (yet generally unstated) reason for Central and Eastern European states to seek NATO membership is to obtain Article V security guarantees. Membership in the EU, or even the WEU, would not provide the same fundamental guarantee (unless NATO enters into formal agreements with EU or WEU members). It will be argued that NATO security guarantees *by themselves* may not necessarily be sufficient but that *conjoint* NATO-WEU-Russian security guarantees would actually provide greater reassurance for Central and Eastern European states, particularly through the formation of a Euro-Atlantic DSI intended to permit sufficient political-military solidarity to resist pressures from any one nuclear power.

While Central and Eastern European hopes to obtain NATO Article V security guarantees are perfectly understandable, it must be pointed out that even the Washington Treaty's Article V provides only for quasi-automatic responses, based on integrated force and command structures and planning for specified contingencies; "no government is obliged to engage in any specific operations."[42] During the Cold War, the automatic nature of the U.S. response was diluted by the strategy of "flexible response," which was intended to give NATO more options for action (short of all-out thermonuclear war).

Moreover, if NATO *alone* is to guarantee the security of Central European states, the major questions have yet to be resolved. How and where are these states to be defended? From which of the NATO/WEU countries would the deployment of troops be acceptable? Would they be sufficient? Can the United States, EU, and WEU truly coordinate strategy? What if the United States refused to deploy troops, either in deference to Moscow or due to isolationist American sentiment? Would Poland and the Czech Republic accept the German *Bundeswehr* on their territory? Most crucially, where would the line of defense be drawn? In Finland, or the Baltic states? The Oder River or the Bug? At what point, if any, should nuclear weapons be deployed on the territory of Central and Eastern European states if they become "full" NATO members?

In regard to the latter question, for example, given the deep-strike range of nuclear weaponry, it is not clear what would be the purpose of the deployment of nuclear weaponry in Poland and the Czech Republic. These weapons would most likely be subject to preemption in case of war, and their deployment would not be conducive to the maintenance of geostrategic *parity*—an issue of prime concern during the Cold War, but which appears to have been overlooked in the post–Cold War strategic debate. Concurrently, NATO nuclear weapons policy prefers to keep options open for all NATO members—nuclear and declared non-nuclear alike. Hence, "full" membership of Central and Eastern

European states in NATO potentially destabilizes the present situation of rough nuclear parity regardless of the fact that new members may not initially deploy nuclear weapons. A Russian reaction would seem likely.[43] (What may appear to be a "peacetime" condition for one state, may be regarded as preparation for war by another.)

Concurrently, what if the Russians (or others) engage in acts of imperialism in regions other than Central Europe, precisely to test American and European resolve? What, for example, would be the American response to a Russian intervention in northern Kazakhstan, or in other areas of Central Asia, or the Far East—areas not considered either American or European spheres of influence and security? What if Russia and China establish a condominium arrangement over Mongolia, Central Asia, and the Far East? How would the U.S. and the EU response to overt acts of Russian imperialism there affect the direction of U.S. and EU policies in other areas (such as the Baltic states or Finland), particularly if the United States and Europe have not worked out a concerted regional and global strategy?[44] Finally, what if Moscow did forge linkages with ultra-nationalist political parties in Western Europe (as has Vladimir Zhirinovsky's Liberal Democratic Party)—so as to fragment European political consensus?

In the Cold War, one scenario for Soviet aggression was a rapid conventional strike, perhaps preceded by tactical or intermediate-range nuclear strikes. Post–Cold War scenarios, however, involve tensions arising from undefined and uncontrolled borders, trade in illicit materials, transnational ethnic disputes, Russian subversion of Central or Eastern European states, or aggression stemming from complex and extended processes involving breaches of treaties (such as the CFE). One scenario may be a major crisis in which Lithuania, suspecting contraband, blocks transit routes to Kaliningrad—possibly resulting in a 1948–49 Berlin Blockade in reverse. Another scenario is Polish-Belarusian border tensions erupting into a major confrontation. In these cases, it is most probable that conflict would not erupt immediately, that a whole series of countermeasures would be taken over an extended period before large-scale aggression was initiated: "The threshold for triggering [NATO] Article V-type obligations would therefore be embedded in a dynamic and ambiguous situation."[45]

Interrelated with the above are issues of threat perception. Front-line states—those closest to the apparent or potential threat—seek the strongest guarantees. Assuming they possess the resources, they must build their own armed forces and seek allies. Yet those very allies *not* on the front line may take a more disengaged attitude. They may not feel the same obligation to defend the state most immediately threatened, or at the exact time demanded. Perceptions of threats also explain Germany's determination to form a "buffer" between itself and instability on its eastern borders and the CIS, by supporting NATO membership for Central European states. (Threat perceptions may also help to explain support received from the "Red Belt" by Communist Party leader Gennady Zyuganov during the 1996 Russian presidential elections. The Red Belt is located largely along Russia's unstable southern borders or in areas of significant ethnic tension.) From this viewpoint, contemporary Germany (with or without a Central European buffer) may take a different view of a potential threat than did West Germany (when the latter was a front-line state).[46]

Poland's position vis-à-vis Kaliningrad and Belarus, for example, helps to explain its eagerness to join NATO. In effect, Poland may have already become the new front-line state vis-à-vis Belarus. The latter in turn may or may not be given unconditional support by Russia, while Poland may or may not obtain *automatic* NATO support, even as a "full" member. Accordingly, Warsaw should obtain clear security guarantees from Russia in the case of Polish-Belarusian conflict (in addition to "full" guarantees from NATO), so as to assure that Moscow will not support Minsk. Concurrently, Warsaw may also want to obtain security assurances from Minsk that it will not join forces with Moscow.

This hypothetical scenario of a dynamic and ambiguous situation ultimately triggering Article V-type obligations is aggravated by the conflicting "missions" of the varying political and security organizations engaged in Europe: NATO (plus the proposed Atlantic Partnership Council), the WEU, the EU, the UN, and the OSCE. At present, each of these security or political regimes possesses a different mission and represents a different constituency with security interests that may not coincide. It is therefore crucial that these regimes and organizations coordinate strategies, thus becoming truly "interlocking" as opposed to "interblocking." Without the assistance of such international regimes as the OSCE, NATO will not be able to deal with all aspects of a crisis, particularly issues involving preventive diplomacy and conflict resolution. (See Chapter 10.)

On the other hand, what if Russia or Belarus attacked NATO-member Poland? A Congressional Budget Office (CBO) report, for example, recognizes that Russia—at present—does not represent a significant threat to Central Europe. At the same time, should a resurgent Russia rebuild itself militarily in the next ten to fifteen years, the CBO report asserts, NATO could defend against an attack on Poland by Russia and Belarus, much as the United States and its allies engaged Iraq in Kuwait in Operation Desert Shield and Storm. While there are certainly some similarities, the analogy appears absurd, as it neglects a number of significant differences. Not only would Russian forces be in greater readiness than those of Iraq, Russian air power, ballistic and cruise missile capabilities, and air defense systems would be more effective. It is thus extremely unlikely that NATO forces would "achieve air superiority after a few days."[47]

Moreover, it appears to be totally forgotten that whereas Iraqi leader Saddam Hussein was armed with dilapidated intermediate-range SCUDs (used primarily for the purpose of political terror against Israel and Saudi Arabia than for striking strictly military targets), a resurgent Russia would be armed with a full panoply of ICBMs, IRBMs, and tactical nuclear weapons, many with MIRVed warheads. Moreover, any Russian attack on Poland would most likely be part of a global war on several fronts, thus making geostrategic calculations even more uncertain and risky. Finally, the analogy forgets that even though Iraq lost the war, Saddam Hussein remains alive and requires permanent vigilance. Even if an Allied coalition could—without significant loss of life, or perhaps destroying the planet—defeat a resurgent Russia much as it defeated Iraq, could the West afford permanent vigilance against a hostile Russia, without occupying it?

At the same time, even if Russia did not wage war on Poland (Polish conflict with Belarus, however, appears more likely in the near term), Moscow could break the INF and START II treaties and engage in missile threats (combined with the development of BMD systems). It is not clear that even forward-deployed NATO forces would be able to defend adequately against tactical and intermediate-range ballistic missile scenarios, among others. From this perspective, it seems more rational to compromise with Moscow than risk permanent political-military instability in Russia, and the permanent threat of global war.

Congress has thus yet to come to terms with the nature of the nuclear commitment that unilateral NATO expansion would entail. Much as was debated in the Cold War, is Washington willing to risk Detroit for Warsaw? Will Washington be able to accept a concerted multilateral approach to nuclear dissuasion, one involving French and British participation? Perhaps these questions will only be answered if U.S. and EU/WEU resolve is actually tested. But rather than waiting for that terrifying moment—an approach known as "brinkmanship" in the Cold War—it appears wiser to enter into a cooperative-collective security arrangement with Moscow involving conjoint NATO, EU/WEU, and Russian security guarantees. A militarily integrated Euro-Atlantic DSI would sustain mutual confidence among the nuclear weapons states by helping each side to know the *limits* of regional military deployments. At the same time, if any of the nuclear states broke away from the agreement, the other nuclear powers would remain committed to the defense of all participating Central and Eastern European states. (See Chapter 11.)

CHAPTER 8

Former Yugoslavia:
The Testing Ground of
Cooperative-Collective Security

THE ROLE OF MAJOR POWERS

The fact that Yugoslavia was at the geostrategic crossroads between the interests of the United States, Germany (and Europe), Russia, Turkey, Ukraine, the Middle Eastern states, and Iran should have indicated that the present conflict could have been defused only by a truly concerted approach from the outset. American interests were directly involved due to the NATO membership of Greece and Turkey. Russian interests were involved because of historical links to Serbia. Germany had historical influence in Croatia, while Turkey, Iran, and Saudi Arabia had interests to support in Bosnia. At the same time, these international linkages tended to be conflictual and contradictory. For example, Greece supported Serbia, while Turkey supported Bosnia. As the conflict escalated, there developed a partial rift within the EU itself: Germany took a pro-Croatian tilt; while the UK and France sought intermediate ground between Croatia and Serbia. Russia supported Serbia, but did not necessarily support Bosnian Serbs. The United States backed Bosnian Moslems, but attempted to bring Bosnian Moslems and Croatians into an alliance (despite their own bitter animosities) against Bosnian Serbs backed by Serbia.

The crisis in former Yugoslavia has represented a testing ground for a potential system of cooperative-collective security throughout Central and Eastern Europe. Aspects of cooperative-collective security, involving concerted, war-preventive, and irenic diplomacy, have all been practiced. Concerted diplomacy is better illustrated by the formation of the Contact Group in April 1994 than by UN deliberation. War-preventive diplomacy is perhaps best illustrated by the UN

Preventive Deployment Force (UNPREDEP) in the Former Yugoslav Republic of Macedonia. Irenic diplomacy is perhaps been best shown in the belated, but engaged, American "armed escort" diplomacy in former Yugoslavia in 1995 that brought three "non-democratic" states into a peace settlement. Overall cooperative-collective security is better illustrated by the multinational deployment of IFOR, involving U.S., EU, and Russian troops and other armed forces under a general UN mandate—as opposed to the belated UN intervention. This chapter will analyze the failure of the major powers to settle the conflict at its origins, the tension between the UN and NATO, the belated advent of concerted Contact Group diplomacy in April 1994, and the subsequent U.S. diplomatic engagement, resulting in the decision to negotiate and implement the Dayton Accords and to deploy IFOR/SFOR (as part of a broad coalition of NATO and non-NATO states), as well as UN forces in Eastern Slavonia as peacekeepers.

The settlement of the Yugoslav crisis is in many ways the key not only to peace in the region but also to the long-term development of U.S.-European-Russian relations—if not the viability and legitimacy of NATO itself. As Secretary of Defense William Perry put it, "It is important to get this right because this will affect security relations in Europe, between NATO and Russia, and between the United States and Russia for years to come."[1] General Leonti Shevtsov, leader of the Russian contingent, argued that NATO-Russian cooperation in the Balkans represented a model for a "concerted action plan which can nip conflict in the bud before it has a chance to spread beyond a given region."[2] Whether NATO-WEU-Russian actions will, however, lead to a "concerted action plan" depends upon the extent of commitment of both the major and other significant actors to the peace process, as well as upon the ability of international regimes to provide adequate developmental assistance and a modicum of stability. At the same time, Moscow's cooperation in this region does not necessarily guarantee its acceptance of NATO enlargement into Central Europe.

BACKGROUND OF THE CONFLICT

In essence, three underlying and interacting factors led to the outbreak of the conflict. First of all, there were the geohistorical claims of each of the republics within the multinational, multiethnic, federated state, in which rival elites jockeyed to expand power and influence within their various republics, particularly following the death of Marshal Josip Tito. Secondly, there was the 1972 closure of the European Community labor market to Yugoslav "guest workers," which helped exacerbate socioeconomic tensions. Finally, there was the retrenchment (then collapse) of the Soviet empire, which presented the "opportunity" to establish an entirely new regional order. At its origins, the Yugoslav conflict represented an *internal* or *civil* war in which an opportunistic Serbia sought to overthrow the domestic *status quo* previously established by Marshal Tito. This essentially internal conflict, however, became *internationalized* with German recognition of Croatia and Slovenia. In essence, Belgrade sought to reestablish the predominant or hegemonic role which Serbia possessed before 1941, but which it lost in the post–1945 Tito regime.[3]

By 1992, Serbian-backed secessionist movements sought either to establish their own independent republics or to merge in a confederation with Serbia proper. President Slobodan Milosevic sought both to establish and consolidate a new power base within Serbia, Kosovo, and Bosnia, while he opposed efforts to forge a looser, confederal state. In effect, between mid-1987 and May–June 1991 Milosevic sought to recentralize the Yugoslav state under Serbian predominance. In this period Milosevic acted illegally to "unify" the formerly autonomous provinces of Vojvodina and Kosovo (autonomous under the federal constitution of 1974). In January 1990, Milosevic worked to overthrow the leadership of the republic of Montenegro.

In an effort to counter Serbian actions, on 4 October 1990 Slovenia (which led the secessionist, or "disassociation," movement) and Croatia jointly proposed a "Confederate Model among South Slavic States"—a proposal that was rejected by Serbia and Montenegro. The latter two insisted upon a federal (yet in reality pro-Serbian), centralized model. Seeking out a middle ground, Bosnia and Macedonia favored a "community" of republics with a "federal" system (including monetary union) but in which each republic would retain its own army.

In December 1990, Serbia illegally obtained $1.7 billion by manipulating Yugoslavia's central bank; Milosevic was then accused of using these funds to augment wages and pensions in Serbia and Montenegro in an effort to assure a communist electoral victory. The imposition of special duties on Serbian imports from Croatia and Slovenia, plus efforts to block a Croatian leader from assuming the federal Yugoslav state presidency, also helped to set off secessionist referendums. Slovenia and Croatia declared independence in May–June 1991. In October 1991, the Bosnian-Herzegovinan parliament adopted a "Resolution of Sovereignty." Likewise, an underground parliament in Kosovo declared independence in 1991. (Yugoslav federal and Serbian leaders had rejected proposals for an independent Kosovo in July.) Concurrently, Serbians in Croatian Krajina demanded immediate secession from an independent Croatia.

From the Serbian perspective, Croatian demands for "national" independence seemed unlikely to result in Serbian minorities being allowed to forge an independent state (or a state linked to Serbia) out of Croatian-claimed territory. This was the rationalization for supporting pan-Serbian secessionist movements.[4] The brief war with Slovenia began in June 1991. Then, in July 1991, the Yugoslav federal army (largely under Serbian control) attacked Croatia to prevent the latter's secession and on the pretext of protecting the Serbian "minority" (representing approximately 13 percent of the population); it seized roughly 30 percent of Croatian territory.

THE ROLES OF THE EUROPEAN UNION, GERMANY, AND THE UNITED STATES

Following the outbreak of full-scale war in 1991, the EU (formerly EC) declared that it would take the lead in mediating the crisis. The president of the European Commission, Jacques Delors, asserted that Yugoslavia remained an all-European, and not at all an American, affair. Delors's declaration, however, did not recognize global geopolitical realities by which the United States, Europe, and Russia each possessed geostrategic interests in the region. At the same time, the EU was in the process of debating the Maastricht Treaty and could not thoroughly engage itself in peace talks to prevent the outbreak of conflict. Jacques Delors did warn in general terms against resort to the use of force by any of the parties involved; he did so, however, without sufficient political backing or force to make the threat credible.

The EU developed its peace plan between July and October 1991 and declared an arms embargo and a freeze on financial assistance to Yugoslavia on 5 July 1991. Serbia rejected the EU's peace plan, but Montenegro accepted, which provoked a feud between the two allies.[5] The EU foreign ministers attempted to reach a cease-fire and presented a draft proposal based on a loose confederation. The EU's proposal, however, did not have strong American or Russian backing. By 26–27 August 1991, the Cyrus Vance mission moved forward under UN/EU auspices. The OSCE endorsed an arms embargo on 3–4 September, and the UN declared a complete arms embargo on Yugoslavia on 25 September 1991 (in UN Resolution 713).

On one hand, the United States, EU, and the Soviet Union initially attempted to sustain the status quo until a compromise could be worked out. However, there was no significant *concerted* effort upon the part of the major powers to *impel* Serbia to compromise. Germany, on the other hand, rejected the notion of compromise. On its own initiative (and in opposition to U.S. policy), Bonn recognized Slovenia and Croatia in December 1991. In effect, German political pressure ultimately led the EU to the recognition of Slovenia and Croatia, on the 15 January 1992.

The EU's overriding concern was that the secession of one state or region would cause others to follow; from this perspective, support for

Slovenian and Croatian secession would risk the widening of the war into Bosnia (which it did). It could also set a precedent for secessionist movements in the USSR (which it did), plus in Czechoslovakia (idem), if not movements in France and Spain (Corsica and the Basque region), Northern Ireland, and even northern Italy. EU states also feared that secessionist movements in Yugoslavia would also influence secessionist movements in India (Kashmir). The breakup of Yugoslavia might additionally regenerate Greek, Bulgarian, and Serbian tensions over Macedonia (the site of ethnic slaughters in the late nineteenth and early twentieth centuries); hence, Greece opposed the Slovenian and Croatian secessionist movements. Another fear was the rise of Greek, Serbian, Albanian, and Turkish disputes over Kosovo province.

U.S.-GERMAN-TURKISH-BOSNIAN LINKS

Rather than attempting to reach a settlement based on a looser confederation, as had been sought by Croatia and, to a certain extent, Bosnia, Bonn pushed for early and rapid recognition of the Yugoslav independence movements. Germany's actions raised tension within the EU as well as Moscow. Bonn argued that the United States and EU should have acted earlier to support the secessionist movements, in particular, that NATO should have backed the secession of the two states by threatening the use of force against Serbia—even though President George Bush had publicly ruled out a proposed NATO intervention on 30 November 1991. Considering that Washington was not willing to deploy ground forces and Germany itself was reluctant to engage in NATO operations (as Bonn engaged in a constitutional debate whether it could legally deploy troops outside Germany), it is doubtful whether Serbian secessionist movements regarded even the threat of limited air strikes by NATO as very credible.

German support for the independence of Slovenia and Croatia forced Bosnia into a choice of either accepting Serbian dominance or declaring independence. (The leaders of Bosnia and Macedonia had openly opposed a Yugoslav breakup, at least initially.)[6] Moreover, Bosnian calls in 1991 for the deployment of at least a thousand UN "blue helmets" as a preventive force were dismissed by an assistant to Cyrus Vance, who argued that the UN was not empowered to engage in such activity. Bosnia was then put in the absurd position of having to wait for the war to begin before it could obtain UN "protection."[7] As the war progressed, Bosnian president Alija Izetbegovic urged the EC and Turkey to resist Serbian plans to partition Bosnia between Serbian and Croatian factions, with Moslems as a buffer. On 6–7 April 1992, the EU recognized Bosnia-Herzegovina, followed by Washington.

Due to Turkey's geostrategic position (see Chapter 6), Washington

was strongly influenced by Ankara's perspective, which supported
Bosnia, Kosovo, and Albania. (The EU, however, appeared more
attuned to Greek interests). Turkey's interests in Bosnia were based on
historical, familial, and ethnic ties to Bosnian Moslems, but at the
same time, larger geostrategic and political economic interests were at
stake within areas that had once been part of the Ottoman Empire.
Partly because of its rivalry with Iran, Ankara did not want to permit
Iranian infiltration of the Bosnian resistance movement, which began
to adopt a pan-Islamic ideology despite its previously secular stance.
Washington generally regarded Turkey as a check on Iranian influence.

To prevent the war from spreading, and in deference to Turkish and
Moslem interests, President Bush warned Serbia in December 1992 that
the United States would intervene if the "civil war" spread to Kosovo.
This statement was reiterated by the Clinton administration in March
1993, and again in December 1994. Although civilian monitors were
deployed by the OSCE in Kosovo until ejected by Serbia, U.S. proposals
to deploy UN preventive forces in Kosovo (and Vojvodina) failed to
materialize, as they had been obstructed by Russia in the UN Security
Council in 1992. Turkey and Albania sought UN peacekeeping forces in
Kosovo, while Albania asked for membership in NATO. President
Izetbegovic additionally urged the UN not to lift sanctions on Serbia
until the latter formally recognized the borders of prewar Bosnia.

Thus while Bonn pushed for secession, the EU supported the concept
of a "looser" confederation but could not implement it. London had
rejected the Franco-German proposal for a WEU peacekeeping force in
September 1991, because it feared a long-term commitment worse than
what it faced in Northern Ireland. It was not until June–July 1992 that
NATO and the WEU sprang into action, at least on a limited basis—
engaging in more or less judicious military actions intended to force a
political settlement.

On the surface, NATO/WEU decisions taken in June–July 1992 to
support a naval blockade of former Yugoslavia were "complementary."
Yet France tended to push for limited intervention (including ground
troops) to protect refugees from the fighting. French actions were in
part taken as a means to counterbalance NATO initiatives and also to
assert political-military *primacy* over Germany, which, for historical
and legal reasons, was initially unable to contribute forces.
Washington and London, however, had been more reluctant to
intervene in what both saw as largely a continental affair, and fearing
that they would be dragged into a quagmire.

INITIAL FAILURE OF THE UNITED STATES

Despite the fact that the CIA had correctly predicted in late 1990
the likelihood of war, Washington largely deferred the initiative to

the EU, the UN, and the OSCE, who were themselves unable to come up with a common foreign policy to deal with the crisis. Washington was not prepared to push NATO into "out of area" operations just after the expensive, "high-tech" war in the Persian Gulf; Washington tended to regard the situation in former Yugoslavia as more akin to Vietnam. Washington determined that an operation to roll back Serbian forces in Bosnia alone would have taken as many as 300,000 soldiers, making for a long-term commitment. Moreover, President Bush was facing a tough reelection campaign.

The Bush administration therefore saw the dispute as an essentially European affair (without fully assessing its implications for two NATO allies, Greece and Turkey). President Bush and Secretary of State James Baker consequently refused to recognize the Croatian and Slovenian governments, resulting in charges of "appeasement" by domestic American critics. The Bush administration thus chose not to *initiate* a concerted strategy involving the EU and Russia that would reinforce Croatian and Slovenian proposals for a looser confederation, in compromise with Serbia.[8]

In other words, rather than seizing the initiative as it had before the Persian Gulf War, the United States was slow to take an active leadership role despite (or because of) the conflicting interests of NATO members in the region. Moreover, while not approving the EU's proposal for a "looser" confederation, Washington did not back the UN plan either. The stillborn Vance plan (December 1991) was followed by the deployment of UN "protection forces" (UNPROFOR) in February 1992. Washington thus adopted a backseat policy rather than supporting a *concerted* U.S./UN-led political-military initiative.

In June 1992, UN Secretary-General Boutros-Boutros Ghali refused to implement a UNSC decision to require Serbians to place heavy arms under UN control—because the UN did not possess sufficient resources to oversee such an operation. In August 1992, plans involving 100,000 troops to open up "relief corridors" were also rejected. Only a less expensive and much more limited "peacekeeping" option was accepted, one which involved sixteen thousand UN "blue helmets." In December 1992, the UN did deploy about 1,500 not entirely symbolic war-preventive forces (UNPREDEP) in the Former Yugoslav Republic of Macedonia to prevent the fighting from spreading there. The deployment of UNPREDEP represented an effort to delimit Serbian expansion and prevent Greek, Bulgarian, and Albanian conflict over the region. (The fact that Macedonia had initially asked Moscow to provide forces may have served as an impetus for Washington to act sooner rather than later, consequently deploying forces in Skopje in 1992.)[9] On the other hand, proposals to deploy forces in Kosovo and Vojvodina were blocked by Russia (in the interests of Belgrade).

By May 1995, UNPROFOR operations involved 43,926 troops, with 160 killed in action. The UN role (at a cost of $1.6 billion a year) was intended to be that of an "honest broker," applying strict rules of engagement designed to protect civilians and bring supplies and relief assistance. As Bosnian Serb forces continued to advance, however, UN policies tended to be regarded as pro-Serbian and incapable of containing pan-Serbian expansionism. As its engagement was largely belated, the UN had tremendous difficulty sustaining sanctions, even in areas occupied by its forces. In early 1992, as part of the UN-negotiated peace Vance-Owen plan for Croatia, UN forces were to monitor the demilitarization of paramilitary forces and to oversee the withdrawal of Croatian army and Yugoslav federal forces from the front line. Yet before UNPROFOR could fully assume the protected areas, the Yugoslav federal army began to distribute heavy weaponry to local Serbian territorial defense forces or paramilitary groups. Both Serbian and Croatian militias moved into areas left by both the Yugoslav army and Croatian army—the very areas supposedly under UN control. By late November 1992, Serbian militias had formed an independent army which pledged itself to the Republic of Serbian Krajina. Croatian forces reestablished a presence along the front line. In effect, UNPROFOR was never able to assume control, resulting in escalation of tensions, violations of cease fires, and "ethnically motivated terrorism."[10]

In January 1993, President Clinton argued that tighter sanctions needed to be placed around Serbia and that a war crimes tribunal should be set up. He also urged the Russians to become more involved in finding a negotiated settlement, but the latter were reluctant to pressure Milosevic to the extent demanded by Washington. Although the Clinton administration appeared to support it in February 1993 (after waffling), the Vance-Owen plan was ultimately opposed by the United States in the spring of 1993, for essentially three reasons. First, it appeared to legitimize Serbian gains and reward "ethnic cleansing." Secondly, it was impossible to enforce by UN peacekeepers, in part due to the fact that UN rules of engagement did not permit armed response even to clearly perceived hostile intent. Thirdly, the United States wanted NATO forces to be deployed under an American commander (SACEUR); the French (who had entered NATO's military committee officially in April 1993) wanted the entire operation under the UN.[11] (The United States did not want UN interference in its military chain of command—if it was to intervene.) The UN had been hit from two sides. On one hand, the UN was late to enter the conflict; on the other, Washington refused to support its efforts.

In effect, Serbia (seizing roughly 70 percent of Bosnian territory) and Croatia (seizing 17 percent) had by 1993 entered into a condominium agreement over Bosnia, prior to the tenuous U.S.-engineered Croatian-Bosnian "confederation" of March 1994 (the previous Croatian-Bosnian alliance of July 1992 had broken down in May 1993). Despite the U.S.-inspired "confederation," Bosnia had regarded Russia, France, and Britain as favoring Serbian and Croatian factions. Moreover, Bosnian Moslems still suspected Croatian intentions, due to the latter's control of access to the Adriatic and its claims to Bosnian territory, particularly Mostar, the "capital" of the Croatian-Bosnian state of Herceg-Bosna. Bosnia continued to press for an end to UN sanctions against obtaining its own arms.

From late 1993 to late 1994, the issue of whether to lift the UN arms embargo to former Yugoslavia as a whole and adopt a "lift and strike" policy split allied opinion and weakened the credibility of the UN. The UN embargo was only partially effective and until 1995 was largely justified as a means to limit the conflict and protect UN forces. States that were lax on controls included Albania, Macedonia, Italy, Greece, Iran, Saudi Arabia, and Hungary. Russia has been accused of permitting at least a thousand "volunteers" to supervise pan-Serbian military operations. The United States itself was accused of overlooking large Iranian shipments of small arms to Bosnia, at least from May 1994, opening the door to closer Iranian-Bosnian ties.

The UN mission was followed by the actions of the 1994 Contact Group. The latter represented a major-power grouping of the United States, Russia, Germany, Britain, and France, finally established in April 1994. It was formed, in part, to draw the Europeans into closer support for the Croatian–Bosnian Moslem Federation (sponsored by Washington), and to prevent the isolation of Russia.[12] Its plan involved the tripartite division of Bosnian territory: it granted Bosnian Serbs roughly 49 percent of former Bosnian territory and Bosnian Croat and Moslems 51 percent—assuming that Bosnian Serbs would ultimately withdraw from some 20 percent of the territory they had seized. (The emphasis was on the formation of separate "ethnic" states, as opposed to a "looser" confederation: The latter option had not been entirely rejected by Serbians in Croatia and Bosnia.) While Turkey, Croatia, and Bosnia endorsed the Contact Group plan, Bosnian Serbs rejected it, stating that it did not include a right of confederation with Serbia and Montenegro, did not provide access to the sea, or define the status of Sarajevo.

Concurrently, the embargo on Serbia appeared to be having a significant effect, and Moscow seemed to be exercising influence on Serbian policy. Prior to this, Moscow had been more concerned with its own domestic crisis than with events in former Yugoslavia. Mikhail Gorbachev had warned that the Soviet Union itself could break up as had Yugoslavia. Following the Soviet collapse, Moscow expected the

United States and Europe to show greater empathy for the Serbian perspective. Although claiming to take an "evenhanded" approach, Moscow was accused of providing overt diplomatic (and also clandestine) support to Serbia (much as Germany had been accused of covertly supporting Croatia). In reality, however, Russian policy flip-flopped between a pro-Western and pro-Serbian policy.

A more or less positive Russian diplomatic role began when UN sanctions (backed by Russia) were placed against Serbia in May 1992, in an effort to keep it from providing significant support to Bosnian Serbs. This action, however, led to attacks by factions attempting to bring down the Yeltsin government; Yeltsin then tilted back to support of the Serbian position. On 12 April 1993 the UN Security Council had postponed a vote to impose stronger sanctions on Serbia until after the 25 April Russian referendum, which would test President Yeltsin's popularity and provide him with a modicum of legitimacy. At the same time, Yeltsin urged President Clinton not to take any action against Serbia that might weaken his chances to win the referendum. Clinton, nonetheless, threatened the Bosnian Serbs two days before the Russian referendum, in response to Serbian advances. Following the Russian referendum, on April 27, Yeltsin menaced Bosnian Serbs as part of a show of support for U.S. and EU efforts. (Interestingly, Russia had agreed to tougher sanctions on Serbia at the G-7 Tokyo meeting on 14–15 April—money talks!) In May 1993, Foreign Minister Kozyrev called on the Serbian leadership to halt supplies to Bosnian Serbs and attempted to pressure the latter to accept uncontested parts of the Vance-Owen peace plan. Bosnian Serbs, however, rejected it. Bosnian Croats went on an offensive against Moslems in areas of Bosnia, such as Mostar, claimed by Croatians. Concurrently, in September 1993, the Bosnian parliament refused the proposed peace accord.

Moscow realized that it was not in Russian interests to permit a more generalized conflict, but its efforts were stymied. Foreign Ministry proposals to engage large numbers of UN troops in Bosnia, for example, had been blocked by very strong parliamentary opposition and by the Russian Security Council and Ministry of Defense. Much like his American counterparts, who opposed a "Vietnam-like" situation, former defense minister General Pavel Grachev called UN intervention a "second Afghanistan."[13] Accordingly, Moscow was capable of only a symbolic deployment, a battalion of airborne troops to Sarajevo in February 1994 (reluctantly accepted by Bosnia) in an effort to counterbalance Western and Serbian interests and to show its support for UN efforts.

In August 1994, Russian influence helped to gain Serbian leader Milosevic's acceptance of the Contact Group's latest peace endeavor. In 14 September, Serbia accepted international monitors on its borders to oversee the enforcement of the blockade on Bosnian Serbs. The Contact Group promised to suspend *selectively* sanctions that had been placed on Serbia in 1992. Serbia had hoped to end the sanctions; otherwise it would face another round of hyperinflation. Belgrade wanted a permanent lifting of the sanctions, access to foreign credits, and as much oil and fuel as possible. To meet Belgrade's demands, however, would be tantamount to "appeasing" the aggressor, from the viewpoint of the American Congress.

The victory of the Republican Party in the November 1994 American congressional elections threatened a crisis among the UN, EU, NATO, and Russia.[14] Despite his own campaign promises to engage in a "lift and strike" strategy, President Clinton had rather ironically engaged in policies similar to those of President Bush. The Bush administration had originally supported the overall embargo (arguing that the situation would otherwise get worse) but then shifted its position under heavy criticism from candidate Bill Clinton; the latter accused Bush of not supporting Slovenian, Croatian, and Bosnian "yearnings" for freedom. Once in power, however, President Clinton attempted to hold the UN embargo in place, against congressional demands to lift it. Senator Robert Dole, in turn, twisted President Clinton's own campaign promises against him, to demand anew a "lift and strike" policy.[15] As Republican (and Democratic) pressure on Clinton grew, Washington threatened to lift the arms embargo. The Administration stalled but then declared that it would no longer provide ships and aerial reconnaissance planes to enforce the arms embargo, on Bosnia in particular.

The turning point in the war came when tensions between the UN (plus the UK and France) and NATO (the United States plus Germany) became increasingly evident. At this point, the United States began to demand an end to the "dual key" approach, by which any military decision had to be accepted by both the UN and the NATO staff. In general, the UK and France opposed U.S. and German proposals to remove the UN total embargo on Bosnia as an action that would widen the war. Both London and Paris attempted to prevent Washington from ending the embargo before November 1994. The UK and France opposed most air raids, because of the fear that their UN "blue helmets" would be taken hostage or used as shields (as they were). France in particular accused the United States of encouraging the Bosnians (to the detriment of peace efforts with Serbia); it generally accused Russia of playing the role of agent for the Serbians and attempting to disrupt efforts by both the UN and WEU. While the United States sought an interventionist stance involving air attacks, the UN commander, General Sir Michael Rose (supported by British and French policy), opted for cautious mediation with Serbian leader Radovan Karadzic, at a time when Bosnian Serbs were about to take over the Bihac "safe area." The United States demanded NATO air strikes to help thwart the Serbian seizure of Bihac (which had been besieged for thirty months). General Rose, however, refused to identify the appropriate targets, thus halting strikes.

Although the Clinton administration publicly supported the British, French, and UN position (and appeared to offer concessions to the Bosnian Serbs), it now secretly began to aid the Croatian and Bosnian Moslem militaries. In November 1994 Washington gave indirect support to Croatia (through a private "consultancy") and organized air drops of weapons and military equipment to the Bosnian Army in Tuzla, in breach of the embargo.[16] Concurrently, Washington cut off satellite intelligence on ship movements in the Adriatic to its own allies, Britain and France.[17] On 11 November Senator Dole stated that the "UN should get off NATO's back" and on 27 November argued that the UN had helped the "Serbian aggressor" by not identifying targets for NATO to bomb (on 25–26 November).[18] The rift widened between the United States and UN, while tensions among the Western allies continued to steam. In general, Britain and France were more willing to make concessions to Serbia than was the United States. The Americans and EU, however, both insisted against Russia that sanctions should be lifted on Serbia only after Belgrade formally recognized Bosnia, Croatia, and the other former Yugoslav republics.

Washington's policy accordingly risked alienating Moscow. Foreign Minister Kozyrev opposed U.S. and EU demands that Serbia recognize the states of Croatia and Bosnia *prior* to the abolition of UN sanctions. In February 1994, Russia had opposed unilateral NATO air strikes, not authorized by the UN. Moscow did support the UN mandated "no-fly zone," but it warned that it would not remain in the Partnership for Peace (PfP) if NATO took action without Moscow's input. In essence, Moscow argued that threats of NATO intervention led to Bosnian intransigence at the negotiating table and new rounds of Serbian-Bosnian imprecations. Consequently, in December 1994 Moscow used its veto in the UN Security Council (for the first time since the breakup of the Soviet Union) to block UN sanctions on Serbia.

THE BREAKDOWN OF THE CARTER CEASE-FIRE

Until 31 May 1995, the Contact Group had hoped to draw Russia into stronger efforts to block pan-Serbian expansion, even in areas such as Kosovo and Vojvodina. The Contact Group attempted to convince Serbia to close its borders with Bosnian Serbs, but there remained a considerable number of holes. The original plan was to give Bosnian Serbs 49 percent of former Bosnian territory. Serbian leader Milosevic tentatively accepted, but Bosnian Serbs, who controlled 70 percent of Bosnian territory, rejected the offer.

Accordingly, by late 1994 and 1995, as Croatia began to demand the total withdrawal of UN forces in Croatia, former president Jimmy Carter was able to bargain a cease-fire in December 1994, which (generally) held until 1 May 1995. The Carter plan, however, was denounced as a "fig leaf" to cover key concessions to the Bosnian Serbs, which included the possible establishment of a confederation between Bosnian Serbs, and Serbia proper. The "peace" itself was also satirized as a "seasonal truce" that would not last past the winter. Bosnian Serb leader Radovan Karadzic opposed the Contact Group's plan. He demanded (1) that Bosnian Serbs obtain defensible natural borders; (2) that there be an equal distribution of natural resources and infrastructure between the Bosnian-Serb and Moslem-Croatian sectors; and (3) that Bosnia be provided access to the sea.

In the meantime, domestic pressure pushed the Croatian government to regain lands taken by Serbia and renounce the truce negotiated by Jimmy Carter. Even though the UN provided Croatia as much as $250 million annually for its economy (including support for tourism), the UN was increasingly regarded as merely appeasing pan-Serbian advances. At same time, the United States (despite congressional criticism) and Europe attempted to coordinate a policy to keep UN troops in place—until Croatia demanded their removal, by 1 May 1995.

In response, NATO developed contingency plans to deploy Alliance forces (involving German soldiers) as part of a rescue mission for UN forces, if UN forces were taken as hostage—a possibility that had been clearly foreseen for at least two years. In May 1995, a minor Croatian victory in western Slavonia was met by Serbian cluster-bomb attacks in Zagreb, nearly striking the American embassy. Bosnia also refused to extend the truce in April 1995; both sides hoped to roll back pan-Serbian gains by means of a two front war, encouraged by the promise of a lifting of the embargo. The UN attempted to negotiate a cease-fire to prevent a wider war, but Croatia refused to withdraw its forces from western Slavonia.

Accordingly, in May 1995, following the breakdown of the cease-fire arranged by Jimmy Carter, Bosnian Serbs took approximately 350 UN "blue helmets" as hostages, as a tactic to pressure NATO into halting its air strikes. Bosnian Serbs also shot down a U.S. F-16 over a "no-fly zone"—once again in an effort to humiliate NATO and the UN. UN operations had proven to be a disaster: heavy weapons remained in the exclusion zone, and air strikes were impossible as long as "blue helmets" were being held hostage. If UN forces were removed, it was feared that Sarajevo itself would fall. In July, Bosnian Serbs were able to seize the so-called UN "safe areas" of Srebrenica and Zepa.

Moscow indicated that it wanted to play a key role in the release of UN "blue helmets" taken hostage by Bosnian Serbs. While condemning the hostage-taking, both Slobodan Milosevic and Boris Yeltsin (despite his own brutal actions in Chechnya) hoped to make political capital out of their efforts to help release UN forces taken hostage. These actions were taken as a means to gain international recognition for Russia as a "peacemaker" and put an end to sanctions placed against Serbia—even if it meant some sacrifice of pan-Serbian goals.

Although they had initially threatened to pull out UN forces, Britain and France now called for the implementation of a ten-thousand-man rapid response force under UN control, to be deployed in August 1995. (Such a force was opposed by Yeltsin unless it was placed under UN control.) Concurrently, Washington angered allies by initially appearing to support the deployment of ground troops as part of the UN rapid response force but then by vacillating on exactly how many troops—if any—it would deploy to help save UN "blue helmets." (These flip-flops were in part due to President Clinton's lack of consultation with Congress as to the nature and full cost of the proposed operation.)[19]

In effect, the belatedly deployed "blue helmets" were unable to fill their intended role of "honest broker." Rather, they served as a temporary, yet porous, buffer which ultimately permitted the rebuilding of military capabilities on all sides. The fact that Serbian regular forces were involved in Bosnia until May 1995 indicated that the only way to deal with the Serbians was to tear up the UN mandate.

TOWARD DAYTON

In April 1995, further evidence of Slobodan Milosevic's direct support for "ethnic cleansing" and "war crimes" (in addition to those of the Bosnian Serb leader, Radovan Karadzic) surfaced, at nearly the same time that the Contact Group looked to Milosevic to recognize Bosnia-Herzegovina and Croatia as a step toward the mutual recognition of all the newly independent states of the former Yugoslavia. Previous reports of concentration camps in western Bosnia, "ethnic cleansing," and other atrocities had been publicized since at least December 1992. At that time, former U.S. Secretary of State Lawrence Eagleburger had publicly accused certain Serbian leaders of being war criminals. Serbian pan-nationalists in turn counter-propagandized against Eagleburger's role in the Vietnam War.

The Serbians—who were accused of committing up to 90 percent of all the offenses—continued their propaganda campaign against the never-forgotten war crimes of the Croatian *Ustasche* during World

War II and counter-accused Croatia of human rights violations in attacks on Serbian enclaves near the Adriatic coast in 1993. Bosnian Moslems in turn accused Croatia of human rights violations during attacks in Mostar. After the war, the image of presumed Bosnian innocence was put in question by the discovery in February 1996 inside what the Bosnian government described as a counter-terrorist training camp of Soviet-style booby traps set in children's toys and shampoo bottles, plus documents and military personnel linked to Iran.[20]

On 25 January 1995, the French foreign minister, Alain Juppé, warned that Washington would cause a "catastrophe" if it did not bolster EU and Russian pressure on all the warring parties to end the dispute. Juppé's call for a summit meeting in Paris of the leaders of Bosnia, Croatia, and Serbia was intended to preclude a new round of fighting that might force the withdrawal of UN peacekeeping forces; but the meeting failed to materialize, largely due to American opposition. A State Department spokesperson, Michael McCurry, countered that "forcing a settlement on the aggrieved parties [Moslem Bosnians] requires a very strange moral calculus." Moreover, Juppé's call went unheeded because the three parties were girding for war in May 1995, and the United States was supporting Croatian and Bosnian efforts by covertly lifting the arms embargo.

Western impotence as a result of the UN hostage crisis permitted the fall of Srebrenica in July 1995. It was reported that UN forces had failed to stop the seizure of Srebrenica. The French president, Jacques Chirac, reportedly ordered General Bernard Javier to cease air strikes in return for the freeing of hostages—a charge denied by Paris.[21] (Later in July 1996, Admiral Leighton Smith, U.S. Navy, called Srebrenica a "tactical victory" for Bosnian Serbs but a "strategic defeat," in that it "galvanized the international community into laying out clear guidelines, which, if violated, would bring NATO Air Strikes at a level not previously contemplated.")[22]

Confronted with a dangerous option involving the retreat of UN forces in the face of renewed combat, the United States engaged itself diplomatically. Washington stole the initiative away from Paris, but only after the Croatian and Bosnian alliance had regained some 20 percent of Bosnian territory by force. Now a cease-fire could be established: "greater Serbian" aspirations were on the retreat, and Belgrade was willing to negotiate. By August, NATO had obtained clear rules of engagement and guidelines for the use of force *on its terms*. From 28 August to 14 September 1995, NATO's Operation "Deliberate Force" began air operations that ultimately helped bring Serbia (backing the Bosnian Serbs) to the negotiating table—despite Bosnian Serb accusations that their leader Milosevic had sold out.

However, NATO airstrikes against Bosnian Serb positions angered

Moscow, which had hoped to influence Belgrade and the Bosnian Serb leadership to accept a peace settlement. In mid-April 1995, the duma urged President Yeltsin to "take decisive measures" to end sanctions against Serbia. (A secret Russian-Serbian agreement was rumored to have been signed in the early spring 1995.) Following the September 1995 use of Tomahawk cruise missiles against Bosnian Serb positions, the duma made a nonbinding demand to suspend the NATO-Russian Individual Partnership agreement signed in May 1995. As Yeltsin put it, NATO strikes on Bosnia were "only the first sign . . . [that] NATO's enlargement" could "reconstitute the two military blocs."[23] The concern for Russia was not related merely to support for Serbia but also to perceptions that NATO military infrastructure was pressing closer to historical Russian spheres of influence and security. NATO's use of Hungarian air space and territory was another issue of concern. Alliance actions represented a calculated risk that NATO could, on one hand, pressure the Bosnian Serb leadership to the negotiating table, and, on the other, sustain cooperation between NATO and Russia.

Russian policy likewise represented a balance of priorities. On the one hand, Moscow had to fend off domestic, pan-Slav, "national-patriot" criticism that had fervently denounced the "democratic" leadership for not standing up for fellow Slavs. Calling for the establishment of "Slavic committees" similar to those set up to support Serbia in the nineteenth century, pan-Slav propagandists argued that Germany, the Vatican, and wealthy Islamic states had worked together to support Croatia and Bosnia against Serbia. If Serbia collapsed, so would Orthodox Russia, Belarus, and Ukraine.[24] On the other hand, Moscow was concerned not only with domestic criticism of its policies but also with the policy of CIS members. Russia's Slavic rival, Ukraine, tended to support Croatia and not Serbia. Moscow also needed to take into account the views of its Moslem populations, which represent between twelve and twenty million people within the Russian Federation, plus those of the predominantly Moslem republics in the CIS. Finally, a wider war was not in Moscow's own interest.

Thus, following the efforts of the Contact Group, Washington engaged in the "armed escort" diplomacy of Assistant Secretary of State Richard C. Holbrooke (and assistants, who died when their vehicle slipped off the roadside). These diplomatic actions were backed by the generally judicious use of force (Operation "Deliberate Strike"). These concerted actions resulted in the Dayton Accords, agreed to 21 November 1995. (Congressional support was uncertain, however; the decisive House and Senate ratification took place only after heated debate and after Bill Clinton had already left Washington for the final signing in Paris in December.)[25]

Each of the antagonists had a different motivation for accepting the peace. The Bosnians realized that it was the best deal they could get, given the stronger Serbian military position; at the same time, they were promised substantial military and economic assistance, and a promise that IFOR would monitor Bosnian Serb actions. The Serbian side saw that the agreement would prevent an even greater loss of territory than suffered in the Bosnian and Croatian offensives in 1995. Serbian leader Milosevic also hoped to put an end to sanctions placed on Serbia, as well as deflect the blame for war crimes onto the Bosnian Serb leadership. Concurrently, the Croatian leader, Franjo Tudjman, realized the agreement would permit Croatia to hold onto close to 25 percent of Bosnian territory (as opposed to 17 percent) and that political-economic benefits could be gained from aligning with Bosnia, including the possibility of integration into the EU. Indeed, Croatia would obtain primacy, if not hegemony, over Bosnia.[26]

THE DAYTON AGREEMENT AND AFTER

Following the November–December 1995 Dayton agreement to settle the war, Russia was very reluctant to offer much assistance without greater financial and political compensation from Washington. Moscow's proposal to put NATO forces under UN command had been refused by Washington. Russia was additionally not permitted to form a fully conjoint NATO-Russian command, ostensibly because Moscow refused to commit significant forces and funds. A "compromise" was finally reached in which Russian peacekeepers would serve as a "special operations unit" under the First Armored Division of the U.S. Army, but not under NATO command. (Ironically, Russian forces were under the command of General George Joulwan, who was both top commander of all U.S. forces in Europe and NATO supreme commander!) All decisions involving Russian forces were to be taken with consent of the latter, as well as the Russian ministry of defense. Russian and American forces were to be deployed in the strategic Posavina corridor, where all three Bosnian parties met. (Interestingly, a Ukrainian battalion was placed under French command, not NATO.)

The issue of NATO enlargement (in addition to its relationship with Serbia) strongly influenced Russian policy; Moscow threatened to quit Bosnia altogether if NATO opted for enlargement in 1996.[27] At the same time, new hopes for a stronger U.S.-Russian relationship were expressed. Meeting then defense minister Pavel Grachev, NATO commander General George Joulwan, U.S. Army, stated on 7 February 1996 that "cooperation between U.S. and Russian troops in Bosnia can create a new relationship between NATO and Russia."[28]

The NATO Implementation Force (mandated by UNSC Resolution 1031) did not altogether marginalize the UN, in that a civilian commission was created and given wide powers, but it had few resources to carry out its mission. The High Representative was to meet with a steering board consisting of the EU presidency, the European Commission, the Organization of Islamic Conference, and the Political Eight (the Group of Seven plus Russia), which in turn was to report to a Peace Implementation Council. The UN was not on the steering board, and actions of the High Representative could be overturned by a majority vote of the UN Security Council. The High Representative (and indirectly, the UN) had absolutely no authority over the military operation, nor could he interfere in the chain of command. An obvious problem accordingly arose in the definition of "military" and "political" issues: Should war crimes be part of the military mandate, and if so, how should alleged war criminals be apprehended, and to what extent should the perpetrators be prosecuted?

IFOR was largely successful in removing heavy weapons, preventing military activity, forcing hostile forces to withdraw from zones of separation but it had difficulties (if not a general reluctance) in implementing key aspects of the Dayton agreement involving: (1) a guarantee of freedom of movement; (2) the right of refugees to return to their homes; and (3) the arrest of indicted "war criminals." For example, IFOR had not been able or willing to stop the plundering of villages to be transferred to the other side. IFOR authorities responded to such accusations by stating that it is not a "police force" or a "fire department," nor will it organize "posses." IFOR did augment its military presence in regions where tensions were highest, through expanded checkpoints. It surrounded the home of Bosnian Serb leader Karadzic with military vehicles to increase the "psychological campaign" against him and others indicted for war crimes.

While the international community has sought the arrest and trial of Radovan Karadzic and Ratko Mladic as indicted war criminals, Washington has maintained that Serbian President Milosevic—and not IFOR—is responsible for their arrest. In the meantime, since Milosevic has claimed that he cannot force Karadzic to resign, Washington has argued that it is best to "neutralize" Karadzic politically. Such an effort was undertaken by Holbrooke in August 1996, but it was initially opposed by Moscow.

Most revealingly, the United States itself refused to allow IFOR into Eastern Slavonia. Washington insisted (against the views of UN Secretary-General Boutros-Boutros Ghali) that the UN should cope with this dangerous area by deploying UNTAES (The UN Transitional Authority in Eastern Slavonia), ostensibly because IFOR forces were overextended in Bosnia and the WEU (except for Belgium) did not agree to deploy forces in that region. A more likely explanation, however, was that Washington (and the EU/WEU) opposed a NATO presence in this region, in deference to Russia and Serbia. (At the same time, however, UNTAES was put under an American command.) This oil-rich region could eventually spark a new round of conflict.

Just as the issue of Eastern Slavonia had not entirely been settled, neither had that of Mostar. Tensions between Croatians and Moslems have been manifest in Mostar, Sarajevo, and Central Bosnia. If the Moslem-Croatian "federation" breaks down, efforts by Moslems to retake territory held by Croatians cannot entirely be ruled out, once Bosnian Moslems have rebuilt their forces. An increasingly isolated Bosnian Serb republic is also subject to Moslem or Croatian attack. On the one hand, Washington has been concerned with the continued presence of Islamic mujahedeen on Bosnian territory, as well as with Bosnian links to Iran. On the other hand, the United States has insisted upon a $700–800 million military assistance plan to bring the Bosnian Moslem-Croatian alliance to "parity" with Bosnian Serbs (and to keep the alliance intact). The United States wanted to a achieve a rough military balance on the ground once IFOR forces withdrew. On 18 June 1996, the arms embargo on former Yugoslavia was ended; a 5:2:2 ratio of Serbian to Croatian and Bosnian military capabilities was to be established. France and the EU, however, argued that "stability and reconstruction" should be the first priorities, not "rearmament."[29]

Bosnian Moslems, Croatians, and Serbians could still appeal to international backers. The Pentagon itself has argued that the strategic goals of each of the warring factions have not changed significantly and that tensions could grow in the months before a NATO pullout.[30] As of April 1996, the United States had shouldered an estimated $2.5 billion of the $6–7 billion total cost of the IFOR mission. Washington began to pull U.S. forces out of Bosnia in June, in accord with President Clinton's promises (complete withdrawal had been scheduled for February 1997). European leaders threatened to pull out their forces, if those of the United States departed. In September 1996, however, Washington began to deploy a smaller force for Bosnia to cover the IFOR withdrawal of sixty thousand troops. By 19–20 December 1996, NATO established the Stabilization Force of between twenty–five to thirty thousand troops, of which five thousand were American. SFOR was to remain for eighteen months. According to Defense Secretary William Cohen, U.S. soldiers were to leave Bosnia "for good" in mid-1998, raising the question whether the WEU or UN (if either) would take over peacekeeping duties, assuming the situation would not stabilize before that time.[31]

Moreover, the Dayton agreement tended to set unrealistic deadlines for reconstruction. There appeared to be no clear philosophy of what was to be done. The fact that there were no real steps being taken to help re-integrate Bosnia into a larger regional economy highlighted the danger of partition. This possibility was also illustrated by the fact that OSCE election rules appeared to legitimize the results of ethnic cleansing rather than promote a multiethnic Bosnia.[32]

Irenic and preventive diplomacy involving an interlocking interaction between the UN, the OSCE, and NATO/WEU forces could ultimately help bring peace to the region—assuming the United States and EU remain engaged and Russia remains on board. Not-so-ironically, Serbia has appeared interested in the PfP initiative (as proposed by the Serbian New Democracy Party, with close ties to the ruling Socialist Party); ultimate Serbian membership in the PfP could be linked to the amelioration of Serbian policies in Kosovo, Sandjak, and Vojvodina. A close NATO-Slovenian relationship could also help sustain psychological-military pressure in the region, so as to make the regional actors think twice about waging war (but assuming a NATO presence does not lead Serbia to fully align with Russia).

On the other hand, conflict could break out in Kosovo, Macedonia, or Vojvodina. Secretary of State Warren Christopher warned that Serbia would never be fully accepted by the international community "until it reconciles the status of Kosovo."[33] Serbian defeat has led democratic and pan-nationalist opposition to intensify against Milosevic and the ruling Socialist party, particularly once the leadership refused to accept the results of municipal elections, leading to significant protest in Belgrade from November 1996 to February 1997. (There are some 200,000 anti–nationalist Serbians in the Serbian Republic.) Milosevic, however, has attempted to deflect popular Serbian attention away from his socialist leadership and toward the situation in Kosovo. Serbian-Albanian tensions in Kosovo, coupled with political-economic instability and full-fledged insurrection in neighboring Albania in early 1997, following the collapse of several "pyramid" financial schemes, do not augur well for stability. Conflict in Albania may further exacerbate tensions between Greece and Turkey.

In summary, the December 1995 Dayton Accord did finally achieve a negotiated truce among the rival former-Yugoslav factions. But will this agreement be able to sustain the peace in the long term, given mutual recriminations and accusations of "war crimes"? For example, can a looser all-Yugoslav confederation (without Slovenia) be created—ironically, similar to what was proposed by the EU before the war began? Or will former Yugoslavia be carved into perpetually hostile camps, each backed by regional and major powers? Will SFOR engagement achieve peace, or will it undermine NATO's credibility, particularly if U.S. forces are removed "for good" in mid-1998 too soon to achieve a permanent settlement, or if war explodes in a neighboring region?

CHAPTER 9

A Critique of Three Approaches to NATO Enlargement

APPROACHES TO EUROPEAN SECURITY

In essence, three very different proposals for a new system of security for the Central and Eastern European countries have been outlined since the collapse of the Soviet bloc. A fourth option—that of cooperative-collective security—has been given less attention than it deserves but is not excluded by the September 1995 *Study on NATO Enlargement.*

Each of these approaches to Central and Eastern European security raises five basic issues of concern: (1) NATO's integrated military command and its ability to cope with new members and sustain a political consensus; (2) the Russian response to NATO "expansion," which in turn involves the extent of Russian participation in decisions that affect its perceived "vital" interests; (3) the precise *security assurances* or *security guarantees* to be granted to Central and Eastern European states, and the possible negative reaction of states that do not obtain some form of assurance or guarantee as "associate" or "full" NATO members; (4) the relationship of NATO and the proposed Atlantic Partnership Council to the UN and the OSCE, as well as to the EU and the WEU; and (5) U.S. congressional reaction to any security commitment promised, as well as to the costs of any proposed system of European security. Also at stake is the question of whether any proposed system of security involving NATO will require a revision of the North Atlantic Treaty (thus needing a two–thirds majority vote in the Senate), or can be dealt with as an *extension* of NATO security guarantees, which can be approved by simple majority vote in each house of Congress.

This chapter will essentially argue four main points. First of all, the "NATO maximalist" approach risks alienating not only both Russia and Belarus but also such states as Ukraine, which would not initially be granted "full" NATO membership. Secondly, the "WEU-first" approach is likely to aggravate U.S.-EU/WEU-Russian relations, particularly if an expanding EU/WEU is regarded by Moscow as absorbing former Soviet (or czarist Russian) spheres of influence and security; in addition, relations will be further exacerbated if NATO and a relatively independent EU/WEU cannot agree on which states should be defended. Thirdly, the NATO "self-limitation" approach (like the maximalist approach) risks a hypertrophy or overextension of Alliance resources and capabilities. Moreover, even the proposed NATO-Russian Charter may not allay Russian suspicions of "encirclement," nor will joint NATO-Russian "security assurances" (by themselves) necessarily mitigate Central and Eastern European fears about Russian intentions. The very process of bringing states into NATO could prove provocative and destabilizing if not thoroughly and carefully negotiated with Moscow. The fourth alternative of "cooperative-collective security" is to be discussed in Chapters 10 and 11; it envisions a militarily-integrated Euro-Atlantic Defense and Security Identity linked to regional self-defense forces, under the political mandate of the UN or the OSCE, and ultimately backed by conjoint NATO, WEU, and Russian *security guarantees*.

THE MAXIMALIST APPROACH

NATO maximalists argue for a rapid expansion of membership to as many states as is feasible but generally regard the defense of the Central European theater (Poland and the Czech Republic, plus Hungary and Slovakia for geostrategic reasons) as the most crucial. A more assertive "neo-containment" faction has pushed for Baltic and Ukrainian membership in NATO. "Full" membership is regarded as the best force for regional stabilization as well as for the "export" of stability to non-NATO members. The adoption of new Alliance members is additionally regarded as a means to preserve newly emerging democracies, protect international investment, and continue progress toward market liberalism in the newly liberated Soviet-bloc states, and toward the "democratization" of civil-military relations for prospective NATO members. Membership is also regarded as the best way to protect Central European states from Russian pressures.

Moreover, NATO enlargement into Central Europe would not only help to create a "buffer" between Germany and the potential for eastern instability but would work to preserve U.S. hegemony over an expanding EU/WEU, as well as over a unified Germany. NATO maximalists fear that Bonn might move toward political-military (and nuclear) independence, or else toward a separate German-Russian pact, if Central Europe is not solidly integrated into the American-led Atlantic Alliance. This approach accordingly argues that Washington must sustain its leadership within the Alliance. It has generally resisted efforts to "Europeanize" NATO through CJTF and ESDI.

The maximalist approach argues that NATO should not "dally." Moscow, in this view, will respect Western resolve and accept compromise only if decisiveness is shown. The West should cooperate with Russia, but it should do so on the basis of toughness and Western interests. (For example, the option to deploy nuclear weapons and foreign forces should be kept "open.") NATO maximalists believe that a decisive enlargement into Central Europe will ultimately attract both Ukraine and Russia toward a stronger NATO; firmness will also bolster the security of the Baltic states, even if the latter do not become full members.[1] In effect, this view holds that Moscow will ultimately see that it is in its own interest to accept enlargement—even into areas of former Soviet and czarist spheres of influence and security.

THE "WEU-FIRST" APPROACH

The WEU-first school proposes what former Senator Sam Nunn has called an "evolutionary" approach to European security. It argues that states in Central and Eastern Europe should first become members of the EU and then the WEU before becoming members of NATO. As a non-isolationist alternative to NATO enlargement, the WEU-first approach has proposed EU, and then full WEU, membership for Poland, the Czech Republic, and Hungary. Once these countries join the WEU, NATO could extend then *security guarantees* to them. These states would thus obtain conjoint NATO-WEU guarantees but not "full" NATO membership. The Baltic–Adriatic belt of states, for example, which do not qualify for WEU membership, could be made subjects of *security assurances* similar to the conjoint U.S. and Russian *assurances* granted a non-nuclear Ukraine in the trilateral agreement of January 1994. Alternatively, Baltic states could obtain full WEU membership.[2]

The non-isolationist, "evolutionary" WEU-first approach is particularly concerned with the possible overextension of the integrated NATO military command. It believes that a crisis within the Atlantic Alliance could arise if NATO cannot reach a political consensus after it expands. It argues that NATO enlargement may well be in the national interests of Central European states but that it is not necessarily in the national interest of the United States, particularly if enlargement results in a revanchist Russian backlash. The WEU-first approach argues that NATO can assist the enlargement of the EU/WEU by permitting lend-lease of key NATO assets for selected missions, and by permitting the formation of Combined Joint Task Forces involving NATO, WEU, and non-NATO members, such as Russia and Ukraine. The WEU-first approach also addresses the domestic political consequences of NATO enlargement; NATO's very legitimacy would be in question if the American Senate (for whatever reason) refused to accept new Central European states as "full" members.

A non-evolutionary (if not shock-oriented) variant of this strategy argues that Washington should, in effect, threaten "isolationism" so as to impel the EU and WEU to strengthen their defense capabilities. The EU would then be in a position to provide security guarantees for new EU/WEU members. Over time, the United States and European Union could develop a more equitable transatlantic political and defense relationship, by forming a U.S.-EU "security coordination council."[3] NATO as an American-led alliance could ultimately wither away.

THE NATO SELF-LIMITATION APPROACH

The NATO self-limitation approach argues that the Alliance can expand into Central Europe without provoking Russia, creating a new Iron Curtain, or isolating those states not included, but only if it simultaneously extends "bridges" to those states not immediately drawn into NATO.[4] The "self-limitation" approach accordingly seeks to grant Russia special rights (but within limits) and argues that a separate treaty forming a "standing consultative committee" with Russia and Ukraine as members can be established to give Russia greater rights of participation in European security issues. It argues that an open treaty, such as the "NATO-Russian Charter" proposed by Warren Christopher in September 1996, would allay Russian fears. Such a Charter would, for example, specify the conditions for the forward deployment of nuclear weapons. (This would place restrictions like Norway's unilaterally imposed non-nuclear status, or the "two-plus-four" agreement not to deploy nuclear weapons or foreign troops into eastern Germany. Another possibility would be to deploy NATO forces a fixed distance from the eastern border of Poland, as has been suggested by Henry Kissinger.) Such a Charter could go a long way to mitigating the fears of not only Russia but also Ukraine, Romania, and other states in the region. Expanding NATO membership should be accompanied by continued U.S.-Russian cooperation on conventional arms, such as the CFE treaty, as well as by the strengthening of UN, OSCE, and EU/WEU mechanisms for guaranteeing peace.

The NATO self-limitation approach argues that once applicants fulfill the conditions for membership, they should join the political structure of NATO as a participant in the North Atlantic Council but not its military structures. (This approach thus parallels the initial

Spanish model; states could join the military structures of the Alliance at a later date, if a threat should arise.) This approach argues against the proposition that Alliance cohesion and decision-making would be impaired by enlargement, particularly since NATO has been moving toward more flexible arrangements involving the ESDI and CJTF. It thus welcomes tendencies that permit Europeans (and Germany) greater "power" and "responsibility." In addition, NATO membership can help to head off "re-nationalization" tendencies, in which Central and Eastern European states re-militarize or else attempt to forge new, potentially destabilizing alliances. Likewise, "democratization" and resolution of minority and ethnic tensions are best done within, and not outside, the Alliance. NATO enlargement would furthermore permit certain Central European countries to help "export stability" to non-NATO members. Finally, the NATO self-limitation approach argues that it is better for the Alliance to expand gradually, but decisively, and in a no-crisis environment: "Precipitous enlargement of the Alliance in a crisis situation could have a potentially disastrous escalatory effect on that crisis."[5]

In general, American proponents of the self-limitation option seek joint agreements with both Russia and Ukraine, and support Poland, the Czech Republic, and Hungary as future "full" members of NATO. France has given strong support to Romania as well; Italy has advocated the addition of Slovenia (and may back Romania). A case can be made that states not previously in Soviet or czarist spheres of influence and security, such as Sweden and Austria, could enter as "full" members under specific conditions. (See following discussion.)

CRITIQUE OF THE NATO MAXIMALISM

NATO maximalists seek a provocative extension of NATO and American influence into a region of the world in which the United States has had only negligible historical experience. NATO enlargement risks drawing the United States into a cauldron of Central and Eastern European disputes, at the same time that it risks exacerbation of Russian political-economic instability, at a minimum, or the breakup of the Russian Federation, or even a Russian revanchist backlash. NATO enlargement (either of the "maximalist" or "self-limitation" varieties) cannot be regarded as a "quick fix" for either internal or external squabbles. Enlargement risks dragging the Atlantic Alliance into disputes that it is not equipped to handle and without the "overarching requirement for unity" it possessed during the Cold War.[6] Moreover, should NATO expand, it should recognize that its very enlargement could provoke shifts in government leaderships and power relationships that could well bring to the forefront irredentist claims or territorial disputes that were previously and officially downplayed. Concurrently, any NATO enlargement must take into consideration the fact that Russian pressures on the "near" and "middle" abroad may not be related to the Russian ethnic diaspora alone but also to such geostrategic, political-economic, and military-technological security concerns as access to markets (including arms sales), warm-water ports, and transit rights to Kaliningrad.

The more moderate breed of NATO maximalist suggests that only Poland, the Czech Republic, and Hungary should join as "full" members as soon as possible. Other states, such as Romania and Slovenia, should wait for the second round of membership talks. The problem, however, is that NATO enlargement into Poland would, in effect, make NATO responsible for Lithuanian security, as well as for that of the other two Baltic states. The de facto enlargement of NATO security guarantees would result from close Polish-Lithuanian defense cooperation, linked in turn to close defense cooperation among the three Baltic states. In effect, an attack by Russia or Belarus on Lithuania would represent an attack on Poland, once it becomes a new NATO member. NATO would be obliged to respond. A crisis, for example, could arise if Lithuania denied Russia transit rights to Kaliningrad because of truly legitimate Lithuanian concerns (the transport of illicit materials, etc.)

Most crucially, prospective NATO enlargement into Central Europe alone may create a backlash in such states as Belarus, Slovakia, Romania, and Ukraine, in addition to the Russian Federation. Slovakia could well become a thorn in the defenses of Poland, the Czech Republic, and Hungary, threatening to break the lines of communication between these states. (Ironically, although not generally proposed by NATO maximalists, Swedish and Austrian membership in NATO is even more crucial to lines of communication with the northeastern and southeastern flanks.)

NATO enlargement to fill the strategic "vacuum" in Central Europe has often been justified by the dubious argument that Belarus and Ukraine represent "buffer" states between NATO and Russia. In addition to the obvious fact that Poland and Russia possess a common border with Kaliningrad, neither Belarus nor Ukraine represent stable "buffers." Their potential instability is only partially due to the so-called "civilization fault-line" that divides Belarus and Ukraine into Catholic and Orthodox regions.[7] The more fundamental issue is the question of historical irredentist claims among these states, claims that are accentuated by political-economic instability as well as by the NATO-EU/WEU-Russian rivalry.

From this perspective, the neo-containment NATO maximalists appear blind to the real dangers of overextension to defend the Russian-Ukrainian border (among other areas of possible disputes) should membership be extended to Ukraine. Even if Ukraine did not become a "full" NATO member, the fact that Warsaw has forged a Polish-Ukrainian "strategic partnership" could drag NATO into a crisis. A crisis scenario could unfold where an unstable Ukraine represents the pivotal state. On the one hand, should Ukraine swing too close to NATO or the EU/WEU (or to the PRC) without a counterbalancing NATO-Russian entente, such an action may be perceived by Moscow as a new form of "encirclement." This would be true if Russia cannot pressure Ukraine and the other CIS states into a "Eurasian" alliance with Beijing. On the other, imposition of Russian hegemony over Ukraine may be perceived as a new threat to Europe, particularly if Russia should deploy troops along the Polish-Ukrainian border. Concurrently, Ukraine is a candidate for disaggregation, a possibility which is potentially exacerbated by Polish, Hungarian, Slovakian, and Romanian official and unofficial irredentist claims to Ukrainian territory. (The latter states are, by the way, all aspirants for NATO membership.) NATO expansion, plus a strong U.S. dollar or *Deutsche Mark*, is certain to attract pro-Western regions away from Kyiv's influence, while eastern regions look to Russia and the Crimea potentially seeks independence.

Precipitous NATO enlargement into Central Europe alone (without careful negotiations) may likewise exacerbate schisms within Belarus and polarize its society with factions seeking relative "neutrality" and others willing to accept Russian hegemony. Citing the intent of Poland and Lithuania to become full members of NATO, the president of Belarus, Aleksandr Lukashenko, stated in February 1995 that Belarus (despite its professed "neutrality") and Russia should seek out closer security cooperation, including joint efforts to protect the Belarusian border.[8] In March 1996, despite evident tensions, Belarus and Russia proclaimed that they had formed a new "union."

Belarus has stated that the "deployment of Alliance troops and, moreover, nuclear weapons on the Polish territory under present circumstances would adversely affect the Republic's public opinion and might create undesirable political unrest. Vice versa, even a small reduction of Polish armed forces after it joins NATO would have a positive effect on the process of washing out the enemy image that has just begun in our country."[9] To a certain respect, Belarus could play a role somewhat like East Germany during the Cold War, except for the fact that Minsk is probably more unstable, and far less under firm Russian control than was Berlin when under the Soviet fist. And finally, NATO expansion to the Polish-Belarusian border would place NATO in defense of a territory in which the boundaries are not at all clearly demarcated, and thus is subject to territorial disputes.

While NATO has recognized the danger of alienating Russia, the

September 1995 *Study on NATO Enlargement* was met with Russian skepticism. Despite claims to be a purely "defensive" Alliance, NATO still commands an awesome offensive capability, which appears even more powerful in light of the breakup of the Soviet integrated command. Soviet retreat from forward positions in eastern Germany, Poland, and the Baltic states has isolated a highly unstable Kaliningrad, Russia's last remaining pressure point in Europe. In 1996, Foreign Minister Primakov stated his intention to check the movement of NATO military infrastructure closer to Russian territory.[10]

In summary, the "NATO maximalist" approach overlooks the risk of provoking Russia, of pressing Belarus closer to Russia, and of isolating Ukraine. Moreover, the Baltic states, Finland, and other Central and Eastern European states, such as Slovakia, Romania, Moldova, and Bulgaria, may be left in a "no-man's-land." The NATO maximalist approach also risks diluting NATO's integrated military command and its well-established force planning. NATO enlargement could result in the hypertrophy and overextension of Alliance capabilities, political consensus, and resources in the event of any major crisis—including that of a revanchist Russian backlash.

SENATOR DOLE'S "NEW REALISM"

American critics of Russian foreign policy believe that Moscow is attempting to regain, step-by-step, much of the former Soviet empire— if not its global reach. The Republican Party opposition (whose foreign policy is supported by many Democrats) have accordingly questioned the Clinton administration's "Russia-first" strategy. By attempting to push NATO expansion "as soon as possible" to the top of the agenda prior to the November 1996 presidential election, Republicans sought to make President Clinton look "weak" on Russia. In a June 1996 speech, then Republican Senator (and 1996 presidential candidate) Robert Dole argued that NATO membership should begin with Poland, Hungary, and the Czech Republic, "but it should not end there."[11] The Republican Party thus attempted to undermine Clinton's leadership by denigrating his multilateral initiatives, particularly those involving Russia and the UN. Where the issue was not of "vital" U.S. concern, Republicans placed an emphasis on unilateral "selective intervention."

Dole had been developing a Republican Party foreign policy to counter what he perceived as Clinton's inability to deal with Russian expansionism. In 1995 he outlined five multifaceted threats to American global interests—what he called the "five realities." The "fifth reality" is that "we must face the fact that geopolitical rivalry with Russia did not end with the demise of Soviet Communism." He illustrated this observation by six points which appeared to indicate a deterioration in U.S.-Russian relations; three of these points included proposed Russian nuclear technology sales to North Korea and Iran, Russia's December 1994 veto of a UN sanctions resolution on Serbia, and Russian maintenance of an electronic monitoring station (which eavesdrops on NASA and East Coast communications) and support personnel in Cuba. (See Chapters 6 and 7.)

Senator Dole's sixth point argued that "Russian pressure, subversion, and intimidation of the sovereign states of the 'near abroad' follows an historical pattern set long before the Bolsheviks took power in 1917." The second point affirms that "Russia continues to threaten prospective NATO members over alliance expansion, thereby confirming the need to enlarge NATO sooner than later."[12] While Russia has undeniably begun to "pressure" states in the "near abroad" and "threaten" prospective members over the issue of expansion, the question remains whether the unilateral expansion of NATO (without Russian input) "sooner" rather than "later" actually represents the appropriate response in terms of long-term American national interests.

As Senator Dole defined the problem, "new realism means that developments like arms sales to Iran, violence in Chechnya and UN vetoes on the behalf of aggressors should not be excused, ignored, or minimized. Our differences with Russia should be identified, laid out on the table. They should be negotiated when possible, and condemned when necessary. Such an approach would ultimately serve both Russian and American people better than defending, denying, or rationalizing Russia's misdeeds."[13] The path of "new realism," however, risks a further escalation of tensions if the Russian leadership perceives that Washington has been either indirectly or directly aiding and abetting particular states or socio-political movements that seek to undermine, if not dismember, the Russian Federation. Judging by "democratic" Russia's actions in Chechnya, it appears extremely doubtful that the Russian Federation will accept its potential disaggregation, as gracefully as the Soviet Union accepted the breakup of its empire in 1991. Thus, contrary to its intended effect, Senator Dole's "new realism" may result in a new round of mutual imprecations rather than compromise. Russia may, indeed, seek to *impel* the United States, the EU, and Japan into an entente or alliance, upon the threat of confrontation.

Moreover, the "new realism" needs not only to take a more critical look at the actions of United States itself but also to examine the actions of U.S. allies or even prospective allies, as Russia would perceive those actions. Moscow has argued that NATO and EU/WEU efforts are designed to isolate Russia in both geostrategic and economic terms, by indirectly assisting the formation of a Central and Eastern European "Baltic–Black Sea" alliance tacitly linked to NATO (what

is also referred to as a "double buffer zone"). U.S. efforts to impose
sanctions, to reduce or eliminate aid to Russia, and to block Russian
nuclear reactor and "dual use" high-technology sales to India, Iran,
and Cuba have been regarded by Moscow as efforts to sustain American
hegemony. In addition, Russian hard-liners have argued that Turkey
is presently attempting to use its membership in NATO as leverage to
uproot Russian influence in Central Asia, and new NATO members in
Central Europe would most likely do the same in that region.

In other words, Washington needs to anticipate more cleverly and
accurately Russian responses to both American *and* allied actions. This
is particularly important because U.S. allies in the post–Cold War era
possess much greater room than previously for actions independent of
the United States or in potential conflict with Russian (or even
American) global interests. The problem of developing an *empathetic*
understanding of the way Russia views the world has been well
characterized by the former NATO Supreme Allied Commander in
Europe, General Jack Galvin. "We won the Cold War, but we're losing
the peace after the Cold War. There's no doubt in my mind about it. We
do not think about the Russians enough, about who they are and what
they're doing. We don't think much about the way they think of us. . . .
We should consider folding NATO into a bigger organization, without
losing what has made NATO effective—sustained political control
over a collective military for decades. . . . [We need] a whole new
organization that brings the Russians on board."[14]

Finally, the question remains: if Washington cannot get the
Russians on board, to what extent would and could Moscow strengthen
its support for those such states as Iraq and Iran, not to overlook the
PRC, which Senator Dole mentions as key threats to U.S. global
interests? Should the United States risk calling the Russian bluff? An
alternative, yet "realistic," global strategy would seek to work more
closely with the Russians in the long term effort to "double contain"
these potential threats as effectively as possible rather than seek to
contain or roll back *both* these emerging powers *and* Russia as well.

CRITIQUE OF THE WEU-FIRST APPROACH

The September 1995 *Study on NATO Enlargement* states that "the
enlargement of NATO is a parallel process with and will complement
that of the European Union," but there remains a fundamental
disagreement among U.S. policy-makers as to how to proceed.[15] The
"WEU-first" approach argues that NATO enlargement into Central
Europe would be "destructive" for U.S.-Russian relations. Furthermore,
from the WEU-first perspective, both the NATO "maximalist" and
"self-limitation" approaches fail to consider the possible negative

consequences of enlargement upon NATO's integrated military command, or the risk of a hypertrophy of resources and capabilities. In other words, rather than risk its overextension to new front-line members in Central and Eastern Europe, who are more likely to prove "consumers" rather than "producers" of security, it is best to keep NATO's power *in the background*. At the same time, however, much as the June 1996 Berlin accord promised, NATO can help build WEU defense capacities through the sharing of assets and by CJTF—similar to deployment of multinational IFOR forces in the former Yugoslavia. Also, international regimes such as the OSCE can help build new systems of security in Europe, in cooperation with NATO and the WEU.

The "WEU-first" approach thus emphasizes that NATO should *extend* security guarantees, but not full membership, to states which have first joined the WEU. The key point in regard to the latter statement is concern for American domestic politics. The "WEU-first" approach posits that it will not be easy to obtain the two–thirds majority vote in the U.S. Senate necessary to revise the North Atlantic Treaty so as to add new "full" members. From a domestic political perspective, it is more feasible to *extend* NATO security guarantees to WEU members than to add new members to NATO. Such an action would take a simple majority in both the House and the Senate, once its intent and costs were fully explained.

In May 1995, Ambassador Richard T. Davies and a group of retired foreign service officers (including former ambassadors John A. Armitage, Jack F. Matlock, and Paul H. Nitze) wrote a letter to Secretary of State Christopher. This group argued that the extension of NATO membership to the Czech Republic, Hungary, and Poland "risks endangering the long-term viability of NATO, significantly exacerbating the instability that now exists in the zone that lies between Germany and Russia, and convincing most Russians that the United States and the West are attempting to isolate, encircle, and subordinate them, rather than integrating them into a new European system of collective security."[16]

To counter this stinging attack from former top officials, Assistant Secretary of State Richard C. Holbrooke replied on 25 July 1995 that WEU membership alone failed to "satisfy the desire of Central Europeans for full integration into western structures which include the United States" and that "NATO must participate in, and indeed help drive" the transformation of European security. Holbrooke additionally argued that "the close link between the respective Article V commitments of the WEU and NATO means that any nation which joins the WEU as a full member has a de facto 'back door' security guarantee as well, but without the direct and formal agreement of the United States." According to Holbrooke, the latter fact produces two problems. The first is "the absence of a strong political consensus between the Administration and Congress," which means that Central European states may not obtain wholehearted American support. The second is that promises of NATO "back door" security guarantees (which may or may not be fulfilled) "could easily destroy the underlying consensus on which U.S. engagement in Europe has been sustained."[17]

In rebuttal, Ambassador Davies argued against Holbrooke's contention that the United States should base its global strategy on the "desires" of the Central Europeans for full integration into the West; rather, the first consideration should be American national interests. Secondly, he asserted that WEU membership did not necessarily represent a "back door" for WEU members to obtain NATO security guarantees. Rather, a "NATO guarantee obtained through full WEU membership could be made *de jure* and a front door one by Congressional passage of a joint resolution recognizing its implications. The passage of such a resolution would require the approval of majorities in both Houses. Such a simple majority should be easier to obtain than the two–thirds majority of the Senate that would be required if the North Atlantic Treaty were revised to include NATO membership for these states."[18] Ambassador Davies added that a decision to enlarge NATO itself would also need a strong political consensus between the president and the Congress. His point was that U.S. political consensus should be easier to obtain through a joint resolution providing for the extension of NATO security guarantees to those states which join the WEU rather than an attempt to revise the North Atlantic Treaty, requiring a two–thirds Senate majority.

The "WEU-first" approach correctly argues that U.S. national interests should dictate U.S. actions, not the desires of Central European states. It is also correct that NATO enlargement might not survive the Senate debate once the full burden of American responsibilities and costs was generally understood. It also appears sound in its assessment that NATO can *extend* security guarantees to particular states rather than invite them to be "full" members. (As will be argued in Chapter 11, NATO can extend security guarantees to a select group of core states that participate in a Euro-Atlantic DSI.)

However, it is still not clear that the WEU-first path itself will mitigate Russian fears. First, the WEU acted much later (December 1994) than NATO to forge a rapprochement with Russia, Belarus, and Ukraine. (The NACC had moved in November–December 1991 toward such a rapprochement.) Second, the possible enlargement of the EU and WEU to Central European states could call into question the scope of the WEU security guarantees (and the Article V commitment).[19] Third, if the EU and WEU are not prepared for a nuclear defense of their own expanding memberships in concert with the United States, their expansion could drag NATO into a crisis, particularly if the United States is not willing to back up all new EU/WEU members (such as Finland) with security guarantees. The UK, France, and Germany have yet to formulate what France has called "concerted deterrence," which involves closer Anglo-French, and possibly German, nuclear cooperation. (See Chapter 2.) Fourth, it is not obvious that the expansion of the EU followed by WEU membership will appear less threatening than the expansion of NATO.[20] Russia's "Full Strategic Doctrine" of November 1993 opposed the expansion of *any* blocs into former Soviet (and czarist) spheres of influence and security which did not simultaneously forge conjoint security guarantees with Moscow, even if these blocs were not perceived to be a "threat."[21] Fifth, the failure to forge a concerted NATO, EU/WEU, and Russian security relationship could ultimately lead EU/WEU states to seek alternative alliances with Ukraine, the PRC, or, more likely, Japan. This final point is the key problem with the "non-evolutionary" WEU-first approach which argues that the United States should threaten "isolationism" in order to impel the EU/WEU to increase its defense capabilities. Such a shock-oriented approach would not only force the EU/WEU to look to alternative alliances but would risk the breakup of NATO and U.S.-European cooperation in general. It could also cause the breakup of the European Union itself—which is to a large extent sustained by the NATO "double-containment" of Germany (as well as French complicity in that "double-containment").

SENATOR NUNN'S TWO-TRACK STRATEGY

Senator Sam Nunn has advocated a "two-track" approach, similar to the "WEU-first" concept, to NATO enlargement. The first, "evolutionary," track proposes that once a country joins the EU it be eligible to join the WEU, which can then prepare it for NATO membership. The second track, accelerated "threat-based" expansion, is conditioned upon Russian behavior. According to Senator Nunn, NATO could expand in case of a clear Russian threat, which could include "aggressive moves against other sovereign states; militarily significant arms control violations; or else the emergence of a non-democratic Russian government that impedes fair elections, suppressed domestic freedoms or institutes a foreign policy incompatible with the existing European security system."[22]

Yet despite his own critique of the PfP as an attempt to "bridge the unbridgeable," Senator Nunn's "first track" retains the uncertainties of the Partnership for Peace initiative. It is not at all clear which states will obtain NATO security guarantees once they enter the EU and then the WEU. Moreover, states which do not enter the WEU will not feel secure; they therefore risk falling into a "no-man's-land" or a Russian orbit. Potential conflicts among EU members and non-EU members may create new confusion as to whom is to be defended. The EU's initial inability to deal with the former Yugoslavia without American backing does not portend well for an even more encompassing all-European security initiative. Moreover, waiting for EU expansion to take place before initiating any *systemic* form of security structure, allows, in effect, regions of potential crisis to fester. It is better to take *preventive* measures before conflicts do arise (as argued in Chapter 11).

From a U.S. perspective, Senator Nunn's approach tends to renounce American leadership. Rather than permitting Washington to take the lead in forging a new system of cooperative-collective security that would incorporate EU/WEU *and* Russian interests *from the outset* and that would engage in preventive diplomacy, Senator Nunn's "first track" strategy suggests that the Washington should follow European timing (and bureaucratic red tape!)[23] States joining the EU would be eligible to join the WEU, and then NATO, only if qualified.

Senator Nunn's statement that his so-called evolutionary "first track" represents a "natural process connecting economic and security interests" may furthermore be disingenuous, i.e., if EU expansion isolates Moscow from trade opportunities, arms sales, as well as key geostrategic positions. Senator Nunn's basic principal is to "do no harm;"[24] if his policy is implemented, however, the United States risks exacerbating U.S.-EU/WEU-Russian tensions more by *omission* (for example, by not acting in concert with *both* the EU *and* Russia) rather than by *commission*.

As neither the nature of guarantees for Russian participation, nor the role of American interests are fully explicated in Senator Nunn's strategy, Russia's "encirclement" may well prove self-fulfilling, thus leading directly to his second track, "threat-based" strategy. Senator Nunn argues that accelerated (or immediate) NATO membership "would depend on Russian behavior." However, his reasoning appears somewhat faulty. First, negative aspects of Russian behavior can be exaggerated (and Russia itself can be provoked) by the efforts of Central and Eastern European states to draw NATO to their support, thus tying membership to Russian actions.

Secondly, it is not entirely clear exactly when Russia would be considered "a clear and present danger." Perceptions of Russian intent may well differ. WEU-first proponent Michael Brown, for example, argues that Alliance support for NATO expansion would be easier to mobilize if Russia either violates the CFE treaty, refuses to respect international borders, absorbs Ukraine or Belarus into the Russian Federation or into the CIS, or else withdraws from START I, START II, or other arms treaties.[25] Yet Russia has already been accused of violation of the CFE treaty, over the issue of flank limitations in November 1995 (until an apparent compromise was reached in June 1996). Perhaps more to the point, Moscow has moved toward a closer political military "union" with Belarus. Moscow has yet to ratify the START II treaty (in large part due to the expense involved in its implementation). Do these acts represent clear examples of an "imperialist agenda" and thus justify a hasty NATO enlargement, as Brown suggests they should? Or would not the implementation of a system of cooperative-collective security be more rational, particularly given the divergence of allied opinion over precisely when Russia would, in fact, represent a clear and present danger?

Thirdly, while Russian threats to the existing European security system could well justify a hasty extension of NATO security guarantees, the emergence of a non-democratic Russian government may not necessarily, as the Senator argues, require it. A non-democratic Russian government may or may not prove to be a rival to the U.S. and EU. Such a regime could seek to repress mafia organizations or revanchist forces, and might be willing to work out compromises with which the U.S. and EU could agree without capitulation, but *only* if that potential dictatorship did not feel directly or indirectly threatened by U.S., European, or Japanese actions.

The fact that the Russian Federation is confronted with the prospect of its own breakup (along with such issues as mafia criminality and political corruption) will make it very be difficult to sustain even a nominal form of "democracy." Russian efforts to quell political-economic instability and the fissiparous tendencies of the CIS and the Russian Federation itself have raised not-unwarranted fears that the new Russia will soon revive its two-headed eagle: autocracy on the one hand and imperialism on the other.

If the Russian two-headed eagle does raise its brutal head, it cannot be presumed that such a Russian "dictatorship" would necessarily pursue an anti–Western foreign policy. Even though internal political dynamics within Russia may not prove congenial for a truly "democratic" regime, due to the twists and turns in Russian domestic policy, it is still in the American, European, and Japanese interest to continue to *channel* Russia in a pro-Western direction in the long term, in an effort to *deflect* Russia from supporting states that are truly hostile to U.S., EU, and Japanese interests. The key question as to whether the United States, the EU, and Japan would be forced to confront, appease, or capitulate to Russian demands—or those of other states, such as the PRC, which may or may not be supported by a resurgent Russia—will depend largely upon the very nature of those demands and the nature of any new alliances formed, as well as the ability of the three allied centers of power and financial influence to negotiate *legitimate* compromises through a concerted strategy that refuses to sacrifice *truly* vital interests.

CRITIQUE OF NATO SELF-LIMITATION

While the self-limitation approach argues that enlargement will not dilute NATO's integrated command, the debate over ESDI, and CJTF, and the "Europeanization" of NATO has, in fact, raised questions as to the ability of NATO to adjust to European demands for relative autonomy, as well as the Alliance's ability to take on new members. (See Chapter 3.) The problem is that NATO may be taking on more than it can handle. In essence, rather than strengthening the Alliance, NATO enlargement (in any form) risks the dilution of its integrated military command and the overextension of its resources, capabilities, and political will. This is particularly true at a time when NATO attention is increasingly being drawn towards the Persian Gulf (Iraq and Iran), former Yugoslavia, Albania, and Algeria (and North Africa generally), in addition to Central and Eastern Europe (which itself raises the prospect for the formation of a Central European "caucus" within NATO). Most crucially, NATO risks the outbreak of a crisis between two of its own members, Greece and Turkey—if not with Ankara alone. The range of potential security concerns thus implies the need for a more concerted global strategy.

THE "PARALLEL TRACK" APPROACH

The September 1996 proposals by Warren Christopher called for three "parallel" tracks in NATO enlargement, which should take place simultaneously: (1) reform of the Atlantic Alliance to permit greater power and responsibility-sharing for NATO allies in Western Europe; (2) extension of invitations to states of Central and Eastern Europe to begin NATO accession talks; and (3) an intensive dialogue with Russia, resulting in a NATO-Russian charter. (A fourth track, a NATO-Ukrainian agreement, was subsequently added.) However, the "parallel track" approach entails a significant element of risk, and a calling of the Russian bluff. Despite promises of a NATO-Russian Charter/Council, or such other palliatives as a promise not to forward-deploy nuclear weapons or foreign forces in peacetime, there is a real danger that the proposed enlargement of NATO may precipitate the very crisis that the self-limitation approach hopes to avert.

The fundamental problem resides in the geohistorical relationship between Russia and the countries that NATO intends to offer "full" membership. Poland, in particular, has been a rival of both Belarus and Russia. Rather than drawing states from former Soviet or czarist spheres of influence, it may prove less controversial to bring in former neutral states. One possibility to consider would be the "full" membership of formerly neutral states such as Austria and Sweden (if these states would accept). Both are highly developed democracies and, unlike Poland, the Czech Republic, and Hungary, have never been part of the Soviet or Russian orbit. They would thus be unlikely to cause friction with either Russia or other Central and Eastern European states. At the same time, should these states seek membership, careful negotiations with Moscow would still be necessary.

ZBIGNIEW BRZEZINSKI'S TWO-TRACK STRATEGY

In many ways, Zbigniew Brzezinski's "two-track" strategy appears to provide some of the basis for the "parallel track" strategy, although the latter has added an extra dimension, the European-ization of NATO (discussed in Chapter 2). However, some of the problems inherent in Brzezinski's two-track strategy may also arise in the Clinton administration's "parallel track."

Zbigniew Brzezinski has argued that NATO should announce the intent to bring in at least Poland and the Czech Republic a members, while simultaneously inviting Moscow "to help create a new transatlantic system of collective security, one that goes beyond the expansion of NATO proper."[26] Largely using the "two-plus-four" agreement leading to German unification as a model, he argues that "periodic joint manoeuvers, coordinated joint planning, prepositioning of equipment, and joint exercises would be sufficient to give substance to the guarantees inherent in NATO's Article V, while the formula of 'no forward deployment' of NATO forces in Central Europe would underline the non-antagonistic character of the expansion. This should mitigate some of Moscow's legitimate concerns."[27] (Neither American nor German troops would initially be deployed.)

Unlike the NATO maximalist approach, Brzezinski's self-limiting proposal does offer, at least in principle, an overall security framework for a new system of transatlantic security that would include Russia. However, although his proposed transatlantic security pact leaves "open the question of Russia's eventual membership [in NATO]," it appears unlikely that Brzezinski's plan would gain Russian confidence and acceptance.[28] Two essential problems arise. First, the prospects of "full" Russian membership in NATO appear highly doubtful from both the American and Russian perspectives, and it is disingenuous to make promises that will not be fulfilled. It is improbable that Russia would serve as a "gendarme" U.S. interests, nor would the United States want to play a role in Central Asia and the Far East in accord with Russian interests. It is also unlikely that either state would want to share nuclear-strategic secrets.

Second, bringing Poland and, to a lesser extent the Czech Republic, into NATO as "full" members could prove problematic—if not dangerously risky. Enlargement to include Poland could place NATO and Russia in confrontation over Kaliningrad (among other possible disputes with Belarus and the Baltic states). Despite promises of an extensive NATO-Russian Charter, Moscow would most likely regard NATO control of the Polish corridor—the historical route of invasion into Russia—as a future threat. Moscow would consequently attempt to upgrade its position in Kaliningrad (pressuring Germany, Poland, Finland, and the Baltic states) and continue to press Belarus into a firm alliance, at the same time that it sought to break the "strategic partnership" between NATO, Poland, and Ukraine.

The acceptance of the Czech Republic would be less provocative to Russia but it could alienate Poland if both states are not brought in together. Although the Czech Republic has no common borders with Russia, Czech membership in NATO may be perceived as cutting a historical Russian-Western link and a "conduit" of Russian influence in Central and southeastern Europe; the Czech Republic (in part due to tensions over the Sudetenland) has generally attempted to counterbalance both Russian and German influence. Moreover, should the United States incorporate *only* Poland and the Czech Republic into NATO (without Russian participation), Moscow could take it as an invitation to incorporate sections of the Baltic states, Finland, Ukraine, or other states into its own sphere of influence and security— resulting in a new partition of Europe.

Brzezinski's plan furthermore appears to *threaten* Russia into accepting NATO membership for Poland and the Czech Republic. Moscow's hand would possibly be forced with a *fait accompli,* if it does not ultimately agree, rather than having been invited into the process of building a new transatlantic security order *from the beginning.* Should Russia fail to participate, NATO could find itself caught in a situation where it must force Moscow's hand. In such a situation, NATO may be forced either to engage in a provocative (and expensive) forward deployment, possibly overextending its capabilities, or give in to Russian threats. Thus, contrary to Brzezinski's assertions, his "transitional phase" may in fact be destabilizing, particularly if Moscow questions NATO's credibility.

While proponents of the "self-limitation" approach argue against forward deployment of nuclear weapons and foreign forces, as factors that could alienate Russia (among other states), they appear to miss a more fundamental question that is at the heart of the Russian security dilemma. It is not as much NATO's actions (or feared actions) that may alienate Moscow but rather the lack of substantial Russian influence in

NATO's decision-making process, particularly in those areas affecting its perceived "vital" interests. This is the heart of the matter.[29] The real question is about *power*; questions of nuclear weapons deployment and foreign troops are secondary. Will NATO, the WEU, and Russia be able to engage in actual power-sharing, in a true partnership? Or will Russia only be permitted limited rights of consultation—with no actual guarantee of influencing those decisions, except by threats? There is thus a real danger that Russia (from a position of relative weakness and in fear of the disaggregation) may engage in *preclusive* actions, even in response to a "self-limiting" enlargement. Proposals that bring Central European states into NATO's political, but not military, structures at least initially, still raise concerns that these states may ultimately press for membership in NATO's integrated military command. Much as was the case with the czarist and Soviet "legal" traditions, *NATO is presumed guilty of the worst possible intentions—that is, until Moscow itself proves it to be innocent.*

From this perspective, a precise conjoint NATO-Russian Charter (coupled with conjoint NATO-WEU-Russian security guarantees) need to be worked out, preferably prior to and not parallel with NATO enlargement. Although the simultaneous invitation of potential NATO members, coupled with negotiations aimed at forging a NATO-Russian Charter, is intended to pressure the Russians into compromise, it is a risky strategy. If new members are to come on board in two years after the July 1997 invitation, there will be very little time for all the issues to be negotiated. If he is still in power, President Boris Yeltsin's illness and incapacity may throw the decision-making process into turmoil, resulting in greater intransigence upon the part of the Russian elite. NATO, Russian, and Central and Eastern European states really need to build regional systems of security, prior to the invitation to NATO membership for any one state—precisely in order to safeguard *both* new members *and* those states which do not join as "full" members. Alternatively, if membership application process begins in July 1997 as proposed, NATO's Atlantic Partnership Council (with full Russian and Ukrainian participation) should begin to implement a regionally integrated system of cooperative-collective security prior to 1999 when selected countries are to become "full-fledged" members, so as to reduce the gap between "members" and "non-members." (See Chapter 11.)

Moreover, the mere announcement of "full" NATO membership for a particular state will not immediately provide full Article V security guarantees until NATO has had time to build up its power-projection capabilities and has put its military-infrastructure in place. (The latter fact, of course, indicates why Russian foreign minister Primakov has opposed the deployment of NATO infrastructure on the territory of new members but not the *extension* of NATO political guarantees.) If

Moscow does not truly perceive itself as part of any agreement reached with NATO (for example, following a change in leadership), it could attempt to block parliamentary ratification of new NATO members through threats of nuclear blackmail, and other forms of obstruction.

On the other hand, *if* the Alliance is determined to enlarge (and to pressure Russia into accepting NATO's resolve to enlarge), then the proposal should be considered that the first states to enter as "full" members not be former members of the Soviet or czarist spheres of influence and security. In other words, if enlargement is to take place, such states as Austria and Sweden would both benefit NATO and make less provocative members. These states have never been part of the Soviet or Russian orbit and would be unlikely to cause friction with either Russia, or Central and Eastern European states. At the same time, as Sweden and Austria are highly developed states, their "full" (but non-nuclear) membership would greatly enhance NATO's capabilities, whereas the defense capacity of former Warsaw Pact states would have to be thoroughly renovated. Sweden and Austria could play a key role in providing logistics to a Euro-Atlantic Defense and Security Identity as proposed in Chapter 11. They would represent security "producers," not security "consumers." Although Moscow has attempted to block NATO's enlargement to these formerly neutral states, the Russians could not claim that such states as Sweden and Austria threaten Russia's "vital" national security interests. Moreover, much as NATO played a role in double-containing Germany, Russia may well see it as in its interests for NATO to continue to "double-contain" the influence of Sweden in the Baltic states and Finland, and that of Austria in southeastern Europe and Ukraine. (If these states do not want to become "full" members of the Alliance at this point, however, their role in the EU/WEU could be enhanced through CJTF and ESDI. See Chapters 3 and 11.)

The key point is that even NATO enlargement to states not within former Soviet or czarist spheres of influence and security should be carefully negotiated with Moscow, as a step toward a viable, more comprehensive system of security for all of Europe. NATO's next step should be to enhance the participation of all Central and Eastern European states in systems of regional defense, linked to a Euro-Atlantic Defense and Security Identity in the period 1997–99. In effect, these latter states would become "associate," as opposed to "full," members of NATO (unless "full" membership is redefined, see Chapter 11.) Failure to forge such a comprehensive system of cooperative-collective security—whether *prior to* or *parallel with* NATO's expansion—would not only risk a new partition of Europe but could jeopardize the very credibility of NATO itself.

CHAPTER 10

Strengthening International Regimes

NATO AND THE OSCE: INTERLOCKING OR INTERBLOCKING?

Working through and with international regimes such as the UN and OSCE, *in cooperative interaction with more traditional multilateral and bilateral alliances*, will prove crucial to the formation of a viable European and global security order lasting into the next millennium. NATO alone is not sufficient; and NATO, whose primary duty is to provide a military backdrop as well as nuclear deterrence, is neither prepared nor equipped to deal with many post–Cold War security issues. NATO thus needs additional support from international regimes, such as the UN and OSCE, to cope with the complex problems arising from actual and potential ethnic, territorial, religious disputes as well as human rights abuses, ecological destruction, drug trafficking, and the smuggling of arms and nuclear materiel, among other vital international security concerns. From this viewpoint, non-constructive criticism of international regimes may well prove counterproductive; it may not only undermine international cooperation but the very solidarity and legitimacy of NATO itself, particularly in the post–Cold War era, in which NATO members themselves often hold diverse and conflicting opinions, and in which there is no commonly perceived threat, as during the Cold War.

American and German demands for unilateral NATO expansion into Central Europe have been countered by Russian demands that the OSCE be strengthened in such a way as to become the international regime most responsible for security in Europe. The Conference on Security and Cooperation in Europe, formed in 1975, was renamed the Organization for Security and Cooperation in Europe (OSCE) at the

Budapest summit in December 1994. Although the name change was symbolic of an intent to strengthen the organization by developing systems of early warning, and crisis prevention and management, the OSCE has yet to be empowered to the extent proposed by Moscow; the Budapest summit rejected Russian proposals for the establishment of an OSCE security council.

In 1992 Boris Yeltsin called for a "Charter for American and Russian Partnership and Friendship," as well for a stronger OSCE and a "Euro-Atlantic Peacekeeping Capability." In many ways, Yeltsin's proposals sought to actualize Secretary of State James Baker's call in Aspen in June 1991 for a "Euro-Atlantic Community" from "Vancouver to Vladivostok." Yeltsin's concepts largely fell on deaf ears. Despite his own (albeit belated) support for the formation of the OSCE in Helsinki in 1975,[1] Henry Kissinger, for example, depicted Yeltsin's proposals as "downgrading NATO."[2] Kissinger's views against a stronger OSCE have tended to predominate in American policy-making circles.

Contrary to Kissinger's skepticism, however, the cooperative-collective security approach need not "downgrade" NATO. In fact, CCS can actually upgrade NATO's role as a supplier of security in Central and Eastern Europe, by facilitating NATO, WEU, and Russian defense cooperation with the UN and OSCE. (See Chapter 11.) In effect, the effort to develop a viable system of cooperative-collective European security represents the first step toward a new global system of security. Accordingly, Germany, Japan, and Russia (and ultimately China) should be drawn into greater support for viable systems of cooperative-collective security in Europe and Asia. The interaction and coordination among the UN and OSCE and NATO, the WEU, and Russia needs to be strengthened, not downgraded.

Cooperative-collective security means the advent of *preventive* diplomacy (which implies efforts taken to deter conflict before it begins), but not overlooking the contemporary renaissance of *irenic* diplomacy (which implies efforts to reduce tensions or end conflict among democratic and non-democratic states). Both preventive and irenic diplomacy may threaten the use of force, but the latter may opt for the use of force in as judicious a manner as is possible given the circumstances. Both preventive and irenic diplomacy seek to mediate the options envisioned by short-term national-interest calculations with the long-term options and interests of interstate cooperation and the international community. States must regard it in their own interest to work through international regimes; in fact, international regimes can help orchestrate the often conflictual interface between national goals and those of the international community. It is moreover essential that ways be found to sustain positive cooperation among international regimes, so as to make certain that these regimes become truly "interlocking" rather than obstructive and "interblocking."[3] At the same time, American leadership in implementing such a system of cooperative-collective security in Central and Eastern Europe—if not much of the world—is crucial.

The September 1995 *Study on NATO Enlargement* argues that "the activities of the OSCE and of NATO are complementary and mutually reinforcing," but the study does not outline the precise nature of the NATO-OSCE-Russian interrelationship, nor does it describe the particular security role of OSCE members that do not expect to become NATO members in the near future. The *Study on NATO Enlargement* also warns against efforts to slow down NATO enlargement: "OSCE discussions on a European Security model for the twenty–first century should reflect the process of NATO enlargement, but not delay it. A strengthened OSCE, an enlarged NATO, an active NACC and PfP would, together with other fora, form complementary parts of a broad, inclusive European security architecture, supporting the objectives of an undivided Europe." The reference to possible efforts to "delay" NATO enlargement is clearly aimed at perceived Russian steps to block that enlargement, through the auspices of the OSCE.

NATO's concern is based upon Moscow's success at the December 1994 OSCE Budapest summit in getting the OSCE to endorse a project for "a common and comprehensive security model for Europe in the twenty-first century." At the same time, the *Study on NATO Enlargement* appears to overlook Boris Yeltsin's statement that there is still room in the OSCE "for reciprocal guarantees between states or groups of states."[4] Accordingly, the cooperative-collective security approach is intended to explore the validity of the often-reiterated Russian demand for "reciprocal" or "conjoint" security guarantees, and to make certain that Russia (and other states) will truly respect Central and Eastern European state sovereignty concerns, so as to prevent Europe from once again being divided into two (or more) blocs, or spheres of influence and security. In essence, mutual U.S.-EU-Russian support for "interlocking" international security regimes can help to keep geopolitical lines from becoming "impermeable."

THE UN, OSCE, AND NATO

In general, only those UN Security Council members with vital concerns or interests at stake have tended to take an active role in managing regional crises. At the same time, it is possible for major states *without* a specific national interest in a particular regional crisis to play the role of "honest broker" or "arbitrator," through UN or OSCE mediation. Although there has been a general tendency in the post–Cold War era to sanction UN actions only in those spheres of influence and security previously established by the major powers, the use of UN forces not only provides a broader mandate, and hence a greater *legitimacy*, for what otherwise might be a unilateral intervention, but it also offers a multilateral forum for the aggrieved party to express its views. UN efforts can help to counterbalance a major state's predominance—that is, as much as possible, given the UN's limited resources and overextended commitments.

NATO has, when it has suited its interests, encouraged greater cooperation with the UN and the OSCE, confirming its position in the September 1995 *Study on NATO Enlargement* as discussed above. The July 1990 NATO summit encouraged the CSCE to endorse free elections, the rule of law, human rights, economic development, and to provide an institutional forum for wider political dialogue among all CSCE members. At its December 1991 summit, in addition to establishing the North Atlantic Cooperation Council, which provided a forum for discussions involving security and defense–related matters among NATO and former Soviet-bloc and newly independent states, NATO first expressed interest in making its collective experience open to the CSCE. (The purpose of NACC, according to former NATO Secretary-General Manfred Wörner, was not to compete with the CSCE but to "strengthen" it by "concentrat[ing] on security and defense related issues where NATO can offer things which the CSCE cannot.")[5]

In the Prague summit of January 1992, the German delegation had proposed that the CSCE organize its own peacekeeping forces. Although the proposal was backed by the Czech and Slovak republics, in addition to NATO allies, Italy and Germany, it was opposed by the United States, Britain, and France. In June 1992, NATO then established a framework for future NATO out-of-area peacekeeping "on a case-by-case basis under a CSCE mandate," but "in accordance with our own procedures." At the same time, however, neither NATO nor the CSCE could agree within itself as to how best to manage the conflict. In July 1992 the CSCE gave warm support to NATO's offer for peacekeeping on a case-by-case basis; it created a Forum for Security Cooperation to meet regularly in Vienna. Poland, for example, called on the CSCE to alleviate security concerns on its borders with Belarus and Kaliningrad. Although the CSCE did establish a framework for an "interlocking" NATO-CSCE relationship, it failed to make it operational. More pertinently, the CSCE failed to act on NATO's request to deal with the Yugoslav crisis under a CSCE mandate.

NATO then turned to the UN for a mandate. At the December 1992 foreign ministers' meeting in Brussels, NATO agreed to make its resources available to the UN, in particular to maintain a no-fly zone over Bosnia.[6] While not discarding the regime altogether, NATO downplayed the CSCE as an interlocking "partner" of NATO from late

1992 to November 1994, emphasizing the UN. By late 1994, however, the failure of the UN to deal effectively with the crisis in Yugoslavia led NATO to reconsider the CSCE/OSCE.

In September 1995, NATO once again discussed the interaction between the OSCE and NATO as part of its *Study on NATO Enlargement*. Proposals for mutual NATO-OSCE representation at headquarters, permanent NATO representation at security-related OSCE deliberations, NATO input to the OSCE High Level Planning Group in Vienna (responsible for peacekeeping planning), an OSCE liaison at the Partnership Co-ordination Cell in Mons, Belgium, among other possibilities for mutual cooperation, were suggested.[7] In July 1996, the OSCE appeared to reciprocate: its Stockholm Declaration proposed "an enlarged NATO" as one pillar of a new comprehensive security order in Europe—a position opposed by the Russian delegation.[8] Yet issues involving OSCE oversight of NATO deployments in the context of enlargement remain problematic. Will Russia and other states be able to inspect and verify the capabilities of new NATO members through the OSCE?

THE OSCE AND THE RUSSIAN "NEAR ABROAD"

The UN has been criticized for supposedly siding with Russia's de facto role as a "policeman" among CIS states rather than lending support to UN or OSCE supervision of Russian actions. Moreover, as Russia appeared to support the OSCE as a alternative to NATO (specifically in 1993), Washington sought to avoid any entanglement in that international regime. By so doing, however, Washington overlooked a possible area of compromise. Russian calls for joint NATO-Russian security guarantees, with the OSCE *and* NACC as decision-making bodies, were generally ignored.

At the December 1993 meeting of OSCE foreign ministers, Russia proposed that the North Atlantic Cooperation Council "coordinate," under OSCE auspices, the peacekeeping efforts of NATO, the WEU, and the CIS. These Russian proposals appeared disingenuous, in part because former Defense Minister Pavel Grachev was concurrently speaking of subordinating NATO and the WEU to the OSCE, and in part due to Russian resistance to OSCE diplomatic intervention in arbitration on Nagorno-Karabakh and Chechnya.[9] Russian proposals were regarded as a cover for permitting Russia to restore its hegemony over the CIS and hence rejected. This rejection, however, was shortsighted. First, Russian peacekeeping efforts in the CIS were an established fact (in part as no other state wanted to intervene). Secondly, the West may actually want or need Russian involvement in the resolution of certain conflicts, such as that in former Yugoslavia.

In January 1994, then Foreign Minister Kozyrev warned that a departure of Russian troops from the "near abroad" would create "a security vacuum" which would be filled by forces "directly hostile to Russian interests." Russia has accordingly been criticized for engaging in "peace prevention" in Georgia and Azerbaijan, in hegemonic efforts to "divide and rule" these countries, forcing them to join the CIS. Moscow has been regarded as "peacemaking" in Tajikistan but "province-making" in Moldova. In the case of Moldova, Lieutenant General Lebed at one point refused to withdraw Russian forces, in order to sustain a military presence there (and in the Balkan region in general). A Russian military presence in Moldova represented (1) an effort to counter-encircle Ukraine; (2) an attempt to block Moldova from merging with Romania; and (3) pressure to impel Moldova to join the CIS.[10] In this example, Russian leaders have hoped to involve other CIS states (where they possess national interests) in conflicts throughout the former USSR. Kyiv (and Bonn), however, categorically rejected any CIS peacekeeping operations on the territory of the former USSR—unless such actions were sanctioned by the UN or OSCE.[11]

Moscow has argued that NATO and the WEU should be delegated certain tasks by the UN and OSCE; while Russia itself should be delegated other "tasks." Moscow has argued that the United States and Europe have, in effect, used the UN to assert their own geopolitical interests. (Following its intervention in Rwanda under UN auspices, for example, France was charged with a reassertion of a traditional French sphere of influence.) This critique has made it difficult for the UN to block intervention by Russian peacekeepers in the "near abroad." Moscow has sought a tacit *quid pro quo*; in other words, if the UN serves U.S. or European interests in one area, the UN should serve Russian interests in another.

Not surprisingly, both the OSCE and the UN have been accused of being "pro-Russian," in that Moscow has not always acted as a disinterested party. Accordingly, Central and Eastern European leaders have generally preferred EU and NATO support (to that of the UN or OSCE) as a means to counterbalance Russian influence. On the other hand, the complaint goes the other way as well. In reference to the Azeri-Armenian conflict over Karabakh, Russian political leaders have accused the OSCE of being used by countries that "are trying to use the CSCE as a cover for their geopolitical interests, rather than as a conflict resolution mechanism. Some people would like to minimize Russia's role and exclude the CIS from the process."[12]

American policy has likewise been reluctant to concede special Russian rights within the former Soviet bloc. In August 1993, the State Department circulated a classified document, "Directive 13," which stated that the United States should be prepared to support UN peacekeeping operations in the CIS, even if these actions opposed Russian interests.[13] Russia did, however, permit UN observers to monitor the cease-fire between Georgia and Abkhazhia in August 1993 and allowed a new peacekeeping force to enter Nagorno-Karabakh, at the December 1994 OSCE summit in Budapest.

On the other hand, Russia's intervention in Chechnya (within the Russian Federation) in December 1994 was regarded as violating rules governing military activities as set forth by the OSCE, including those agreed to by Russia at the December Budapest summit, in that: (1) Russia failed to honor the CFE treaty on armed forces and arms cutbacks, violating the section dealing with flank violations; (2) it failed to notify the OSCE countries of the introduction of troop contingents in excess of nine thousand troops and did not give forty–two days notice of military manoeuvres; and (3) it omitted to prove that the "operation" was of a peacekeeping or peace-restoring nature. Former Foreign Minister Kozyrev, however, justified the intervention on the ground that OSCE member states must not permit the existence of armed forces beyond the control of the constitutional authorities.[14] Under EU and French pressure in particular, Russia did permit a limited number of OSCE observers to go into Chechnya.[15]

Here is the crux of the dilemma: to what extent should the United States and the EU grant Russia a *legitimate* role in regional and global affairs at the same time that the United States and EU seek to limit and dampen revanchist or revisionist Russian claims, which Central and Eastern European, as well as Caucasian and Central Asian states, rightly fear? That is, how can the United States and EU account for Russia's continuing role as a major power with both global *and* regional rights and responsibilities? How can Russia possess a *legitimate* monopoly over nuclear weaponry, which in effect grants Russia de facto *primacy* or *hegemony* over the CIS and other former Soviet-bloc states, without a risk of even more overt forms of imperialism or revanchism?

As long as Moscow seeks to protect the Russian "diaspora" through OSCE diplomatic intervention, the OSCE can also seek to influence Russian behavior in other areas of the "near abroad"—unless Russia declares such areas off limits or to be "vital security." A constant trade-off between Russian and non-Russian interests within Russian-designated "spheres of influence and security" should help to sustain OSCE influence (even if limited) within the Russian "near abroad." However, this should only be the case when such influence is consistent with *legitimate* U.S. and EU security interests and concerns. At the same time, the United States and EU will not, and should not, be able to influence Russian actions in those regions which do *not* interact with "vital" spheres of their security. The United States and EU may thus have tacitly to accept various aspects of Russian *primacy, hegemony,* or *predominance* in specific regions, in a long-term effort to draw or "co-opt" Moscow into a more concerted relationship and to look for openings which might lead to a *devolution* of Russian controls.

On one hand, the United States and Russia must find new ways of cooperation. On the other, the United States must help Europe build new systems of security so that Central and Eastern European states are not threatened either by their own conflicting irredentist claims or by the threat that Russian revanchism may go beyond the present regime's pressures on the "near abroad." To attempt to deny Russia's role as a major power with both global and regional rights and responsibilities is to deny the United States and EU an important partner (if not fuel the possibility of Russian revanchism). Yet not to attempt to mitigate Russian behavior through concerted dialogue and pressure is to abdicate responsibility.[16]

CONTRADICTIONS IN U.S. POLICY

The UN's mixed record does not at all justify congressional threats to cut U.S. support for the actions of the United Nations. These threats could paralyze the UN, if not prevent effective action that may actually serve American interests. Working through the UN can help to keep the United States itself from becoming overextended in its pursuit of global security and stability. Working *effectively* through the UN can also help to reduce pressures for risky unilateral U.S. interventionism. Working through the UN and OSCE can also make NATO operations more effective.

The so-called UN "failure" in Somalia, for example, was more a result of American political ineptitude than a case of bungling by the UN. The U.S.-UN intervention (from December 1992 through August 1993) was an instance in which the United States did *not* work *effectively* through, and in interaction with, the UN.[17] Following that fiasco, in October 1993 Congress sought to block U.S.-UN actions in Haiti and planned to overhaul the War Powers Act. Presidential Decision Directive 25 (PDD-25) of May 1994 outlined strict guidelines for U.S. participation in UN peacekeeping operations—as had Secretary of Defense Les Aspin's 1993 "Bottom-Up Review" of Pentagon activities. The latter particularly questioned the feasibility of multilateral efforts and the wisdom of UN interventions. PDD-25 required clear objectives, a thorough assessment of the risks to international peace and security, strong support from the international community for dealing with the crisis on a multilateral basis, assessment of financial costs and availability of manpower, identification of the circumstances in which UN intervention might take place, and a definable end-point.

In November 1994, the Republican Party accused the UN of "appeasing" Serbia (see previous chapter); the Republican leadership promised a "Contract with America" involving a "national security restoration act" that would bar the deployment of U.S. troops under UN command and cut back funds on "non-traditional" programs such as defense conversion and UN peacekeeping assessments.[18] Yet, contrary to the Republican leadership's views, some 45 to 50 percent of the population consistently support U.S. involvement in the UN, and only a small, hard-core faction oppose it. But to gain popular support, any mission involving U.S. troops must be clearly perceived as part of a UN peacekeeping operation and as consistent with U.S. interests. The operation must also be perceived as having a potential for success.[19]

Although PDD-25 may represent another historical "about face" in regard to the American relationship with international regimes (starting with the congressional rejection of U.S. membership in the League of Nations), this does not necessarily preclude American support for UN-OSCE operations that do, in fact, serve both U.S. national and global interests.[20] In regard to the American backing for the UN intervention in Kuwait, for example, General Colin Powell did not initially support the UN intervention, but President Bush still ordered the U.S.-led operation, under the flag of the UN. Whereas U.S.-UN actions in Somalia were later deemed a "failure," that action in support of Kuwait has generally been judged as a "success," despite efforts by Saddam Hussein to escape UN-imposed sanctions after the Persian Gulf War. The intervention against Iraq was largely U.S.-initiated; the United States obtained a Russian stamp of approval and an abstention from China on UN Resolution 676. Moreover, bringing in the UN helped to legitimize an action which convinced Arab states to combat a fellow Arab power alongside the United States (the ally of Israel). It is unlikely that Washington could have as easily built the same coalition against Iraq if it had not gone through UN channels.

Multilateral diplomacy through UN auspices is evidently not easy to achieve, and U.S. interests may not always win out, but compromises on less "vital" issues can be made. Washington, for example, purportedly had to make a number of concessions on human rights, trade, and arms sales in order to obtain Beijing's cooperation in regard to the Persian Gulf War. Beijing's reluctance to support the intervention against Kuwait could be based on the fact that Beijing could rationalize a seizure of Taiwan (which the PRC considers a "province" of the mainland) as being similar to that of Iraq's seizure of its "former province" Kuwait.

Interestingly, although the United States became increasingly hesitant to involve itself in UN activities, it was not as hesitant to support UN activities within the CIS states. In August 1993,

"Directive 13" stated that Washington should be prepared to support UN peacekeeping operations in the CIS, even if these opposed Russian interests. U.S. policy thus appeared to contradict itself: Washington was prepared to support UN peacekeeping in the CIS (because it served U.S. interests *against Russian efforts to achieve hegemony*), but not necessarily to support UN operations in other regions, where they might interfere in global U.S. spheres of influence and security.

A further contradiction in U.S. policy toward the UN can be seen in the former Yugoslavia. Despite American criticism of UN actions during the war, the United States has not entirely abandoned the UN as a security organization. Even since the turnover of UN operations to the NATO IFOR at the Dayton agreement of December 1995, a number of contradictions in U.S. policy in regard to the UN can be pointed out. First, under strong U.S. insistence, the UN (not IFOR) was to supervise the demilitarization of Serbian-occupied Eastern Slavonia and prepare for its return to Zagreb. The UN was to increase its forces under UNTAES from 1,600 peacekeepers up to 5,000. Ironically, UN Secretary-General Boutros-Boutros Ghali strongly supported the deployment of IFOR (a position also backed by Croatia). The official U.S. position was that NATO forces were overextended in Bosnia and that the WEU states (except for Belgium) did not want to provide the necessary troops for a role in Eastern Slavonia. It thus appeared that neither NATO nor the WEU wanted to be involved in this region. Their refusal appears to be based on geopolitical concerns, deference to Russian and Serbian interests, and on an effort to keep Russia "on board." At the same time, the five thousand peacekeepers of UNTAES were put under American command (and both IFOR and SFOR were to provide support for UNTAES).

Secondly, Washington has been reluctant to involve NATO forces in tracking down war criminals. In January 1996, the Secretary of Defense, William Perry, stated that IFOR was not a "police force;"[21] human rights issues would be better handled, he asserted, by the international UN police force and the OSCE (despite the fact that both are heavily underfunded). NATO does not want to compromise its position as an "honest broker" (after learning its lesson from Somalia).[22]

Washington has likewise given its support to the UN preventive deployment force (UNPREDEP) stationed in the Former Yugoslav Republic of Macedonia which as of February 1996 is to be independent of NATO command in other parts of Yugoslavia and report directly to UN headquarters. The United States has deployed approximately five hundred troops. Ironically, had PDD-25 guidelines been in effect in 1992, it may not have been possible to deploy these forces as part of a UN operation, in what has thus far been deemed successful in deterring potential conflict among Serbia, Albania, Greece, and Bulgaria. The key issue has been that there is no identifiable "end-point" for the UN involvement in this region. (Insurrection leading to mass migration from neighboring Albania could, however, destabilize Macedonia.)

In regard to tensions in Moldova, an unnamed NATO official was quoted in 1995 as being opposed to NATO involvement in the Transdniester dispute, which is to be settled by the UN and OSCE. He stated that any decision in Moldova should take Russia's interests and the situation there in consideration, and be taken only with the approval of the OSCE. At the same time, however, an OSCE spokesperson stated that it lacked funds to conduct peacekeeping by means of multilateral forces in areas such as Moldova and that therefore it could only engage in "preventive diplomacy." Thus, despite U.S. acknowledgment that Moldova should be under OSCE jurisdiction, the OSCE has had to plead for international support. (Ukrainians and Russians have, however, both considered providing "blue helmets" for an OSCE peacekeeping mission in Moldova.) In addition, the OSCE has asked for the return of the OSCE missions to Kosovo, Sandjak, and Vojvodina. However, it is clear that both the UN and OSCE are hamstrung by lack of funding and can generally play only secondary roles—even if it is in the long-term U.S. interest to strengthen and to work through these international regimes (in interaction with NATO, the WEU, and Russia). From this perspective, the UN can serve and legitimize U.S. global interests by helping to build coalitions that support vital U.S. interests. At the same time, Washington must expect to compromise with states (including Russia) on those issues considered less "vital" to American interests.

UN OVEREXTENSION

Speaking in support of a strengthened UN, General Jack Galvin, following his retirement as Supreme Allied Commander in Europe, declared that the UN "resembles a military organization with a division headquarters, but no brigades, no battalions, no command and control infrastructure. We are attempting to operate the UN, currently 19 operations, with some radio antennae on top of a highrise in downtown Manhattan. And we complain that this does not work?"[23]

Whereas the UN did engage in traditional peacekeeping activities and peace-enforcement in the Cold War, the post–1989 era has vastly expanded its activity, to the point of overextension. The UN's nineteen operations have involved traditional peacekeeping, peace-enforcement, humanitarian intervention, and preventive action. In former Yugoslavia alone, UN activities run the gamut from traditional peacekeeping (as in Croatia), humanitarian intervention (as in Bosnia), peace-enforcement (against pan-Serbian movements in

Croatia and Bosnia) and preventive actions (as in the Former Yugoslav Republic of Macedonia). These operations have not always worked successfully and have often been at cross-purposes, which has resulted in stinging, but not entirely justified, criticism.

Since 1948, the UN has mobilized at three different force levels: (1) high-level enforcement operations with a single-nation command structure (the Korean War and the Persian Gulf War); (2) mid-level operations (Congo, Cambodia, Somalia, with twenty to twenty-five thousand troops); and (3) low-level interpositional forces, observers, and transitional and verification missions (seven thousand troops and below).[24] The former Yugoslavia has represented an in-between case, somewhere between a mid-level and a high-level operation. But unlike high-level enforcement during the Cold War, UN actions in the former Yugoslavia did not have a single-nation command structure.

The essential weakness of the UN has been not so much the hastily constructed and overextended nature of its command structure but the *unwillingness* of UN Security Council members to act, combined with the lack of a significant *rapid reaction force*, which could engage when called to duty. The concepts of preventive diplomacy and war-preventive deployments had not yet been accepted in 1991; then, largely due to its Cold War impotence, the UN was completely unprepared to move war-preventive forces into Bosnia when needed and asked by the Bosnian leadership. Thus, rather than engaging war-preventive forces rapidly and in mass *before the conflict spread*, the UN built up peacekeeping forces in former Yugoslavia *during* the conflict, thus making for a less effective military presence. Any future peacekeeping, peacemaking, or war-preventive deployments should be more capable of significant operations—once again, depending upon the geopolitical circumstances and resources available. Most importantly, the concept that *militarily integrated* Euro-Atlantic war-preventive forces be deployed throughout Central and Eastern Europe—backed by the UN/OSCE, NATO and a strengthened Atlantic Partnership Council—should also be considered. (See Chapters 9 and 11.)

The general overextension of UN peacekeeping actions in post–Cold War conflicts since 1989 should not jeopardize the prospects for a new system of cooperative-collective security, particularly in Central and Eastern Europe. The concern here is that apparently morally justifiable UN-backed interventions in Somalia or Haiti, for example, are generally secondary *in a global geostrategic perspective* to the necessity to secure states in Central and Eastern Europe. This is true if only because conflict in Central and Eastern Europe is more likely to spill over into a wider war—if not become the flash-point of another global conflict. This is *not* to argue that the UN should not intervene in crises throughout Asia, Africa, or Latin America, but only that the UN can only act with what resources it possesses, given the political will of the UN Security Council plus the will of the other major powers to finance and support UN operations that truly reflect "vital" international security concerns.

The dilemma is that UN intervention on ostensibly "humanitarian" grounds does risk a double standard: the assertion of spheres of influence and security under the "fig leaf" of the UN flag raises questions. Such interventions risk the political and financial overextension of the UN and can weaken the credibility and legitimacy of the UN as a security organization. Nevertheless, the UN and OSCE need to learn from mistakes and expand their roles in the security and peacemaking spheres, even if they only provide a general mandate for NATO, Russian, or WEU actions. Doing so would (1) provide, where possible, a legitimate international security alternative to unilateral state interventions; and (2) avert the formation of exclusive alliance networks or spheres of influence and security, which would result in the alienation of third powers.

A further dilemma is that failure to set up stronger regional international security regimes could, in the fairly near future, undermine present American alliances and global stability in general. American failure to coordinate global strategy in the UN could result not only in the alienation of Russia but also alienate NATO and European allies.[25] The very fact that both the United States and Russia have been in arrears with UN regular and peacekeeping dues has not augured well for a greater commitment to international security regimes.[26] At the same time, U.S. citizens have obtained more posts and influence in the organization than any other state. In addition, the organization was deliberately located in New York City so that UN revenues would largely be spent in the United States. Congress, with White House support, has pushed to reduce its percentage of peacekeeping costs to 25 percent, even though the annual cost to the United States for UN peacekeeping is less than half of 1 percent of the U.S. military budget, as of October 1996. Even after fiscal 1997 dues are paid, Washington will owe the UN $976 million (according to U.S. figures) and $1.5 billion (according to the UN). Washington has based its peacekeeping rate at 25 percent, while the UN has charged 30.4 percent.[27]

The dilemma is that cooperative-collective security is exposed to the pressures of national political expediency. Although cooperative-collective security should prove cost-effective in the long-term, it is cost-intensive in the short-run and thus may prove difficult to implement from a domestic political standpoint, unless clearly shown to be in the national interest.[28] On the one hand, Congress has rightly been concerned with the UN's evident overextension and "aggressive multilateralism"; the fairness of the U.S. burden with respect to the UN peacekeeping budget; the uncertain long-term costs of peacekeeping operations; exposure of U.S. military personnel to danger under UN command; and the necessity for the president to consult with Congress more candidly as to the nature, extent, and expense of UN operations. The Pentagon is rightly concerned with the fact that UN peacekeepers have largely been paid with dollars allocated to operations and maintenance which tends to drain resources and weaken force readiness and morale. (Since Congress has refused supplemental appropriations, U.S. involvement in the UN operations has been paid for out of the Pentagon budget.) In addition, UN peacekeeping activities are regarded as "eroding the unit skills that forces need in combat."[29] On the other hand, many of these issues can be dealt with only through *strengthening* UN or OSCE operations, but in coordination with NATO and the Atlantic Partnership Council. Also, the development of a truly integrated system of Euro-Atlantic war-preventive deployments (and an Euro-Atlantic DSI would involve *real* training.

International regimes will obviously not work if there is no coordination of strategy among the major powers. On the other hand, international regimes can forge linkages that can draw *willing* states into even more extensively interlocking aspects of cooperation, because of the promise that multilateral cooperation will *ultimately serve the national interest* of each state in the long-term. From this viewpoint, it may be possible to find a compromise in regard to NATO support for Euro-Atlantic war-preventive forces mandated by the UN or OSCE and deployed in regions other than the Former Yugoslav Republic of Macedonia and Eastern Slavonia, for example—*if* it is shown that these international forces would in fact serve American global security interests.

Moreover, by placing greater political emphasis on the OSCE (than the UN) as a conjoint European, Russian, and American effort to sustain peace in Central and Eastern Europe, the United States may be able to provide diplomatic support for the OSCE at the same time that NATO cooperates with OSCE operations. From this standpoint, it may thus be possible to diffuse congressional criticism of U.S. involvement in UN peacekeeping. This can only be done if U.S. troop deployments are kept to a minimum, for domestic political reasons, and if it can be shown that such efforts work in both the American and global interest.

EMPOWERING THE OSCE AND UN

Warren Christopher, former Secretary of State, spoke vaguely of a "strengthened OSCE with a peacekeeping formula under which they would be able to engage the armed forces of various countries."[30] But

Washington has yet to frame this concept into a viable cooperative-collective security pact. The Russian Foreign Intelligence Service has likewise hinted at a system of "collective security that would somehow range between NATO on the one hand and the CSCE and the United Nations on the other."[31] Additionally, Moscow has proposed strengthening the OSCE by forming a UN-type security council, the members of which would have veto power. This position has thus far been opposed by Washington, and it was rejected at the December 1994 OSCE summit in Budapest. American and European leaders feared that Moscow's proposals could result in a subordination of NATO and the WEU to the OSCE. In totally rejecting the Russian proposals, Washington further weakened former Foreign Minister Kozyrev's position vis-à-vis anti–Western forces in Russia.

This seemingly anti–NATO Russian position may, however, represent a bargaining stance: a compromise position that may be acceptable to the United States had been stated by Vladimir Shustov (Russia's chief delegate to the Vienna talks): "We do not mean that the [OSCE] should be a commanding body. . . [but that] the [OSCE] should be the central organization coordinating activities by these other organizations, particularly in regard to security and peace."[32] From this perspective, Washington's fears appear unjustified, a stronger OSCE could never supplant NATO.[33] Accordingly, one way to forge a close U.S., EU, and Russian relationship is to strengthen the OSCE as an international security regime seeking to *coordinate*, but not necessarily *control*, NATO, WEU, and Russian political-economic and security interests in Central and Eastern Europe. At the same time, Washington could strengthen NATO's proposed Atlantic Partnership Council, as the latter cooperates with the OSCE.

The Russian view should not altogether be ruled out, an OSCE security council may not merely serve Russian interests alone, as feared, but may actually help counterbalance the viewpoints of the key states in the new Europe. Members of the OSCE security council could include the United States, Russia, Austria, Poland, Sweden, and Ukraine. Western European states like France, Germany, Italy, or the UK could rotate as members of an OSCE security council. (However, would Russia accept Ukraine as an OSCE security council member?) As Poland would be represented, it should be seen as in the interest of such a state to support the formation of an OSCE security council.[34] Lesser states would look to the support of a more influential power. (Washington has, however, spoken of creating an "inner group" within the OSCE.)[35]

A step towards a stronger OSCE, but stopping short of a "security council," was implied by the "OSCE first" proposal of Germany and the Netherlands in 1995. This proposal argued that all disputes of the region should be handled by the OSCE before being referred to the UN.

The German-Dutch proposal also called for a new "arms control regime" and a "common CSCE security area" which would not compromise the existing CFE treaty. The Dutch, in particular, argued that, at present, the CSCE has no teeth for conflict prevention and that "it is better to prevent crises than to address them once they have erupted." In a similar declaration apparently supporting a stronger OSCE, German Foreign Minister Klaus Kinkel stated that if it is to become a credible security organization, it must be capable of taking "resolute action in response to the threat of the use of force against the sovereign or territorial integrity of a member state."[36]

The German-Dutch proposal, however, did not advocate strengthening the OSCE to the extent promoted by former German foreign minister Hans Dietrich Genscher. The latter argued that the OSCE would live up to its claims in the long run only if it is "put on a basis that is binding in international law," if both its decision-making structure and presidency's capacity to act are bolstered, and if it obtains "a European security council with the same scope as the UN Security Council."[37] Ultimately, a truly strengthened OSCE could give impetus to security arrangements and a system of crisis prevention managed by the proposed Atlantic Partnership Council, which would include militarily-integrated war-preventive deployments, peacemaking, and peacekeeping under Chapter VI of the UN Charter. Operations similar to those under Chapter VI could be carried out on the basis of the 1992 Helsinki document.[38] (To work toward the prevention of crises, another option would be to establish more powerful "contact groups," which, much like the Contact Group mechanism for former Yugoslavia, would formulate policies concerning specific regions. These contact groups, however, would not possess the full weight of a security council in that the latter would permit bargaining and trade-offs among the states involved.)

Creating a new OSCE security council may not altogether reduce the sovereignty of lesser states if the OSCE as a whole becomes more effective. A stronger OSCE could reduce some of the pressure on an overburdened UN, if the two organizations do not have to compete for decreased international funding. Such a regime would also permit those states (most closely involved in the issues) to resolve those issues without interference from powers outside the region. This also would take some of the political (and economic) burden off the UN. However, if these states are not able to resolve their disputes on their own accord through the OSCE process, the UN could be brought in as a higher authority. An OSCE security council would not serve Russian interests alone but might counterbalance the viewpoints of the key states in the new Europe, depending precisely which were members of such a council.

BRINGING JAPAN AND GERMANY ONTO THE UN SECURITY COUNCIL

The United States should support eventual German and Japanese membership on the UN Security Council, on the condition that they support cooperative-collective security regimes in Europe and Asia. As proposed by the Clinton administration in 1993 (and in opposition to the UK's views), these steps should likewise help reduce, but not eliminate, the U.S. share of the political, economic, and military "responsibility." If Germany and Japan were to enter the UN Security Council, it would be necessary to rescind the "enemy states" clause of the UN Charter (Article 53 and Article 107). The enemy state clause has, in effect, legitimized the Soviet/Russian role, as well as that of other members of the UN Security Council, in the "double containment" of both Germany and Japan, by authorizing the Security Council to take measures against any "enemy state." This clause perhaps represents the final obstacle to full German (and Japanese) sovereignty, but a sovereignty which should still be carefully constrained within international cooperative-collective security regimes.[39]

While German unification proceeded through the "two plus four" process, which required approval by the four victorious allies, Japanese accession to the Security Council would need to be preceded by a U.S.-Japanese-Chinese-Russian peace treaty to end formally World War II in Asia. In becoming members of the UN Security Council, both Japan and Germany would need to extend greater diplomatic, financial, and military support for aspects of cooperative-collective security throughout Europe and Asia. (See below.)

In addition to German efforts to support UN operations in former Yugoslavia (and acceptance of a reinterpretation of the Basic Law by the German *Bundestag* in July 1994 for a German role in UN or OSCE out-of-area peacekeeping), the Japanese have taken positive steps in support of UN operations in Cambodia and Mozambique, following the 1992 International Peace Keeping Law. Moreover, in April 1994 Tokyo's deputy ambassador to the UN called for the abolishment of the UN's enemy clause. However, Article IX of the Japanese constitution forbids Japan from threatening or using force to settle international disputes, thus raising the question whether this would ban Japanese military action under UN command. Japanese leaders have remained split, between those who want Tokyo to push for a permanent seat on the UNSC and those who wish to remain a "civilian" power. A third, more threatening Japanese option would reject both American hegemony and the UN—a position that could come to the forefront if Japan believes that Washington intends to decouple itself from Japanese defense interests.[40] (For 1997–98, Tokyo intended to seek a non-permanent seat on the UN Security Council; at the same time, the issue of using "comfort women" for Japanese troops during World War II was seen as undermining Japan's chance for a permanent seat.)

To solidify a concerted relationship (and finally put an end to World War II), the United States, Japan, and Russia can form an entente over the Kurile Islands (Northern Territories). Such an entente would require the establishment of confidence and security–building measures, coupled with a reduction of Russian military capabilities and a significant increase in Japanese aid to Moscow and investment in Russia, to obtain Russian military approval. Russia and Japan could engage in joint development projects in the region. This entente would also have to include conjoint U.S.-Russian security guarantees to Japan. Another option is to place the Kuriles under a UN trusteeship for a specified number of years.[41]

Similar regionalized international regimes could also be established in Asia (with the United States, Russia, Japan, and the PRC as the key actors) and Central Asia (with the U.S., Russia, Kazakhstan, Turkey, and the PRC). The deployment of international war-preventive forces in key conflict regions of Asia could also be considered. (Perhaps a more enlightened Chinese leadership would permit international war-preventive forces in Tibet, for example!) Such deployments would, of course, require financial and political commitment on all sides. Three Central Asian states (Kazakhstan, Kirgystan, and Uzbekistan, which presently operate under CIS auspices in Tajikistan) have sought UN approval to form a joint peacekeeping battalion to be trained by the PfP and stationed in Tajikistan in late 1996.[42] These states have also established a conference on interaction and confidence–building measures in Asia, which joins Russia, China, India, Turkey, Iran, Azerbaijan, and the five Central Asian states (not Turkmenistan). (See also Chapter V.)

A formal end to the Korean War should also be negotiated; it could perhaps ultimately be achieved by nudging the two Koreas towards a loose confederal arrangement acceptable to both sides. Steps towards a U.S.-EU-Russian-Japanese entente must not alienate the PRC but work to guarantee security of both the PRC and Taiwan by defusing tensions in the South China Sea (in regard to the Spratly Islands) and across the Taiwan Straits. The efforts of ASEAN to forge a rapprochement with China, involving aspects of both cooperation and containment, represent a positive step. Joint renunciation of the use of force (overseen by the UN or by an Asian security forum), coupled with a closer PRC-Taiwan confederal arrangement (one that would not permit the deployment of People's Liberation Army forces on Taiwan), may represent a possible option in the fairly near term.

CHAPTER 11

Toward Cooperative-Collective Security

POTENTIAL COSTS OF NATO ENLARGEMENT

In March 1996 the U.S. Congressional Budget Office estimated the potential costs of NATO enlargement, under the assumption that the so-called Visegrad states of Poland, the Czech Republic, Hungary, and Slovakia will be the next to enter. These costs are *above* the estimated $90–120 billion that is allocated to forces that might be made available to NATO out of the yearly $260 billion U.S. defense budget. These costs are likewise to be spread out over the 1996–2010 period among the NATO allies, which presently spend a total of roughly $160 billion yearly on their defense.[1] In February 1997, the White House estimated the costs of NATO enlargement to run between $27 billion to $35 billion over the thirteen year period from 1997–2010; NATO's own figures put the cost "very close" to the $35 billion figure. All of these estimates, however, really depend upon which options are finally chosen, and the reaction of those states not invited to join the Alliance.

The CBO has concretely outlined five defense options:

Option I: Enhance Visegrad defense and facilitate NATO supplemental reinforcement. According to the CBO report, enhancing Visegrad defense forces would mean upgrading the militaries and infrastructures of new NATO members, making them more compatible with NATO forces, and provide "C⁴I" capabilities (Command, Control, Communications, Computers, and Intelligence). At the same time, NATO would have to improve its own military capabilities and increase the range of its aircraft. The CBO option also envisions improvements in the Polish military, making it more mobile and improving the navy's submarine and mine-sweeping capabilities. As the report states, "The major disadvantage is that such efforts might only permit the Visegrad states to deter and defend themselves against lesser threats, such as a border skirmish with a neighbor, or a limited war with a regional power." This option would cost the United States, $4.8 billion; NATO allies, a total of $13.8 billion; and new members, $42 billion, for a total of $60.6 billion.

The CBO report acknowledged that Central European states probably cannot afford a $42 billion defense upgrade and then absorb a 60 percent increase in defense spending to meet NATO modernization requirements. Thus, improvements may well be selective, involving increased training and exercises, enhancing C^4I, and improving air defenses and integrating them with NATO. This latter option represents a "budget plan" and would cost the United States $1.9 billion, NATO allies $3.7 billion, and new members $15.6 billion for a total of $21.2 billion. The CBO states, however, this proposal would only marginally improve Central European defenses. (The "budget plan" appears to parallel the first official February 1997 cost estimates of the Clinton administration. See below.)

Option II: Project NATO air power eastward to defend Central European states. Projecting NATO air power would mean to reinforce Central European states, and it would most likely involve the establishment of prepared bases—"colocated operating bases" (COBs). At the same time, projecting air power into COBs in Central Europe is likely to be regarded as threatening to Russia (possibly resulting in preemption); thus the CBO argues that it is better that NATO operate from German bases. This option would cost the United States $4.6 billion, NATO allies $10.3 billion, and new members $3.6 billion for a total of $18.6 billion.

Option III: Project power eastward, with NATO ground forces based in Germany. This option would add ground forces (ten NATO divisions), based in Germany, to air power. The CBO regards this option as a greater symbol of commitment than air power alone. Reception facilities would need to be established in the Central European countries. This option would cost the United States $3.6 billion, NATO allies $20.3 billion, new members $6.2 billion for a total of $30.1 billion in all.

Option IV: Move stocks of prepositioned equipment eastward. This assumes that stocks of equipment could be permanently stationed in Central Europe at a relatively low cost. The CBO states that the Pentagon has already shifted equipment nearer Dutch and Belgian ports in case of an overseas crisis; placing large stocks in Central Europe would make displacement for out-of-area operations more difficult and slower. In addition, such stocks could be targets of preemption or sabotage. This option would cost the United States about $300 million,

NATO allies $900 million, new members, $100 million, a total of $1.2 billion.

Option V: Station a limited number of forces forward. This most ambitious option is meant to reassure Central European allies of NATO's full commitment. The CBO argues that whereas Russia might react to a deployment of a large force, a limited one might not be perceived as a threat. Permanent deployment of a large force would also require either German or American forces—considering that not all NATO members would contribute. This option would cost the United States $5.5 billion, NATO allies $8.7 billion and new members, nothing, $14.2 billion in all.

If all five options are chosen, overall costs would be predicted to be at $18.9 billion for the United States; $54 billion for NATO allies; $51.8 billion for new members—for a sum total of $124.7 billion. If, however, only the "budget plan" under Option I is accepted, costs would be roughly $21.2 billion, but security gains would be minimal.

The "budget plan" appears to parallel the first official February 1997 cost estimates of the Clinton administration, involving an total outlay of between $27 billion to $35 billion over a thirteen year period. The United States would pay roughly between $2.1 billion to $2.7 billion (about $200 million a year). New members would spend $10 billion to $13 billion to bring ground and air defenses to alliance levels. Current NATO allies would pay $8 to $10 billion bolstering rapid-reaction forces; and both new and old members would spend about $9 to $12 billion to link their communication and command systems. Initial administration estimates most likely assume only gradual improvements in the armed forces and communications of new member states. Poland and other new members, for example, would have only four divisions and six fighter wings designated for defense.[2]

A CRITIQUE

An immediate problem not raised by the CBO report is that each of the options assumes that all four Visegrad states enter NATO together; but what if Slovakia does not? What, if any, would be the additional costs should Slovakia prove a thorn in NATO defenses and break up a geomilitarily integrated system? Moreover, what if Romania and Slovenia, pushed by Canada, France, and Italy, do enter as "full" members? What then would be the additional costs involved?

The second issue revolves around the cost of an adequate defense, particularly given that it could take up to ten or fifteen years for new members that had been Warsaw Pact states to upgrade their forces to NATO qualifications. Due to the dependence and training of Central European militaries on outdated Soviet-bloc equipment, it may not be economically feasible to revamp thoroughly their military-technological infrastructure. An adequate defense thus entails that NATO begin to operate its forces side-by-side with former Warsaw Pact forces, rather than intermeshing with them. NATO forces may also need to be restructured for out-of-area force projection.[3] NATO's experiments with IFOR and CJTF in the former Yugoslavia appear to move in this latter direction.

The third point is, precisely what kind of force projection would it take to make NATO membership credible? NATO enlargement to the Central European states would prove meaningless if it were not also in a position to protect the Baltic states (or Finland). The fact that it appears Russia will not be capable of mounting an offensive deep into Central Europe or against China for next ten to fifteen years does not necessarily preclude actions against the Baltic states. The problem, however, is that regional defense linkages (for example, between Poland and Lithuania) essentially mean that an attack on the Baltic states could represent an attack on a new NATO member, as Poland and then NATO could be drawn into such a clash. As the Baltic states lack strategic depth, they would be difficult to hold and to retake by amphibious assault, across waters that are mined and guarded by submarines. Moreover, the CBO report itself has recognized that membership for the Baltic states "might entail much risk for NATO and little reward."[4] Protecting Central Europe alone, however, while being unable to protect the rest of Central or Eastern Europe, could thus result in a new partition and a renewed Cold War—but in highly unstable and dangerous conditions in which a clear "victory" would appear extremely doubtful.

The dilemma is that it is not certain if Central European countries will feel totally reassured by a limited NATO deployment. (They may demand a greater tangible commitment.) Whether Moscow will *not* regard even very limited steps to improve NATO infrastructure as a potential threat is also uncertain. Concurrently, it is not clear to what extent Germany will want to play a key role—if NATO decides to deploy ground or air forces on German territory (rather than on the territory of new member states) or if German forces are to be deployed outside Germany. It is also not certain how Central and Eastern European states might react to a German troop presence, if deemed necessary. And finally, U.S. efforts to export most of the costs of NATO enlargement onto both new and old Alliance members may cause significant acrimony in an era of defense and budget cutting.

In contrast to the CBO report, a RAND study on the costs of NATO enlargement has argued that the costs are likely to be "modest"—$30 to $52 billion over a ten-to-fifteen year period, depending upon the level of capabilities deemed necessary. In essence, the RAND study cut troop deployments in half. Rather than deploying ten divisions (16,000 men each) and ten fighter wings (ninety fighter jets, plus eighteen support aircraft, each) as suggested by the CBO, the RAND study proposed five divisions and ten fighter wings. The RAND report has argued that self-defense support would cost a total of $10–12 billion; air power projection would cost $20–30 billion; joint-power projection, $30–52 billion; while a forward presence would cost $55–110 billion. (These costs are likewise to be spread out among the NATO allies.)

Largely ignoring the CBO's "budget plan," the RAND report justifies its lower cost estimates by stating that the CBO approach is "threat-based" (against Russia), while its own approach is "goal" and "capacity-based"—and aimed at "providing political reassurance."[5] At the same time, however, the RAND cost estimates make the uncertain assumption that Russia and other states not initially accepted into NATO will truly be "on board" and that Moscow will not engage in an *obstructionist* if not a *preclusive* strategy to thwart NATO enlargement.

From this perspective, costs (such as those estimated by the Clinton administration in February 1997) could be much higher if Russia (or such states as Belarus) opt to obstruct NATO's enlargement. Moreover, the Clinton administration may have purposely "low-balled" the potential costs so as to reassure both the Congress and the Russians. An anonymous Senior official was quoted as saying: "There was a strong political imperative to low-ball the figures. Everybody realized the main priority was to keep costs down so as to reassure Congress as well as the Russians."[6]

The potential costs of enlargement must also be seen in light of the overall global geostrategic and military balance. Despite maintaining a relatively high level of defense spending, the Clinton administration presently admits a $40 billion shortfall in its own defense plan—*prior to* any additional costs involving proposed NATO enlargement. The real American defense costs could even be as high as $50–200 billion over the next six to ten years, in terms of what critics have deemed the "strategy–resources" mismatch in the first term Clinton administration plans to prepare for two nearly simultaneous regional conflicts.[7]

The expansion of overseas commitments, for example, has already threatened to overextend U.S. capabilities. While Kuwait and Saudi Arabia have been paying for the indefinite deployment of a Marine amphibious ready group in the Persian Gulf, U.S. participation in UN peacekeeping in Haiti, Somalia, Rwanda, Bosnia, and Macedonia has largely been paid for by funds originally allocated to the Pentagon. Even though Washington has reduced its military presence, continued NATO engagement (for at least eighteen months after December 1996 under SFOR) in former Yugoslavia has also raised significant financial questions—as has the deployment of U.S. aircraft carriers in the Taiwan Straits. The number of troops on contingency missions has increased by 500 percent since 1989, while the GDP devoted to U.S. defense has declined by 30 percent since 1991.

Concurrently, shoring up force readiness (whether NATO expands or not) may mean additional costs. NATO's nuclear weaponry (that deployed on European territory) has been cut by 80 percent. (See Chapter 7.) NATO defense ministers warned in mid-December 1995 that the Alliance faced shortfalls especially in support for reaction forces, ground-based air defense, and strategic mobility, due to the fact that NATO infrastructure has shrunk by 60 percent since 1991. This point has raised fears that NATO may lack a credible projection strategy—at the very time that an enlargement of the Alliance has been proposed. Moreover, as European allies have all been cutting defense costs, they may oppose the increased burden of NATO enlargement, and may press the United States to pay a greater proportion of the costs.

It is highly ironic that unilateral NATO enlargement to the Central European theater has been proposed at a time when not only U.S. forces risk hypertrophy but also when Russia and Ukraine have been cutting the size of their armed forces. (Belarus, however, may be increasing the size of its army. See Chapter 5.) In the Soviet era, weapons acquisition represented two–thirds of Soviet defense spending; in the post–Cold War period, weapons acquisition takes roughly 25 percent, and military personnel 67 percent. (The military itself has been cut to 30 percent its former size: the Russian army now has about 1.5 million troops as compared to 4.5 million in the Soviet era.) Most of defense spending goes to the Strategic Rocket Forces and to a lesser extent, air defense. This leaves both the army and navy in a state of disarray, in which both soldiers and firms can go for months without pay.[8] In August 1996, the state debt to the Russian armed forces was estimated at more than 15 million rubles. Concurrently, an increasing amount of Russian defense spending has been allocated to prevent mass unrest *within* the Russian Federation itself. The number of interior troops has reportedly increased to 1.5 times that of the Soviet era.[9] This fact indicates that Moscow is presently preparing for the contingency of domestic repression rather than for external expansion.

The war in Chechnya has illustrated the obsolescence of Russian military methods, and its lack of coordination, leadership, discipline, as well as its sheer corruption. The military will continue to have difficulty in reforming itself, due to internal political discord, which is often fueled by political factions. Moreover, in 1996 roughly only a quarter of a million soldiers met modern standards of readiness, the rate of modernization of equipment has been falling so drastically that the proportion of modern weaponry in service may well drop from 55–65 percent in 1995 to 40 percent after 2000. Russian strategic nuclear potential is roughly 2.5 times lower than that of the United States (and may drop even lower). It may take up from ten to fifteen years to set up an air defense system capable of withstanding American ICBMs, SLBMs, and cruise missiles. The Russian navy has been in a state of disrepair, and even advances in its nuclear submarine fleet have been offset by poor support and maintenance. Inadequate maintenance, lack of supplies, and inability to modernize have weakened the reliability and readiness of its land and sea-based nuclear missiles.[10]

Defense Minister Igor Rodionov stated that it would be "difficult but not impossible" to transform Russian military into an all-professional force by the year 2000, given the "necessary economic conditions." As advocated by Rodionov, Russian military reform (intended to coordinate the often isolated decisions of separate ministries) may require the creation of a new military council that would have the power to make binding decisions for all ministries and agencies that have armed forces under their jurisdiction.[11] Despite current problems involving excessive waste, lack of coordination among the armed services, and redundancy of weapons systems, training facilities, and command staff, both Rodionov and former Security Council secretary Alexandr Lebed have protested the 1997 budget plan of 101 trillion rubles ($20 billion), which fell far short of the 260 trillion rubles requested by the defense ministry. Defense spending has been estimated at around 80 trillion rubles ($17 billion) in 1996, or only 10 percent of the U.S. level, although real defense spending may be as much as two times that amount.[12] Lebed warned of military insurrection and declared that the Chernomyrdin government had "conclusively" decided to "undermine the armed forces."[13]

As the Russian military cannot obtain the necessary finance, Russia would seem to represent no immediate threat to Central Europe—at least for ten or fifteen years. (The Baltic states, however, may represent a different category.) At the same time, the very fact that the United States could well become overextended implies the necessity to cultivate and secure Russia as a potential ally. For their own global interests, the United States, the European Union, and Japan must work to draw Russia into a new system of European security (so as to draw Moscow away from directly supporting the geopolitical and military-technological potential of third powers, such as the PRC). The United States already spends more than double the *real* defense spending of potential *separate* "threats," that include Russia, China, Iran, Iraq, Syria, Libya, India, and North Korea.[14] NATO enlargement, however, could press Russia to seek stronger, military alliances with these lesser powers (despite the evident clash of interests among the latter), thus potentially magnifying the American defense burden. The tighter the military alliance, the greater the danger that a clash between lesser powers could draw in the major ones. Russia needs assistance from the United States, Europe, and Japan to prevent its own isolation. On the other hand, the latter need Russian cooperation in order to lessen the chances of a self-fulfilling prophecy.

THE COOPERATIVE-COLLECTIVE SECURITY APPROACH

The CCS approach seeks to synthesize the geostrategic and political economic aspects of European security issues. Its first, and most important, purpose is to avoid the overextension of NATO's integrated military command. If not carefully managed, the enlargement of NATO's "full" membership could weaken its consensus and political will to act, particularly with no common threat to unify members, as there was during the Cold War. NATO could also become overextended if it does not truly possess the capabilities to meet its promised Article V obligations. NATO's very legitimacy could be undermined if the American public (and domestic constituencies of NATO member countries) oppose the costs and burdens of NATO enlargement.

The second aim of the CCS approach is to resolve the potential intra-West conflict of interest between the enlargement of the EU or WEU, or both, to Finland and other Eastern European states, and U.S. congressional/German demands to incorporate only the states of Poland, the Czech Republic, and Hungary into NATO. The CCS approach likewise seeks to avoid a NATO-Russian (or even German-Russian) partition of Central and Eastern Europe, and to dampen the possibility that NATO enlargement could provoke a Russian revanchist backlash.

The CCS approach is intended to hold in check the potential irredentist claims of Central and Eastern European states against Russia or its allies, and to deter conflicts among the Central and Eastern European states themselves. The CCS approach argues that the primary and immediate threat to Central and Eastern European security stems from interethnic disputes, the trafficking of illegal materials, and disputed borders. It accordingly seeks Russian cooperation *from the beginning*, so that misperceptions of intent will not escalate into tensions and conflict. Most importantly, instead of attempting to *impose* a structure of security *from above*, in accord with essentially American and German geostrategic and political-economic criteria, the CCS approach would attempt to construct a regional system of defense *from the ground up*, building upon preexisting defense and strategic linkages and partnerships, but again without alienating Moscow.

The CCS approach seeks to spread the overall potential defense burden and responsibilities in regard to Central and Eastern Europe to as many states as is possible, and thus reduce the relative burden for the United States in terms of both financial and political commitments. American and European aid should not be perceived by Russia as subsidizing future NATO members against Russian interests but as supporting regional cooperation in which Russia and Central and Eastern European states participate fully.[15] Finally, the ultimate goal is to form a Euro-Atlantic Defense and Security Identity backed by NATO, EU/WEU, and Russian *security guarantees.*

TOWARD A EURO-ATLANTIC DEFENSE AND SECURITY IDENTITY

The CCS approach looks to a non-threatening, militarily integrated Euro-Atlantic DSI linked to regional Central and Eastern European, Finnish, and Baltic state self-defense forces. It represents a transition to a new system of global security. The basic approach is to expand the deployments of Euro-Atlantic war-preventive forces into regions of potential contention throughout much of the former Soviet bloc *before* conflict actually erupts.[16] These forces would be somewhat similar to the UNPREDEP deployed in the Former Yugoslav Republic of Macedonia, or UNTAES in Eastern Slavonia, but should seek the military integration of defense capabilities of as many Central and East European states as is possible under the auspices of a strengthened Atlantic Partnership Council. In many ways, this concept represents a regional "PfP plus," as the Partnership for Peace initiative has already helped to create the infrastructure for defense and peacekeeping cooperation necessary for this proposal.[17]

A strengthened Atlantic Partnership Council can accordingly decide the nature, number, and nationality of war-preventive forces to be deployed under a general UN or OSCE mandate. These deployments must be acceptable to each of the participating states. Military infrastructure and weapons systems, including sophisticated anti-tactical ballistic missile systems, would also be deployed after collective agreement and in respect to the CFE treaty. The stationing of Euro-Atlantic war-preventive forces would involve forces from any state trained by the PfP initiative. It is unlikely that American, Russian, or German forces would be deployed—except in special circumstances. If, however, the forces of these latter states were to be deployed, they would be brought in together by collective agreement (as Combined Joint Task Forces) and deployed in such a way so as to counterbalance the geopolitical interests of each state in the region. A joint American-Russian brigade, as proposed by Secretary of State Madeleine Albright in February 1997, represents only one possible combination of forces. Moreover, as Russia could have a say in what forces and what kinds of defensive weapons systems would be deployed, it would not be alienated. Concurrently, NATO allies (in cooperation with Russia) would develop an ability to project air power eastward and operate forces side-by-side Euro-Atlantic war-preventive forces, which may or may not include troops from "full-fledged" NATO member states.

In effect, Euro-Atlantic peacekeeping and war-preventive forces (trained by PfP and grafted onto existing Central and Eastern European self-defense forces) would seek to form a triangular system of nonthreatening defense initially radiating out from eastern Germany to Finland, from Finland to Slovenia, covering the Baltic states, Poland, the Czech and Slovak republics, Hungary, and Romania. More specifically, Euro-Atlantic war-preventive forces could be deployed along the Russo-Finnish border, the disputed areas of the Estonian-Russian border, the Lithuanian and Polish borders with Belarus, the Polish border with Kaliningrad, the German and Czech borders and into disputed regions among Slovakia, Hungary, Romania, and Ukraine. War-preventive forces could be deployed as well in other areas, such as the eastern Ukraine, or regions of Belarus, or the Crimea. Similar deployments in Kosovo (parallel to UNPREDEP) may not prove altogether unrealistic, particularly if Serbia ultimately joins the PfP initiative. But, of course, any deployments depend upon the resources available, as well as the political will to commit such forces.

Evidently, new cooperative-collective security arrangements must be given support by the states caught between both German and Russian pincers, particularly Poland and the Czech Republic. Both Polish and Czech spokespersons have indicated that the NATO alliance can help to contain German pressures and that NATO must simultaneously sustain "cooperation" with Russia.[18] While this latter position may appear tenable (if it is at all possible for Central and Eastern European states to become "full" NATO members and not alienate Moscow), it ignores the burgeoning role of Germany within both NATO and the WEU. As indicated by U.S. congressional reluctance to sustain IFOR forces in the former Yugoslavia over a year, and SFOR for only eighteen months, the United States may increasingly take a back seat in the NATO alliance, which would permit Europeans greater "power" and "burden"-sharing through ESDI and CJTF. Hence, from this perspective, an enlarged NATO may increasingly be influenced by Germany and the EU/WEU, rather than the United States, in possible opposition to the interests of states such as the Czech Republic and Poland. By contrast, a system of cooperative-collective security involving an Euro-Atlantic Defense and Security Identity may be better able to counterbalance Russian and German pressures and those of other states, and concurrently provide reassurance against fears of a U.S.-Russian condominium.

Rather than seeking multilateral cooperative-collective security arrangements, however, both Poland and the Czech Republic (as well as other Central and Eastern European countries) have sought "full" NATO membership, as a means to guarantee their long-term security. These states (particularly Prague) have tended to downplay regional defense cooperation and have opposed proposals involving NATO-Russian "cross guarantees." (See Chapters 3 and 7.) On the other hand, the CCS approach argues that NATO-EU/WEU-Russian "cross guarantees" may actually be preferable to NATO security guarantees alone. States such as Poland and Lithuania may need Russian security guarantees, for example, against Belarus (if not against Germany as well); at the same time, NATO and the WEU will need to cooperate to back these states against potential Belarusian and Russian threats. Central and Eastern European cooperation that is *reinforced* by a Euro-Atlantic DSI regime would not only counterbalance German, Belarusian, Ukrainian, and Russian pressures and interests but also help mitigate Russian efforts to sustain hegemony over CIS states. Moscow could then permit a more *proportional* relationship of power to develop between itself and former Soviet-bloc states.

From this perspective, rather than unilaterally and prematurely expanding NATO or the WEU into Central and Eastern Europe, Washington should first strengthen cooperative *security assurances*. As argued above, this could be achieved by the not entirely symbolic deployment of Euro-Atlantic war-preventive forces throughout much of the former Soviet bloc under a general UN or OSCE mandate in the period 1997–99, to achieve greater credibility for those security assurances. During this interim phase the United States would be able to work more confidently with Russia and the EU/WEU to forge more effective conjoint "hard" security guarantees, to be backed by NATO, the EU/WEU, and Russia.

THE NORDIC STATES, KALININGRAD, AND THE KOLA PENINSULA

A shift in the Nordic geostrategic and political-economic equilibrium is best illustrated by: (1) Swedish and Finnish membership in the EU; (2) Nordic support for Baltic state independence; (3) perceived Nordic political-economic support for autonomy or independence movements in Karelia and Komi (if not St. Petersburg); (4) potential political-military instability in Kaliningrad and Murmansk (as well as within Russia in general); and (5) potential tensions between Poland and Belarus, among other states. From this standpoint, Nordic states can no longer rely upon "neutrality" to guarantee regional security.

As the thorn in any European defense posture is the Russian geostrategic pressure point at Kaliningrad, all efforts should be taken to permit Russia to withdraw over a certain period, thus dampening any need for a substantial defense buildup of the northern or former Leningrad Military District.[19] The danger, however, is that political-economic-military instability in Kaliningrad risks spilling over into the rest of the region. To prevent conflict, the UN or OSCE could supervise transit routes to and from Kaliningrad through Lithuania (assuming the latter accepts) until the region is demilitarized, if not ultimately "internationalized," as part of an overarching cooperative-collective security pact. (American congressional calls to demilitarize Kaliningrad and transfer the region to an international administration were condemned by Russian foreign minister Kozyrev in July 1995, but Russia may ultimately be inclined to accept Kaliningrad's "internationalization" once all states in the region become part of a cooperative-collective security arrangement—but only if it involves significant Russian input.)[20] There has been one suggestion that NATO headquarters should be shifted to Kaliningrad should the Russian Federation join NATO.[21] It would be more appropriate, however, to place one of the primary headquarters of Atlantic Partnership Council in this district, to symbolize the implementation of a Euro-Atlantic DSI. To establish Kaliningrad as an Atlantic Partnership Council headquarters should help to build the confidence of the Russian military and help to stabilize Kaliningrad itself. (Mutual representation at Supreme Allied Headquarters, and at the headquarters of the Russian General Staff, has been proposed by NATO spokesmen, in addition to other steps to formalize a permanent political consultation mechanism.)

The potential for political-military instability in Kaliningrad, Murmansk, and Russia in general means that the extension of *positive security assurances* to Finland and the Baltic states (similar to those extended to Ukraine through the UN and the NPT) would not be not sufficient to guarantee the security of these states.[22] At the same time, NATO membership for these states risks Alliance overextension. As argued previously in this Chapter, to provide Article V security guarantees to the Baltic states in particular would require the forward deployment of NATO conventional and nuclear forces. In April 1996 the Finnish and Swedish foreign ministers proposed the concept of a EU peace project under the mandate of the UN and OSCE;[23] but this proposal would still need conjoint NATO, WEU and Russian backing to guarantee adequately the security of this region. Accordingly, to guarantee sufficiently Nordic state security and other Eastern European states, UN or OSCE security assurances must be reinforced by the deployment of Euro-Atlantic war-preventive units. Once a militarily integrated Euro-Atlantic DSI is fully in place under general UN/OSCE "soft" security assurances, NATO—in conjunction with the WEU and Russia—could extend more formal "hard" security guarantees.[24]

Moreover, NATO's credibility to back up the Baltic states *and* Finland would certainly be strengthened if Sweden joined, on a non-nuclear basis. Although delicate negotiations would still have to take place, Russia should have no justification to oppose a self-limited, non-nuclear Swedish membership in NATO as a means to guarantee regional stability, as the latter was never part of a czarist or Soviet sphere of influence and security. At the same time, Finland and the Baltic states (the latter would take further steps toward military and economic integration) would play a role in the "arch of cooperation" between Norway and Sweden, Russia and Belarus. ("Full" NATO membership for Sweden could also reduce any pressures for the renationalization of Swedish and Finnish defenses and concurrently help to "double contain" any potential Nordic alliance against Russian interests. While Germany should be likewise encouraged to support a system of cooperative-collective security that would provide stability along its eastern borders, the pressures on Germany to meet defense obligations along the Central Front, as well as in northeastern and southeastern Europe, could be substantially diminished if Sweden and Austria both joined NATO as "full" but non-nuclear members. See discussion below.)

THE CENTRAL FRONT AND GERMANY

In this proposal, Germany is positioned at the vertex of the defensive triangle. Under the CCS option, however, there is really no need to press for the "full" membership of Central European states in NATO as a security buffer for Germany, since a Euro-Atlantic DSI could play the role of a buffer against the threat of "instability" from the East. At the same time, incorporating Germany into active and visible support for a militarily integrated system of Central and Eastern European security is crucial to allay fears of a resurgence of German militarism. The deployment of Euro-Atlantic war-preventive forces in eastern Germany is thus not intended only to allay Russian fears of a revisionist Germany or of a NATO-WEU forward deployment. Rather, such a deployment is also intended to *channel* German diplomatic and financial energies into a positive role in a viable system of cooperative-collective security for Central and Eastern Europe.[25]

The purpose is thus to retain German membership in NATO and to link German support for a militarily integrated system of cooperative-collective security with a permanent seat for Germany on the UN Security Council, coupled with an enhanced role on a more powerful OSCE. (See Chapter 10.) Such an option could actually enhance the *positive* aspects of German influence throughout Central and Eastern Europe. The deployment of Euro-Atlantic war-preventive forces could be framed as the price to pay for *full-fledged* European unification (to prevent a threatened partition), as well as the price of sustaining the interest of a potentially isolationist United States in the long-term process of European integration.

There is no reason why Germany cannot be integrate its forces into NATO, the WEU, and the European Corps, and also assign forces or assets under a general UN or OSCE mandate to the disposal of a strengthened Atlantic Partnership Council. As Germany has voted to support out-of-area UN missions, Bonn can provide greater support to a cooperative-collective security pact (and remain within NATO), particularly if German diplomatic and financial support for a Central and Eastern European system of cooperative-collective security is linked to German membership on the UN (and OSCE) security councils.[26] If the Franco-German brigade can parade down the Champs d'Elysées on 14 July 1994, a Euro-Atlantic war-preventive force could also march through the Brandenburg Gate!

THE ROLE OF THE PFP

The PfP should accordingly "go fast" to actualize its vague-sounding formulas, to establish a new Central and Eastern European system of cooperative-collective security. The key problems of the CCS approach are primarily those of building credibility and of finding a viable working relationship between NATO, the EU, the WEU, Russia, the UN, and the OSCE. On the one hand, the UN, NACC, and NATO (minus France) all possess different peacekeeping doctrines, and the WEU has been developing its own.[27] On the other hand, NATO would need to coordinate more closely war-preventive deployments and peacekeeping actions with the UN and the OSCE, partly by learning from the experience of IFOR and SFOR in the former Yugoslavia. NATO efforts to bring Moscow into the peace process there (and to make certain Russia does not feel itself to be a "junior partner") may well prove decisive for the future of the NATO-WEU-Russian geostrategic relationship.

Negotiations involving the choice of troop nationalities, as well as the nature of military-technology to be deployed (perhaps involving a quota for Russian/Eastern European weapons systems) may prove to be complex. (In addition to a revision of the CFE Treaty, NATO-Russian arms cooperation has been considered by NATO authorities.) Accordingly, U.S., Russian, or German forces may or may not be deployed, according to the circumstances, and only with agreement of all the states concerned. Would Poland, or the Czech Republic, accept German troops, even if these countries did become "full" members of NATO? What if the United States, in an isolationist mood, refused to deploy its forces? The question, then, is precisely *who decides* what forces and defense systems should be deployed? NATO alone? Or will it be a conjoint NATO, EU/WEU, and Russian decision, through a strengthened Atlantic Partnership Council?

A Central and Eastern European system of collective-cooperative security should be designed so that all states can benefit by remaining in it, and so that if any state decided to withdraw, it would face an alliance of all the remaining members. In other words, if a revanchist Russia (or a revisionist Hungary, Romania, Belarus, Ukraine, or Germany) should drop out of such a security system, then Euro-Atlantic war-preventive forces would still be in place to counter any threat. The renegade state (or states) would then risk confronting the international community. At the same time, NATO's "full" members would remain independent. NATO would decide at what point it would act, and in what measure.

This perspective accordingly supports the "go slow" approach to NATO's eastward expansion, but it argues that the United States and EU/WEU must *not* "go slow" in taking appropriate steps toward a new Central and Eastern European system of cooperative-collective security. This is to argue not that NATO should not enlarge but that the public debate over NATO enlargement into Central Europe has been misdirected; any steps toward NATO enlargement must take place *with* the cooperation of Russia, Ukraine, and other states not selected as "full" members.

From this perspective, only two or three states appear appropriate for "full" NATO membership (in the traditional *exclusive* sense) in the short-term. If these formerly neutral states accept, NATO could enlarge to include Austria, as well as Sweden, on a "self-limiting," nonnuclear basis, as a means to provide logistical support for Euro-Atlantic war-preventive force deployments in the Baltic–Barents Sea region, as well as in central and southeastern Europe. As highly developed democracies and politically stable states, already well integrated into Western political-economic structures, Sweden and Austria should not represent a drag on NATO's political will or resources.

In addition, neither Sweden nor Austria has ever been part of a Russian sphere of influence and security, and their membership could actually "double contain" their influence over states in northeast and southeast Europe respectively. If Sweden and Austria, however, decline "full" NATO membership, or if they are not accepted by the American Senate as such, NATO assets could still made available to them through ESDI and CJTF. However, the question of "full" NATO Article V security guarantees would still be left hanging—unless these states become "associate" members to which NATO would extend its security guarantees.

A third state which could possibly enter NATO as a "full" member (or at least sustain a close relationship with NATO) is Slovenia, which appears to have no unreconcilable disputes with either its Yugoslav or Italian neighbors. With a close relationship to NATO, Slovenia could help place a military-psychological check on future conflict or irredentist actions in that tumultuous region. (This proposal assumes that Slovenian membership would not arouse the jealousy of Croatia or Serbia—and lead the latter to fully align with Russia).

In effect, *all* states (primarily those which once belonged to the Soviet bloc, the Warsaw Pact, or Yugoslavia) that participate in such a Euro-Atlantic Defense and Security Identity could become "associate" members of NATO and would obtain conjoint NATO, WEU, and Russian *security guarantees.* "Full" NATO membership (for states such as Sweden and Austria, if these states would accept it) would be reserved for those states in which NATO held an *exclusive* sphere of security and influence. (Sweden and Austria may possibly join NATO, but only if they begin to perceive Russia or Belarus to be an imminent threat.)

Accordingly, a realistic alternative to the traditionally exclusive approach to NATO enlargement would be to *extend* security guarantees to members of a Euro-Atlantic DSI in coordination with Russia and the EU/WEU. If NATO chose this approach, as opposed to the traditional path, NATO security guarantees for certain key states could be stronger than those for less strategically important states. A *hierarchy* of states could be established within the Euro-Atlantic DSI in which some states would achieve "full" membership status after two years and others remain "associate" members, based upon the extent of each state's contribution to the overall system of security. This approach would seek to reduce the gap between "full" and "associate" membership in such a way that Hungarian membership in NATO would not alienate Romania or Slovakia, for example. This would represent a reinforcement, if not an acceleration, of the PfP initiative.

By enlarging NATO's "full" membership to include Romania and Slovenia (countries supported by France, Italy, and Canada for NATO membership), as well as Poland, the Czech Republic, and Hungary (the three countries supported by the United States), NATO could help mend its apparent rift with France (and other allies) who have sought a *wider* enlargement, partly as a means to counter-balance German influence in Central and Eastern Europe. This latter option would permit Poland, the Czech Republic, Hungary, as well as Romania and Slovenia, to enter NATO, but only within the overall confines of a Euro-Atlantic DSI and the Atlantic Partnership Council. Moreover, as these latter states would play a key role in the regional defense of Central and Eastern Europe, but not in NATO's integrated military command, this option would make it more plausible for NATO to accept *power sharing with Russia and to implement conjoint NATO-EU/WEU-Russian security guarantees for the entire region.* NATO would not risk either the overexposure or the overextension of its integrated military command through a forward deployment.

This option would represent a historic Euro-Atlantic compromise intended to prevent a possible breakdown in the political consensus of NATO's present membership. It could help bring France back into NATO's integrated command. Concurrently, this approach could also prove problematic in that it would require a redefinition of "full" membership. States which now seek membership in NATO may fear that they will not obtain adequate security guarantees as their right to "full" NATO membership would, in effect, be qualified. In addition, the U.S. House and Senate would be concerned—if the change in "full" membership status is not carefully explicated. Yet if NATO has truly changed its role in the post–Cold war era, then a reformulation of roles and duties of "full" members should not be ruled out. At the same time, given this formulation, Russia could tacitly be considered as a "full" member, and thus be less likely to obstruct the arrangement.

The path of cooperative-collective security cannot absolutely guarantee that Moscow will not move in a revanchist direction, but it can mitigate the influence of revanchist factions within the Russian Federation. To be successful, the CCS approach must be implemented soon enough and in such a way as to help *channel* Russian pressures away from Europe. The intent is to draw Moscow step by step into greater responsibility for global affairs, while international cooperative-collective security measures seek to provide checks and balances adequate to forestall Russia or any other any state from taking unilateral advantage. Such a system of cooperative-collective security would likewise attempt to prevent states from forming exclusive spheres of influence and security, and hence keep the new lines from becoming "impermeable." In essence, the CCS approach seeks to forge a militarily integrated regional system of defense against any revisionist or revanchist movements (Russian-initiated or not) which refuse to abide by international norms.

OBTAINING AMERICAN SUPPORT

The cooperative-collective security approach should thus create a political-military solidarity sufficient for Central and Eastern European states to resist the pressure of any power. In effect, by forming a regional counterpoise to Belarusian, German, Russian, or Ukrainian influence (if not that of other states), a Euro-Atlantic DSI would seek to sustain an "arch" of active cooperation between the EU and Germany, and the CIS and Russia, and to mediate among all the states in the region. Poland and the Czech Republic (and possibly Finland) could take the lead as intermediaries. The three Baltic states would seek greater defense and economic integration and likewise seek to play a role as intermediaries between the EU, Russia, and Belarus. Rather than pushing Belarus even closer towards Russia, and isolating Ukraine, the cooperative-collective security approach would seek to reduce pressures on Belarus to align with Russia and of Russia to align with Belarus; Ukraine could retain its role as a "non-aligned" state straddling the EU and the CIS. Ironically, NATO expansion into Central Europe alone (but not into the Baltic states and Ukraine) would actually cut into regional defense linkages already being initiated, for example, between Poland and Lithuania. By contrast, the CCS approach would build upon regional alliances, thus strengthening Baltic state cooperation, as well as that among the Visegrad states of Poland, the Czech Republic, Hungary, and Slovakia. It would also seek out cooperation among Poland, Belarus, and Ukraine, as well as Hungary, Romania, and Ukraine among others—but in coordination with Russia.

Such a system of cooperative-collective security would primarily aim at forming a credible system of nonthreatening defense capable of peacemaking and peacekeeping actions, and at providing early warning in case of hostile action by Russia or other states. Secondly, a CCS regime would help reassure Russia that NATO does not intend a NATO-WEU "forward deployment" of nuclear weapons systems or hostile forces. Finally, it would seek to prevent disputes among Central and Eastern European states themselves from drawing in the major powers, and to reassure Russia that these states would not advance irredentist claims. Such a system would not represent the "Baltic–Black Sea alliance" or "double buffer zone" dreaded by Russian strategic analysts. (See Chapter 1.) Rather, such a system would coordinate defense policy among all the states of Central and Eastern Europe in a long-term effort to integrate Central and Eastern Europe and Russia into a more concerted relationship.

The view that Moscow has sought to "veto" expansion is not entirely justified in that it has tacitly accepted NATO enlargement by arguing for the establishment and implementation of conjoint NATO-

Russian security guarantees for Central and Eastern European states. Assistant Secretary of State Richard C. Holbrooke, however, argued in July 1995 that Eastern European states, as well as unspecified NATO allies, have rejected the idea of NATO-Russian security assurances as "historically discredited" and that Eastern European states "fear being dependent on others for a concept of security in which they are 'beneficiaries,' but not 'participants.'"[28] There is no doubt that Russia has in the past played roles of both hegemonic "divide and rule" and imperialist "divide and conquer" but, in the contemporary situation, the relative independence of both Ukraine and Belarus (among other states) from Moscow's controls means that Moscow does not *yet* possess sufficient power and influence to dictate policy in all of Central and eastern Europe.

Despite efforts to achieve a closer Russian-Belarusian alliance, for example, there is still room for the United States and Europe to play Moscow against Minsk. Russian abilities to pressure and force concessions upon individual Central and Eastern European states can furthermore be mitigated, through an Euro-Atlantic Defense and Security Identity that would provide a militarily integrated "coalition framework." A Euro-Atlantic DSI would provide Central and Eastern European countries an independent voice among the major powers, but without siding with one faction or the other. At the same time, this approach recognizes that Central and Eastern European states, *in realistic terms,* will continue for some time to represent *beneficiaries*—rather than substantial *providers*—of security.

Moreover, the strength of a Russian *droit de regard* and fears of a potential Russian pressures or intervention (under any pretext) can thus be counterbalanced by an internationalized Central and Eastern European security regime, reinforced by the deployment of Euro-Atlantic war-preventive forces, but also backed by NATO and the WEU. Conjoint NATO-Russian security assurances would in fact raise fears of a NATO-Russian condominium and would represent worthless "paper promises"—but only if *not* reinforced by the deployment of Euro-Atlantic war-preventive forces that would help provide the credibility and reassurance necessary to make cooperative-collective security work. A militarily integrated system of Euro-Atlantic war-preventive forces linked to regional defense forces would represent a real deterrent to potential aggressors and help prevent more powerful states from playing one Central or Eastern European state against another.

No approach—including that of NATO maximalism—can absolutely guarantee that Moscow will not pressure states or intervene. Isolating and alienating Russia would definitely risk provoking it to acts of subversion. Ironically, however, by granting Russia a *legitimate* oversight, Moscow would actually be less tempted to subvert or counter such a system. At the same time, a *legitimate* Russian *droit de regard* could be contained and counterbalanced by the influence of NATO and the WEU, as well as that of other states such as Germany or Ukraine.

American congressional support for an Euro-Atlantic Defense and Security Identity should be easier to obtain than "full" NATO membership for Central and Eastern European states, but still not without considerable debate. First of all, the system is largely based on self-help; as in the 1948 Brussels Treaty, which helped to draw congressional support for the formation of NATO, Central and Eastern European states would participate in the development of their own security community. The approach is essentially pragmatic and carries no "ideological baggage." It recognizes that there will continue to be significant problems in implementing democratic principles and practices in each of the Central and East European countries in the foreseeable future. The fact that each country may introduce very different political and economic systems should not be permitted to sharpen divisions and preclude the possibility of general regional cooperation. Besides expected contributions for participation, there would thus be no *initial* political-ideological preconditions for joining. Moreover, *long-term* democratic goals would ultimately need to be achieved under OSCE guidelines.

This approach should help mitigate trends toward a "re-nationalization" of defense and the formation of potentially destabilizing alliances with third powers, as well as minimize the potential for tensions with Belarus and Russia. Central and Eastern European states have, in the past, feared that the formation of regional self-defense forces or that the deployment of UN war-preventive units might be interpreted as a substitute for *real* security offered by NATO. However, this point of view overlooks the need, from the American perspective, to show a willingness to defend one's own region. It also overlooks the fact that even "full" NATO membership may not absolutely guarantee *automatic* support (see Chapter 7). At the same time, a thoroughly integrated Euro-Atlantic DSI could help to prod Central and East European states toward *real* regional cooperation, rather than attempting to rely solely upon NATO. Third, a thoroughly integrated Euro-Atlantic DSI should reduce redundancy and the overall costs of European defenses, particularly as the burden would be shared among Atlantic Partnership Council and OSCE members. The fact that the costs would be spread out (and not placed upon "full" NATO members alone), should help mitigate criticism from a populist American "isolationism" (or what has been deemed "selective interventionism") that could seek to disengage the United States from Europe altogether.

Such a cooperative-collective security system should be considered truly nonthreatening to Belarus, Russia, and Ukraine. Yet if any of the latter states (or others) should drop out of this system of cooperative-collective security, the rest of the states would keep their war-preventive units on alert, backed by the NATO and WEU alliances. The cooperative-collective security approach affirms that NATO will not dilute its integrated military command. Russia would not hold a "veto" over NATO, nor would NATO become a "subcontractor" of the UN or the OSCE.

Perhaps most importantly, from a domestic American political perspective, congressional backing for this proposal would not require the two–thirds majority vote that would be needed in the Senate to revise the North Atlantic Treaty, but rather a simple majority vote in both houses of Congress on the passage of a joint resolution. Thus, much as the "WEU-first" approach advocated (see Chapter 9), NATO would be permitted to *extend* security guarantees to a select group of core states participating in a Euro-Atlantic DSI. As the real potential costs of NATO enlargement (without Russian input) are uncertain, and as the make-up of the U.S. Senate has changed in recent years, a two–thirds majority vote in support of the expansion of NATO's "full" membership cannot be guaranteed. There is no reason to risk the disapproval of the U.S. Senate and NATO parliaments—or a Russian backlash—if a viable alternative can be implemented. (Russian threats or obstructionism may or may not impel Congress to press ahead with enlargement in its traditional sense, but why risk a spiraling of tensions, if a viable alternative path can be pursued?)

The cooperative-collective security approach requires American guidance. By working through the UN and OSCE as well as a strengthened Atlantic Partnership Council, Washington should reach out for a "strategic partnership" with Russia while helping to build the infrastructure for a viable, nonthreatening, yet militarily integrated, Euro-Atlantic Defense and Security Identity. The implementation of a such a regime should preferably take place *prior* to any unilateral expansion of NATO or WEU membership to states in Central and Eastern Europe. This action could thus take place in the period 1997–99 before the proposed new NATO members are expected to come on board as "full" members. It is possible that Washington may need to mobilize the UN and OSCE (in much the same way as it mobilized the UN before the Gulf War) to gain global support for such an initiative, and to begin the deployments of OSCE-Atlantic Partnership war-preventive forces as soon as possible.

How the vital question of Central and Eastern European security will be handled by American leadership will largely determine whether the next millennium will behold a renaissance or a further descent into hell. NATO's decision at the July 1997 summit to offer "full" membership to Poland, the Czech Republic, and Hungary risks dividing NATO's attention between conflicting imperatives. As proposed, NATO's Atlantic Partnership Council—in coordination with the OSCE and UN—should begin to implement an Euro-Atlantic DSI in the period 1997–99, before these three Central European states are to become "full-fledged" members. At the same time, the considerable resources devoted to integrate only these states could begin to crowd out funds available for a more comprehensive system of security *for the entire region*. Lack of resources could then alienate states that had hoped to enter NATO on a promised second wave, while Ukraine may find itself impelled to choose between NATO or Russia. Concurrently, despite NATO efforts to cooperate with the UN and OSCE, and to engage in joint consultations with Russia, the integration of NATO's exclusive command structure with Central European states could raise the suspicions of Russia, Belarus, and other non-NATO members.

In February 1997, Ambassador George F. Kennan warned that NATO expansion "would be the most fatal error of American policy in the entire post–Cold War era"; Secretary of State Madeleine Albright responded that such criticism represents an example of "old system thinking" in that it assumes that NATO is still carrying out its Cold War mission.[29] NATO may claim that it has adopted a "new" role, but its public rhetoric and pressure to achieve a "timetable" for expansion so as to sustain its credibility and political promises may prove alienating—if Moscow is not given substantial input into the decision-making process affecting its perceived "vital" security interests and involving the formulation of conjoint NATO-EU/WEU-Russian security guarantees. Moscow's ruling circles may be impelled by domestic opposition groups to obstruct NATO enlargement (in any compromised form) as Russia's global status and prestige is at stake.

While Russia may appear too weak to counter NATO enlargement at present, a delayed reaction cannot be ruled out, given continued political and economic instability and factional rivalry within Russia, the possible formation of an anti–Western Eurasian alliance, and Russia's still powerful conventional, not-so-conventional, and nuclear capabilities. Pressure to expand NATO may well help provoke the rise to power of an anti–Western regime in Russia, one that totally distrusts cooperative-collective security, as well as NATO's promises, and that seeks to *impel* the United States into a "comprehensive" European "settlement" through the threat or use of force. Concurrently, the real potential for NATO hypertrophy—the inability to meet burgeoning strategic demands with appropriate resources and political consensus—may prevent NATO (and other American allies) from effectively managing a whole range of challenges—and not only from Russia alone.

Notes

GENERAL INTRODUCTION:

1. See for example, Michael Mandelbaum, *The Dawn of Peace in Europe* (New York: The Twentieth Century Fund Press, 1996), 12–24.

2. Cited in Helmut Wagner, *The Interim Solution of NATO: Continental Region-Building as* un fait providentiel, paper delivered at the Committee on Atlantic Studies conference, Paris: The American University of Paris, 4–6 November 1994.

3. The American-Soviet relationship during the Cold War was characterized by Janus-faced elements of collaboration and confrontation. On the one hand, both "superpowers" engaged in a "double containment" of German ambitions. On the other, the United States pursued a strategy of containment of the Soviet Union, while the latter sought to counter-contain the United States and its allies, partly as an effort to influence the behavior of Germany and Europe as a whole. See Hall Gardner, *Surviving the Millennium: American Global Strategy, the Collapse of the Soviet Empire, and the Question of Peace* (Westport and London: Praeger, 1994).

4. In an address, "From Containment to Enlargement," delivered in September 1993 at the Johns Hopkins Paul H. Nitze School of Advanced International Studies, then National Security Advisor Anthony Lake stated, "Our nation's policies toward the world stand at a historic crossroads."

5. It is not entirely accidental that the revanchist Vladimir Zhirinovsky endorsed the American populist and isolationist Pat Buchanan during the latter's failed bid to obtain the Republican Party's nomination for president.

CHAPTER 1:

1. To join the PfP, states must sign a "framework document" whereby they are to "develop a capability in their military to contribute to operations under the authority of the UN and/or the responsibility of the OSCE." The document also states that participants in PfP are to build cooperative relations with NATO for

the purposes of joint planning and of training for joint peacekeeping, search and rescue, and humanitarian operations. However, no mention is made of war-preventive enforcement or systems of cooperative-collective security.

2. General Klaus Naumann, "From Cooperation to Interoperability," *NATO Review* 4, 1996, 17, in *SIPRI Yearbook* (Oxford, 1995), 279–80.

3. Bruce George, *Continental Drift* (Brussels: North Atlantic Assembly: International Secretariat, November 1994).

4. Hans Binnendjik, "NATO Enlargement: Sailing between Scylla and Charybdis," *Strategic Forum*, Institute for National Strategic Studies, no. 55, November 1995, 1.

5. See Paul R.S. Gebhard, *The United States and European Security*, Adelphi Paper 286 (London: International Institute for Strategic Studies, February 1994), A17. See also William T. Johnsen, *NATO Strategy in the 1990s* (Carlisle Barracks, PA: U.S. Army War College, 25 May 1995).

6. Dmitrii Gornostaev, "Commentary on Opening to NATO," trans. Natalia Lechmanova, *Nezavisimaya Gazeta*, 19 October 1996,

7. *OMRI Daily Digest*, no. 236, II, 6 December 1995.

8. *International Herald Tribune*, 23 October 1996, 7.

9. Henry Kissinger, *Washington Post*, 25 January 1994.

10. "Moving from Theory to Action: Conference Conclusions" *Strategic Forum*, Institute for National Strategic Studies, no. 12, November 1994.

11. William T. Johnsen, *NATO Strategy in the 1990s* (Carlisle Barracks, PA: U.S. Army War College, 25 May 1995).

12. "Clinton Hints NATO Would Defend East From Attack," *International Herald Tribune*, 13 January 1994.

13. Vladislav Chernov, "Moscow Should Think Carefully," *The Current Digest of the Post-Soviet Press* [CDPSP] 46, no. 8 (1994), 11.

14. The NATO Participation Act of 1994 does not, on the surface, exclude Russian (or European) military technology. On one hand, it calls for "increased standardization"; on the other, it calls for enhanced "interoperability of equipment and weapons systems." *Defense* (Paris: USIS, 27 October 1994).

15. Vladislav Chernov, ibid; and 11. Dmitry Yevstafev, "Russia faces New Containment," *CDPSP*, 46 no. 8 (1994), 12–13.

16. "The West should use its political and economic leverage to ensure that the Polish-Ukrainian partnership does not emerge as an anti–Russian axis. See Ian J. Brzezinski, "Polish-Ukrainian Relations: Europe's Neglected Strategic Axis," *Survival* 35, no. 3, Autumn 1993. In my view, however, it has been NATO's failure to articulate an adequate cooperative-collective security conception that has contributed to both Polish and Ukrainian insecurity.

17. "Interview: General Shevtsov Gnaws on NATO Bone," *Moscow News* no. 36, 12–18 September 1996, 5.

18. Mikhail Gorbachev, *Pravo* (Right), trans. Natalia Lechmanova, (Bratislava, Slovakia), 6 December 1995.

19. W.R. Snyder, "USSR-Germany—A Link Restored," *Foreign Policy*, Fall 1991.

20. *SIPRI* Yearbook 1995 (Oxford: Oxford University, 1995), 276.

21. Henry Kissinger, "Charter of Confusion: The Limits of U.S.-Russian

Cooperation," *International Herald Tribune,* 6 July 1992.

22. *Wall Street Journal Europe,* 2 December 1994.

23. *Keesing's Record of World Events,* 39, nos. 7/8, July–August 1993, 39607.

24. Ukrainian Americans appear as "real votes" in the states of Pennsylvania, New Jersey, and New York. *Congressional Quarterly Weekly Report,* 6 August 1994, 2267, cited in Steve Woehrl, "Ukraine's Uncertain Future and U.S. Policy," *CRS Report for Congress* (Washington, DC: CRS, 21 September 1994)

25. See Peter van Ham, *Ukraine, Russia, and European Security* (Paris: WEU Institute for Security Studies, February 1994).

26. See *Atlantic News,* 22 September 1993, cited in Peter van Ham, op. cit.

27. On Ukrainian threats to hold onto nuclear weapons, see Stephen J. Blank, *Proliferation and Non-proliferation in Ukraine* (Carlisle Barracks, PA: U.S. Army War College, Strategic Studies Institute, 1 July 1994), 7.

28. See Van Ham, ibid, 7–8.

29. The Russian defense ministry claimed that it obtained "the upper hand" against Kozyrev's "opportunist course." (*Segodnya,* 31 April 1995, cited in *Analytica Moscow,* 2, no. 20 [27 May to 2 June 1995]).

30. From *Segodnya,* cited in *Analytica Moscow,* 2, no. 11 (18–24 March 1995), 5. Critics linked Russian membership in the G-7 with the PfP—hence the formation of the "Political Eight." Russia renewed its demand for "full" membership in the "G-7" in early 1997 in the context of a NATO-Russian Charter.

31. *Financial Times,* 24 March 1995. In late 1992, Kozyrev had warned that the U.S.-Russian "honeymoon" would soon come to an end—if the specific interests of "democratic" Russia were not taken into account in Iraq and the former Yugoslavia. At the December 1992 Stockholm CSCE conference, Kozyrev pretended that Russia had decided to give full military support to Serbia, as "an illustration of how things could be if other forces took command in Russia." *Europe,* no. 5879, Mon./Tues. 14/15 December 1992.

32. Statement by Russian foreign minister Kozyrev, "Acceptance of the PfP Individual Partnership and Broad Enhanced NATO-Russian Dialogue and Cooperation going Beyond PfP" (Brussels: NATO Press, 31 May 1995).

33. *OMRI Daily Digest,* 248, I, 22 December 1995.

34. Scott Parish, "NATO and Russia Talk Compromise on Expansion Issue," *OMRI Analytical Brief,* no. 1, 145, 4 June 1996.

35. Scott Parrish, "Russia Fails to Budge Poland on NATO Expansion," *OMRI Analytical Brief,* 1, no. 64, 19 April 1996; and *OMRI Daily Digest,* II, no. 54, 15 March 1996, and II, no. 55, 18 March 1996. The Polish foreign minister Dariusz Rosati has argued that Polish membership in NATO would help to protect Poland from Germany and that thus Warsaw would support a doctrine calling for NATO cooperation with Russia. See "NATO Means Protection for Poland," trans. Natalia Lechmanova, *Pravo* (Right) (Bratislava) 2 February 1996.

36. Summary of Speech by Secretary-General Solana at the International Institute for Strategic Studies, London, 19 September 1996 (Brussels: NATODATA, 1996).

37. *OMRI Daily Digest,* 184, I, 23 September 1996.

38. NATO Secretary-General Solana, in *Press Conference of the Secretary–General and General Lebed* (Brussels: NATODATA, 7 October 1996).

39. Ibid.

40. Ibid.

41. Ibid. See also Almar Latour, "Lebed Warns NATO to Stall Plans to Expand Eastward," *The Wall Street Journal*, 8 October 1996.

42. *Le Monde*, 24 March 1997; *International Herald Tribune*, 22-23 March; 24 March; 12 March 1997.

43. *International Herald Tribune*, 7–8 September 1996, 10; and *International Herald Tribune*, 23 October 1996. To counter V. M. Molotov's opposition to the separation of the Ruhr and the Rhineland, James Byrnes renounced the Oder-Neisse line, siding with Bonn's claims to its 1937 borders, and looked to the integration of Allied occupation zones in West Germany. In many ways the closest geohistorical parallel to the PfP initiative is the 1947 Marshall Plan. Much as the sincerity of the Marshall Plan in truly assisting the Soviet Union was questionable, American sincerity in extending "full" NATO membership to Russia is also questionable. Much as Eastern European states were eager to obtain Marshall Plan assistance then, so too are Eastern European states eager to become "full" members of NATO today. See George Liska, *Return to the Heartland and the Rebirth of the Old Order* (Washington, DC: Johns Hopkins SAIS Foreign Policy Institute/Institute of International Politics, Prague, 1994), 89, n. 16. See also Scott D. Parrish and Mikhail M. Narinsky, *New Evidence on the Soviet Rejection of the Marshall Plan, 1947*, Cold War International History Project Report (Washington, DC: Woodrow Wilson Center for Scholars, March 1994.) In the cases of both the Marshall Plan and the PfP initiative, Moscow has feared American efforts to create an anti–Soviet anti–Russian bloc. Much as has been the case in regard to PfP, Moscow then believed it was better to stay in the Marshall program for as long as possible, as Soviet participation in the Marshall Plan would have actually hindered the creation of an anti–Soviet bloc.

44. The possibility of "associate" membership in NATO was raised by Jeffrey Simon, "Does Eastern Europe Belong to NATO?" *Orbis*, Winter 1993.

CHAPTER 2:

1. In addition to the economic aspects of "burden sharing," the term "responsibility sharing" implies monetary, defense spending, alliance and treaty commitments, foreign aid, peacekeeping contributions, a role in non-proliferation efforts, etc.

2. Mathias Jopp, ed., *The Implications of the Yugoslav Crisis for Western Europe's Foreign Relations* Chaillot Paper 17 (Paris: WEU Institute for Security Studies, October 1994), 4–7.

3. Stanley R. Sloan, "NATO Adapts for New Missions: The Berlin Accord and Combined Joint Task Forces (CJTF)," *CRS Report for Congress*, 19 June 1996, 6.

4. *International Herald Tribune*, 5 July 1995, 12.

5. *Strategic Forum*, "Moving From Theory to Action," Institute for National Strategic Studies, no. 12, November 1994.

6. Javier Solana, "NATO's Role in Bosnia," *NATO Review*, no. 2, March 1996, 3–6.

7. See Stanley R. Sloan, "NATO Adapts for New Missions," 4. Multiple-hatting became known as the "Deputies Proposal."

8. See interview, Hervé de Charette, *Le Figaro*, 10 June 1996.

9. Allies may establish CJTF headquarters within selected Alliance headquarters; during an operation there would be consultations between the North Atlantic Council (NAC) and the WEU Council, and with the NAC over the use of NATO assets. For details, see Antony Cragg, "The Combined Joint Task Force Concept," *NATO Review*, no. 4 (1996), 7–10.

10. *International Herald Tribune*, 26 September 1996.

11. Sloan, 4.

12. See interview, Hervé de Charette.

13. Stanley R. Sloan, "NATO Nuclear Strategy: issues for U.S. Policy" (Washington, D.C.: CRS Report for Congress, 26 July 1996)

14. *Le Monde*, 25 January 1997. The French parliament learned of the document in *Le Monde*!

15. Marcel van Herpen, "A European Role for French Nuclear Weapons?" *Cicero Paper*, 1 (Maastricht: Cicero Foundation, 1996). See also, Paul Cornish, "European Security: the end of architecture and the new NATO," *International Affairs*, 72, 4 (1996), 756.

16. *Europe: The Day in Politics*, no. 6369, 2 December 1994.

17. See European Report, *Treaty on European Union* (Bruxelles: Supplement to European Report, no. 1746, 22 February 1992).

18. *OMRI Daily Digest*, 105, II, 30 May 1996.

19. George Kolankiewicz, "Consensus and Competition in the Eastern Enlargement of the EU," *International Affairs*, 70, no. 3, July 1994.

20. *OMRI Daily Digest*, 138, II, 18 July 1996.

21. *OMRI Daily Digest*, 178, II, 13 September 1996.

22. On EU and WEU relations, see Stefano Silvestri, Nicole Gnesotto, and Alvaro Vasconcelos, "Decision-Making and Institutions," in *Towards a Common Defense Policy*, eds. Laurence Martin and John Roper (Paris: WEU Institute for Security Studies, 1995), 51–57. An additional problem arises in that not all EU members are part of NATO's 1991 strategic concept. On the latter, see *NATO Handbook* (Brussels: NATO Office of Information and Press, 1995), 235–248.

23. Ibid., 57–68.

24. *The Economist*, 10 September 1994.

25. John Andrews, "Core-Europe—A British View" paper delivered in France, Germany, Benelux—Towards a 'Core' Europe of Five, International Experts Seminar (Paris: Cicero Foundation, 7 April 1995).

26. For proposals to improve the structural relationship between the EU and WEU, see Silvestri, Gnesotto, and Vasconcelos. In March 1997, France and Italy proposed a linking of the EU and WEU; the proposal would form a coalition of the willing, including France, Germany, Belgium, Luxembourg, Spain, and Italy (mostly NATO members). The position has been opposed by the UK, as well as new EU members Finland, Sweden, Austria. *International Herald Tribune*, 25 March 1997. See also Chapter 7, n. 44.

27. France's reentry into NATO's Military Committee is to help resolve disputes over ESDI and CJTF. Paris also intended to press for a NATO-Russian Charter. *Le Monde*, 7 December 1995; and *Financial Times*, 6 December 1995.

28. In May 1994, the WEU's Forum of Consultation brought the three Baltic

states, the Czech Republic, Hungary, Poland, Romania, and Slovakia into "associated partner" status, which permits these states to participate in the Common Foreign and Security Policy (CFSP) of the EU. In addition, the conditions for membership in the WEU could be linked to acceptance as NATO members. Non-NATO, non-EU members can become observers of the WEU.

29. Article IV, line 27, of the "Resolution on Future Relations between the European Union, the WEU and the Atlantic Alliance" (adopted by the European Parliament 24 February 1994) supports actions within the framework of the Atlantic Alliance but "if consensus cannot be found within the Alliance, the European member states should be able to take decisions and actions within the Council of the European Union."

30. *Financial Times*, 20 March 1995. French foreign minister Alain Juppé raised the idea of a revamped OSCE, a new Atlantic Charter giving a revitalized WEU a greater voice in NATO as well as a greater voice in NATO expansion eastward—combined with a NATO-Russian non-aggression pact. See Jonathan Clayton, "NATO Prepared to Offer Moscow Deal," *Reuters*, 16 February 1995.

31. *OMRI Daily Digest*, 14, II, 19 January 1996.

32. Jonathan Dean, "Losing Russia or Keeping NATO: Must We Choose," *Arms Control Today* (June 1995), 6. See also, Michael Mihalka, "Squaring the Circle: NATO's Offer to the East," *RFE/RL Research Report*, 3, no. 12, 25 March 1994.

33. "Russia's Full Strategic Doctrine," *Foreign Report* (London: *The Economist*, 18 November 1993), 1.

34. *Europe: The Day in Politics*, no. 6369 (2 December 1994), 4.

35. *OMRI Daily Digest*, 111, I, 7 June 1996.

36. *Analytica Moscow*, 20, II. (27 May–2 June 1995).

37. *OMRI Daily Digest*, 31, I, 21 February 1997.

38. *The Economist*, 1 March 1997, 30; *OMRI Daily Digest*, 244, I, 19 December 1996.

39. *RFE/RL Research Reports*, 192 (10 October 1994).

40. *OMRI Daily Digest*, 99, II, 22 May 1996.

41. See report of Vladimir Abarinov, *Segodnya*, (26 January ; 30, 1996) in *CDPSP*, 48, no. 4 (1996).

42. *OMRI Daily Digest*, 19, I, 26 January 1996.

43. *OMRI Daily Digest*, 87, I, 3 May 1996.

44. See Council on Foreign and Defense Policy, "Russia and NATO: Theses of the Council on Foreign and Defense Policy" (Moscow: 25 May 1995), 11.

45. See the *CDU/CSU-Fraktion des Deutschen Bundestages*, "Reflections on European Policy" (Bonn: 1 September 1994).

46. James Kitfield, "Kohl's Answer," *The National Journal* (7 December 1996), 2637–2640.

47. Serguei Kurguinjan has argued that closer U.S.-Russian ties may bring about new "encircling" alliances. "As for the Baltic–Black Sea confederation, then the more firmly are the USA and Russia related, the more solid alliances will be formed between Ukraine and Germany, Kazakhstan and China, Central Asian Union (CARS) and Turkey. In [these] cases Russia will find itself between two fires. And the geopolitical stability of Europe will be undermined, and not to the

benefit of notorious 'American imperialism.'" See Serguei Kurguinjan, *Lessons of Bloody October* (Moscow: International Foundation, EDT, 1994), 47. On the possibility of alternative alliances formed outside U.S. or Russian influence, see my fifth "pessimistic scenario," in *Surviving the Millennium*, 229–230.

CHAPTER 3:

1. For a definition of "strategic leveraging," see Gardner, *Surviving the Millennium*, 27

2. Swedish prime minister Göran Person met with President Clinton to discuss security in the Baltic states. *OMRI Daily Digest*, 152, II, 7 August 1996.

3. *OMRI Daily Digest*, 165, II, 26 August 1996.

4. *OMRI Daily Digest*, 152, II, 7 August 1996.

5. Hans Binnendijk and Jeffrey Simon, "Baltic Security and NATO Enlargement," *Strategic Forum*, Institute for National Strategic Studies, no. 57, December 1995, 2. Russia and Estonia held talks 9–10 July 1996, in Tallinn. See also OMRI *Daily Digest*, 7, I, 10 January 1997.

6. *OMRI Daily Digest*, 147, II, 31 July 1996.

7. See, Rene Nyberg, "The Baltic Countries and the Northwest of Russia: A European Challenge," *European Security*, 3, no. 3 (Autumn 1994), 534; and Phillip Petersen, "Security Policy in the Post–Soviet Baltic States," *European Security*, 1, no. 1 (Spring 1992), 46.

8. Segodnya, 2 March 1996, cited in *Analytica Moscow CIS Weekly*, 3, no. 9, 2–8 March 1996.

9. Polish-Lithuanian military "ties tend to assuage Lithuanian doubts that Kaliningrad could disqualify them for NATO candidacy. In sum, Poland may more closely tie the Baltic states generally and Lithuania specifically, to NATO as the Alliance enlarges." Binnendijk and Simon, 3.

10. *OMRI Daily Digest*, 106, I, 31 May 1996.

11. *OMRI Daily Digest*, 152, II, 7 August 1996.

12. Stephen J. Blank, *Prague, NATO, and European Security*, Strategic Studies Institute (Carlisle Barracks, PA: U.S. Army War College, 17 April 1996.

13. See Ustina Markus, "Belarus: A 'Weak Link' in Eastern Europe," *RFE/RL Research Reports*, 2, no. 49 (10 December 1993). Both Poland and Ukraine have categorically denied having any border disputes, as alleged by Senator Kay Hutchinson. *OMRI Daily Digest*, 203, II, 18 October 1995.

14. On Poland and Kaliningrad, see Jeffrey Simon, "Central Europe: 'Return to Europe' or Descent to Chaos," *Strategic Review*, 21, no. 3, Winter 1993, 20.

15. *OMRI Daily Digest*, 34, II, February 16, 1996.

16. Ivo Samson, "Between East and West—Slovakia's Uncertain Security Situation" *Cicero Paper*, 1 (Maastricht: Cicero Foundation, 1996).

17. *OMRI Daily Digest*, 141, II, 23 July 1996; *OMRI Daily Digest*, 142, II, 24 July 1996; *OMRI Daily Digest*, 140, II, 22 July 1996.

18. *OMRI Daily Digest*, 156, II, 11 August 1995; *OMRI Daily Digest*, 58, II, 22 March 1996;

19. *The Economist*, 1 March 1997; *OMRI Daily Digest*, 31, II, 30 January 1997.

20. *OMRI Daily Digest*, 140, II, 22 July 1996. In February 1997, after a change in government, Bulgaria requested NATO membership. Interestingly, both

Bulgaria and Romania (as well as the USSR) opposed Turkish membership in NATO, when Turkey joined with Greece.

21. *Radio Prague*, E-News, 21 January 1997. OMRI *Daily Digest*, 14, II, 19 January, 1996.

22. Following the 1994 NATO Participation Act, the National Security Revitalization Act (HR7), which passed in the House in February 1995, initially demanded Visegrad state membership by 1999, to be followed by the Baltic states and Ukrainian membership. These latter demands were deleted at White House request before being passed by the House. Companion legislation by the Senate stalled after Senator Nunn's 22 June 1995 speech at SacLant, which opposed NATO enlargement on grounds that it would heighten instability, particularly at a time in which security responsibilities appeared to be expanding but defense budgets were dwindling. (See critique of Nunn's views, Chapter 9.) The NATO Enlargement Facilitation Act of April 1996 mentioned only Poland, Hungary, and the Czech Republic as potential NATO members, dropping Slovakia, and promised $60 million in U.S. assistance to prospective NATO members. (Sharon Fisher, "NATO Enlargement and Slovakia," *OMRI Analytical Brief*, 1, no. 77, 23 April 1996.) On the other hand, former Secretary-General Willy Claes stated that neither President Clinton nor members of Congress attempted to press him to select any particular countries for membership. (Discussion with Willy Claes, International Experts Seminar, Cicero Foundation [Paris: 13–14 June 1996.])

23. As Slovak foreign minister Pavol Hamzik put it, "The first enlargement will change the political *status quo* in Europe. It is not sure that there will be a second group." *International Herald Tribune*, 23 October 1996.

24. *Defense* (Paris: USIS, 27 October 1994), 3–6.

25. Much as West Germany was able to seek German unification under a NATO aegis, other states could seek similar goals. Yet, unlike the case with West Germany in regard to East Germany, these demands may not lead to peaceful change, particularly if the Russian, Belarus, or Ukrainian leaderships remain unstable. See my argument in Gardner, *Surviving the Millennium*.

26. *Defense* (Paris: USIS, 27 October 1994), 3–6.

27. The 1973 War Powers Act, for example, remains in contention in the United States. The problem arises as to what is meant by "democratic" control. The latter involves parliamentary oversight, the nature of military-civilian relations, military-government relations, as well as the nature of defense reform itself, including military organization and military psychology. See Chris Donnelly, *NATO Review*, 1, 45 (January 1997), 1519.

28. The choice of Marian Zacharski as head of Poland's Civil Intelligence Service raised questions as to the credibility of the Polish leadership. (Zacharski had procured military-oriented technology for the Polish People's Republic in 1977–81, until caught by the FBI.) A communiqué released by President Lech Walesa stated that the appointment of Zacharski would jeopardize Polish "integration with the West." *RFE/RL Daily Report*, 156 (18 August 1994). Zacharski subsequently resigned. See also Polish accusations of Russian "provocations" to sabotage Polish efforts to join the EU/NATO in *OMRI Daily Digest*, 33, II, 17 February 1997.

29. *OMRI Daily Digest*, 148, II, 1 July 1996.

30. On popular opposition to nuclear weapons in Hungary, see *OMRI Daily Digest*, 145, II, 29 July 1996. Jiri Pehe, "Czech Parties' Views of the EU and NATO," *OMRI Analytical Brief*, 1, no. 121, 20 May 1996; and "Czechs and NATO After Elections," *OMRI Analytical Brief*, Vol. 1, No. 217, 10 July 1996.

31. *International Herald Tribune*, 20 February 1995, 4.

32. To meet NATO standards, Polish defense spending would have to increase from 2.4 percent to 3.8 percent of GDP; Hungary from 1.5 percent to 2.6 percent; the Czech Republic from 2.5 percent to 3.6 percent, and Slovakia from 3.1 percent to 4.6 percent, once again depending upon force goals. See *Congressional Budget Office*, "The Costs of Expanding the NATO Alliance" (Washington, DC: CBO, March 1996), 40, 65–66.

33. Data provided by Public Opinion Research Center, cited in *OMRI Daily Digest*, 136, II, 16 July 1996.

34. *OMRI Daily Digest*, 149, I, 2 August 1996.

35. See Stanley R. Sloan, "NATO Enlargement and the Former European Neutrals" (Washington, D.C.: CRS Report for Congress, 18 February 1997). In late May 1996, the North Atlantic Assembly discussed the accession of neutral states of Finland and Austria to NATO. Neutral states may be interested in NATO to cut defense costs: Neutrals spend roughly seven percent of GDP on defense; NATO members spend about three percent. See also, Nils Andrén, "NATO and Peacekeeping: The Nordic Countries and NATO" (paper delivered at the Committee on Atlantic Studies Conference, Warsaw, 21 March 1997).

36. IMAS Research Institute, cited in *Reuters* News Report, 17 July 1996.

37. See proposals of Lena Hjelm-Nullen and Tarja Halonen, *Europe* no. 67, 13, 23/24 April 1996.

38. *Radio Sweden News*, 29 March 1996.

39. *OMRI Daily Digest*, No. 105, II, 30 May 1996.

40. *OMRI Daily Digest*, 116, II, 27 August 1996.

41. See viewpoint of Mr. Onyszkiewicz in Mr. Baumel, *Organizing Security in Europe: Defense Aspects*, Document 1510E-4, Appendix II (Brussels: NATODATA, 8 February 1996).

42. Former Czech foreign minister Jiri Dienstbier put the issue this way: "Neutral and buffer zones have always been a source of tension in history and sooner or later become a reason for competition among various powers in order to conquer them." Radio Prague E-News, 7 February 1996.

43. Wlodzimierz Cimoszewicz, "Building Poland's Security," *NATO Review*, no. 3, May 1996.

44. Ceslovas V. Stankevicius, "NATO Enlargement and the Indivisibility of Security in Europe," *NATO Review*, no. 5, 1996.

45. Colonel Juris Dalbins, "Baltic Cooperation: The Key to Wider Security," *NATO Review*, 44, no. 1, January 1996, 7–10.

46. See views of Gregore-Kalev Stoicescu, of the Estonian Ministry of Foreign Affairs, in Philip Petersen, "Security Policy in the Post-Soviet Baltic States."

47. *RFE/RL Research Reports*, 16 May 1994.

48. Sharon Fisher, "Meciar Looks for Allies in the Balkans," *OMRI Analytical Brief*, 1, II, 15 February 1996.

49. Blank.

50. See "NATO Means Protection for Poland," trans. Natalia Lechmanova, *Pravo* (Right) (Bratislava) 2 February 1996.

51. *OMRI Daily Digest*, 54, II, 15 March 1996; and 55, II, 18 March 1996.

52. Ceslovas V. Stankevicius, "NATO Enlargement and the Indivisibility of Security in Europe."

53. Strobe Talbott, *Defense File*, 15 (Paris: USIS, 25 September 1995).

54. William T. Johnsen, *NATO Strategy in the 1990s* (Carlisle Barracks, PA: U.S. Army War College, 25 May 1995). "The question should not be whether there will be new lines, but how to prevent those lines from becoming impermeable. And, even if these lines harden, that result might be preferable to a security vacuum that leaves Central and Eastern European states in the wind. Finally, notwithstanding NATO actions, Russian leaders will make the final decision on how to respond. Given the fact and historical failure of appeasement, NATO should carefully consider the cost-benefit calculus of placating Russia on this issue."

55. See Janne E. Nolan, "The Concept of Cooperative Security," in Janne E. Nolan (ed.) *Global Engagement* (Washington, DC: Brookings, 1994), 5.

CHAPTER 4:

1. Lieutenant General William E. Odom, testimony, Senate Foreign Relations Committee on Europe, 22 August 1995, *Defense File* no. 14 (Paris: USIS, 14 September 1995), 8.

2. Russian opinion polls (which are not "scientific") increasingly viewed NATO as "hostile" as opposed to "friendly" or "neutral." In May 1994, 18.6 percent of Russians polled viewed NATO as friendly, 31.8 percent as neutral, and 14.6 percent as hostile (with 35.0 percent uncertain). By September 1995, 10.7 percent of Russians polled saw NATO as friendly, 30.4 percent as neutral, and 29.9 percent as hostile (with 24.9 percent uncertain, and 4.0 percent no opinion). Poll published in *Who is Who*, no. 18, 1995, 2. See *Analytica Moscow*, 2, no. 39, 7–13 October 1995. In early 1997, anti–NATO lobby groups were formed in both Moscow and Kyiv. The Russian group advocated developing a new generation of tactical nuclear weapons. See *OMRI Daily Digest*, 21, I, 30 January 1997.

3. "The question of NATO's eastward expansion brings out an almost unheard-of unanimity among Russian academics and politicians." Pavel Baev, "Drifting Away From Europe," *Transition*, 1, no. 11, 30 June 1995.

4. Gregorii Yavlinsky, "Russian Generals Desire a New Division of Europe," trans. Natalia Lechmanova, *National Revival* (Bratislava: November 29, 1995)

5. "Interview: General Shevtsov Gnaws on NATO's Bone," *Moscow News*, no. 36, 12–18 September 1996, 5.

6. James Bryant Conant, in *Department of State Foreign Relations of the United States*, 1950, vol. II (Washington, DC: GPO, 1977), 176–87

7. Stephen F. Cohen, "Yeltsin Was Supposed to Build Democratic Consensus," *International Herald Tribune*, 13 October 1993.

8. *OMRI Daily Digest*, 61, I, 26 March 1996. The view that the Belovezhskaya accords should be renounced at a later date was purportedly overruled by the Communist Party Executive Committee, to subordinate Zyuganov.

9. Yeltsin obtained only 35.28 percent to Zyuganov's 32.04 percent on the first

round. Lebed obtained 14.52 percent.

10. *OMRI Daily Digest*, 134, I, 12 July 1996. The 1993 constitution stated that there should be a law governing the exact nature of the powers of the National Security Council, but it had yet to be adopted. *OMRI Daily Digest*, 131, I, 9 July 1996. Proposals to create a new military council (which would make decisions binding on all ministries and agencies which involve the armed forces) would also enhance the powers of the secretary of the Security Council who would chair the Military Council in case of the President's absence (which has been frequent in the case of Yeltsin). *OMRI Daily Digest*, 139, I, 19 July 1996.

11. *Analytica Moscow,*, 3, no. 26, 6–12 July 1996.

12. See Alexei Pushkov, "Solo for Primakov," *Moscow News* 36 (12–18 September 1996).

13. *OMRI Daily Digest*, 54, I, 15 March 1996.

14. *OMRI Russian Regional Report*, 4, I, 18 September 1996.

15. *CDPSP* 47, 6 (8 March 1995). Mark Smith, "Russia's Regions—Attitudes to Central Authority," Conflict Studies Research Center, The Royal Military Academy Sandhurst, Camberley, Surrey, May 1994.

16. In September 1996, Foreign Minister Primakov permitted the regions in the Russian Federation to manage their own foreign economic relations. *OMRI Daily Digest* 187, I, 26 September 1996. This change could prove beneficial, if tax collection becomes more efficient!

17. Stephan Black, "Russia's Real Drive to the South," *Orbis*, Summer 1995.

18. *CDPSP* 47, no. 2 (1995), 22; *CDPSP* 47, no. 3 (1995), 13; and *CDPSP* 47, no. 5 (1995), 16.

19. See *Obshchaya Gazeta*, no. 5 (1996), cited in *Analytica Moscow* 3, no. 6, 10–16 February 1996.

20. The OSCE has strongly condemned Russian actions. *OMRI Daily Digest*, 62, I, 27 March 1996.

21. Igor Birman, "Gloomy Prospects for the Russian Economy," *Europe–Asia Studies*, Vol. 48, No. 5 (1996); *OMRI Daily Digest*, 154, I, 9 July 1996.

22. See debate on costs of the Chechen war, *CDPSP* 47, no. 1, 10 January 1995, 47; *CDPSP* 4, no. 2, 8 February 1995.

23. *OECD Economic Outlook*, no. 56 (Paris: OECD, December 1994), 120–22. According to the Russian minister of labor, Gennady Milikyan, some 4.8–4.9 million people work a shortened week or are on forced leave.

24. See *CDPSP* 47, no. 1 (1 February 1995), 18–19.

25. *Financial Times*, 14 October 1993, 3.

26. Mikhail Glazachev, cited in *OMRI Special Report: Russian Election Survey*, no. 3, 3 November 1995.

27. See *CDPSP*, 46, no. 38, 19 October 1994, 27. The Congressional Research Service states that Russia had surpassed U.S. arms sales in 1995, to become the world's largest exporter to developing countries (up to $6 billion from $3.7 billion in 1994), selling primarily to the PRC. The Stockholm Peace Research Institute (SIPRI) estimated, however, that Russian exports reached a lesser figure of $3.9 billion, while Moscow stated it was $2.5 billion. U.S. sales in 1995 were $3.8 billion, down from $6.3 billion in 1994. See *International Herald Tribune*, 21 August 1996. See also *OMRI Daily Digest*, 161, I, 20 August 1996.

28. *CDPSP*, no. 41 (1995), 24.

29. Valeri Borisenko, "Whose Muscles are Growing?" *Moscow News* no. 6 (1996).

30. *OMRI Daily Digest*, 165, I, 26 August 1996. The Armed Forces received only 56.6 trillion rubles ($10.2 billion) out of 68.8 trillion awarded to them in the 1996 budget. (37 trillion paid in cash; the remainder in credits and securities). The 1997 draft budget promised 104 trillion. The Defense Ministry asked for 160 trillion rubles. *OMRI Daily Digest* 3, I, 6 January 1997. On the other hand, in March 1997, Izvestiya cited documents stating that the military wasted hundreds of millions of rubles yearly on redundant weapons systems, training facilities, and command staff. *OMRI Daily Digest*, 49, I, 11 March 1997.

31. *OMRI Daily Digest*, 161, I, 20 August 1996; and *OMRI Daily Digest*, 154, I, 9 July 1996.

32. *CDPSP* 43, no. 43 (1991), 10–12.

33. Alexander Zhilin, "Russian Army: Lost and Lonely," *Moscow News*, 36, 12–18 September 1996.

34. Ibid.

35. *OMRI Daily Digest*, 145, I, 29 July 1996.

CHAPTER 5:

1. Paul Goble, "Ten Issues in Search of a Policy," *Current History*, October 1993, 305–08.

2. Bogdan Szajkowski, "Will Russia Disintegrate into Bantustans?" *The World Today*, August/September 1993.

3. *International Herald Tribune*, 10–11 June 1995. For background, see Roman Solchanyk, "The Politics of State Building: Centre-Periphery Relations in Post–Soviet Ukraine," *Europe–Asia Studies* 46, 1, 1994. The Pereiaslav agreement continues to affect the political psychology of Ukrainian-Russian relations. For background, see Orest Subtelny, *Ukraine: A History* (Toronto: University of Toronto, 1994), 134–154.

4. *OMRI Daily Digest* 147, II, 31 July 1996. By August 1996, the main stumbling block was the basing of both the Ukrainian and Russian navies at Sevastopol. Both states were against the deployment of nuclear weapons in Eastern Europe. Ukraine had no intention of joining NATO or the CIS Collective Security Pact, but it would continue developing ties with NATO. *OMRI Daily Digest* 152, II, 7 August 1996.

5. *OMRI Daily Digest* 123, II, 25 June 1996.

6. *OMRI Daily Digest*, 37, II, 21 February 1997.

7. Ukraine owes about $5 billion to Russia and $3 billion to the IMF. See *OMRI Daily Digest*, 36, II, 20 February 1997.

8. *OMRI Daily Digest*, 45, II, 5 March 1997.

9. See Ustina Markus, "Belarus: A 'Weak Link' in Eastern Europe," *RFE/RL Research Reports* 2, 49, 10 December 1993.

10. From *Commersant Daily*, 26 June 1996, cited in *Analytica Moscow Commonwealth of Independent States (CIS)* III, no. 24 (22–28 June 1996).

11. Belarus has sent contradictory signals to Lithuania and Poland; see Jan Zaprudnik, *Belarus: At a Crossroads in History* (Boulder, CO.: Westview Press,

1993), 205–228; Stephen R. Burant, "International Relations in a Regional Context: Poland and its Eastern Neighbors," *Europe–Asia Studies*, 45, no. 3, (1993).

12. *OMRI Daily Digest*, 140, II, 22 July 1996.

13. *Segodnya*, 2 March 1996, cited in *Analytica Moscow* III, no. 9 (2–8 March 1996).

14. See *CDPSP* 47, no. 7 (1995), 21.

15. This action led Washington and other states to augment aid through the IMF and the World Bank. In September 1995, however, the IMF stopped granting credits to Belarus because the nation's budget deficit had surpassed 2.7 percent of total GDP. See *OMRI Daily Digest*, 62, II, 27 March 1996.

16. See Eugene B. Rumer, "Can Russia be CIS Security Manager," *Moscow News*, no. 12 (31 March–6 April 1995), 4.

17. Quoted in Larisa Sayenko, "Belarus: A Coup Up Top," *Moscow News*, no. 30 (1–7 August 1996).

18. See *Analytica Moscow CIS Weekly Press Summary* 3, no. 18 (18–27 May 1996). See also *OMRI Daily Digest* 145, II, 29 July 1996; and *OMRI Daily Digest* 146, II, 30 July 1996.

19. Roland Dannreuther, "Creating New States in Central Asia," *Adelphi Paper* no. 288 (London: IISS, March 1994), 46. See also Anthony Hyman, "Moving out of Moscow's Orbit," *International Affairs* 69, no. 2 (April 1993).

20. *OMRI Daily Digest*, 60, I, 25 March 1996.

21. Oleg Dorojevets, "Kiev à la lueur du Croissant," *Courrier International*, no. 225 (23 February–1 March 1995), 15. Russia, for example, has sought to block Ukrainian efforts to sell tanks worth $550 million to Pakistan.

22. Roland Dannreuther, 48–49.

23. *OMRI Daily Digest*, 56, I, 19 March 1996.

24. For details of the duma's vote, *OMRI Daily Digest*, 56, I, 19 March 1996.

25. *OMRI Daily Digest*, 55, II, 18 March 1996.

26. Sergei Rogov has three scenarios for the CIS: (1) Russia emphasizes bilateral relations with all the former Soviet republics (hegemony); (2) Russia recreates a unified structure, by force (dominance); and (3) Russia should "recognize in practice the equality of all the former Soviet republics. . . and [abandon] attempts to subordinate any CIS body to itself" (parity). A nonthreatening system of cooperative-collective security could help move Russia toward the latter. See *CDPSP* 47, no. 1 (1995), 22–24.

27. Peter Rutland, "A New Study of Russia's Role in the 'Post–Soviet Space'," *OMRI Analytical Brief* 1, no. 127 (24 May 1996). See also *Nezavisimaya Gazeta*, 23 May 1996.

28. CIS figures for 1995 show that Russia's GDP fell by 4 percent (as compared to 15 percent in 1994) and industrial production fell by only 3 percent in 1995, as compared with 21 percent in 1994. GDP dropped in Ukraine by 12 percent; industrial output for the CIS as a whole fell by 6.1 percent in 1995.

29. *Financial Times*, 12 May 1993.

30. *OMRI Daily Digest*, 62, I, 27 March 1996.

31. According to a 1996 report by the UN Conference on Trade and Development (UNCTAD), direct foreign investment in Russia in 1995 amounted

only to $2 billion; Hungary obtained $3.5 billion. Poland and the Czech Republic each obtained $2.5 billion, Kazakhstan obtained $284 million, Ukraine $200 million, Uzbekistan $115 million, Azerbaijan $110 million, Moldova $32 million, and Belarus $20 million. Kirgystan and Tajikistan each obtained $15 million. China, however, obtained $35 billion out $315 billion in worldwide investments.

32. Dov D. Zakheim, "A Top-Down Plan for the Pentagon," *Orbis*, Spring 1995. For estimates of U.S. defense spending during the Cold War, see Scott Adler, *New York Times Magazine*, 22 August 1993.

33. *OMRI Daily Digest*, 1, I, 2 January 1995.

34. Ukraine was offered $900 million in IMF credits in 1996, $200 million more than previously promised. *OMRI Daily Digest* 39, II, 23 February 1996. Yet if aid is measured in per capita terms, Armenia, for example, has been obtaining more aid than Russia: Russia has obtained $11.60 per person, while Armenia has obtained $97, and Azerbaijan, $7. *OMRI Daily Digest*, 1, I, 2 January 1995; and *OMRI Daily Digest*, 4, I, 5 January 1995.

35. For a critical view of U.S. foreign policy, see Jerry F. Hough, "America's Russia Policy: A Triumph of Neglect," *Current History*, October 1994, 308–12.

36. U.S. General Accounting Office, *Former Soviet Union: U.S. Bilateral Program Lacks Effective Coordination* (Washington, DC: GAO, February 1995).

37. *Analytica Moscow, Politica Weekly* 3, no. 27 (13–19 July 1996)

38. *OMRI Daily Digest*, 143, I, 25 July 1996. According to the *Daily Telegraph* (24 September 1996), Lebed stated that Russia should threaten sanctions against U.S. and German firms—if NATO opted to enlarge. Lebed's spokesperson subsequently denied that the interview ever took place.

39. The threat of crime gangs, coupled with ineffective Russian police efforts, brought FBI director William Webster in 1994 to Moscow to look into strengthening of joint police actions, assuming that the two sides can agree to focus on the same problems!

40. Boris Chichlo, "Geopolitics of Siberia"; and Oleg Kobtzeff, "Geopolitics of the Northeast," Conference on the Northeast Pacific, American University of Paris, 1 April 1996. See *OMRI Russian Regional Report*, 4, I, 1 September 1996.

CHAPTER 6:

1. Mark Smith, *Russia and the Far Abroad*, Conflict Studies Research Centre, The Royal Military Academy, Sandhurst, Camberley, Surrey (May 1994).

2. Quoted in *Wall Street Journal*, 24 April 1996.

3. In his April 1996 address to the Chinese leadership, Yeltsin stated that Russian communists were impeding reforms and "if they win, it will mean civil war in Russia, it will mean the end of reforms." The room, of course, was filled with Chinese communist officials! See Pavel Shinkarmko, "A Partnership Directed Toward the 21st Century," in *CDPSP* 48, no. 17 (22 May 1996), 6–7.

4. As Russian General Shevtsov has noted, NATO may not be afraid of a Russian Eurasian strategy, but NATO is "afraid. . . of China." On the other hand, NATO is quite sure that China will not become a partner of Russia, as China has its own geopolitical interests and ambitions. Accordingly, since Russia and China cannot form an alliance, Russia "will have to gnaw on the NATO bone." "Interview: General Shevtsov Gnaws on NATO's Bone," *Moscow News* 36, 12–

18 September 1995.

5. On Turkey, see Eric Rouleau, "Turkey: Beyond Ataturk," *Foreign Policy,* Summer 1996; and *OMRI Daily Digest* 242, II, 14 December 1995.

6. Russian ships have been detained 249 times since new rules governing the straits went into effect. Ankara (reportedly pressed by a Greek environmental group) says it fears an accident; Russia says Turkey is trying block Russian oil deals and trade in the region. Vessels can pass the Straits only in daytime, with twenty–four hour notice. *OMRI Daily Digest*, II, 229, 27 November 1996.

7. Georgy Bost, "Compromise Struck on Caspian Oil Pipeline Routes," *CDPSP* 47, no. 41 (1995), 8–10. U.S. policy change apparently arose came from a dispute between the Chevron Corporation and the Russian-backed Caspian Pipeline Consortium (CPC) over equity shares in a CPC pipeline. Chevron came to the conclusion "that the northern route needed competition." For details see James M. Dorsey, "Sea of Troubles," *Wall Street Journal,* 26 April 1995, 1, 8.

8. See Stephen Blank, "Russia's Real Drive to the South," *Orbis,* Summer 1995, 373.

9. Dmitry Yevstafyev, *CDPSP* 46, no. 8 (1994).

10. According to Russian academician Vladimir Loborev, Russian reactors were just as dangerous for nuclear proliferation as gas centrifuge systems. For details, See *Moscow News*, no. 18 (12–18 May 1995).

11. See Steve Coll and Steve LeVine, "A Global Militant Network," *Washington Post National Weekly Edition,* 16–22 August 1993, 6–7.

12. *Le Monde,* 20 February 1995.

13. *International Herald Tribune,* 15 March 1995.

14. On the one hand, Russia has tried to bring in Iran, Pakistan, and Saudi Arabia to resolve the conflict diplomatically. On the other hand, Russia could attempt a rapprochement with the Afghan and Tajik rebels against Western interests. On radical, pro-Russian, pan-Islamic movements, see Gulnar Kendirbaeva, "Time and Independence, Time of Trial," *Asian Affairs,* 34, no. 3 (October 1993); and Richard K. Herriman, "Russian Policy in the Middle East," *Middle East Journal,* 48, 3 Summer 1994.

15. Jyotirmoy Banerjee, "Implications for Asian Pacific Security," *Asian Survey* 34, no. 6, June 1994, 554–551. U.S. threats to impose sanctions, reduce or eliminate financial aid, and block Russian efforts to enter GATT combined to halt the sale of rocket manufacturing technology to India. After U.S. threats, Moscow supplied the rocket engines but not the technology that can reproduce those engines. *Radio Free Europe/ Radio Liberty Research Reports*, 140, 26 July 1994

16. This action may strengthen the position of the Hurriyat coalition of political parties, which seeks UN sponsored elections to decide the fate of Kashmir. *Le Figaro,* 15 March 1995. The UN, however, sustains only a very limited presence of about forty officers. See Robert G. Wirsing, "The Kashmir Conflict" *Current History,* April 1996. For a Pakistani perspective, see I.H. Malik, "Beyond Ayodhya: Implications for Regional Security in South Asia," *Asian Affairs* 24, no. 3, (October 1993). In June 1995, Pakistan stated that India had deployed eighty thousand troops in Kashmir in addition to about 600,000 already there. *International Herald Tribune,* 9 June 1995, 4. On Russia and India, see Anita Inder Singh, "India's relations with Russia and Central Asia,"

International Affairs 71, no. 1, (January 1995).

17. Could Indian opposition to the 1996 Comprehensive Nuclear Test Ban Treaty (in opposition to both Russian and American views) represent a gambit designed to win back Russian nuclear guarantees? Or will New Delhi opt for nuclear independence to counter the "threat" posed by Pakistan and the PRC?

18. Rajon Menon, "Japan-Russia Relations and North-east Asian Security," *Survival* 38, no. 2, (Summer 1996), 77.

19. *RFE/RL Daily Report,* no. 190 (6 October 1994).

20. *Le Figaro,* 2 July 1995, 4-B.

21. On the other hand, in compensating Beijing for rising repayment costs of yen-denominated loans, "Japan backed away from its 1992 Overseas Development Aid charter that would make aid conditional upon human rights, the environment, arms exports, and development of weapons of mass destruction." See *Far Eastern Economic Review* 158, no. 4, 26 January 1995, 25–26.

22. Michael J. Green and Benjamin L. Self, "Japan's Changing China Policy: From Commercial Liberalism to Reluctant Realism," *Survival* 38, no. 2 (Summer 1996), p 36–37.

23. Ibid.

24. See Hall Gardner, "China and the World after Tiananmen Square," *SAIS Review,* Spring 1990.

25. See the Russian argument for collective security in Asia, in Shim Jae Hoon, "Silent Partner," *Far Eastern Economic Review,* 29 December–5 January, 1994–95, 14–15. See also a proposal for a token Russian naval presence in Cam Ranh Bay as part of a peacekeeping force, jointly with U.S. units, in Jyotirmoy Banerjee, "Implications for Asia Pacific Security," 552.

26. Manwoo Lee, "North Korea: The Cold War Continues," *Current History,* December 1996. *OMRI Daily Digest,* 140, I, 22 July 1996.

27. According to North Korean defector Lee Chung Kuk, North Korea may have held three nuclear tests (one in Russia and two in Ukraine in 1992). North Korea may also be building a missile site capable of threatening the PRC (which recognized South Korea). See Lee Chung Kuk, *The Atom and the Military of Kim Jong Il* (Tokyo: Kodansya, 1994), 230, 238–39 (in Japanese).

28. On North Korea's nuclear program, see analysis by Joseph A. Yager, *Future U.S. Roles in Northeast Asian Security* (McClean, VA: SAIC, 14 September 1994.) See also *Far Eastern Economic Review,* 9 September 1993.

29. *OMRI Analytical Brief,* 1, 90, 29 April 1996

30. Douglas L. Clark, "Hollow Russian Military Force in Asia," *Transition,* 22 September 1995. See also *International Herald Tribune,* 8 February 1996, 4.

31. Chinese intra-industry debt forewarns of stagflation and socio-economic crisis, as does the fact that it may have become a net importer of oil since 1994. On China's socio-economy, see Weijian Shan, "Privatization or Stagflation—China's Dilemma," *Wall Street Journal Europe,* 17 January 1995, 8.

32. James Shinn, "Engaging China: Exploiting the Fissures in the Alliance" *Current History* Vol. 95, no. 602, September 1996. R.I.D. Taylor, "Chinese Policy Towards the Asia–Pacific Region," *Asian Affairs* 25, Part 3, October 1994, 263.

33. Sino-Vietnamese tension has pitted two conglomerates against each other: a Mobil Oil bloc has been backed by Vietnam, and Crestone, backed by the PRC.

Chinese pressures also prompted Australia to enter into a closer security pact with Indonesia, in December 1995.

34. *Far Eastern Economic Review*, 16 September 1993, 28.

35. George T. Crane, "China and Taiwan: Not Yet 'Greater China,'" *International Affairs* 69, no. 1 (October 1993), 705–723.

36. For a debate on the extent of the Chinese threat, see Denny Roy, "Hegemon on the Horizon"; and Michael G. Gallagher, "China's Illusory Threat to the South China Sea," both in *International Security* 19, no. 1 (Summer 1994). Gallagher's view that China's threat is largely "illusory" due to lack of sufficient air cover for its forces in the Spratlys and its previous failure in combat with Vietnam in 1979 does not rule out a more gradual strategy of harassment over the next decade (as its military-technological capabilities increase)—particularly *if* Beijing perceives that Washington is willing to appease its demands. See also Charles A. Goldman, *Managing Policy toward China under Clinton* (Santa Monica, CA: RAND, July 1995).

CHAPTER 7:

1. Paul H. Nitze and Robert W. Chandler, "At What Price an Enlarged NATO," draft editorial, unpublished (16 May 1995).

2. While reaffirming that NATO's present nuclear posture "will, for the foreseeable future, continue to meet the requirements on an enlarged alliance," the September 1995 *Study on NATO Enlargement* still keeps its options open: "NATO should retain its existing nuclear capabilities along with its right to modify its nuclear posture as the circumstances warrant."

3. Nitze and Chandler.

4. In an effort to recover debt conservatively estimated at more than $20 billion, Russia has opted to trade oil for sugar (though generally at a loss) and sustain its position in the Cuban nuclear power industry; to create joint enterprises for producing arms to penetrate the Latin American market (including states such as Columbia). See *CDPSP* 47, no. 7 (1995), 26.

5. Alexander Zhilin, "Rodionov to NATO: Don't Bait a Wounded Bear," *Moscow News*, no. 51, 26–31 December 1996.

6. General Lebed, press conference of Secretary-General Solana and General Lebed (Brussels: NATODATA, 7 October 1996).

7. *Radio Prague E-News*: 29 September 1995. For Russian views on NATO expansion, see synopsis of *Commersant-Daily*, 22 September 1995, in *Analytica Moscow* 2, no. 36, (September 16–22) 1995.

8. *OMRI Daily Digest*, 112, I, 10 June 1996.

9. *International Herald Tribune*, 22-23 February 1997.

10. Hennadii Udovenko, "European Stability and NATO Enlargement," *NATO Review* 6, no. 43 (November 1995). See also *OMRI Daily Digest* 198, II, 11 October 1995.

11. The August 1991 coup attempt raised world fears as to who was in control of Russian strategic nuclear weapons, as did Boris Yeltsin's September–October 1993 crackdown on the Russian parliament. Contrary to general belief, the Russian (and American) military possess all the codes necessary to launch an all-out strategic nuclear attack without need for presidential authorization. See

Bruce G. Balir, "Russia's Doomsday Machine: The View from the Brink," *International Herald Tribune*, 9–10 October 1993.

12. See John Mearsheimer, "The Case for a Ukrainian Nuclear Deterrent," *Foreign Affairs* 72, no. 3 (Summer 1993), 67–80.

13. On Kazakhstan, see *Facts on File*, 1 December 1994, 900C. *Defense* (Paris: USIS, 9 December 1994), 62; *Facts on File*, 1 December 1994, 900C.

14. *OMRI Daily Digest*, 107, II, 3 June 1996.

15. *OMRI Daily Digest*, 179, II, 16 September, 1996.

16. *Defense* (Paris: USIS, 9 December 1994), 81; and Paul Balkovsky, "Bigger NATO Could Make Ukraine a Buffer," *Reuters*, 16 February 1995.

17. Ustina Markus, "Ukrainian-Chinese Relations," *RFE/RL Research Reports* 2, no. 45 (12 November 1993); and Ustina Markus, "To Counterbalance Russian Power, China Leans toward Ukraine," *Transition* 1, no. 17 (22 September 1995), 34–36. See also *OMRI Daily Digest* 99, I, 22 May 1996, 18.

18. Editorial, *Washington Post*, 14 January 1994, A22.

19. *OMRI Daily Digest* 165, I, 26 August 1996.

20. *OMRI Daily Digest* 229, I, ,27 November 1995.

21. Mr. Baumel, *Organizing Security in Europe—Defense Aspects*, Assembly of the WEU, Document 1510, Part I (NATODATA: 8 February 1996).

22. "Draft Document: Russian National Security Policy," in *Nezavisimaya Gazeta*, 25 April 1996, cited in *OMRI Daily Digest*, 83, I, 26 April 1996.

23. See *CDPSP* 47, no. 46 (1995).

24. *OMRI Daily Digest*, 181, I, 18 September 1996; *OMRI Daily Digest*, 185, I, 24 September 1996. In March 1997, the commander of the Russian Strategic Rocket Forces, Igor Sergeev, stated that despite shortcomings, there was no alternative to ratifying START II, but that the treaty should be linked to a strict U.S. adherence to the ABM treaty; the deadline for implementing the treaty should be extended from 2003 to 2006 or 2007. *OMRI Daily Digest*, I, II, 11 March 1997.

25. Stepan Kisseliov, "Ou va la Russie," *Moscow News* (French version) 42 (22 October 1991), 1–3.

26. *CDPSP*, 47, no. 42 (1995), 22; Facts on File, 15 February 1996.

27. *International Herald Tribune*, 25 September 1996, 2; and *OMRI Daily Digest*, 109, I, 5 June 1996. See analysis by Alexei Arbatov, "The ABM Treaty and Theater Ballistic Missile Defense," *SIPRI Yearbook 1995*.

28. Clive Archer, "New Threat Perceptions: Danish and Norwegian Official Views," *European Security* 3, no. 4 (Winter 1994), 608.

29. See views of V. Viktorov, *The Enlargement of the Alliance*, eds. Karsten Voigt and Tamas Wachsler, Annex III, correspondence between Karsten Voigt and Associate Delegations (Brussels: International Secretariat, May 1995).

30. *Defense* (Paris: USIS, 30 May 1995), 1.

31. *OMRI Daily Digest*, 185, I, 22 September 1995.

32. *Keesling Contemporary Archives*, 21 February 1995, 40421.

33. See *OMRI Daily Digest*, 216, I, 6 November 1995.

34. John W.R. Lepingwell, "The Russian Military and Security Policy in the 'Near Abroad,'" *Survival* 36, no. 3, (Autumn 1994).

35. *International Herald Tribune*, 1 October 1993.

36. *Moscow News*, no. 84 (3–10 December 1995), 11. The Norwegian

government was divided on the timing of the NATO exercises. On accidental political-military tensions between Moscow and Oslo brought about by the firing of a Norwegian meteorological rocket in January 1995, see *CDPSP* 48, no. 9 (27 March 1996); *CDPSP* 47, no 4 (1995).

37. Rene Nyberg, "The Baltic Countries and the Northwest of Russia," *European Security* 3, no. 3 (Autumn 1994), 534.

38. *OMRI Daily Digest*, 88, I, 6, May 1996.

39. *OMRI Daily Digest*, 107, I, 3 June 1996.

40. The Atlantic Council, "The Indivisibility of Arms Control: Saving the CFE Treaty," *Bulletin* 6, no. 9 (14 September 1995).

41. *OMRI Daily Digest*, 31, I 21 February 1997

42. Uwe Nerlich, "The Relationship between a European Common Defense, NATO, the OSCE, and the United Nations," in *Towards a Common Defense Policy*, eds. Laurence Martin and John Roper (Paris: WEU Institute for Security Studies, 1995), 85.

43. As "full" membership in NATO means that the Alliance must keep its nuclear options "open," the enlargement of non-nuclear "associate" NATO membership should appear less provocative, if *coordinated* with the WEU and Russia. This position could also permit NATO to drop its opposition to a nuclear-free zone in Central and Eastern Europe—particularly if a treaty could ultimately eliminate the deployment of tactical nuclear weapons in the western military districts of Russia.

44. Credible implementation of Article V (for the Baltic states) "would require nuclear deterrence and significant forward deployment of troops, a dangerous and expensive option in the former Soviet republics. A hollow commitment, on the other hand, could undermine the credibility of all NATO's Article V commitments." Hans Binnendijk and Jeffrey Simon, "Baltic Security and NATO Enlargement," *Strategic Forum*, Institute for National Strategic Studies, no. 57, (December 1995), 3.

45. Nerlich, 85. Nerlich argues that Article V of the Brussels Treaty is virtually ineffective because "it is not related to any decision-making structure, nor to force structures for collective defense. If this is to change, it can only happen as a result of major changes in the relationship between the EU/CFSP and the WEU which make the latter an organic part of the former." If a Common Defense Policy can ever be forged within the EU, he argues that "the common basis for collective defense obligations would be stronger among EU members than among NATO members." Needless to say, a closer organic relationship between the EU and WEU has been opposed by Washington (and London).

46. Nerlich.

47. Congressional Budget Office, *The Costs of Expanding the NATO Alliance* (Washington, DC: CBO, March 1996), 17.

CHAPTER 8:

1. Quoted in *Washington Post*, 29 November 1995, cited in Michael Mihalka, "Cauldron of the Emerging Security Order," *Transition* 12, January 1996.

2. "Interview: General Shevtsov Gnaws on NATO's Bone," *Moscow News* 36, 12–18 September 1996.

3. For a "pro-Croatian" position, see Reneo Lukic, *The Wars of South Slavic Succession: Yugoslavia 1991–93*, Graduate Institute of International Studies, no. 2 (1993). For a "pro-Serbian" position, see John Zametica, *The Yugoslav Conflict*, Adelphi Paper, no. 270 (London: IISS 1992). Zametica (p. 14) questions the sincerity of Slovenia's offers of confederation as opposed to "secession."

4. Christopher Civic, "Implications of the Crisis in South-eastern Europe," in *Adelphi Papers*, no. 265, *New Dimensions of International Security*, Part I, Winter 1991, 92, 88.

5. Zametica, 63.

6. See Flora Lewis, "Reassembling Yugoslavia," *Foreign Policy*, no. 98 (Spring 1995). *Keesling's Record of World Events* 37, no. 10, October 1991.

7. Interview with Bosnian vice-president Ejup Ganic, *Tribune de Geneve*, 4 January 1993. Had significant numbers of UN war-preventive forces been deployed in Bosnia in 1991—as had been requested by the Bosnian leadership—would Serbia and Croatia have extended their conflict into Bosnian territory?

8. See also Flora Lewis.

9. Discussion with Vladlen Sirotkin, Professor, Diplomatic Academy, Russian Ministry of Foreign Affairs, May 1995.

10. Mats R. Berdal, "Whither UN Peacekeeping," *Adelphi Paper* no. 281, 23, (London: IISS, 1993), 47.

11. Nicole Gnesotto, *Lessons of Yugoslavia*, Chaillot Paper 14 (WEU Institute for Security Studies, March 1994), 21–41.

12. The UN's Vance-Owen plan was followed by the Owen-Stoltenberg plan. See Pauline Neville-Jones, "Dayton, IFOR, and Alliance Relations in Bosnia," *Survival*, 38, 4 (Winter 1996–97), 46–47. The Contact Group tended to displace the role of the UN, as well as that of the EU presidency and the troika. At the same time, it helped reassert European influence; it helped develop a single policy line; it reduced the ability of the warring parties to play outside powers against each other; and it created a greater capacity than previously to match political objectives with the situation on the ground and with UN force capabilities.

13. Alexei G. Arbatov, "Russia's Foreign Policy Alternatives," *International Security* 18, no. 2 (Fall 1993), 32.

14. On 9 June 1994, the Defense and State departments and the Joint Chiefs of Staff issued a joint statement arguing that the unilateral lifting of the arms embargo "would seriously sour our relations with our NATO and UN allies and undermine our partnership with Russia." David C. Morrison, "How Bosnia Is Becoming a Priority," *National Journal* 26, no. 34–35 (20 August 1994), 1976. See also *International Herald Tribune*, 18 November 1994.

15. William Schneider, "Making a Political Issue of Bosnia," *National Journal* 26, no. 50, 10 December, 1994.

16. Ed Vulliamy, "Bosnia: The Secret War," *The Guardian*, 29 January 1996.

17. *International Herald Tribune*, 4 July 1995, 12.

18. Schneider.

19. The cost of the UN rapid response force was estimated at $520 million annually—assuming the United States is assessed at 31 percent of the UN costs. *International Herald Tribune*, 15 June 1995, 10.

20. *OMRI Special Report: Pursuing Balkan Peace*, no. 7, 20 February 1996.

21. *OMRI, Pursuing Balkan Peace*, 1, 22, 4 June 1996.
22. Address of Admiral Leighton W. Smith to the North Atlantic Council, 17 July 1996. (Brussels: NATODATA, 2 August 1996).
23. *International Herald Tribune*, 11 September 1995, 5. *Le Figaro*, 9–10 September 1995.
24. *CDPSP*, 45, no. 3 (1993), 19.
25. *Facts on File*, 14 December 1995, 922–23.
26. Janusz Bugajski, "Policy Forum—After the Troops Leave," *The Washington Quarterly*, 19, no. 3, 1996, 62.
27. *Pravda* (Bratislava) trans. by Natalia Lechmanova, 11 December 1995.
28. *OMRI Daily Digest*, 28, II, 8 February 1996.
29. *OMRI Daily Digest*, 53, II, 14 March 1996.
30. Lt. General Patrick M. Hughes, quoted in *International Herald Tribune*, 21 March 1996.
31. *OMRI Daily Digest*, 46, II, 6 March 1997.
32. "Lessons Forgotten," *OMRI Special Report:* Pursuing Balkan Peace, 19, I, 14 May 1996. The World Bank sought $5.1 billion in pledges by April 1996 but had only obtained $520 million by December 1995.
33. *OMRI Daily Digest*, 6, II, 26 February 1996.

CHAPTER 9:

1. See Lieutenant General William Odom, testimony, Senate Foreign Relations Committee on Europe, 22 August 1995, *Defense File*, no. 14 (Paris: USIS, 14 September 1995), 8.
2. Ambassador Richard T. Davies, letter to Secretary of State Warren Christopher, 15 May 1995, ibid. See also Jonathan Dean, "Losing Russia or Keeping NATO: Must We Choose?" *Arms Control Today*, June 1995.
3. Ted Galen Carpenter argues for a U.S.-EU "security coordination council" to replace NATO but says nothing about a possible Russian role in such a council. See Ted Galen Carpenter, *Beyond NATO: Staying Out of Europe's Wars* (Washington, DC: Cato Institute, 1994), 65.
4. Karsten Voigt and Tamas Wachsler, *The Enlargement of the Alliance*, Draft Special Report of the Working Group on NATO Enlargement (Brussels: International Secretariat, May 1995). See also Deputy Secretary of State Strobe Talbott, remarks in Poland, *Defense File*, 15 (Paris: USIS, 25 September 1995), 38.
5. Voigt and Wachsler.
6. Paul H. Nitze, "Alliance's Military Role Means Less Is More," *Insight*, 5 December 1994, 22.
7. Samuel Huntington, "The Clash of Civilizations?" *Foreign Affairs*, Summer 1993.
8. Michael Mihalka, "Eastern and Central Europe's Great Divide over Membership in NATO," *Transition* 1, no. 4, (11 August 1995).
9. Mr. I Tsyareshka, Belarusian Delegation, in Voigt and Wachsler, Annex III.
10. *OMRI Daily Digest*, 248, I, 22 December 1995.
11. Senator Dole further stated that he would not grant Russia a veto over enlargement but would "offer Russia a serious dialogue on long-term relations with NATO. NATO is a defensive organization. . . and its interests collide with

Russia only where Russia intrudes upon sovereign nations. A non-expansionist Russia is not threatened by any enlargement of NATO." Senator Dole, 25 June 1996 speech to the Philadelphia World Affairs Council, cited in U.S. Foreign Policy Agenda, *Foreign Policy and the 1996 Presidential Election USIA Electronic Journals* 1, no. 14 [October 1996]. This is not the way Moscow sees it.

12. *International Affairs*, no. 8 (Paris: USIS, 21 March 1995), 20–21.

13. Ibid., 21.

14. General Jack Galvin, "Closing Plenary Session," co-chairs Walther Leisler Kiep and Robert D. Blackwill, *American Council on Germany, Atlantik-Brücke Conference* (Berlin: 17 June 1995).

15. NATO, *Study on NATO Enlargement* (Brussels: NATODATA, September 1995).

16. Davies, letter to Christopher.

17. Assistant Secretary of State, Richard C. Holbrooke, Letter to Ambassador Davies, 25 July 1995, 1.

18. Ambassador Davies, reply to Assistant Secretary of State Richard C. Holbrooke's letter of 25 July 1995.

19. Germany has considered speeding the move of Central European states, which are "associate partners" of the WEU, to full membership, but without any *automatic* promise of a security commitment. If pursued, Article V of the modified Brussels Treaty would be "temporarily frozen." See Lord Finsberg, in Mr. Baumel, *Organizing Security in Europe—Defense Aspects*, Assembly of the WEU, Document 1510, (NATODATA: 8 February 1996), Part II, sections 65–69. In addition to its legal ramifications (involving parliamentary ratification of such a modification), it is doubtful that this would mitigate Russian opposition to WEU enlargement tacitly backed by NATO—as seemingly intended.

20. Jonathan Dean, "Losing Russia or Keeping NATO: Must We Choose?" *Arms Control Today*, June 1995, 6; Michael Mihalka, "Squaring the Circle: NATO's Offer to the East," *RFE/RL Research Report* 3, no. 12 (25 March 1994).

21. "Russia's Full Strategic Doctrine," *Foreign Report* (London: *The Economist*, 18 November 1993), 1.

22. Senator Sam Nunn, "The Future of NATO in an Uncertain World," speech to SacLant (Norfolk, VA: NATODATA, 22 June 1995).

23. Peter W. Rodman notes that Warren Christopher linked NATO and the EU "on a parallel track" in January 1996, just after the EU itself had refused to set any date for membership talks with Central European states, at its Madrid Conference. In January 1996, President Clinton delinked NATO enlargement from the EU process, in a letter to Sam Nunn. See Peter W. Rodman, *America Adrift* (Washington, DC: Nixon Center for Peace and Freedom, 1996), 80, n. 27.

24. Nunn.

25. Michael E. Brown, "The Flawed Logic of NATO Expansion," *Survival* 37, no. 1, (Spring 1995), 48.

26. Zbigniew Brzezinski, "A Plan for Europe," *Foreign Affairs*, Jan./ Feb. 1995, 35. See his less polished editorial, "Two Tracks for NATO Toward Central Europe and Russia," *International Herald Tribune*, 30 December 1994, 4.

27. Zbigniew Brzezinski, "A Plan for Europe," 34.

28. Ibid, 35.

NOTES

257

29. Vyacheslav Nikonov, in *Transatlantic Security: Beyond NATO*, NAA Draft Special Report (Brussels: NATODATA, 28 December 1995).

CHAPTER 10:

1. Henry Kissinger realized that U.S. backing for the OSCE (then CSCE) undercut Soviet influence due to that organization's opposition to human rights abuses in the Eastern bloc and by permitting Eastern and Western European states to communicate for the first time. Moreover, rather than freezing Soviet controls over East Germany and Eastern Europe, as critics feared at the time of the signing of the Helsinki Final Act in 1975, the OSCE actually opened the door to peaceful territorial revision—and German unification. See John J. Maresca, *To Helsinki* (Durham, NC: Duke University Press, 1985).

2. Henry Kissinger, "Charter of Confusion: The Limits of U.S.-Russian Cooperation," *International Herald Tribune*, 6 July 1992.

3. See commentary of Robert J. Jackson, in *NATO's Role in European Stability*, ed. Stephen A. Cambone (Washington, DC: CSIS, 1995), 57.

4. *Europe: The Day in Politics*, no. 6371, 5/6 December 1994, 3.

5. Sean Kay, "NATO and the CSCE: A New Russian Challenge," in *NATO in the Post-Cold War Era*, ed. S. Victor Papacosma and Mary Ann Heiss (New York: St. Martin's 1995), 117.

6. Ibid., 130. See also Piotr Switalski, "An Ally for the Central and Eastern European States," *Transition*, 30 June 1995, 28.

7. Bruce George, "Forging the NATO-OSCE Partnership," *OSCE ODIHR Bulletin* 4, no. 3, (1996), 47.

8. See OSCE Parliamentary Assembly, Stockholm Declaration, "Towards a Common and Comprehensive Security Model for Europe For the Twenty-First Century," Stockholm, 9 July 1996, Article 26t. "Full recognition that the enlargement of security organizations cannot be considered in isolation but only as part of a wider process in which the OSCE, a wide-ranging partnership among NATO, Russia and Ukraine, an enlarged NATO, and an active Partnership for Peace and the WEU form complementary parts of a broad, inclusive European security architecture based on mutual confidence and supporting the objective of an undivided Europe." In Article 26u, the Stockholm Declaration also entrusts "the Forum for Security Cooperation with questions of preventive and qualitative arms control, with a particular regard to the impact of new developments in weapons technology." See also *OMRI Daily Digest*, 134, I, 12 July 1996. In the Lisbon OSCE summit in December 1996, Russia obtained support from France and Germany for a strengthened OSCE, *CDPSP*, 48, no. 49 (1996).

9. See Michael Mihalka, "Trawling for Legitimacy," *Transition* 1, no. 11 (30 June 1995), 20.

10. Renée de Nevers, "Russia's Strategic Renovation," *Adelphi Papers* no. 289 (London: IISS, July 1994), 54–57.

11. *Ukrainian Quarterly* 1, no. 2 (Summer 1994), 183-84.

12. Vladimir Kazimirov, in *RFE/RL Daily Report* 190, 6 October 1994.

13. *Wall Street Journal*, 19 August 1993. See analysis by Peter van Ham, *Ukraine, Russia and European Security: Implications for Western Policy*, Chaillot Papers 13 (Paris: WEU Institute for Security Studies, February 1994), 39–40. Roy

Allison, *Peacekeeping in the Soviet Successor States*, Chaillot Papers 18 (Paris: WEU Institute for Security Studies, November 1994).

14. Andrei Kozyrev, "Partnership or Cold Peace," *Foreign Policy*, no. 99 (Summer 1995).

15. See *International Herald Tribune*, 28 September 1994; *International Herald Tribune*, 7 December 1994; and *Financial Times*, 14 December 1994.

16. Hall Gardner, "The Military Integration of Eastern Europe: Toward an Eastern Locarno," in *Defense: Next Step in European Integration?*" Cicero Paper, 1 (Maastricht: 1996).

17. For details, see Mats R. Berdal, "Fateful Encounter: The United States and UN Peacekeeping," *Survival* 36, no. 1 (Spring 1994), 40. Berdal furthermore states that it was "not only inaccurate to assert, but also factually inaccurate to assert, as was done in Congress, that Americans had died in Somalia because they were operating under UN command."

18. *Notes on Economic Affairs*, (Paris: USIS, 22 November 1994), 17.

19. Steven Kull, "Misreading the Public Mood," *The Bulletin of the Atomic Scientists*, March/April 1995, 59.

20. On shifting U.S. attitudes toward the UN, see Robert W. Gregg, *About Face: The United States and the United Nations* (Boulder, CO: Lynne Rienner, 1993).

21. *OMRI Daily Digest*, 3, II, January 1996.

22. K.C. Swanson, "Troubled Tribunal," *National Journal*, 30 March 1996.

23. General Jack Galvin, "Closing Plenary Session," co-chairs Walther Leisler Kiep and Robert D. Blackwill, *American Council on Germany-Atlantik-Brücke Conference* (Berlin: 17 June 1995).

24. In 1948–49, the United States considered a multilateral UN intervention in Manchuria to block a communist Chinese victory, and the deployment of UN forces to neutralize Taiwan. But these actions were never initiated. In addition, similar to contemporary efforts to deploy UN peacekeepers on CIS territory, the UN's Relief and Rehabilitation Administration (UNRRA) permitted U.S. citizens access to Soviet territory in Belarus and Ukraine—before UNNRA was shut down as being "pro-Communist" in 1947, following Khrushchev's 1946 purges.

25. David C. Morrison, "How Bosnia is Becoming a Priority," *National Journal* 26, no. 34035 (20 August 1994), 1976.

26. In December 1995, Moscow owed the UN $63 million, but began to repay arrears on its peacekeeping budget. OMRI *Daily Digest*, 240, I, 12 December 1995.

27. See James Kitfield, "Not-So-United," *National Journal*, 1 January 1997, 72. *International Herald Tribune*, 17 March 1995, 6. *International Affairs* (Paris: USIS, 11 January 1995), 30. Even Senator Jesse Helms stated that he did not like to "veto the mission" because Washington had to pay 31.7 percent of the cost. Helms argued that the United States should let peacekeeping missions go forward without U.S. funding. He threatened to pull the United States out of the UN by the year 2000—if the latter does not reform itself. Jesse Helms, "Saving the UN," *Foreign Affairs*, September/October 1996.

28. Thomas G. Weiss, "The UN and Civil Wars," *Washington Quarterly* 17, no. 4 (Autumn 1994).

29. Dov. S. Zakheim, "A Top-Down Plan for the Pentagon," *Orbis*, Spring 1995. IFOR purportedly cost $1.5 billion as of late 1995.

30. *International Affairs* (Paris: USIS, 9 December 1994), 27.

31. Cited in Hannes Adomeit, "Russia as a 'Greatpower,'" *International Affairs* 70, no. 3 (1994), 49.

32. *RFE/RL Daily Report*, 139, 25 July 1994.

33. Jonathan Dean, "Losing Russia or Keeping NATO: Must We Choose?" *Arms Control Today*, June 1995.

34. On Polish opposition, see Michael Mihalka, "Restructuring European Security," *Transition* 1, no. 2, (30 June 1995).

35. Stanley R. Sloan, "U.S. Perspectives on NATO's Future," *International Affairs* 71, no. 2 (1995), 223.

36. Milhalka.

37. *OSCE Newsletter* 2, no. 8 (August 1995), Special Edition.

38. See Report to Minister by the NACC Ad Hoc Group on Cooperation in Peacekeeping, NATO Press Release, M-NACC 1 (93) 40, 11 June 1993.

39. It is not certain that Bonn's membership on the UN Security Council in 1991 would have restrained Germany from recognizing Croatia contrary to UN counsel. At the same time, German (and Japanese) membership on the UNSC should help to persuade these states not to engage in unilateral actions. (Bonn's membership in NATO did not prevent it from engaging in an independent diplomatic and political-economic strategy either.)

40. Mike M. Mochizuki, *Japan: Domestic Change and Foreign Policy* (Santa Monica, CA: RAND, 1995)

41. U.S. bargaining leverage to counter Japanese nationalist demands to regain the Kuriles could perhaps take the form of a tacit or quasi-apology for the dropping of the second atomic bomb on Nagasaki in exchange for Japanese acceptance of compromise over the Northern Territories.

42. *OMRI Daily Digest*, no. 245, I, 19 December 1995.

CHAPTER 11:

1. Congressional Budget Office, *The Costs of Expanding the NATO Alliance* (Washington, DC: CBO, March 1996), xix.

2. *International Herald Tribune*, 13 March 1997, 7.

3. See Jeffrey Simon, "NATO Enlargement," *Strategic Forum*, Institute for National Strategic Studies, no. 31 (May 1995), 4.

4. CBO. 61. On credible implementation of Article V, see Hans Binnendijk and Jeffrey Simon, "Baltic Security and NATO Enlargement," 3. (Quotation cited Chap. 7, n. 43.)

5. See Ronald D. Asmus, Richard L. Kugler, and F. Stephen Larrabee, "What Will NATO Enlargement Cost?" *Survival* 3, no. 3 (Autumn 1996).

6. *International Herald Tribune*, 13 March 1997, 7. The other domestic political imperative was to export as much of the cost as possible onto present and future NATO members—an option that is likely to be strongly contested. Senator Richard Lugar has realized that the NATO enlargement debate in Congress may not be easy: "Suddenly, somebody is going to say, 'You mean American soldiers [could] be sent to the border of Poland and Russia in the event of an attack.'" See *Wall Street Journal*, 9 August 1996, A6.

7. Andrew Krepinevich, "Train Wreck Coming," *National Review*, 31 July

1995, 42–43; and Dov S. Zakheim, "A Top-Down Plan for the Pentagon," *Orbis*, Spring 1995, 177. The GAO asserted that the Defense Department had underestimated the costs of the Bottom-Up Review by as much as $150 billion by the year 2000; The CBO put the shortfall at $50 billion. See James Kitfield, "Fit to Fight?" *National Journal*, 16 May 1996, 582.

8. Stephen M. Meyer, "Devolution of Russian Military Power," *Current History*, October 1995.

9. Valeri Borisenko, "Whose Muscles are Growing?" *Moscow News*, no. 6 (1996).

10. Alexander Zhilin, "Russian Army: Lost and Lonely," *Moscow News*, no. 36 (September 1996).

11. *OMRI Daily Digest*, 139, I, 19 July 1996.

12. *OMRI Daily Digest* 165, I 26 August 1996.

13. *OMRI Daily Digest* 186, I, 25 September 1996.

14. On the continuing debate over defense preparedness, see John D. Steinbruner, *The Brookings Review*, Winter 1993.

15. In 1991–96 (estimated) NATO spent $66.8 million on NACC and PfP, and, in addition to its contribution through NATO common budgets, Washington spent $53 million in 1995 to PfP member countries through five bilateral programs. By 1996, this assistance was to increase to about $125 million. The United States also provided $130 million in bilateral assistance to support the PfP program over two years in Defense Department support programs and State Department bilateral assistance. Indicating the thrust of U.S. geostrategic interests, Poland was expected to be the largest recipient of aid, at $25 million; the Czech Republic, Hungary, Romania and Ukraine each received $10 million, while Russia is expected to receive only $7 million, including $5 million to help Russian troops participate in PfP exercises. Interestingly Bulgaria ($5 million), Slovakia ($4.5 million), and Albania ($3.25 million) were next in order of support. Government Accounting Office, *NATO Enlargement: NATO and U.S. Actions Taken to Facilitate Enlargement* (Washington, DC: GAO/NSIAD-96-92, May 1996)

16. See Gardner, *Surviving the Millennium*. The purpose is thus not at all that of UN or OSCE forces intervening in "hot spots," as Francis Fukuyama has totally misinterpreted it, but to deploy Euro-Atlantic war-preventive forces (trained by PfP) under a general UN or OSCE mandate in strategically significant regions to forge a militarily integrated system of regional security *before*, rather than after, hot spots begin to fester. The term "preventive" obviously implies the capability for foresight. See Francis Fukuyama, review of *Surviving the Millennium*, by Hall Gardner, *Foreign Affairs*, April/May 1995.

17. On war-preventive forces, see Gabriel Munera, *Preventing Armed Conflict in Europe*, Chaillot Papers, nos. 15/16 (Paris: WEU Institute for Security Studies, June 1994). The initial political support for the concept of war-preventive forces has been traced to Mikhail Gorbachev. *International Affairs* (Paris: USIS, no. 29, 9 December 1994.)

18. See statements by Dariusz Rosati, in "NATO Means Protection for Poland," *Pravo* (Right), trans. by Natalia Lechmanova (Bratislava) 2 February 1996. See also *OMRI Daily Digest*, II, no. 54, 15 March 1996.

19. *RFL/RL Daily Report*, 174 (13 September 1994).

20. Jim Nichol, *Conventional Forces in Europe Treaty* (Washington, DC: CRS, September 1995).

21. Lithuanian government advisor Dmitrii Kopelman, cited in Phillip Petersen, "Security Policy in the Post–Soviet Baltic States," *European Security* 1, no. 1 (Spring 1992), 45. Petersen warns that Kaliningrad represents "another of those issues which will rise up to 'surprise' those unwilling to anticipate it and seek a preemptory solution." (Ibid., 45.) Preventing the rise of rogue militaries implies the necessity to stabilize the central government in Moscow.

22. Jonathan Dean, 7.

23. See proposals of Lena Hjelm-Nullen and Tarja Halonen, *Europe*, no. 6713, 23/24 April 1996.

24. Mikhail Gorbachev has argued, "it is possible to envision an agreement that would provide joint guarantees by NATO and Russia to those European countries seeking membership in the Atlantic Alliance." *International Herald Tribune*, 22–23 February 1997. In addition to the CFE Treaty, there have been two cooperative-collective security pacts with Russian participation in Europe since 1989, the "two plus four" agreement leading to German unification and the trilateral U.S-Russian-Ukrainian nuclear disarmament pact of January 1994. Rather than make any explicit deal with Moscow, the Alliance has made unilateral statements that it will forego the deployment of foreign troops and nuclear weapons in Central Europe.

25. Another misinterpretation by Francis Fukuyama, review of *Surviving the Millennium*. Contrary to Fukuyama's views, as I redefine the concept, I do *not* argue that the American side of the "double containment" has collapsed, thus opening up the possibility global conflict, but that of the Russian side has. It is thus the increasing inability of Russia to retain its collaborative role in "double containing" the emergence of third powers that now threatens global peace.

26. Gardner, *Surviving the Millennium.*, 210.

27. Mr. Bruce George, *Continental Drift*, draft general report (Brussels: International Secretariat, November 1994).

28. Holbrooke, letter to Davies, July 25, 1995.

29. George F. Kennan, "NATO Expansion Would Be a Fateful Blunder," *International Herald Tribune*, 6 February 1997. For Madeleine Albright's reply, see *OMRI Daily Digest*, 33, I, 17 February 1997. Critics of George Kennan may accuse him of "crying wolf" but what if the wolf opens its fangs in the guise of a Russian pan-nationalist movement? Is it worth taking the risk and calling the Russian bluff? Or to change metaphors, isn't better to dampen the coals, than to continue to throw fuel on a smouldering fire?

Selected Bibliography

Arbatov, Alexei G. "Russia's Foreign Policy Alternatives." *International Security*, vol. 18, no. 2 (Fall 1993).

Binnendijk, Hans, and Jeffrey Simon. "Baltic Security and NATO Enlargement." *Strategic Forum*, no. 57, Institute for National Strategy Studies (December 1995).

Blank, Stephen J. *Prague, NATO, and European Security*. Carlisle Barracks, PA: U.S. Army War College, Strategic Studies Institute (17 April 1996).

Brezezinski, Ian J. "Polish-Ukrainian Relations: Europe's Neglected Strategic Axis." *Survival*, vol. 35, no. 3 (Autumn 1993).

Bugajski, Janusz. "Policy Forum—After the Troops Leave." *The Washington Quarterly*, vol. 19, no. 3 (1996).

Burant, Stephen R. "International Relations in a Regional Context: Poland and its Eastern Neighbours." *Europe-Asia Studies*, vol. 45, no. 3 (1993).

Carpenter, Ted Galen. *Beyond NATO: Staying Out of Europe's Wars*. Washington, DC: Cato Institute, 1994.

Cicero Paper. *Defence: Next Step Toward European Integration?* vol. 1. Maastricht: Cicero Foundation, 1996.

Congressional Budget Office. *The Costs of Expanding the NATO Alliance*. Washington, DC: CBO, March 1996.

Cornish, Paul. "European Security: the end of architecture and the new NATO." *International Affairs*, vol. 72, no. 4 (1996).

Crane, George T. "China and Taiwan: Not Yet 'Greater China.'" *International Affairs*, vol. 69, no. 1 (October 1993).

Dean, Jonathan, "Losing Russia or Keeping NATO: Must We Choose?" *Arms Control Today*. June 1995.

Gardner, Hall. *Surviving the Millennium*. Westport, CT and London: Praeger, 1994.

Johnsen, William T. *NATO Strategy in the 1990s*. Carlisle Barracks, PA: U.S. Army War College, 25 May 1995.

Kitfield, James. "Kohl's Answer." *The National Journal*. 7 December 1996.

Kurguinjan, Serguei. *Lessons of Bloody October*. Moscow: International Foundation, EDT, 1994

Lepingwell, John W.R. "The Russian Military and Security Policy in the 'Near Abroad.'" *Survival*, vol. 36, no. 3 (Autumn 1994).

Liska, George. *Return to the Heartland and Rebirth of the Old Order*. Washington, DC: Johns Hopkins Foreign Policy Institute, 1994.

Mandelbaum, Michael. *The Dawn of Peace in Europe*. New York: The Twentieth Century Fund, 1996.

Marcus, Ustina. "To Counterbalance Russian Power, China Leans to Ukraine." *Transition*, vol. 1, no. 17 (22 September 1995).

Maresca, John J. *To Helsinki*. Durham, NC: Duke University Press, 1985.

Martin, Laurence and John Roper eds. *Towards a Common Defense Policy*. Paris: WEU Institute for Security Studies, 1995.

Munera, Gabriel. *Preventing Armed Conflict*. Chaillot Papers, nos. 15/16. Paris: WEU Institute for Security Studies, June 1994.

Nitze, Paul H. "Alliance's Military Role Means Less is More." *Insight*. 5 December 1994.

Nolan, Janne E. (ed.) *Global Engagement*. Washington, D.C.: Brookings, 1994.

Nyberg, Rene. "The Baltic Countries and the Northwest of Russia." *European Security*, vol. 3, no. 3 (Autumn 1994).

Papacosma, S. Victor and Heiss, Mary Ann, eds. *NATO in the Post–Cold War Era*. New York: St Martin's Press, 1995.

Petersen, Phillip. "Security Policy in the Post–Soviet Baltic States." *European Security*, vol. 1, no. 1 (Spring 1992).

Simon, Jeffrey. "Central Europe: Return to Europe or Descent to Chaos." *Strategic Review*, vol. 3, no. 21 (Winter 1993).

Sloan, Stanley R. *NATO's Future: Beyond Collective Defense*. McNair Paper, no. 46. Washington, DC: Institute for National Strategic Studies, National Defense University, December 1995.

Subtelny, Orest, *Ukraine: A History*. Toronto: University of Toronto Press, 1994.

Van Ham, Peter. *Ukraine, Russia and European Security: Implications for Western Policy*. Chaillot Paper, no. 13. Paris: WEU Institute for Security Studies, February 1994.

Zaprudnik, Jan. *Belarus: At a Crossroads in History*. Boulder, CO: Westview Press, 1993.

Name Index

Subject Index

About the Author

HALL GARDNER is Associate Professor and Chair of the Department of International Affairs and Politics at The American University of Paris. He is the author of *Surviving the Millennium: American Global Strategy, the Collapse of the Soviet Empire, and the Question of Peace* (Praeger, 1994).

ISBN 0-275-95857-4

90000>

9 780275 958572

EAN

HARDCOVER BAR CODE

www.ingramcontent.com/pod-product-compliance
Lightning Source LLC
Chambersburg PA
CBHW071842270326
41929CB00013B/2078

* 9 7 9 8 7 6 5 1 4 1 9 1 5 *